Great Transformations

Economic Ideas and Institutional Change in the Twentieth Century

This book picks up where Karl Polanyi's study of economic and political change left off. Building on Polanyi's conception of the double movement, Mark Blyth analyzes the two periods of deep-seated institutional change that characterized the twentieth century: the 1930s and the 1970s. Blyth views both sets of changes as part of the same dynamic. In the 1930s, labor reacted against the exigencies of the market and demanded state action to mitigate the market's effects by "embedding liberalism." In the 1970s, those who benefited least from such "embedding" institutions, namely business, reacted against these constraints and sought to overturn that institutional order. Blyth demonstrates the critical role that economic ideas played in making institutional change possible. *Great Transformations* rethinks the relationship between uncertainty, ideas, and interests, achieving profound new insights on how, and under what conditions, institutional change takes place.

Mark Blyth is an assistant professor of political science at the Johns Hopkins University. He specializes in comparative political economy, with interests in how ideas affect political and economic outcomes, and in institutional change. He has taught at Columbia University and the University of Birmingham (UK) and is a member of the editorial board of the *Review of International Political Economy*.

In formal theory, an economy is usually described by endowments, preferences and technology. . . . We think it is important that something more be added: the beliefs held by the various participants in the economy. "Beliefs" include . . . attitudes and even theories about the way the economy works. The way the economy actually does work can depend on the way agents believe the economy to work . . . [and] . . . the way the economy responds to a policy move by the government can depend on the interpretation that other agents place on it, and therefore on the beliefs about the way things work . . . . If participants believe that every increase in the money supply will be fully translated into the price level, irrespective of any other characteristics of the situation, then they are likely to behave in ways that will make it happen.

Frank Hahn and Robert Solow, *A Critical Essay on Macroeconomic Theory* (Oxford: Blackwell Publishers, 1995), p. 150.

Great Transformations

Economic Ideas and Institutional Change in the Twentieth Century

MARK BLYTH
The Johns Hopkins University

 CAMBRIDGE
UNIVERSITY PRESS

CAMBRIDGE UNIVERSITY PRESS
Cambridge, New York, Melbourne, Madrid, Cape Town,
Singapore, São Paulo, Delhi, Tokyo, Mexico City

Cambridge University Press
32 Avenue of the Americas, New York, NY 10013-2473, USA

www.cambridge.org
Information on this title: www.cambridge.org/9780521010528

First published 2002
8th printing 2011

A catalog record for this publication is available from the British Library.

Library of Congress Cataloging in Publication Data
Blyth, Mark, 1967–
Great transformations : the rise and decline of embedded liberalism / Mark Blyth.
   p.   cm.
Includes bibliographical references and index.
ISBN 0-521-81176-7 – ISBN 0-521-01052-7 (pb.)
   1. Liberalism – United States – History – 20th century.   2. Liberalism – Sweden –
History – 20th century.   3. Economic history – 20th century.   4. Social history –
20th century.   5. Polanyi, Karl, 1886-1964.   I. Title.
JC574.2.U6 B59   2002
320.51´3´09485 – dc21   2002067685

ISBN 978-0-521-81176-7 Hardback
ISBN 978-0-521-01052-8 Paperback

Contents

Preface

My desire to write this book is perhaps best explained by a true story. My father was a butcher. He never took a course in economics. Yet sitting in his car just before the 1987 British election he told me that he would not vote Labour. I inquired why he would not. Because, said my father, "once they get elected, Labour will spend all this money on creating jobs, which is fair enough, but it never works. It just means prices go up. They'll try it again and again and prices will go up and up. Then they will have spent all this money and there will be none left for the schools and the hospitals, so they will have to borrow. But because there is inflation, it will cost more money to borrow, which means there will be less money for everyone else. This means we will all have to pay more on loans and such things, so people will have less money to spend. The less people spend, the more the economy slows down, and so there are fewer people in work. If the Tories get in again, they'll cut taxes, people will spend more, and there will be more jobs."

My father had just regurgitated at least fifty years of contested economic thought in less than one minute flat. Buchanan, Friedman, Laffer, Nordhaus, and even Pigou had been deployed to diagnose the state of the British economy quicker than many a graduate student. Both bemused and impressed, I asked, "So why does the money you spend that comes from a tax cut create jobs while the money spent by a Labour government creates inflation?" He sat for a minute, and then he said, "Because it does. Governments shouldn't do that kind of thing."

Reflecting upon this incident some ten years later at graduate school, I realized something very interesting. Ideas matter because they can actually alter people's conception of their own self-interest. From every conceivable materialist position imaginable, my father should have been a Labour voter, but he was not. He bought into a series of ideas that not only shaped his interests, but did so irrespective of their truth content. This led me to the idea that so long as something about the economy is believed by a large enough group of people, then because they believe it, it becomes true. So if being believed is functionally equivalent to being true, then belief itself becomes politically and economically efficacious. Ideas therefore do not "really" need to correspond to the "real" world in order to be important in that world.

Building upon this insight, this book seeks to explain how such ideas have shaped the institutional contours of democratic capitalism during the twentieth century. This book investigates the role of ideas, specifically economic ideas, as crucial elements in the construction and transformation of institutional orders. Following the pioneering work of Karl Polanyi, this book seeks to understand how such ideas have been used by business, the state, and labor, to help them understand moments of economic uncertainty and to construct institutional solutions to the crises such moments engender.

The key to understanding these dynamics is to pay attention to how people think about the world. For those who are not social scientists, this is hardly a revelation. Yet to those who are, particularly in large parts of political science and political economy, the idea that "ideas matter" in and of themselves is regarded with deep suspicion. Instead, self-interest is taken to be the unambiguous and ever-ready tool of explanation. This book shows how blunt an instrument structurally given interests really are, why we need to rethink what people do in light of their beliefs and desires, and why our commonly understood relationships between interests, ideas, and institutions also need to be overhauled. The George Grosz cartoon on the cover of this book, *Friede Zwischen Kapital und Arbeit* (Peace between Capital and Labor), represents the essence of this exercise.

If one looks at the emaciated worker and the bloated capitalist, one may wonder what on earth they have in common. Seeing this, the political scientist would ask what their common interests are. Going by Grosz's cartoon, the answer is, nothing much at all. Yet they walk side by side, mutually supporting one another, with peace between them – at least at that particular moment. So why would this peace between capital and labor break out given that the interests of capital and labor are so often opposed? In answering this question, the dominant materialist strain in political science and political economy would look for common interests. Despite interests being, in John Maynard Keynes' words, "fickle things," such materialist theorists act as if interests are real objects in the world that are anterior to us. Like David Hume's passions, interests are seen as somehow beyond our ken. They animate us, they determine our action, but they are not affected by our own wills. Instead, our interests are said to be given by structural factors such as class position, asset specificity, sectoral location, etc.

Given such a view of the world, one might hypothesize that this particular bloated capitalist happens to own a steel mill that has mainly foreign customers. One might further hypothesize that the skinny chap on the right is one of his workers. One might then deduce that since they are walking arm in arm, they must share some common interest. One might then learn that their government has just devalued the currency. While this might harm workers in general – for example, by making imported food more expensive – this particular worker, being employed in the export sector, is delighted. He and his boss can see only good times ahead. Their common interests, a function of their similar structural locations, have become realized in the increased demand for their exports. Our bloated capitalist gets profits; our skinny worker gets increased wages; and most interestingly, the politics of this situation gets completely exogenized.

In this world, our capitalist and worker form coalitions and cross-class alliances without regard for ideology, misunderstandings, past and present violence, local politics, or even the institutional context of action. Agency is reduced to a set of price changes in the world economy to which agents passively respond. Politics is reduced to whatever price movements dictate. As a consequence, our understandings rest upon tautologies that explain behavior in terms of hypothesized interests whose existence is confirmed by the observation of the behavior. The theoretical aim of this book is to show the limits of such explanations and replace them with a better understanding of political change that puts ideas front and center.

Acknowledgments

The book took far too long to write and involved innumerable conversations with too many people to ever do justice to their contributions in full. If I miss anyone who should be mentioned, I apologize in advance. What prompts the omission is my defective memory rather than any judgment call on your contribution to this project. Special thanks must go to the principal members of my dissertation committee at Columbia University, Mark Kesselman and Henrick Spruyt. Also, the other members of my committee – Allan Silver, Dick Nelson, and Jack Snyder – deserve special mention, not only for agreeing to be on the committee but for actually reading such a behemoth closely and offering such good advice.

At Johns Hopkins, special thanks go to Kellee Tsai, Adam Sheingate, and William Connolly, who read closely and helped improve the argument so much. Thanks also to Colin Hay, Dave Marsh, Matt Watson, and Jonathan Hopkin at the University of Birmingham (UK) – those to whom the proposition that ideas matter was always important. My dearest intellectual debts are, however, to Robin Varghese, Alex Cooley, Sven Steinmo, and Sheri Berman. Not only have conversations with them improved my thinking immensely, I could never have written this without their friendship and encouragement as well as their unique insights.

To the others who have made this possible at its various stages, I can only offer a heartfelt thank you for listening to and aiding and abetting this project. To mention names is to prompt exclusion, but nonetheless, and in no particular order, I would like to sincerely thank the following people who have made this book both possible, and due to their efforts, better: Sheri Berman, Kate McNamara, Peter Hall, Peter Katzenstein, Ilene Grabel, Anna Seleney, Chris Ball, Brian Burgoon, Anna Ellisson, Paula Blomqvist, Victor Pestoff, Kjell Olof Feldt, Per Olof Edin, Bo Rothstein, Kristina Boreus, Jonathan Kirshner, Rawi Abdelal, Alex Motyl, Arvid Lukauskas, Sven Steinmo, Fran Piven, Kent Worcester, Mark Wickham Jones, Ira Katznelson, Doug Chalmers, Johannes Lindvall, Lenny Benardo, Patrick

Jackson, John Ruggie, Bent Sofus Trannoy, Martin Marcussen, Chris Howell, Andy Martin, David Baker, P. J. Anders Linder, Glenda Rosenthal, the Scottish International Educational Trust, the Arbetslivcentrum, the Council for European Studies, the Institute for the Study of World Politics, the Josephine DeKarman Fellowship, and the late Peggy Freund.

PART I

THEORY

I

Karl Polanyi and Institutional Change

> In retrospect our age will be credited with having seen the end of the self-
> regulating market. . . . Hundreds of millions had been afflicted by the scourge
> of inflation . . . stabilization of currencies became the focal point of the polit-
> ical thought of peoples and governments. The repayment of foreign loans and
> the return to stable currencies were recognized as the touchstones of ration-
> ality in politics; and no private suffering, no infringement of national sover-
> eignty, was deemed too great a sacrifice for the recovery of monetary integrity.
>
> Karl Polanyi, *The Great Transformation: The Political and Economic
> Origins of Our Time* (Boston: Beacon Press, 1944).

While Polanyi's description of the economic disorder caused by the self-
regulating market still has great resonance, his prediction of that same
market's denouement seems precipitous, at least with the benefit of
hindsight. For at the onset of the twenty-first century, we find that stable
currencies, the fight against inflation, and the unfettered mobility of
capital have once again come to be seen as "the touchstones of rationality
in politics" throughout the world. Yet Polanyi's analysis contains within it
an insight that is still of great value: his concept of the "double movement"
as the motor of institutional change.[1]

Polanyi argued, contrary to conventional economic wisdom, that
markets were neither neutral in their distributionary effects nor natural in
their origins. In particular, Polanyi saw labor as "embedded" in a series of
quite "natural" social relationships that made the construction of market
institutions and impersonal exchange extremely difficult. However, the
advance of capitalism and the commodification of labor created "disembedded" markets. In reaction to this, labor mobilized and demanded protection from the state against the strictures of the market.[2] This was

[1] Karl Polanyi, *The Great Transformation: The Political and Economic Origins of Our Time*
(Boston: Beacon Press, 1944), p. 142.
[2] See Polanyi, *The Great Transformation*, pp. 56–86, 135–63.

3

Polanyi's great insight, the double movement: Those dislocated by the market will use of the state to protect themselves, the consequence of which is large-scale institutional change.

However, a problem within the double movement thesis as a *theory* of institutional change is immediately apparent. Polanyi concluded that the new institutions that states developed in response to the double move- ment of his time, welfare states within an institutional order that heavily regulated the movement of capital and scope of markets, marked a perma- nent change in the institutional make-up of capitalism. In short, the great transformation was seen to be a one-way process. Yet, in drawing this conclusion, Polanyi replicated a fallacy he rightly denounced in the liberal economists of his day: the tendency to see market society as the "end of history." Yet in critiquing such a view, Polanyi paradoxically posited his own historical end: an institutional form of capitalism that authors following him have termed "embedded liberalism."[3]

The fallacy is, of course, that Polanyi's thought the double movement would end there. After all, if disembedding the market led to a double movement where labor demanded protection through an institutional re- embedding, then was it not reasonable to expect, in turn, another reaction against those "embedding" institutions by those most affected, namely capitalists? In fact, the political struggle between disembedding and re- embedding the market continues today, even though its contours have shifted. The contemporary neoliberal economic order can be seen as merely the latest iteration of Polanyi's double movement. It is an attempt once again to disembed the market from society, to roll back the institutions of social protection and replace them with a more market-conforming insti- tutional order. In short, despite its problems as a sufficient theory of change, the double movement does seem to have had another iteration or, more pre- cisely, a reversal. That is, the transformations of both the embedded markets of the postwar era *and* of the self-regulating markets of the 1920s follow a common pattern. The purpose of this book is to explain *both* of these great transformations.

The Double Movements of the Twentieth Century
Throughout the 1920s and 1930s, as the economic and regulatory insti- tutions of liberal capitalist states became unstable during the Great Depres- sion, the majority of such states rejected the ideas of classical liberalism as

---

[3] John Gerald Ruggie, "International Regimes, Transactions, and Change: Embedded Liberalism in the Postwar Economic Order," *International Organization* 36 (2) Spring (1982); Jonathan Kirshner, "Keynes, Capital Mobility and the Crisis of Embedded Liberal- ism," *Review of International Political Economy* 6 (3) Autumn (1999); Eric Helleiner, *States and the Reemergence of Global Finance* (Ithaca: Cornell University Press, 1994); Kathleen R. McNamara, *The Currency of Ideas: Monetary Politics and the European Union* (Ithaca: Cornell University Press, 1998), esp. pp. 54–5, 82–7.

the cornerstone of economic management. In response to this destabilization and uncertainty, a variety of reflationary and redistributive economic ideas, ranging from Keynesianism to fascism, were developed and deployed by different states. Such economic ideas, in their Keynesian rather than fascist forms, served as the ideological basis of the postwar "embedded liberal" order foreseen by Polanyi and others.[4]

These economic ideas postulated that governments could, and should, seek to control the national economy by active market manipulation since the private economy as a whole was perceived as inherently unstable and incapable of delivering socially optimal outcomes. In particular, massive and prolonged unemployment was seen to be an inevitable outcome of the capitalist process. In light of these new ideas, the state had a duty to socialize the conditions of investment to minimize the inherent instability of the business cycle and its associated unemployment.[5] These ideas were the means through which the end product of Polanyi's double movement was fulfilled: the creation of the institutions of embedded liberalism. Polanyi's double movement indeed wrought progressive institutional change. However, it did not stop there.

The economic downturn of the 1970s and early 1980s witnessed a *counter* double movement away from these embedded liberal ideas as states began to experience problems such as stagflation that existing ideas and institutions seemed unable to address.[6] In this situation, those institutions that had served as the basis of the embedded liberal order themselves became objects of critique and contestation. Institutions and instruments such as dependent central banks and active fiscal policies were now diagnosed as "part of the problem" rather than as "part of the solution" to the downturn of the period and were systematically delegitimated and dismantled. Moreover, in contrast to the previous double movement, organized business groups and their political allies displaced states as the principal

---

[4] On the failure of Keynesian ideas in Germany in the 1930s, see Sheri Berman, *The Social Democratic Moment: Ideas and Politics in the Making of Interwar Europe* (Cambridge: Harvard University Press, 1998), esp. pp. 183–6.

[5] See John Maynard Keynes, *The General Theory of Employment, Interest and Money* (New York: Harcourt Brace, 1964), pp. 245–57, 372–85. This study sees embedded liberalism as a distinct form of state. While Ruggie et al., have tended to view the Bretton Woods exchange rate mechanism as embedded liberalism, this book sees that system as merely the international monetary regime that made particular market-reforming domestic regimes – embedded liberal states – possible. Such states were characterized by relatively closed capital markets, demand-side fiscal policies, a belief in an activist state, and a view of unemployment as being due to a general failure of demand.

[6] "Seemed unable to address" is the appropriate qualifier in this case. Indeed, even some monetarist economists concede that the simple "supply-shock" model, which posited the inflation of the 1970s as a function of oil price increases, remains the single best explanation of the disruptions of the period. See Thomas Mayer, *Monetary Policy and the Great Inflation in the United States* (Cheltenham: Edward Elgar, 1999).

actors responding to economic dislocation. Such business groups used a variety of monetarist and other "neoclassical" ideas to redefine the boundaries of political economy away from the Keynesian emphasis on redistribution and growth and toward the neoliberal emphasis on inflation control and monetary stability.

In sum, just as labor and the state reacted to the collapse of the classical liberal order during the 1930s and 1940s by re-embedding the market, so business reacted against this embedded liberal order during the 1970s and 1980s and sought to "disembed liberalism" once again. In this effort, business and its political allies were quite successful, and by the 1990s a new neoliberal institutional order had been established in many advanced capitalist states with remarkable similarities to the regime discredited in the 1930s. That is, both classical liberalism and neoliberalism are characterized by high capital mobility, large private capital flows, market-conforming tools of macroeconomic management, a willingness to ride out balance of payments and other disequilibria by deflation, and a view of the rate of employment as dependent upon the market-clearing price of labor. Polanyi's double movement, it seems, has indeed been put into reverse gear.

In order to explain both sets of transformations, it is nonetheless necessary to develop a better understanding of institutional change than that provided by the framework of the double movement. To do so, this book focuses upon two factors mentioned previously that are generally given short shrift in political economy explanations: the political uses of economic ideas and politics of organized business.[7] As well as "bringing business back in," this book contributes to institutionalist scholarship by developing a theoretical understanding of how ideas, specifically economic ideas, are vitally important components of institutional construction and change. In particular, by challenging the way that political scientists often think about the relationship between ideas, interests, and institutions under uncertainty, the theory elaborated and tested here neither reduces ideas to interests nor

---

[7] Historically, a remarkable feature of comparative political economy has been the clear preference of scholars to undertake research on the state and labor, to the relative exclusion of the role of business in politics. However, the late 1990s saw a flowering of excellent scholarship on business as a political actor. For seminal contributions, see Peter Swenson, "Arranged Alliance: Business Interests in the New Deal," *Politics and Society* 25 (1) (1997); Torben Iversen, Jonas Pontusson, and David Soskice, eds., *Unions, Employers, and Central Banks: Macroeconomic Coordination and Institutional Change in Social Market Economies* (New York: Cambridge University Press, 2000); Peter A. Hall and David Soskice, eds., *Varieties of Capitalism: The Institutional Foundations of Comparative Advantage* (New York: Oxford University Press, 2001). Yet, despite the impressive theoretical contributions of this scholarship, it cannot accommodate within its methodological ambit such phenomena as why the Swedish Institute of Trade (HUI) publishes studies claiming that the average Swede is now poorer than inner-city African Americans (http://www.reuters.com/news article.jhtml?type=search&StoryID=918506). The politics of business is as much the politics of interest construction as it is equlibria construction.

treats them as simple adjuncts to existing institutional explanations. This book attempts to push the boundaries of ideational and institutional scholarship forward by moving beyond reductive interest-based explanations toward one that sees ideas and interests together as essentially embedded elements of institutional change.[8]

Structures Do Not Come with an Instruction Sheet: Rethinking Institutional Change

While Polanyi's double movement offers a plausible heuristic, it suffers from a serious limitation as a theory of institutional change and must be reconceptualized. The double movement, in common with other interest-based explanations of institutional change, sees change as a problem of comparative statics.[9] That is, in order to explain institutional change, the elements of a present set of institutions are juxtaposed to those of a previous set, and then a (usually exogenous) variable is imputed that "explains" why the latter emerged out of the former.[10] Such arguments implicitly posit the model, "institutional equilibrium → punctuation → new institutional equilibrium."[11] Putting this in terms of the double movement, the shift from disembedded to embedded institutions is explained by the punctuation of

[8] For an account of ideas that subordinates them to interests, see Judith Goldstein and Robert Keohane, eds., *Ideas and Foreign Policy: Beliefs, Institutions, and Political Change* (Ithaca: Cornell University Press, 1993). For attempts to overcome this dichotomy between ideas and interests, see Kathryn Sikkink, *Ideas and Institutions: Developmentalism in Argentina and Brazil* (Ithaca: Cornell University Press, 1991); Berman, *The Social Democratic Moment*; McNamara, *The Currency of Ideas*; Ngaire Woods, "Economic Ideas and International Relations: Beyond Rational Neglect," *International Studies Quarterly* 39 (2) (1995).

[9] For examples of such structural explanations, see Ronald Rogowski, *Commerce and Coalitions: How Trade Affects Domestic Political Alignments* (Princeton: Princeton University Press, 1989); Douglass C. North and Robert P. Thomas, *The Rise of the Western World: A New Economic History* (Cambridge University Press, 1973). For agent-centered but still static alternatives, see Douglass North, *Institutions, Institutional Change, and Economic Performance* (Cambridge: Cambridge University Press, 1990); Elinor Ostrom, *Governing the Commons: The Evolution of Institutions for Collective Action* (Cambridge: Cambridge University Press, 1990).

[10] To take an example of this logic, the embedded liberal order emerged because of the crisis engendered by a negative change in banking liquidity in the 1920s. This change produced institutions that provided excess liquidity, and thus inflation, in the 1960s and 1970s. See Milton Friedman and Anna J. Shwartz, *A Monetary History of the United States 1867–1960* (Princeton: Princeton University Press, 1963).

[11] For a discussion of the advantages and disadvantages of such punctuationist logics in political science, see Stephen Krasner, "Approaches to the State: Alternative Conceptions and Historical Dynamics," *Comparative Politics* 16 (2) January (1984); Hendrik Spruyt, *The Sovereign State and Its Competitors* (Princeton: Princeton University Press, 1994).

the 1920s and 1930s, with the institutions of the latter period being a reaction to the outcomes produced by the former. Given such a model, the new institutional equilibrium is seen to reconstitute itself automatically.

Such a model of institutional change is unsatisfactory for two related reasons. The first is rather straightforward. The logic behind such a model is *post hoc, ergo proptor hoc* – that is, that which comes after explains that which comes before. Unfortunately, that which comes after *does not* explain that which comes before, *unless* one can specify the causal links between the former and latter objects.[12] Second, such a model does not specify such links. By identifying agents' intentions in terms of observed outcomes, the mechanism of institutional change remains at best underspecified and at worst circular.[13]

While the institutions of embedded liberalism were indeed a reaction to the failures of classical liberalism, and the institutions of neoliberalism were also a reaction to the failures of embedded liberalism, such "failures" are not self-apparent phenomena obvious to agents on the ground that demand obvious solutions. This is because while exogenous material changes may help to explain why a particular institutional order becomes unstable, such infusions of instability do not in themselves explain how the new or modified order takes the form that it does.[14] In short, structural theories of institutional supply are indeterminate as to subsequent institutional form. Theoretically, no exogenous factor can in and of itself explain the specific forms that institutional change takes. While the destabilization of existing institutions can be exogenously driven, moving from such a position to a new stable institutional order must be seen as an *endogenous* process. Specifically, how agents redesign and rebuild institutional orders, *and the conditions under which these activities take place*, need to be analyzed.

Uncertainty and "Crisis" in Institutional Change

Such theories of institutional change that rely on comparative statics are burdened by two conditions commonly ignored in static theories: the type of uncertainty faced by agents and the set of ideas available to them. While some institutionalist theories explicitly posit uncertainty as the reason for the existence of institutions, in doing so they tend to discount the importance of uncertainty by turning it into risk. In such models, institutional

---

[12] That is to say, *post hoc* does not necessarily lead to *proptor hoc*.

[13] As Robert Wade argues, it is necessary to recognize these failings since such theories "do lend themselves to some of the sloppiest reasoning in . . . political science. The existence [of agents] is often inferred from the asserted fact of common interests, and their influence is in turn inferred from policy outcomes in line with those interests . . . to yield . . . one great tautology." Robert Wade, "East Asia's Economic Success: Conflicting Perspectives, Partial Insights, Shaky Evidence," *World Politics* 44 (2) (1992), p. 309.

[14] Specifically, once a given equilibrium has become unstable, there is no *a priori* way of predicting the new equilibrium by reference to its collapse.

supply follows from the "need" for agents to realize their "given" interests in a "risky" environment. However, as we shall see in detail in the next chapter, such a reduction is not always warranted because the situations we are interested in here – that is, situations of economic crisis – are not best understood as situations of risk.[15] Instead, they are situations of what I shall call throughout this book "Knightian" uncertainty[16] – that is, situations regarded by contemporary agents as unique events where the agents are unsure as to what their interests actually are, let alone how to realize them.

Static models of change eliminate Knightian uncertainty as an issue by making the content of new institutions a determinate function of the problems faced by previous institutions. Consequently, both uncertainty and the issue of agents' interests (and thus actions) under uncertainty are avoided. However, if periods of economic instability are seen as situations of Knightian uncertainty, then two conditions change. First, agents' interests become *something to be explained*, rather than something with which to do the explaining. Second, the notion of what an economic crisis under such conditions *actually is* becomes much more problematic and much more theoretically important than is usually acknowledged. This is because what constitutes an economic crisis *as a crisis* is not a self-apparent phenomenon.[17] While the destabilization of institutions may produce uncertainty, and while such uncertainty may manifest itself in effects such as currency collapses or rising prices deleterious to the agents involved, neither the causes of nor the solutions to such uncertainty are given by the conditions of the collapse. Agents must argue over, diagnose, proselytize, and impose on others their notion of what a crisis actually *is* before collective action to resolve the uncertainty facing them can take any meaningful institutional form. As Colin Hay argues, "the mobilization of perceptions of crisis . . . involves the formation and triumph of a simplifying ideology which must

---

[15] That is, situations where agents are sure of their interests but are unsure of how to achieve them.

[16] On Knightian uncertainty, see Frank Knight's original conception in Frank H. Knight, *Risk, Uncertainty and Profit* (Boston and New York: Houghton Mifflin Company, 1921). A perspective on uncertainty that has been very influential in my thinking and which I draw upon here is Jens Beckert, "What Is Sociological about Economic Sociology? Uncertainty and the Embeddedness of Economic Action," *Theory and Society* 25 (6) (1996).

[17] See Colin Hay, "Narrating Crisis: the Discursive Construction of the 'Winter of Discontent,'" *Sociology* (30) 2 May (1996); Deborah A. Stone, "Causal Stories and the Formation of Policy Agendas," *Political Science Quarterly* (104) 2 (1989). For example, the German hyperinflation of the 1920s was clearly a crisis in the sense that the basic mechanisms of the economy ceased to function. But what caused that crisis was very much open to interpretation. Similarly, in 1979 the British Conservative Party was elected to resolve Britain's crisis of six hundred thousand unemployed. By 1983 Britain had over five times this number unemployed, but the situation was no longer diagnosed, nor narrated by the state, as a crisis. Crises need to be narrated and explained. They are not self-apparent phenomena.

find and construct points of resonance with a multitude of individuated experiences."[18] Crisis thus becomes an act of intervention where sources of uncertainty are diagnosed and constructed. Given this, the set of available ideas with which to interpret the environment, reduce uncertainty, and make purposeful collective action possible becomes crucially important in determining the form of new institutions.[19]

Since structures do not come with an instruction sheet, economic ideas make such an institutional resolution possible by providing the authoritative diagnosis as to what a crisis *actually is* and when a given situation *actually constitutes a crisis*. They diagnose "what has gone wrong" and thus "what is to be done." In short, the nature of a crisis is not simply given by its effects, dislocations, or casualties, nor are the actions of agents simply determined by their "given" interests. Instead, the diagnosis of a situation as a "crisis" by a particular set of ideas is a construction that makes the uncertainty that agents perceive explicable, manageable, and indeed, actionable. Therefore, in periods of *economic crisis*, it is imperative to attend to the *economic ideas* that key economic agents have.[20]

Rethinking Ideas

Acknowledging these conditions opens up the space for an ideational account of institutional change that builds upon Polanyi's original concept of the double movement. While Polanyi saw the double movement as a function of agents with structurally given interests reacting to self-apparent crises, what this and other static accounts of institutional change miss is the importance of uncertainty and ideas in determining the form and content of institutional change. Economic ideas are causally powerful in this way because they do not simply reflect the world that precedes them. Of course, ideas do reflect the world to some degree, especially during times of institutional stability, but they are also constructions that allow agents to define a crisis *as a crisis*, and thereby both plan and politic their way forward.

---

[18] Colin Hay, "Crisis and the Structural Transformation of the State: Interrogating Processes of Change," *British Journal of Politics and International Relations* 1 (3) October (1999), p. 321.

[19] Such ideas are generated to respond in a new way to new conditions and are a creative element in political economy, for better or worse. Such ideas do not "come from nowhere" precisely because they arise out of confusion and uncertainty in times of instability. However, because they are a response to uncertainty, they are not simply reducible to a given and self-apparent crisis. Such ideas are generative, not correspondence theories. I thank Bill Connolly for this insight.

[20] For significant attempts to explain states responses to economic dislocations that assume interests as given and crises as unambiguous, see Peter A. Gourevitch, *Politics in Hard Times: Comparative Responses to International Economic Crises* (Ithaca: Cornell University Press, 1986); Helen V. Milner, *Resisting Protectionism: Global Industries and the Politics of International Trade* (Princeton: Princeton University Press, 1988).

Economic ideas provide agents with an interpretive framework, which describes and accounts for the workings of the economy by defining its constitutive elements and "proper" (and therefore "improper") interrelations. Economic ideas provide agents with both a "scientific" and a "normative" account of the existing economy and polity, and a vision that specifies how these elements *should* be constructed.[21] That is, economic ideas also act as blueprints for new institutions. In sum, ideas allow agents to reduce uncertainty, propose a particular solution to a moment of crisis, and empower agents to resolve that crisis by constructing new institutions in line with these new ideas.

Moreover, such an analysis of institutional change suggests that the reduction of uncertainty, the specification of causes, and the actual supply of new institutions are parts of a temporally distinct sequence of events where ideas have different effects at different junctures. Such a sequential understanding of change is what the double movement and other static models of institutional change miss and what taking ideas seriously makes possible: a way of making institutional change dynamic, contingent, and political. Process and contingency cannot be understood within a model of comparative statics because such a model does not even acknowledge such conditions. Once reconceptualized in this way, the double movement offers us a powerful understanding of patterns of large-scale institutional change. This is *not* to say that only ideas matter, nor that institutional change is purely an ideational affair; they do not and it is not.[22] But economic ideas certainly do matter in periods when existing institutional frameworks and the distributions they make possible fail and uncertainty prevails. At these junctures, it is ideas that tell agents what to do and what future to construct.

The Choice of Cases: The United States and Sweden

In the investigation of the double movements of the twentieth century, the rise and fall of the embedded liberal institutions of the United States and Sweden represent examples of "most different" and "crucial" case

---

[21] Economic ideas are scientific and normative in so far as all positive statements about the causal order of the economy necessarily imply value trade-offs and hence different patterns of distribution. For example, if one accepts the proposition that individual incentives to invest are the most important source of growth (a positive statement), then cutting taxes and public expenditure (a policy preference) implies a normative statement (that such spending by the state is bad).

[22] A group of financiers, for example, responding to new and uncertain conditions, would be unlikely to accept a set of ideas that they could see would diminish their own role. Yet, in such moments of uncertainty, before such a threshold is reached, such a group may accept new patterns of diagnosis and response, leading the group to change its conceptions of its interests in the process.

strategies.[23] The logic of a "most different" selection criterion is that if a variable of significance is found in two cases, which are different in all respects apart from the hypothesized independent and dependent variables, then the importance of those variables – in this case, ideas and institutional change – is highlighted.

A most different case strategy is also appropriate on the grounds that the United States and Sweden tend to be seen as two ends of the liberal – capitalist continuum. Sweden is often seen as the social democracy *par excellence*, characterized by universal welfare provision, high labor density, and until recently, highly regulated capital movements.[24] In contrast, the United States tends to be seen as the exemplar of the liberal political economy with residualist welfare provisions, low union density, and free capital movements.[25] Indeed, these states are often seen as the exemplars of exclusive "worlds of welfare" given that the paths taken to democracy, the structures of representation and organization, and their relative positions in the international economy are radically different.[26] Given these conditions, a most different case strategy appears to be optimal.

Furthermore, the juxtaposition of these two cases constitutes a variation on a "crucial case" strategy. Taking these cases together pairs them as the most and least likely environments in which to find the phenomena of interest. As the premier liberal political economy, the United States can be seen as the case where the influence of business and the power of market-conforming ideas would be most likely to be apparent. In contrast, Sweden's

---

[23] On most- and least-likely case logics, see Jack Snyder, "Richness, Rigor, and Relevance in the Study of Soviet Foreign-Policy," *International Security* 9 (3) (1985). On the logic of crucial cases, see Alexander George, "Case Studies and Theory Development: The Method of Structured, Focused Comparison," in Paul Gordon Lauren, ed., *Diplomacy: New Approaches in History, Theory, and Policy* (New York: Free Press, 1979); Harry Eckstein, "Case Study and Theory in Political Science," in Fred I. Greenstein and Nelson R. Polsby, eds., *The Handbook of Political Science* (Reading, MA: Addison-Wesley Publishing, 1975). For a recent attempt to combine case study and statistical logics in a single logic of inference, see Gary King, Robert O. Keohane, and Sidney Verba, *Designing Social Inquiry: Scientific Inference in Qualitative Research* (Princeton: Princeton University Press, 1994).

[24] On Sweden, see Bo Rothstein, *The Social Democratic State: The Swedish Model and the Bureaucratic Problem of Social Reforms* (Pittsburgh: University of Pittsburgh Press, 1996); Hugh Heclo and Henrik Madsen, *Policy and Politics in Sweden: Principled Pragmatism* (Philadelphia: Temple University Press, 1987); Klaus Misgeld, Karl Molin, and Klas Åmark, eds., *Creating Social Democracy: A Century of the Social Democratic Labor Party in Sweden* (Pennsylvania: Pennsylvania State Press, 1992).

[25] On the distinctiveness of the United States version of capitalism, see the classic statement by Andrew Shonfeld, *Modern Capitalism: The Changing Balance of Public and Private Power* (Oxford: Oxford University Press, 1966). For the United States in comparative, perspective, see Peter J. Katzenstein, ed., *Between Power and Plenty: Foreign Economic Policies of Advanced Industrial States* (Madison: University of Wisconsin Press, 1978).

[26] On this typology, see Gosta Esping Anderson, *The Three Worlds of Welfare Capitalism* (Princeton: Princeton University Press, 1990).

social democratic institutions and strong encompassing labor organizations would constitute the least likely environment where such dynamics would be apparent. Thus, if the same institutional changes, as a function of the same ideas, occur in these very different states, and if one can explain the impact and relevance of this variable theoretically, then the case for the causal importance of ideas can be powerfully demonstrated. Finally, as James D. Fearon has recognized, in "small N" case studies where degrees of freedom are either small or negative, counterfactuals must be used to strengthen the claims made in the cases.[27] Therefore, the conclusion will apply a strategy of highlighting relevant counterfactuals. Given this combination of strategies and selection criteria, the cases of the United States and Sweden are justifiable selections on both methodological and substantive grounds.

The Units of Analysis

This book focuses upon three main actors: the state, organized labor, and organized business. While rational choice theorists, through their insistence on microfoundations, have done great service in pointing out the problems inherent in collective action and the construction of collective agents, this position sometimes seems to turn a methodological postulate – that individuals are appropriate units of analysis – into an ontological one – that only individuals are "real."[28] This book rejects this position and argues instead that it is wholly reasonable to focus on collectivities as agents.

First, if the barriers to collective action were as insurmountable as some theorists suggest, then being able to talk meaningfully about states, unions, parties, etc., as agents of change would be impossible. Collective action barriers are often overcome and, as we shall see in the next chapter, ideas are important resources in this regard. Second, given that agents do act collectively, identifying the appropriate unit of analysis in a given case is not given by *a priori* theorizing. Rather, the relevant unit of analysis depends upon the view of the crisis that the agents in question operationalize and act upon. That is, the ideas that agents have about the sources of the "crisis" they face set limits on the types of collectivities, and thus collective actions, that are possible.

For example, during the first great transformation, the failure of liberal economic institutions and ideas to make sense of the depression, coupled with the dislocations it caused, produced a growth of the state *as an actor*

---

[27] James D. Fearon, "Counterfactuals and Hypothesis Testing in Political Science," *World Politics* 43 (2) (1991).

[28] For such a position, see Jon Elster, ed., *Rational Choice* (New York: New York University Press, 1986), esp. pp. 1–19. For an application, see Michael Taylor, "Structure, Culture and Action in the Explanation of Social-Change: Explaining the Origins of Social-Structures," *Politics and Society* 17 (2) (1989).

in new policy areas.[29] Given the ideas used by the state to make sense of the crisis at hand, the state actively "organized" labor and encouraged the same organization in business, with a view to active cooperation with these collectivities to resolve the crisis.[30] Similarly, during the second great transformation, given the failure of embedded liberal institutions and ideas to limit institutionally generated uncertainty, business reorganized itself as a collective agent so that it could argue for the demobilization of the state and labor as economic agents.

Neither the actions that these collectivities undertook nor these collectivities themselves are theoretical abstractions that can be identified by *a priori* reasoning. Instead, such collective agents can only be identified – and indeed can only be constituted by – the conditions faced by agents and, crucially, by the interpretations of those conditions held by such agents. The ideas, arguments, and struggles produced by these collectivities helped to constitute these transformations. Given these factors, focusing upon the state, business, and labor as the units of analysis employed in this study is justifiable on both theoretical and empirical grounds.[31]

The Plan of the Book

The book is divided thematically and functionally into four parts. Part I, comprising Chapters 1 and 2, sets out the objectives of the book and

---

[29] On the state as an actor, see Theda Skocpol, "Bringing the State Back In: Strategies of Analysis in Current Research," in Peter Evans, Dietrich Rueschemeyer, and Theda Skocpol, eds., *Bringing the State Back In* (Cambridge: Cambridge University Press, 1985). Given the clear institutional differences found in the American and Swedish "states," throughout this book the "state" in the American case shall denote the executive branch of government and associated federal institutions and agencies controlled by the governing party. In the Swedish case, the "state" refers to the totality of governmental institutions both inside and outside parliament controlled by the governing party. Given the weak nature of party in the American case, Congress is not held to be identical with the state.

[30] I am not saying that states have ideas and think. Clearly agents within the state who are empowered to act in the name of the state, with the resources of the state, do the thinking and have ideas. However, making this an issue strikes me as trivially true. After all, the Works Progress Administration built things; the head of the Works Progress Administration did not.

[31] Given this, an *a priori* desire simply to focus on abstract individuals or equally vague "structures" as sources of change regardless of the conditions of action, and agents' perceptions of those conditions, seems to miss the empirical woods for the theoretical trees. Viewing only individuals as "real" is just an aggregation fallacy in reverse. While methodological individualists were quite correct to criticize structural theories for being all product and no producer, by insisting on individualist microfoundations (*qua* ontological individualism), rather than the whole being greater than the sum of its parts, it is argued that all historical change is reducible to the actions of discrete individuals. If this were the case, given collective action problems, it would be almost impossible to explain why much change occurs. States, to take one example, are more than just an aggregation of bureaucrats. States "act" as states, not as individuals, and to reduce the question of state action to what individual bureaucrats do is to rob the question of "what states do" of any meaning.

develops the theory of ideas and institutional change used to analyze the great transformations of the 1930s and 1970s. Chapter 2 expands upon the claims made in this chapter by developing a theory of how, in periods of economic crisis, ideas both give substance to interests and determine the form and content of new institutions. From this theory, five specific hypotheses about ideas are generated. Specifically, it is hypothesized that as part of an overall sequence of institutional change, ideas reduce uncertainty, act as coalition-building resources, empower agents to contest existing institutions, act as resources in the construction of new institutions, and finally coordinate agents' expectations, thereby reproducing institutional stability. Viewing institutional change ideationally and sequentially offers a better explanation of the cases that follow than purely structural or interest-based models can offer.

Following Part I's discussion of what ideas do in theory, Part II details the ideas used in practice to make the embedded liberal orders of the United States and Sweden. Chapters 3 and 4 discuss the actual formation of American and Swedish embedded liberalism during the 1930s and 1940s. This is done from the perspectives of the state, business, and labor, given the ideas that were used by these groups to make sense of the Great Depression and construct an institutional order to resolve it.

In the United States, the key ideas used to transform institutions appeared outside the economic mainstream and included the administered prices thesis, institutional economics, and various underconsumption and secular stagnation theories.[32] In contrast, in Sweden, the key transformative economic ideas were developed inside the economic mainstream, albeit by junior economists and politicians, and revolved around the development of a reflationary yet "supply-side" model of intensive export-oriented growth.

Part III discusses the ideas used by business in America and Sweden in the 1970s and 1980s to attack and dismantle the embedded liberal order and replace it with neoliberalism: monetarism, rational expectations theory, public choice theory, and various theories of "credibility" and "Normpolitik."[33] Chapter 5 details the changing international and

---

[32] For examples of each of these types of arguments, see, among many others, Adolphus Berle and Gardiner Means, *The Modern Corporation and Private Property* (New York: Legal Classics Library, 1993); William Trufant Foster, *Business without a Buyer* (New York: Houghton Mifflin Company, 1927); Alvin Hansen, *Fiscal Policy and Business Cycles* (New York: W.W. Norton and Company, 1941).

[33] For examples of each of these types of arguments, see Milton Friedman, "The Role of Monetary Policy," *American Economic Review* 58 (1) March (1968); John Muth, "Rational Expectations and the Theory of Price Movements," *Econometrica* 29 (3) July (1961); Robert E. Lucas, Jr., "Expectations and the Neutrality of Money," *Journal of Economic Theory* 4 (2) April (1972); James M. Buchanan and Richard E. Wagner, *Democracy in Deficit: The Political Legacy of Lord Keynes* (New York: Academic Press, 1977); Hans Tson Soderstrom, *Normer och ekonomisk politik* (Stockholm: SNS Forlag, 1996).

domestic environmental factors that destabilized the existing institutional order and then goes on to discuss the alternative economic ideas that were developed to narrate this new and unexpected period of uncertainty. Following this, Chapters 6 and 7 detail the actual development and deployment of these ideas by business and its allies in the United States and Sweden in the 1970s and 1980s and the great transformations that these new economic ideas wrought.

Chapter 8 draws together the conclusions of this study. First, the five hypotheses about ideas developed in Chapter 2 are reexamined and the importance of a sequential understanding of institutional change is reiterated. Following this, broad theoretical comparisons are drawn from the examination of the cases as a whole. Specifically, Chapter 8 critically reexamines the relevance of this study for existing theories of institutional change, and the hypothesized causal factors that such theories rest upon. Third, by way of further comparison, the *extent* of the second set of institutional transformations under study here is discussed. While it is concluded that these transformations do not constitute a simple return to an institutional *status quo ante*, it is nonetheless stressed that contrary to many other studies, the scope of such changes should not be underrated.

Finally, Polanyi's double movement is revisited and the general nature of change in advanced capitalist societies is discussed. In doing so, it is reiterated, based upon the evidence marshaled in the cases, that while ideas do not "matter" all the time, in certain specific circumstances – particularly in moments of economic crisis, ideas, and the political control of those ideas – matter most of all. Making political and economic analysts take *this* idea seriously is, above all other objectives, the fundamental goal of this book.

2

A Theory of Institutional Change

Kathryn Sikkink noted that "it is a paradox that scholars, whose entire existence is centered on the production and understanding of ideas, should grant ideas so little significance for explaining political life."[1] The source of this paradox lies in the way contemporary political science has conceptualized the relationship among institutions, interests, and ideas. The purpose of this chapter is to reformulate these concepts and resolve this and other paradoxes in a theoretically productive way.

The first section of this chapter reviews existing ideational approaches in political science and argues that the current literature fails to take ideas seriously as both objects of inquiry and significant explanatory categories. This failure is principally due to the tendency of both the major schools of ideational analysis, historical institutionalism and rationalist institutionalism, to use ideas as "fillers" or auxiliary hypotheses to solve preexisting problems within their respective research programs. Given this tendency, neither school fully investigates ideas as explanatory factors in their own right. Further, by building a theory of ideas out of a prior theory of institutions, ideas become derivative of the mode of analysis in which they are operationalized. This creates a homology of ideas and institutions that precludes the development of a theory of ideas and institutional change that takes ideas seriously as explanatory categories.

This homology of ideas and institutions is not the only problem encountered in developing a better theory of institutional change. A parallel problem that limits the usefulness of current ideational explanations is the tendency within such studies, and within political science in general, to treat ideas and interests as radically different and unrelated concepts. That is, there is a tendency to mistake an analytic distinction, that one can hold

[1] Kathryn Sikkink, *Ideas and Institutions: Developmentalism in Argentina and Brazil* (Ithaca: Cornell University Press, 1991), p. 3.

ideas and interests as separate *for purposes of analysis*, for a synthetic one, that ideas and interests are *in fact different things* in the world.[2]

The point of problematizing this distinction is to demonstrate that not only is such a position logically untenable, it also inhibits practical theorizing about the role of ideas in explaining both institutional stability and change. Current ideational approaches generally force analysts to choose between ideas and interests as an "all or nothing" proposition, and underplay, as noted in the previous chapter, the importance of uncertainty. This study, in contrast, aims to demonstrate not only that ideas matter, but precisely when, why, and under what conditions they matter, by building a sequential theory of ideas and institutional change under uncertainty. However, before developing this new theory, we need to examine contemporary approaches to the study of ideas and institutions and note their strengths and weaknesses.

Studying Ideas

Contemporary Ideational Approaches: Ideas and the "New" Institutionalisms

Broadly speaking, there are two schools of ideational literature in contemporary political science. These can be categorized as separate historical and rationalist research programs.[3] The historicist usage of ideas developed out of the "historical institutionalist" research program that emerged during the early 1990s, while rationalist treatments of ideas followed the "institutional turn" of rational choice theory of the same period.[4] While these approaches helped place the question of ideas at the forefront of scholarship, such studies suffered from several basic limitations.

---

[2] See Hilary Putnam, "The Analytic and the Synthetic," in Herbert Feigel and Grover Maxwell, eds., *Minnesota Studies in the Philosophy of Science* (Minneapolis: University of Minnesota Press, 1962); William Connolly, *The Terms Of Political Discourse* (Princeton: Princeton University Press, 1963).

[3] There are other bodies of literature on ideas, but ideas in such theories tend to be conceptualized in a wholly different manner than that undertaken here – for example, as norms or identities in the international relations literature. Although some of this work is excellent, it is less appropriate for this study than the institutional literature reviewed here. For exemplars in the international relations traditions, see Peter J. Katzenstein, ed., *The Culture of National Security: Norms and Identity in World Politics* (New York: Columbia University Press, 1996); Alexander Wendt, *The Social Theory of International Politics* (Cambridge: Cambridge University Press, 1999). There is also an immense sociological literature on ideas that is omitted here for reasons of space.

[4] The literature of both schools is now enormous. For important statements of each, see Douglass C. North, *Institutions, Institutional Change and Economic Performance* (Cambridge: Cambridge University Press, 1990); Sven Steinmo, Kathleen Thelen, and Frank Longstreth, eds., *Structuring Politics: Historical Institutionalism in Comparative Analysis* (Cambridge: Cambridge University Press, 1992).

Because their models are grounded in the basic assumptions of microeconomics, rationalists hold agents' preferences to be the primitives, the uncaused cause of the theory. Given that all social structures and institutions are (and by definition must be) reducible to individual utility calculi, nothing *a priori* to the individual exists that another individual did not put there. Because of this, all social phenomena and outcomes must at base be intentional, and institutions can therefore only be seen as instrumental products used by individuals to maximize their respective utilities. Given these assumptions, rationalists' theories predict a world in flux, replete with cycling, multiple equilibria, and the like, where institutions are both formed and changed according to rapidly shifting contract curves and cost/benefit trade-offs.[5]

However, since the world around us seems to be much more stable than rationalists' theories would predict, these theorists needed some mechanism to explain the apparent anomaly of stability. At first, institutions were invoked to solve this problem. However, it was soon appreciated that if institutions are themselves instrumental products, and producing institutions is itself a collective action problem, then existing rationalist theories contained no endogenous mechanism of institutional supply.[6] Given this theoretical problem, ideas became the focal point of investigation for explaining institutional supply and stability.

Historical institutionalist scholarship's problem is the mirror image of rationalism's dilemma. Rather than holding individuals' preferences as primitives, historical institutionalists hold institutions themselves as theoretical primitives.[7] For historical institutionalists, institutions are ontologically prior to the individuals who constitute them. Therefore, the preferences of "historical" individuals are themselves a *reducta* of institutions. For historical institutionalists, institutions "structure" individuals' preferences, whereas for rationalists, the preferences of individuals "structure" institutions.[8]

Under these assumptions, historical institutionalist theories, especially their earlier works, predicted a world of stability, path-dependence, and persistence.[9] Yet such a perspective created a problem for historicists, for if

[5] Mark Blyth, "'Any More Bright Ideas?': The Ideational Turn of Comparative Political Economy," *Comparative Politics* 29 (2) January (1997), pp. 230–1, 238–9.

[6] Robert H. Bates, "Contra Contractarianism: Some Reflections on the New Institutionalism," *Politics and Society* 16 (2–3) (1988).

[7] James March and James Olsen, "The New Institutionalism: Organizational Factors in Political Life," *American Political Science Review* 78 (3) (1984); Peter A. Hall, *Governing the Economy: The Politics of State Intervention in Britain and France* (Oxford: Oxford University Press, 1986); Steinmo et al., *Structuring Politics*, esp. pp. 1–32.

[8] Blyth, "'Any More Bright Ideas?,'" esp. pp. 230, 235–7.

[9] For example, see Paul Pierson, *Dismantling the Welfare State: Reagan, Thatcher and the Politics of Retrenchment* (Cambridge: Cambridge University Press, 1994); Hall, *Governing the Economy*, Steinmo et al., *Structuring Politics*.

individuals' interests were institutionally derived, then it made little sense to appeal to individuals as sources of institutional change. Consequently, change within institutions became hard to explain unless it was seen to result from rather *ad hoc* exogenous "punctuations."[10] However, institutions do change, sometimes without obvious punctuations, and because of this theoretical problem, ideas also became attractive to historical institutionalists as an *endogenous* source of change.

Paradoxically, then, given these radically opposing views of institutions and what they do, both schools faced a similar problem. Despite one school seeking to explain stability and the other seeking to explain change, there was nonetheless an underlying similarity in both rationalist and historicist efforts to "bring ideas back in." Both approaches tended to treat ideas as auxiliary hypotheses to solve prior theoretical problems inherent in already existing research programs. To see why this is the case, consider some of the exemplars of both schools.

Ideas and Historical Institutionalism: Strengths and Weaknesses

In the historical institutionalist tradition, the seminal works on ideas are perhaps Theda Skocpol and Margaret Weir's account of policy responses to the Great Depression, and Peter A. Hall's work on the spread of Keynesian ideas and "policy paradigms."[11] Skocpol and Weir argued that variations in preexisting institutional arrangements – that is, the degree to which they were open or closed to new ideas – were the critical factors that explained the divergent policy responses of states during the Great Depression.[12] Unless existing state institutions and policy instruments are congruent with new ideas, then new ideas will neither be proposed nor readily accepted by the state and other elites. Seen in this way, state structures and policy legacies acted as filters for policy-relevant ideas.[13]

Placing this argument in a wider comparative context, Hall et al. focused on the international spread of Keynesian ideas.[14] Once again, this study sug-

---

[10] For a discussion of such punctuation logics in political science, see Stephen Krasner, "Approaches to the State: Alternative Conceptions and Historical Dynamics," *Comparative Politics* 16 (2) January (1984).

[11] Theda Skocpol and Margaret Weir, "State Structures and the Possibilities for Keynesian Responses to the Depression in Sweden, Britain and the United States," in Peter B. Evans, Dietrich Rueschemeyer, Theda Skocpol, eds., *Bringing the State Back In* (Cambridge: Cambridge University Press, 1985); Peter A. Hall, *The Political Power of Economic Ideas: Keynesianism across Nations* (Princeton: Princeton University Press, 1989); Peter A. Hall, "Policy Paradigms, Social Learning and the State: The Case of Economic Policymaking in Britain," *Comparative Politics* 25 (2) (1993).

[12] Skocpol and Weir, "State Structures," p. 109.

[13] As Skocpol and Weir put it, "we must ask not about the presence of individual persons or ideas in the abstract, but whether key state agencies were open or closed to the use or development of innovative perspectives." Skocpol and Weir, "State Structures," p. 126.

[14] Hall, ed., *Political Power*.

gested that the critical determinants of whether or not ideas promote policy change were institutional. In explaining the spread of Keynesian policies, Hall hypothesized that new economic ideas must be aligned with administrative and political arrangements to ensure their adoption and spread. Specifically, new ideas must be able to serve the interests of ruling parties by strengthening their political position in the state and must also be "actionable" within state institutions. That is, the state must have the capacity to implement the policies stemming from these new ideas.[15]

Expanding the role of ideas in his later work, Hall, borrowing from Kuhn, developed the concept of "policy paradigms."[16] In this model, Hall outlined a threefold typology of levels of policy intervention: "overarching goals, techniques used to attain these goals, and specific policy instruments."[17] Hall defines change in each of these levels as examples of third-, second-, and first-order changes in economic policy that are themselves engendered by two different patterns of state learning: simple (change in instruments and means) and complex (change in goals and ends). Change in levels one and two are seen as equivalent to changes within a paradigm, while change in level three would correspond to a change of paradigm. For Hall, the British government's economic policy shifts in the period 1976–81 were a clear example of third-order change in that the basic goals of policy, the role of the state, and the nature of economic life were radically reformulated. Given this analysis, a change in ideas, specifically the replacement of one policy paradigm by another, results in institutional as well as policy change.

Later scholars have expanded the scope of historical institutionalism's turn to ideas. For example, Eric Helleiner's study of the reemergence of global finance lays weight on ideas as causal factors in both the development and in the denouement of the international financial institutions of the postwar era.[18] Kathleen R. McNamara's study of the European Monetary Union (EMU) argues that greater European unity in the 1980s did not lead teleologically toward a monetary union, especially one based upon an idea of monetary discipline and price stabilization. Rather, McNamara explains EMU's content and trajectory by reference to the ideas held by central bankers and their insulated institutional position.[19] Similarly, in the study of democratization, Sheri Berman argues that the differential

---

[15] Peter A. Hall, "Conclusion: The Politics of Keynesian Ideas," in Hall, ed., *Political Power*. On state capacity, see Theda Skocpol, "Bringing the State Back In: Strategies of Analysis in Current Research," in Evans et al., *Bringing the State Back In*, esp. pp. 9–20.

[16] Hall, "Policy Paradigms," *passim*.

[17] Hall, "Policy Paradigms," p. 278.

[18] Eric Helleiner, *States and the Reemergence of Global Finance: From Bretton Woods to the 1990's* (Ithaca: Cornell University Press, 1994).

[19] Kathleen R. McNamara, *The Currency of Ideas: Monetary Politics and the European Union* (Ithaca: Cornell University Press, 1998).

trajectories of Germany and Sweden in the 1930s, into fascism and social democracy respectively, are best explained by the ideas held by key academics, labor unions, and political parties in each state.[20]

We can see within these examples both the promises and the problems of using ideas to explain change within an historical institutionalist framework. According to Skocpol and Weir, ideas are relevant causal variables only if a prior institutional configuration selects for them. That is, ideas must somehow fit with preexisting institutions. However, if this is the case, then one must question to what extent such ideas are genuinely transformative. If new ideas are readily accepted by existing institutions, then two conclusions are possible: Either such ideas act as catalysts that speed up change, or, far from ideas being powerful forces for change, the ideas in question can be readily accommodated and pose little challenge to existing policies and practices.[21] Unfortunately, neither position suggests that ideas are transformative in their own right.

Hall's analysis of the spread of Keynesian ideas echoed Skocpol and Weir's by suggesting that new ideas are powerful only when they are congruent with the "structure of political discourse" of a nation.[22] In other words, only when existing policies and practices are interpretable within the framework offered by new ideas will they succeed in promoting policy change. However, such a notion sits awkwardly with Hall's later notion of paradigmatic shifts. For example, if periods of third-order change involve ideas that are transformative of institutions themselves, then surely the power of such ideas is their ability to reinterpret existing practices and policies. Far from being congruent with a nation's political discourse, ideas appear to be powerful only to the extent that they can challenge and subvert existing discourses and thus transform institutions. Moreover, such a position would need to specify where such ideas come from if their adoption and influence are not to be seen as another type of exogenous punctuation.[23]

Despite later historical institutionalist analyses opening up more fully to ideas as independent causal elements, some problems remain. For example, Helleiner's study, explaining why ideas about the role and function of finance changed in the 1930s and the 1970s, relies on the ostensible "facts" of economic difficulties promoting new ideas. However, positing that the supply of new ideas is reducible to material changes itself relegates ideas to being autonomic responses to periods of crisis. If this is the case, then

---

[20] Sheri Berman, *The Social Democratic Moment: Ideas and Politics in the Making of Interwar Europe* (Cambridge: Harvard University Press, 1998).

[21] I thank Dick Katz for this insight.

[22] Hall, "Conclusion: The Politics of Keynesian Ideas," in Hall, ed., *Political Power*, p. 383.

[23] The point of turning to ideas is to endogenize change, yet third-order paradigm changes seem to be unavoidably exogenous to the institutional framework.

the transformative role of ideas is limited at best.[24] Similarly, although McNamara's and other recent historical institutionalist scholarship has been increasingly open to viewing ideas and interests "not as competing causal factors, but as . . . inherent[ly] interconnect[ed]," such scholarship has not, as yet, explicitly theorized exactly how this occurs.[25]

In sum, historical institutionalist scholarship has been critical in bringing ideas "back in" and opening up the possibility that ideas are themselves transformative of institutions. However, the assumptions behind this body of theory – and the lack of explicit theorizing about the relationship between ideas, interests, and institutions – dictate that ideas tend to be seen, especially in earlier works, as auxiliary hypotheses employed to account for the anomaly of change within otherwise static theories. Ideas within such analyses have, until recently, seldom been seen as causal factors in their own right.[26]

Ideas and Rationalist Institutionalism: Strengths and Weaknesses

In the rationalist institutionalist tradition, the seminal works that deal with ideas are perhaps those of Douglass North and of Judith Goldstein and Robert O. Keohane.[27] Dissatisfied with the inability of orthodox economic theories to deal with the issue of institutional change, North developed a theory of institutional supply based on the concepts of transactions costs, uncertainty, and ideology. For North, the incorporation of ideology (*pace* ideas) into his previous work on institutional design and economic development was necessary because of three problems that bedeviled previous rationalist analyses.

The first problem was one of explaining institutional supply from rationalist microfoundations. Basically, it was logically impossible for an agent to make a "rational choice" of institutions from a set of possible

---

[24] If ideas are invariant and accurate reflections of underlying structural conditions, then they would offer a pure correspondence theory. If this were the case, there be no "politics of ideas," since there would be no debate as to what to do and who or what was to blame.

[25] McNamara, *The Currency of Ideas*, p. 8. For a notable exception, see Ngaire Woods, "Economic Ideas and International Relations: Beyond Rational Neglect," *International Studies Quarterly* 39 (2) (1995).

[26] For an elaboration of this thesis, see Blyth, "'Any More Bright Ideas?'" This criticism is less relevant to historical institutionalist scholars such as McNamara and Berman, who do see ideas as genuinely transformative of interests and institutions, but have not as yet developed a systematic theory of such transformations as a general process. This book represents a positive attempt to build upon such historical institutionalist scholarship by theorizing and investigating these connections more thoroughly.

[27] Douglass C. North and Robert Thomas, *The Rise of the Western World* (Cambridge: Cambridge University Press, 1973); Douglass C. North, *Institutions, Institutional Change and Economic Performance* (Cambridge: Cambridge University Press, 1990); Judith Goldstein and Robert O. Keohane, eds., *Ideas and Foreign Policy: Beliefs, Institutions and Political Change* (Ithaca: Cornell University Press, 1993).

alternatives given that no agent could know *a priori* the total transactions costs of any given set of institutions. Thus, notions of deliberate institutional design became questionable.[28] Second, while institutions are a rational response to transacting problems, their generation is itself a collective action problem that has no endogenous solution.[29] Third was the problem of commitment. Put simply, why would rational egoists adhere to institutions, even when they are established, if they are merely "self-enforced constraints"? What makes the "self" in "self-enforcing" do something other than defect?[30]

North attempted to provide answers to these questions by incorporating ideas into a transactions cost theory of institutions. North argued that the ideas individuals hold cheapen the price of having and adhering to one's convictions. That is, the demand curve for collective action is negatively sloped and the cheaper the price of action due to ideological precommitment, the lower the barriers to collective action and hence the greater the amount forthcoming.[31] Turning to ideas allows North to explain how agents overcome collective action problems and produce institutions while still adhering to individualist microfoundations.[32]

Building upon the work of scholars such as North, Goldstein and Keohane attempted to provide a more sophisticated explanation as to how self-interested individuals could use ideas to overcome the problems of explaining institutional supply and stability.[33] Rather than seeing ideas simply as functional devices developed by individuals to increase institutional supply, Goldstein and Keohane posit a tripartite distinction between different types of ideas – namely, principled beliefs, causal beliefs, and worldviews – and suggest different effects for each type of idea. Principled beliefs are seen as the normative bases and justifications for particular decisions, while "causal beliefs imply strategies for the attainment of goals,

---

[28] If institutions exist to reduce transaction costs, one would have to know which set of institutions would in fact perform this function *a priori* to having any experience of them. See Alexander J. Field, "The Problem with Neo-Classical Institutional Economics: A Critique with Special Reference to the North/Thomas Model of Pre-1500 Europe," *Explorations in Economic History* 18 (1981). See also Robert Brenner's comments on the North and Thomas model in Trevor H. Aston and Charles H. Philpin, eds., *The Brenner Debate: Agrarian Class Structure and Economic Development in Pre-Industrial Europe* (Cambridge: Cambridge University Press, 1985), esp. p. 16 fn. 12.

[29] Bates, "Contra Contractarianism."

[30] North, *Institutions*, pp. 36–45.

[31] *Ibid.*, pp. 22, 44–5, 90.

[32] North's later work sought to respecify the relationship between ideas and collective action by appealing to shared mental models. However, this new approach engenders an even more serious problem, for it effectively reduces rationality to various individual psychological states. See Arthur T. Denzau and Douglass C. North, "Shared Mental Models: Ideologies and Institutions," *Kyklos* 47 (1) (1994).

[33] Goldstein and Keohane, eds., *Ideas and Foreign Policy*, esp. pp. 3–30.

[understandable] because of shared principles."[34] Worldviews, on the other hand, are the entire cognitive framework of an agent and/or cultural repertoires of entire groups and classes.[35]

Ideational analysis for Goldstein and Keohane is therefore more variegated than for North. First, ideas are seen as functional devices that promote cooperation among agents whose interests are "given" but not yet realizable.[36] Second, ideas become "focal points" for convergence in conditions of multiple equilibria.[37] Third, ideas are seen as "the normative context that helps define the interests of actors."[38] Therefore, by conceptualizing ideas as performing these functions, the authors posit a solution to the problems of institutional supply (overcoming free riding) and institutional stability (multiple equilibria). However, in a manner similar to that exhibited by historical institutionalist theorists, the works of these scholars demonstrate how ideas are often used to explain disconfirming outcomes (*qua* stability) within existing frameworks rather than investigate what ideas do *per se*.

For example, North's explanation of institutional supply rests upon a paradox. While he notes that ideas make collective action, and thus institutional supply, possible, he also argues that "*institutions*, by reducing the price we pay for our convictions, *make ideas*, dogmas, and fads important *sources* of institutional change."[39] On the one hand, then, ideas create institutions by allowing agents to overcome collective action problems. On the other hand, however, North also seems to argue that *existing* institutions make ideas powerful by reducing the costs of action. Thus, a "chicken and egg" – or more accurately, an "agency and structure" – paradox appears. If institutions make ideas "actionable," then one cannot appeal to ideas to create institutions.[40] However, if one argues that ideas create institutions,

---

[34] Goldstein and Keohane, eds., *Ideas and Foreign Policy*, p. 10.

[35] This definition of worldviews is my extrapolation, as the authors do not provide one.

[36] See G. John Ikenberry, "Creating Yesterday's New World Order: Keynesian 'New Thinking' and the Anglo-American Post-War Settlement," in Goldstein and Keohane, eds., *Ideas and Foreign Policy*, pp. 57–87.

[37] See Geoffery Garrett and Barry R. Weingast, "Ideas, Interests And Institutions: Constructing the European Communities Internal Market," in Goldstein and Keohane, eds., *Ideas and Foreign Policy*, pp. 173–207.

[38] However, theoretical adhering to this latter position within a rationalist framework is problematic at best. An exception that succeeds precisely because it breaks with a strictly rationalist framework is Peter J. Katzenstein, "Coping with Terrorism: Norms and Internal Security in Germany and Japan," in Goldstein and Keohane, eds., *Ideas and Foreign Policy*, pp. 265–97.

[39] North, *Institutions*, pp. 85–6. My italics. This formulation also begs the question about how such costs could be measured in the absence of ideas that define cost. I thank Kellee Tsai for this observation.

[40] That is, unless one has ideas about the institutions that would make ideas possible. However, there is still an economic problem with this use of ideas. If ideas are value goods, that is, they are involved in some sort of production, one needs to know the marginal value of competing ideas. However, one cannot know the marginal value of ideas in the same way as a

then one cannot appeal to institutions to explain ideational and thus institutional change.[41]

Similarly, Goldstein and Keohane's work is unable to resolve the problems of explaining supply and stability despite invoking ideas to do so. First, if agents have fixed interests, which are in principle reconcilable but are unattainable due to problems such as contracting ambiguities, then why appeal to ideas? Indeed, while common ideas may be important in promoting cooperation among egoists, more traditional instruments such as side payments can perform the same function more efficiently.[42]

Second, while ideas may serve as focal points, this is not the same thing as saying that ideas are constitutive of focal points. While there may be a multiplicity of ideas available to diagnose a situation or signal convergence, it is not readily apparent why a specific idea gets chosen as *the* focal point. In order to explain this, rather than relying on institutions to overcome collective action problems, the theorist relies upon ideas. However, just as positing institutions as the solution to collective action problems offers no real solution since institutions are themselves collective action problems, so appealing to ideas cannot solve this problem either. Invoking ideas merely pushes the problems of supply and stability back along the causal chain.

Specifically, if institutions are themselves what might be termed a second-order collective action problem, then ideas must be third-order problems since the supply of ideas is hardly a costless affair either. Invoking ideas as focal points simply begs the questions, "Why that idea?" and, "Why would anyone bother to develop and promulgate ideas in the first place given problems of free-riding?" As such, the problem of multiple equilibria persists despite the invocation of ideas to solve it.[43] In sum, while rationalist scholarship on ideas has made several important conceptual contributions, its underlying assumptions, like that of the historicist alternative, create theories in which ideas can only be important *ex post* as auxiliary hypotheses designed to explain disconfirming outcomes.[44]

---

person cannot know the marginal value of information until he or she already has it. The search cost problem applies to ideas themselves. As such, an agent would have to have ideas about ideas, and so on, into infinite regress. I thank Robin Varghese for this insight.

[41] North tries to resolve this paradox by arguing that, "Ideas and ideologies shape the subjective mental constructs that individuals use to interpret the world around them and make choices. Moreover, by structuring the interaction of human beings in certain ways, formal institutions affect the price we pay for our actions, and to the degree the formal institutions ... lower the price of acting on one's ideas." However, this is more a restatement of the problem than a solution to it, unless one has a theory of how such phenomena interact over time. North, *Institutions*, p. 111.

[42] In fact, if one assumes common interests from the outset, appealing to common ideas would seem to be a very inefficient strategy.

[43] Bates, "Contra Contractarianism," *passim.*

[44] Studying ideas within existing frameworks is further complicated by the fact that ideas operationalized within such theories are necessarily derivative of the mode of analysis within which they are employed. See Blyth, "'Any More Bright Ideas?,'" p. 231.

Given all this, how then does one take ideas seriously? Having made the case for the separation of ideas from their current institutional moorings, we require a further conceptual reformulation – that is, to break the long-standing tendency within political science to hold ideas and interests as mutually exclusive analytic categories. To do so, the "usual suspects" employed in ideational analyses – ideas, interests, and institutions – have to be recast. In particular, social scientists have to reconsider the link between ideas and interests, particularly in periods of uncertainty, such that ideas are not seen as something anterior and external to interests.[45] Building upon these reconceptualizations, the chapter develops a sequential understanding of institutional change that neither reduces institutions to individual choices, nor posits them as immutable structures. Only by doing so is it possible to develop a theory of institutional change that views ideas as genuinely transformative.

Theory

Ideas and Interests

While interests are the weapons of choice in political science for explaining outcomes, the concept of interest is far from unproblematic. Consider what we mean when we say that a given policy is in an agent's interest. When we say that y policy is in agent X's interest, we are making two statements. First, if agent X chooses policy y over policy z, then we can assume that because the agent did so, the choice made was rational.[46] Second, given this assumption, we can similarly conclude that the choice was in fact "reasonable." That is, as far as X is concerned, X's interest was served better by y than by z. Actually, we have explained no such thing. The first statement merely says that an agent's interest is defined in terms of the agent's observed behavior, and that the agent's behavior is explicable only in terms of the agent's hypothesized interest, which is rather self-confirmatory to say the least.[47] The second statement says even less than the first one. To conclude from the choice of y over z that X's interests were best served by this action is to smuggle in a counterfactual to the effect that X acted on the agent's own conception of its best interests.

Unfortunately, such a position cannot be counterfactually supported and it reduces the idea of choice to a bit of a trope. As Raymond Geuss has

---

[45] Despite the importance of this topic, political scientists have paid it little attention. For exceptions, see McNamara, *The Currency of Ideas*, esp. p. 8 and pp. 56–60. For perhaps the most theoretically sophisticated discussion of these issues to date, see Wendt, *Social Theory*.

[46] One can bolster this position, as rational expectations theorists do, by claiming that consistently acting against one's interests is expensive and irrational.

[47] On the circular logic of economic theory, see Amartya Sen, "Rational Fools: A Critique of the Behavioral Foundations of Economic Theory," in Frank Hahn and Martin Hollis, eds., *Philosophy and Economic Theory* (Oxford: Oxford University Press, 1977), pp. 87–110.

noted, acting on one's interests unavoidably carries the baggage that one is acting on one's "true" interests.[48] That is, as the judge of one's own best interests, an agent makes a choice that the observer can only assume to be the best the agent can choose given subjective expected utility limitations.[49] To put it bluntly, "interests are interests," and by definition must be those held "truly" by the agents in question. Yet as Geuss demonstrates, "true" interests can be assessed, and therefore acted upon, only under optimal conditions with perfect information. Only under such conditions are the full range of alternatives and their relative costs apparent to the agent. Furthermore, this position also implicitly assumes that even with perfect information, agents' processing abilities are equivalent. Thus any two agents from the same class, sector, or position, given conditions of optimal choice and perfect information, would make the same objective evaluation and come to the same choice.

These conditions are rather implausible and are perhaps never found in situations of political interest. If information is processed differently by agents, or if information is asymmetrically distributed, then interests cannot be given by structural location or revealed *ex post* in behavior.[50] Yet, it is precisely these situations that are of interest to political scientists. Otherwise, we are simply redescribing the obvious in a rather circular manner.[51] If our analysis holds ideas apart from interests, rather than seeing them as mutually constitutive, then all we are really saying is "because they wanted to do it, they did it, and because we know they did it (assuming everyone acts on his or her own best interests), this shows they wanted to do it."

---

[48] Raymond Geuss, *The Idea of a Critical Theory* (Cambridge, UK: Cambridge University Press, 1981), pp. 45–55.

[49] This is not to say that the choice is "true" in the sense that some omniscient being would make the same choice. Given the way the model is specified, by expressing or revealing his or her preference, the agent is acting on the subjective conception of his or her own best interest.

[50] I would in fact go further than Geuss on this point. While informational asymmetries between agents can lead to situations of moral hazard and other agency problems, such a position actually still assumes that agents are aware of what their interests are. They are just unsure how to pursue them given the behavior of others. Under conditions of Knightian uncertainty, however, information is not the problem as it is in, for example, a principal-agent model since agents have no priors to rank. Improving information under Knightian uncertainty would do little to resolve strategic ambiguity given that agents are unsure as to what their interests actually are in the first place. The text that follows elaborates the concept of Knightian uncertainty.

[51] Furthermore, having an interest and acting upon it logically presupposes having a preference for policy *y* over *z* in a given set of alternatives. But is this assumption really tenable? Assuming that all agents wish to improve their material well-being and act accordingly, this is tantamount to assuming, as Connolly notes, that unarticulated interests simply do not occur and that all alternatives are known to all agents. That is, all agents are aware of their interests *and can also act on them*. Such an assumption is, to say the least, rather strong. See Connolly, *The Terms of Political Discourse*, p. 49.

Within such a framework, we can never answer the really interesting question: "Why did they do it?"

The analyst ends up in this position because of a conceptual error present in most formulations of interest: conceiving of interest as a singular concept. Positing that an agent did something because his or her "interest" lay in x over y ignores the fact that the *concept* of interest presupposes unacknowledged but very important *cognates* of interest, such as wants, beliefs, and desires. As decision theorists have demonstrated, however, these cognates are *not* analytically separate from interests and must be considered as part of the concept of interest itself.[52] If this position is accepted, then specifying interests becomes less about structural determination and more about the construction of "wants" as mediated by beliefs and desires – that is, ideas.

In developing this line of argument, Alexander Wendt has suggested that in order to specify the content of interests, one must have previously specified the beliefs that an agent has about what is desirable in the first place. As such, we should focus "our attention to the schemas or representations through which . . . [agents] define their interests and the roles that such schemas imply."[53] The need to consider "what is desired" as a sociological construction rather than a material given, argues Wendt, lies in modern social sciences' continuing acceptance of a Humean dualism between beliefs and desires. By this logic, "desire is not constitutionally related to belief. Desire is a matter of passion, not cognition; and while beliefs activate and channel desires, they cannot be desires."[54] In the Humean view, desires are seen as material, and as a consequence, ideas are epiphenomenal to explanations of action. Wendt insists that the acceptance of this dualism is untenable since it confuses an analytic distinction in theory with a synthetic distinction in the real world. Instead, Wendt contends that in the real world, "we want what we want because of how we think about it," and not because of any innate properties of the object desired.[55] When seen in this way, the Humean distinction between desires and beliefs collapses, and a richer understanding of interests becomes possible.[56]

---

[52] For elaborations of this basic theme, see Isaac Levi, *Hard Choices: Decision Making under Unresolved Conflict* (New York: Cambridge University Press, 1986); Donald Davidson, *Essays on Actions and Events* (Oxford: Clarendon Press, 1980); Connolly, *The Terms Of Political Discourse*; Giovanni Sartori, ed., *Social Science Concepts: A Systematic Analysis* (Beverly Hills, CA: Sage Publications, 1984); Robert Jervis, *Perception and Misperception in International Politics* (Princeton: Princeton University Press, 1976).

[53] Wendt, *Social Theory*, p. 124.

[54] *Ibid.*, p. 119.

[55] *Ibid.*

[56] Wendt does not wish to go down a poststructuralist path with such reasoning, and even posits a quasi-Maslowian "hierarchy of needs" and a "rump materialism" that limits what one can in fact want. The world, for Wendt, is not *ideas all the way down*. However, I would go further than Wendt on this and accept a position I would characterize as *ideas*

Abandoning this dualism allows interests to be seen as a "cluster" concept – a concept whose intention or core meaning is intimately bound up with its extension: its cognates, such as beliefs and desires. Recognizing this is theoretically consequential. For example, to suppose an agent has an interest in policy y presupposes that she has a "want" for y given her beliefs and desires. However, the stability of this cluster cannot be taken for granted.[57] If interests are a function of beliefs and desires, and if agents are confused about their desires – for example, in situations of high uncertainty – then logically agents' interests must be unstable too. Given this, holding ideas apart from interests, even analytically, makes little sense.

Indeed, understanding how agents respond when the different elements of this cluster are out of alignment with one another holds the key to explaining institutional change. In situations of institutional *stability*, agents' interests are relatively unproblematic since any ambiguities they have over strategies are a function of two factors: risk and complexity.[58] Under such conditions, agents' interests are stable; they are just more or less "sure" of how, and how likely they are, to achieve them. In situations of institutional *instability*, how interests are conceptualized changes drastically. To understand why this is the case, and how recognizing this opens up the space for an alternative theory of change, consider by way of comparison North's treatment of uncertainty as a problem of complexity.[59]

Interests and Uncertainty

For North, uncertainty is the result of "the complexity of the problems to be solved . . . the problem solving software . . . possessed by the individual" and incomplete information between agents.[60] Given these problems, the

---

all the way through – that is, a situation where ideas permeate all aspects of materiality and determine agents' orientations to social objects. This is not to say that ideas are all there is. I can drop a brick on my foot and it will hurt. This is a material fact. But whether I jump for joy or cry out in pain will depend upon whether the brick is made of rock or gold. Yet gold being valuable, like currency, is merely a social construct and not an innate property of the material of the brick. Ideas go all the way through social reality, but not all the way down into an a-material nothingness.

[57] For example, to give a purely interest-based explanation, one has to assume that an agent has transitive preferences. However, if a situation is uncertain because possible outcomes cannot be probabilistically ranked, then the agent's beliefs about the outcomes may be discordant with the agent's desires. As such, the agent's ability to define her interests may be in flux, and the assumption of transitivity, which is central to notions of choice and acting coherently on one's "given" interest, fails.

[58] That is, uncertainty applies to agents' strategies and is a product of the difficulty of assigning probabilities to outcomes plus the processing of information needed to gauge probabilities in the first instance.

[59] This is also true for historical institutionalist scholars such as McNamara, who also see uncertainty as a problem of complexity. See McNamara, *The Currency of Ideas*, pp. 57–61.

[60] North, *Institutions*, p. 25.

"institutional framework, by structuring human interaction, limits the choice set of the actors."[61] North's concept of uncertainty is similar to that of Herbert Simon, who argues that the cognitive processing limits of individuals leads to satisficing rather than maximizing behavior.[62] In sum, for such theorists, uncertainty is a function of computational failings and environmental complexities that cause agents to devise institutions to cope with uncertainty by limiting the choice set available to them.

However, this way of viewing uncertainty as a problem of complexity poses an interesting counterfactual. If agents could overcome their computational limitations, could they design optimal institutions, or better, would they even need institutions? If cognitive limitations were overcome, then all the previously noted considerations concerning how ideas constitute interests would be irrelevant. In contrast to what Geuss argued, interests, in the absence of computational limits and informational asymmetries, would be those truly held by agents, and ideas would be redundant. What stops fulfillment of this counterfactual, however, is not the limits of reason. Rather, it is the limits of viewing uncertainty as a problem of complexity.

As Jens Beckert argues, "uncertainty is [commonly] understood as the character of situations in which agents cannot anticipate the outcome of a decision and cannot assign probabilities to the outcome."[63] However, Beckert further notes, echoing Knight, that uncertainty is much more than a probability distribution problem. Uncertain situations are *qualitatively* different from situations of risk, because in situations of risk, "the distribution of the outcome in a group of instances is known . . . [that is, probabilities can be assigned to possible outcomes] . . . while in the case of uncertainty . . . it is impossible to form a group of instances because the situation dealt with *is in a high degree unique*."[64]

The point of making this distinction is that situations of "Knightian" uncertainty are *not* the same as the situations of "uncertainty as complexity" posited by theorists such as North and Simon. Under "uncertainty as complexity," agents are sure of their interests, but unsure of how to realize them. Therefore, such theories reduce uncertainty to risk insofar as uncertainty as complexity presupposes that agents know their interests but cannot calculate how to achieve them without first reducing the set of

---

[61] *Ibid.*

[62] Herbert Simon, Massimo Egidi, and Robin Marris, eds., *Economics, Bounded Rationality and the Cognitive Revolution* (Brookfield, VT: Edward Elgar, 1992).

[63] Jens Beckert, "What Is Sociological about Economic Sociology? Uncertainty and the Embeddedness of Economic Action," *Theory and Society* 25 (6) (1996), p. 804.

[64] Frank H. Knight, *Risk, Uncertainty and Profit* (Boston and New York: Houghton Mifflin Company, 1921), p. 229, quoted in Beckert, "What Is Sociological," p. 807, my italics. See also Susan Strange, *Casino Capitalism* (Manchester: Manchester University Press, 1997), esp. pp. 107–9; Paul Davidson, "Is Probability Theory Relevant for Uncertainty? A Post-Keynesian Perspective," *Journal of Economic Perspectives* 5 (1) (1991).

possible strategies.[65] Knightian uncertainty, however, does not reduce uncertainty to risk.[66]

Because the situation is "in a high degree unique," agents can have no conception as to what possible outcomes are likely, and hence what their interests in such a situation in fact are. As agents are unable to form a series of instances of like-type events and thus project probabilities, agents' interests in such an environment cannot be given by either assumption or structural location and can be defined only in terms of the ideas that agents themselves have about the causes of uncertainty. Without reference to such ideas, neither interests nor strategies would have meaning under conditions of Knightian uncertainty.[67] As Beckert cautions, "if one can argue . . . [that] . . . uncertainty . . . does not allow actors to deduce actions from preferences . . . it becomes important to look at those *cognitive*, structural and cultural *mechanisms* that agents rely upon when determining their actions."[68]

Cognitive mechanisms, *pace* ideas, are important because without having ideas as to how the world is put together, it would be cognitively impossible for agents to act in that world in any meaningful sense, particularly in situations of Knightian uncertainty that occur during the periodic breakdowns of capitalist economies. Contrary to Bayesian models, individuals do not intervene in the world on the basis of ad hoc generalizations distilled from randomly gathered information. Instead, complex sets of ideas, such as ideas about the workings of the economy, allow agents to order and intervene in the world by aligning agents' beliefs, desires, and goals. Only then can agents diagnose the crisis they are facing.[69]

---

[65] In such a situation, ideas may indeed act as "road maps" or "focal points," as suggested by rationalists – but only if one assumes interests themselves as unproblematic. See Goldstein and Keohane, eds., *Ideas and Foreign Policy*. Moreover, the conflation of risk and uncertainty within economics is commonplace. See Beckert, "What Is Sociological," p. 813.

[66] *Ibid.*, pp. 807–9.

[67] For example, during the economic crisis of the 1930s, agents' interests could not be separated from how agents diagnosed the crisis. To take an example from this period, if one accepts a diagnosis of the economic slump as a result of insufficient purchasing power, then one's interest lies in voting for a reflationary social democratic party. If one accepts the diagnosis of the crisis as due to the machinations of "World Jewry," then regardless of factoral position, structural location, or asset specificity, one's interest lies in promoting genocide. Being a worker in such a situation *tells us nothing* about the politics that such locations will engender.

[68] Beckert, "What Is Sociological," p. 814, my italics.

[69] To reiterate, this is not the same as turning situations of uncertainty into situations of risk since it does not operate from the assumption that agents in fact know what their interests are. Nor is it the equivalent to processes that economists have devised for reducing uncertainty to risk in non-ergodic situations, such as equilibrium revelation and refinement in game theory and hysteresis models in macroeconomics. For discussions of these strategies, see Rod Cross, ed., *The Natural Rate of Unemployment: Reflections on 25 Years of the Hypothesis* (Cambridge: Cambridge University Press, 1995); Davidson, "Is Probability Theory Relevant," esp. pp. 130–36.

Furthermore, conditions of Knightian uncertainty are complicated by another factor apart from their "uniqueness." If agents' interests in such situations can be defined only in terms of their ideas about their interests, then the outcomes that such situations produce will also be a function of those ideas. A contrast with the natural world is useful here. Causes in the natural world may be highly complex, but our understandings of those causes have no impact on the outcomes we observe. For example, what we believe about the motions of the planets has no impact whatsoever upon those motions. In the economic world, however, the problem is qualitatively different because the ideas that agents have about the impacts of their actions, and those of others, shape outcomes themselves. If agents in the economy hold different ideas about how the economy works, this can lead to such agents taking a variety of actions, thereby producing radically different outcomes in the same circumstances.[70] In contrast, agents can have a multiplicity of ideas concerning planetary motion, but such ideas will have no effect on those causal relationships.

In contrast to rationalist and materialist theories, economic ideas under Knightian uncertainty do not simply identify a given causal relationship in the economy for agents. Such ideas also serve to restructure those causal relationships by altering the agents' own beliefs about the interests of others, upon which the realization of the agents' own ideationally derived interests depend.[71] This is why, in part, whether an economic idea is deemed to be "true" or not depends on how widely it is held.[72] Moreover, this is what makes the assignment of probability values to outcomes, and hence the concept of "given" interests in periods of Knightian uncertainty, impossible: The equilibrium set of institutions to resolve a crisis is a moving

---

[70] As Frank Hahn and Robert Solow put it in the epigraph, "The way the economy actually does work can depend on the way agents believe the economy to work . . . [and] . . . the way the economy responds to a policy move by the government can depend on the interpretation that other agents place on it, and therefore on the beliefs about the way things work. . . . If participants believe that every increase in the money supply will be fully translated into the price level, irrespective of any other characteristics of the situation, then they are likely to behave in ways that will make it happen." Frank Hahn and Robert Solow, *A Critical Essay on Macroeconomic Theory* (Oxford: Blackwell Publishers, 1995), p. 150. For the formal elaboration of this phenomenon, see Michael Woodford, "Three Questions about Sunspot Equilibria as an Explanation of Economic Fluctuations," *American Economic Review* 77 (2) (1987); Kunal K. Sen, "The Sunspot Theorists and Keynes," *Journal of Post Keynesian Economics* 12 (4) (1990).

[71] I thank Robin Varghese for pointing out to me this lacunae in Knight's own conception of uncertainty.

[72] Again, as Hahn and Solow note, "It may be worth noting that one of the ways in which governments influence the economy is by propagating theories about the economy." Hahn and Solow, *A Critical Essay*, p. 150. While it is undoubtedly true that some people's ideas may matter more than others – Alan Greenspan versus my grandmother, for example – the fact that Greenspan's pronouncements (that is, the ideas he propagates) are such critical coordinating devices for markets surely bolsters, rather than weakens, the case made here.

target pushed around by the beliefs of agents themselves.[73] In sum, what is critically important in understanding agents' behaviors are the ideas held by agents, not their structurally derived interests. Such a category has little meaning in moments of Knightian uncertainty such as economic crises.

Because of these factors, the explanatory import of ideas cannot be appreciated so long as the analyst maintains a separation of ideas and interests. Instead, analysts should see interests as being necessarily ideationally bound, particularly in situations of Knightian uncertainty such as periods of economic crisis. When reconceptualized in this way, ideas are indeed intimately related to interests but are not reducible to them. Accepting this position as a theoretical primitive, rather than prioritizing either interests or institutions, can only lead to more precise theorizing and better explanations. Given these conceptual reformulations, we can now begin to specify in detail the causal effect of ideas in moments of uncertainty and crisis.

Five Hypotheses about Ideas

This section builds upon the previous conceptual reformulations by developing a sequential model of ideas and institutional change that hypothesizes five specific causal effects of ideas.[74] The objective is to develop a model of institutional change as a sequence of distanciated events that enables us to understand the empirical cases to follow.[75] First, it is hypothesized that

---

[73] For example, if agents believe that deficits cause inflation, then deficits will cause inflation because as in central bank watching, the belief becomes self-fulfilling. If this claim seems problematic, consider that during the 1980s the United States federal budget deficit grew fourfold while inflation fell threefold *simultaneously*. Despite this, investors, especially in the bond market, still acted *as if* deficits caused inflation and demanded higher real effective interest rates despite falling inflation. Conventions, rather than fundamentals, matter. For a similar argument regarding movements on foreign exchange markets, see Gregory P. Hopper, "What Determines the Exchange Rate: Economic Factors or Market Sentiment?" *Federal Reserve Bank of Philadelphia Business Review*, September–October (1997).

[74] The importance of theorizing sequence in social scientific explanation has recently undergone a rebirth. See, in particular, Paul Pierson, "Increasing Returns, Path Dependence, and the Study of Politics," *American Political Science Review* 94 (2) June (2000); *Idem.*, "Not Just What, But When: Timing and Sequence in Political Process," *Studies in American Political Development* 14 Spring (2000). Whereas Pierson has concentrated upon increasing returns arguments to explain institutional persistence, the theory presented here uses an argument about sequence to understand change.

[75] The works of William Sewell have been very influential on my thinking in this regard. See William H. Sewell, "Historical Events as Transformations of Structures: Inventing Revolution at the Bastille," *Theory and Society* 25 (6) December (1996); *Idem.*, "A Theory Of Structure – Duality, Agency, and Transformation," *American Journal of Sociology* 98 (1) (1992).

given an initial position of institutional disequilibrium and uncertainty, economic ideas allow agents to reduce uncertainty by interpreting the nature of the crisis around them as a first step to constructing new institutions.[76] Second, it is hypothesized that economic ideas serve as collective action and coalition-building resources. The third hypothesis is that agents use ideas as weapons that allow them to attack and delegitimate existing institutions. Fourth, ideas are seen as institutional blueprints that agents use *after* a period of contestation to construct new institutions. Finally, once a new set of ideas has become embedded within these new institutions, such institutions serve to coordinate expectations, thereby making institutional stability, and a particular distributional politics, possible over time.

Periods of institutional change thus follow a specific temporal sequence, with ideas having five different causal effects at different time points during periods of economic crisis: uncertainty reduction, coalition building, institutional contestation, institutional construction, and expectational coordination.[77] Although these periods are not entirely distinct from one another empirically, it is nonetheless worthwhile to make such distinctions analytically so that the importance of economic ideas in making institutional supply, stability, and change possible can be better understood. By seeing ideas as having different causal effects in different time periods as part of a sequence of change, we can explain both stability and change within the same framework without creating the kinds of problems and paradoxes encountered in previous theories.

Hypothesis One
In periods of economic crisis, ideas (not institutions) reduce uncertainty.

The first causal effect of ideas is to reduce uncertainty during periods of economic crisis. In contrast to studies that see institutions as themselves reducing uncertainty, this study makes a temporal distinction between the reduction of uncertainty by ideas and the subsequent creation of institutions. As noted in Chapter 1, periods of institutional change cannot be understood as a shift of comparative statics. Institutional change is a dynamic process that occurs over time. Consequently, it is hypothesized that

---

[76] For reasons of space, this book does not fully specify the reasons for the underlying destabilization of existing institutions. For an attempt to specify why these institutional orders originally became unstable during the 1930s and the 1970s through a Keynes/Kalecki/Minsky model of how uncertainty is generated, see the dissertation version of this argument, Mark M. Blyth, "Great Transformations: Economics, Ideas and Political Change in the Twentieth Century," unpublished Ph.D. dissertation, Columbia University, (1999). Available from University Microfilms International.

[77] As Pierson argues, "the significance of temporal processes in historical institutionalist analysis is often left implicit." Pierson, "Increasing Returns," p. 265. This theory is an attempt to make explicit the importance of a sequential understanding of institutional change.

while institutions structure agents' expectations and make stability possible over the long run (an argument elaborated under hypothesis five), such institutions are both temporally subsequent to, and a function of, the ideas used by agents to reduce uncertainty during moments of crisis.

To understand this, consider again the distinction between uncertainty as complexity and Knightian uncertainty. This distinction turns on the former being a problem of assigning probabilities to outcomes given fixed interests, and the latter being unique situations where interests are themselves unclear. In the former case, information-processing limitations make agents construct institutions to narrow the choice set – that is, institutions themselves reduce "uncertainty as complexity." However, this position is predicated on the assumption *that there are indeed prior choices among institutional alternatives to be ranked*; it is just that agents are unsure about which alternatives to choose.

This position is tenable only as long as the uncertainty faced by the agent is computational rather than Knightian. Under Knightian uncertainty, which is much more akin to periods of economic crisis, the situation is radically different. In such an environment, agents have no idea what institutions to construct to reduce uncertainty precisely because "under the condition of [Knightian] uncertainty it becomes *ex-ante* impossible to determine whether a chosen means is rational or irrational for the achievement of . . . [a] . . . goal."[78] In such a situation, agents cannot take institutions "off the shelf" to reduce uncertainty, as institutional supply would be random at best, and at worst impossible. That is, one cannot argue that institutions reduce uncertainty if one is unsure which institutions would in fact perform this function given the indeterminacy of interests.[79] Conceiving of uncertainty as a computational problem solved by institutions fails to explain both the importance of ideas and the supply of institutions during periods of economic crisis.

Uncertainty reduction and institutional supply must therefore be seen as temporally distinct events since *before* agents can institutionally respond to a crisis they must have some idea about what the crisis is and what caused it. Uncertainty must be reduced *prior* to institutional supply, otherwise institutional supply itself would be impossible. If institutional supply under Knightian uncertainty is a "shot in the dark," probabilistically, then agents must reduce uncertainty *before* any choice of institutions can be made.

---

[78] Beckert, "What Is Sociological," p. 818.

[79] And this is exactly what theorists such as North are forced to argue given their conception of uncertainty as complexity. Given the previously noted problems of multiple equilibria in institutional selection and the supply of institutions being a free-rider problem, if uncertainty were conceptualized as Knightian uncertainty rather than uncertainty as complexity, then the supply of institutions could only ever be a "shot in the dark." As such, they cannot not be seen as purely instrumental products. This is precisely the conclusion that rationalist theorists sought to avoid, and why they turned to ideas to avoid it.

Economic ideas make it possible for agents to reduce uncertainty by acting as interpretive frameworks that describe and systematically account for the workings of the economy by defining its constitutive elements and providing a general understanding of their "proper" (and therefore improper) interrelations. Such ideas provide agents with both a scientific and a normative critique of the existing economy and polity, and a blueprint that specifies how these elements *should* be constructed.[80] Economic ideas thus enable agents to interpret, rather than merely simplify, the environment they face such that subsequent institutional construction can take place. Only by using ideas in this way can uncertainty be reduced sufficiently so that an institutional resolution to a crisis can be formed.

By developing and deploying such ideas, agents reduce uncertainty by narrowing possible interpretations of the crisis, and hence courses of action, to a significant degree. As Paul Pierson argues, "once established, [such] basic outlooks . . . are generally tenacious. They are path dependent."[81] Such intellectual path dependency radically alters the environment by coordinating agents expectations around a common interpretation of the crisis at hand. Absent such ideas, uncertainty reduction and subsequent collective action would be impossible. In sum, in moments of economic crisis, ideas are important explanatory devices that *themselves* reduce uncertainty. Only then can *subsequent* institutional construction take place. Ideas are thus the *predicates* of institutional construction, while institutions, as we shall see in hypothesis five, are the *products* that promote long-term stability by coordinating agents' expectations. In short, ideas reduce uncertainty while institutions promote stability.

Hypothesis Two
Following uncertainty reduction, ideas make collective action and coalition-building possible.

Reducing uncertainty is merely the first part of a sequence of institutional supply. Only by overcoming the barriers to collective action can the actual transformation of existing institutions occur. Economic ideas facilitate the reduction of such barriers by acting as coalition-building resources among agents who, in periods of crisis, attempt to resolve the crisis by restructuring the distributional relationships that pertain among the principal collective agents in advanced capitalist nations: business, labor, and the state. Economic ideas make collective action possible by allowing agents

---

[80] This definition is influenced by North's discussion of ideologies as "the subjective perceptions (models, theories) all people possess to explain the world around them . . . the *theories* individuals construct are *colored* by normative views of how the world should be organized." North, *Institutions*, p. 23, fn. 7, author's italics. I differ with this in so far as rather than seeing theories as being *colored* by normative views, I would argue that such norms are inextricable parts of any theory.

[81] Pierson, "Increasing Returns," p. 260.

to redefine existing interests under uncertainty and thereby redistribute the perception of existing political costs and benefits regarding alternative courses of action. Such ideas overcome free-riding problems in two principal ways: by building bridges across class and consumption categories through the redefinition of agents' interests, and by defining the common ends of action.

In periods of uncertainty, ideas do not merely reduce uncertainty for agents with preexisting interests. Instead, they change and reconstitute those interests by providing alternative narratives through which uncertain situations can be understood.[82] In doing so, economic ideas allow agents to overcome free-rider problems by acting as "causal stories" that account for the workings and the dysfunctions of the economy and allow the redefinition of an agent's relationship to the crisis at hand. As Andrew Polsky argues, moments of crisis "upset routine calculations of interest, invalidating rational short-cuts and injecting a large dose of uncertainty. Enter the political entrepreneur, who touts an analysis that sorts out the confusion of other political actors by suggesting a plausible account of why the world no longer works as it did, and proposes a new programmatic menu grounded in this analysis."[83] The economic ideas that allow agents to do this are therefore crucial resources in the promotion of collective action. They allow agents to define the solutions to their problems, and perhaps more importantly, to define the very problems that agents face in the first place.

This is, to reiterate, why reconceptualizing ideas apart from interests *and* institutions is so theoretically important. By providing an interpretive framework for dealing with conflicting data and a rationale for belief, economic ideas define what the common end of collective action should in fact be.[84] Such ideas empower agents affected by economic crises to restructure existing institutions in line with the ideas they use to interpret their interests under uncertainty. By promoting specific diagnosis of a crisis as "the way things really are," such a systematization allows agents to represent that "reality" as being for or against different groups. Specifically, under Knightian uncertainty, by defining a "crisis" as being a function of x and y factors to the exclusion of other elements, economic ideas empower agents to restructure the relationship between these factors in the name of resolv-

---

[82] Deborah A. Stone, "Causal Stories and the Formation of Policy Agendas," *Political Science Quarterly* (104) 2 (1989).

[83] Andrew Polsky, "When Business Speaks: Political Entrepreneurship, Discourse and Mobilization in American Partisan Regimes," *Journal of Theoretical Politics* 12 (4) (2000), p. 466.

[84] As Berman puts it, "ideas determine the goals towards which actors will strive; they provide actors with a way of conceptualizing the ends of political activity." Berman, *The Social Democratic Moment*, p. 29.

ing the crisis. In short, while agents always have interests, ideas make them collectively "actionable."[85]

Economic ideas therefore serve as the basis of political coalitions. They enable agents to overcome free-rider problems by specifying the ends of collective action. In moments of uncertainty and crisis, such coalitions attempt to establish specific configurations of distributionary institutions in a given state, in line with the economic ideas agents use to organize and give meaning to their collective endeavors. If successful, these institutions, once established, maintain and reconstitute the coalition over time by making possible and legitimating those distributive arrangements that enshrine and support its members. Seen in this way, economic ideas enable us to understand both the creation and maintenance of a stable institutionalized political coalition and the institutions that support it.

Hypothesis Three
In the struggle over existing institutions, ideas are weapons.

While the reduction of uncertainty and the generation of collective action create the necessary conditions for institutional transformation, the sufficient conditions lie in the subsequent roles that ideas play as weapons and blueprints with which agents can contest and replace existing institutions. Put simply, economic ideas not only facilitate collective action and radical policy change but are in fact prerequisites for them. Building upon the notion of ideas as resources, which specify the ends of collective action, it is hypothesized that such ideas also provide agents with the means of achieving those ends.

Specifically, identifying the cause of a given crisis as being a function of a particular set of institutions – for example, the gold standard or the welfare state – merely targets those institutions as being "part of the problem." In order to replace them, agents must delegitimate such institutions by contesting the ideas that underlie them. Economic ideas are effectual weapons for transforming existing institutions precisely because *existing* political and economic institutions are the result of *past* economic ideas about how the economy works.[86] Therefore, when agents attempt to replace existing economic institutions and policies, economic ideas provide these agents with an essential resource to attack and restructure them.

Such a view of ideas, while instrumentalist, does not reduce them to preexisting interests. Given the role of ideas in reducing uncertainty and

---

[85] To take a notable example, did white middle-class college students risk injury in the Southern states of the United States in the struggle for civil rights because of the instrumental payoff of having Jim Crow abolished, or did such collective actions come about because the idea of segregation within a liberal society was intolerable?

[86] As Sven Steinmo put it, institutions are perhaps best thought of as "crystallized ideas." Sven Steinmo, personal communication.

making a crisis interpretable and actionable, positing preexisting interests ignores how agents' interests are in fact reconstituted in the very action of wielding those ideas as weapons.[87] By challenging the "accepted" view of the economic world upon which existing institutions are based and the distributional outcomes they make possible, such ideas delegitimate those institutions and, in the process, alter those same agents' conceptions of their own interests.

Hypothesis Four
Following the delegitimation of existing institutions, new ideas act as institutional blueprints.

Building upon the claim that ideas are weapons agents can use to attack existing institutions, one can further hypothesize that the fourth causal effect of economic ideas is to act as institutional blueprints. That is, new institutions are derivative of new economic ideas. As the discussion of uncertainty suggested, it is cognitively impossible for agents to construct economic institutions without having an idea as to what has caused a given crisis. Therefore, any notions as to what institutions are in fact supposed to do must be predicated upon those same ideas; hence ideas are blueprints for institutional design. Economic ideas therefore not only reduce uncertainty, set the ends of collective action, and facilitate the dismantling of existing institutions. They also dictate the form and content of the institutions that agents *should* construct to resolve a given economic crisis.

As the cases will demonstrate, the sheer variety of institutional solutions that states have attempted to develop to manage economic crises in the twentieth century bespeaks a variety of different ways of conceptualizing and acting upon the problem of an economic crisis. Because of this, it is only by reference to the ideas held by the institution builders in question that the constructions attempted make any sense. Structural and material factors alone simply cannot account for such variation.

For example, during the late 1920s, the Swedish state was wedded to an interpretation of the crisis of the period as a misalignment of wages and commodity prices. Given this diagnosis, the Swedes attempted to ride out the crisis by deflation. However, by the early 1930s the state had radically restructured and extended its institutions of economic management to encourage reflation. Such a rapid change in institutional form and policy content is explicable only in terms of changes in the way that state actors reinterpreted the crisis they were facing. Similarly, in the United States in

---

[87] For example, a worker in the 1930s may have an interest in higher wages and may use the Marxist rhetoric of expropriation to explain why this occurs. However, in articulating this understanding, the worker may decide, given these ideas, that his interest now lies in revolution, not a fatter paycheck.

the early 1930s, the state sought to cartelize industry, banking, and agriculture in order to stabilize prices. Yet within a few years, such institutional solutions were abandoned and a new set of institutions based upon consumption maintenance had taken their place. Again, such radical institutional changes make little sense without reference to the ideas that agents were able to use to form the authoritative diagnosis of the crisis at specific historical moments.[88] What is important here is that none of these institutional solutions were determined by the "true" nature of the crisis that each state "objectively" faced. Instead each solution was predicated on a particular notion as to "what went wrong" and therefore "what had to be done." It is therefore only by reference to the ideas that agents use to interpret their situation that understanding the design of new institutions becomes possible.

So far we have argued that ideas have four important causal effects: They reduce uncertainty, promote collective action, provide weapons, and serve as blueprints for institutional replacement and design. What remains, however, is to specify the end of this sequence, the long-term stabilization of new institutions. By disaggregating the four causal effects of ideas that we have just noted, we can now specify the fifth with much greater precision.

Hypothesis Five
Following institutional construction, ideas make institutional stability possible.

The fifth hypothesis regarding the role of ideas in explaining institutional change is that, in addition to promoting change, such ideas also promote stability over time by generating conventions that make the institutional coordination of agents' expectations possible. In short, in addition to telling agents what institutions to construct, ideas tell agents what possible futures to expect. These new institutions bring about stability, not by reducing uncertainty, but by managing and coordinating agents' expectations about the future such that they converge and become self-stabilizing over time. Economic ideas thus make stability as well as change possible through the generation of conventions.

The concept of ideas as conventions refers to the intersubjective understandings that agents share regarding how the economy is put together and how it should operate in normal times. Conventions are shared ideas that coordinate agents' expectations, with such conventions themselves being a function of the ideas that have been used to dismantle and replace the previous institutional order. Promoting economic stability depends upon expectational coordination through the maintenance of these conventions within newly supplied institutions.

---

[88] See Sewell, "Historical Events," *passim*, on this point.

The concept of conventions within institutions as coordinating devices for expectational coordination developed here comes from Keynes.[89] For Keynes, "rational knowledge" and economic interests are not based upon "given" interests, but rest instead on intuitive beliefs. Consequently, interests are "fickle things" that behave nonrationally and are constituted by ideas. In essence, the economy for Keynes is as much a subjective construct as an objective reality. This claim is far removed from most understandings of Keynes as being composed of discussions of the "real" economy, multipliers, consumption propensities, etc. However, for Keynes, these subjective elements are actually more important in understanding stability and change in capitalist economies than is generally appreciated.[90] Keynes points out that

We have, as a rule, only the vaguest idea of any but the most direct consequences of our acts. Now the whole object of the accumulation of wealth is to produce results, or potential results, at a comparatively distant, and sometimes an indefinitely distant date. Thus the fact that our knowledge of the future is fluctuating, vague, and uncertain, renders wealth a peculiarly unsuitable topic for the methods of classical economic theory ... [A]bout these matters there is no scientific basis on which to form any calculable probability whatever. We simply do not know.[91]

Keynes then goes on to list "three techniques" that economic agents have devised for dealing with this situation, all of which are inherently subjective. First, "we assume that the present is a much more serviceable guide

---

[89] This position also supports Beckert's earlier contention that under Knightian uncertainty, agents rely on structural as well as cognitive mechanisms. This model of change gives this claim theoretical specificity by separating in time the cognitive (ideational) and the structural (institutional) factors that Beckert correctly identifies. See footnote 68 for Beckert's original insight. The claims made here about expectational coordination parallel the arguments concerning adaptive expectations causing increasing returns that Pierson draws upon. See Pierson, "Increasing Returns," p. 254.

[90] Those who read Keynes through Samuelson or in the Neoclassical tradition may find this claim surprising. After all, Keynes was known to have made some comments about markets being controlled by "animal spirits" and "beauty pageants," but the conventional wisdom is that *The General Theory of Employment, Interest and Money* is a tortuous book whose import was not really made apparent until authors such as Lawrence Klein and Paul Samuelson formalized the propositions therein. As such, Keynes' scattered insights about the role of economic ideas and expectations were held to be just that, insights. However, in this case, the conventional wisdom is wrong. Keynes provides us with a very sophisticated understanding of the role of economic ideas in politics, particularly in fostering stability. It is perhaps fitting, then, that Keynes, the quintessential builder of economic ideas, should provide us with an understanding of how ideas structure the economy. Refer to the following passages of the *General Theory* to accept the plausibility of this argument. See John Maynard Keynes, *The General Theory of Employment, Interest and Money* (London: Harcourt Brace, 1964), esp. pp. 3–23, 46–52, 89–112, 135–64, 245–57 and 372–85.

[91] John Maynard Keynes, "The General Theory of Employment," *Quarterly Journal of Economics* 51 (2) February (1937), pp. 213–4.

to the future than a candid examination of the past would show it to have been hitherto." Second, "we assume that the existing state of opinion . . . is based on a correct summing up of future prospects." Third, "knowing that our own judgment is worthless, we endeavor to fall back on the judgment of the rest of the world . . . that is, we endeavor to conform with the behavior of the majority or average . . . to copy the others . . . [to follow] . . . a *conventional* judgment."[92] In short, Keynes' macroeconomy rests upon conventions – that is, shared ideas about how the economy *should* work.

Keynes arrives at this conclusion because of the inherent uncertainty surrounding expectations of the future. As he notes, "the most probable forecast we can make . . . depends upon the confidence with which we make this forecast."[93] The problem is that the state of confidence itself rests upon agents' expectations of the future, and for Keynes, agents' expectations are neither naturally convergent nor self-stabilizing. Rather than agents' expectations being an accurate reflection of an invariant underlying structure, as pure "interest-based" arguments assume, agents' expectations are instead seen as being naturally divergent and inherently unstable. Therefore, instead of assuming both that expectations converge and that agents know what the "fundamentals" actually are, Keynes assumes that economic agents are myopic and look to each other for signals, which explains why conventions become so important in producing stability. In short, there is no truth about markets "out there" apart from the prevailing wisdom that markets have about markets themselves, and this can be a very fickle thing.[94]

Given this understanding of agents' expectations, it follows that once new institutions are constructed out of new ideas, it is ideas as conventions that underpin these institutions and make stability possible. Ideas tell agents which institutions to construct, and once in place, such institutions reinforce those ideas.[95] Both general conventions such as "the state of confidence" and specific ones such as "deficits cause inflation" are ultimately intersubjective constructions that have at best a tenuous relationship to market fundamentals and no precise calculable metric.[96] Indeed, as Keynes

---

[92] Keynes, "The General Theory of Employment," p. 214. Similarly, as Keynes summarizes the *General Theory*, "we can regard our ultimate independent variables as consisting of . . . three fundamental psychological factors, namely, the *psychological* propensity to consume, the *psychological* attitude to liquidity and the *psychological* expectation of future yield from capital assets." Keynes, *The General Theory*, pp. 246–7.

[93] Keynes, *The General Theory*, p. 148.

[94] For discussion of this problem of conventionally based knowledge, see Hillary Putnam, *Reason, Truth and History* (Cambridge: Cambridge University Press, 1981), esp. pp. 103–26; David Wayne Parsons, "Was Keynes Khunian? Keynes and the Idea of Theoretical Revolutions," *British Journal of Political Science* 15 (2) (1981).

[95] See Pierson, "Increasing Returns," *passim*.

[96] This is different from contemporary "cascade" and "mimicking" hypotheses employed in macroeconomics since these are strategies employed by rational agents with fixed interests.

notes, "the above conventional method of calculation will be compatible with a considerable measure of continuity and stability, in our affairs, *so long as we can rely upon the maintenance of the convention.*"[97] Seen in this way, the maintenance of such conventions produces stability, and stability itself therefore rests upon the *institutional* coordination of expectations through the maintenance of conventions.[98] Only then are stable institutional orders possible, the end point of this sequential understanding of ideas and institutional change.

Ultimately agents construct institutions not to reduce uncertainty per se, for as we have seen this is a function of ideas. Rather, once agents have used ideas to reduce uncertainty, redefine their interests, and contest and replace institutions, then the new institutions they construct – given the ideas that inform their interests – structure agents' expectations about the future by reaffirming conventions.[99] In doing so, such conventions make stability over time possible. In understanding the role of ideas in institutional change, sequence is everything.[100]

Conclusions: Ideas and Institutional Change

In conclusion, this analysis suggests that earlier ideational studies were more incomplete than they were incorrect. Given how previous theories conceptualized institutions, ideas, and interests, such analyses invariably saw the problem of change as a problem of explaining shifts in comparative statics. However, while exogenous economic shocks and internal distributional battles may destabilize institutions and create uncertainty, as noted earlier, simply making an existing institutional equilibrium unstable does not auto-

---

[97] Keynes, *The General Theory*, p. 152, my italics.

[98] For example, in the embedded liberal order, Keynes' "traditional functions of government" had to be extended to create the convergence of expectations necessary for stability to occur. It is for this reason that Keynes called for a socialization of the "conditions of investment" by extending the "traditional functions of government," such that the "natural propensity to barter and truck" could be channeled in a socially optimal direction. Therefore, by altering the *conventions* governing investment *institutionally*, without attacking the principle of private accumulation *politically*, the state could achieve its goals. Socializing investment, extending governmental control, and reforming state institutions all work to influence behavior by institutionally altering the subjective conventions of economic agents. Such policies are concrete means to a subjective end – that being, to control expectations by institutionally structuring conventions.

[99] This also suggests that uncertainty itself may be more or less important given the nature of the governing conventions present. I thank Kellee Tsai for this insight. For a discussion of why the attempted elimination of uncertainty in financial markets may actually precipitate crises, see Jacqueline M. Best, "Economies of Uncertainty: The Constitutive Role of Ambiguity in International Finance," unpublished Ph.D. dissertation, Department of Political Science, Johns Hopkins University, Baltimore, MD (2002).

[100] As Pierson puts it, "it is not the past per se, but the unfolding of processes over time that is theoretically central." Pierson, "Increasing Returns," p. 264.

matically create a new one. Any new equilibrium settlement has to be defined, argued over, and implemented, none of which is a given function of changing structural conditions.

Without a set of ideas to diagnose the nature of the uncertainty facing agents, institutional change – that is, the deliberate replacement of one set of economic institutions with another – can only be understood theoretically as a random "shot in the dark." Understanding the role of ideas in effecting institutional transformation resolves this dilemma by enabling the analyst to view the making and breaking of institutional orders as a sequential phenomenon of uncertainty reduction, mobilization, contestation, and institutional replacement that occurs through time. Moreover, seeing economic ideas as important elements of a sequential understanding of change highlights how the control and manipulation of ideas are indeed profoundly important political resources.[101] In sum, by taking ideas seriously and sequentially, it is hoped that this theory can both resolve many of the paradoxes that bedeviled previous analysis and provide us with a better understanding of how the double movement works in practice. So much for what ideas "do" in theory. It is now necessary to specify the content of those ideas that mattered, and then go on to analyze how they made possible the institutional transformations in question.

---

[101] As Milton Friedman noted, "what mattered in the world of ideas was not what was true, but what was believed to be true. And it was believed at that time [at the time of writing the *General Theory*] that monetary policy was tried and found wanting." Milton Friedman, "The Counter-Revolution in Monetary Theory," *Institute of Economic Affairs Occasional Paper*, number 33 (1970), p. 5. A more dramatic testament to the ideational bases of economics comes from Friedrich A. Hayek, who declared that it would be "one of the worst things that would ever befall us if the general public should ever again cease to believe in the elementary propositions of the quantity theory." Fredrick Von Hayek, *Prices and Production* (London: George Routledge, 1931), p. 3, quoted in Nick Bosanquet, *Economics: After the New Right* (The Hague: Kluwer-Nijhoff Publishing, 1982), p. 31.

PART II

CASES

3

Building American Embedded Liberalism

Governing state, business, and labor's responses to the Great Depression in the United States was a complex bundle of ideas that contained elements that often worked at counterpoint to one another. At various times, different combinations were accepted, appropriated, deployed, and contested by the state, business, and labor, in order both to explain the economic crisis and to construct an institutional solution to it. The first set of ideas, employed variously by the state, business, and academic economists, explained the depression as a result of the failure of the government to adhere to the principles of "sound finance" and fiscal orthodoxy. These ideas dictated that the role of the state was reducible to a policy of maintaining balanced budgets and protecting private property. The academic version of this argument, modern business cycle theory, argued that the Great Depression was not a depression at all – that is, a secular downward shift in the long-run performance of the economy.[1] Rather it was merely a regular, cyclical, and expected dip in performance that was both therapeutic and would soon cure itself.[2]

Following the failure of these ideas either to make sense of the depression or to build a sustainable political coalition around them, a new set of ideas developed by legal reformers and progressive thinkers inside the state came to prominence. These ideas explained the depression as the result of

---

[1] This body of theory was quite distinct from the business cycle theory being developed, for example, by Knut Wicksell in Sweden and by Keynes in England.

[2] As Columbia University economist Wesley Mitchell argued, "a period of depression produces after some time certain conditions which favor an increase of business activity . . . [that paradoxically] . . . also cause the accumulation of stresses within the balanced system of business, stresses which ultimately undermine the conditions upon which prosperity rests." Wesley C. Mitchell, "Business Cycles," in *Committee of the President's Conference on Unemployment, Business Cycles and Unemployment* (New York: McGraw-Hill 1923), p. 10, quoted in Dean L. May, *From New Deal to New Economics: The American Response to the Recession of 1937* (New York: Garland Press, 1981), p. 69.

monopolistic practices, particularly those of large corporations and trusts. Basically, cartelized industrial structures had choked the economy, and a vigorous dose of antitrust laws was seen to be the tonic for recovery.[3]

Working at complete counterpoint to these classical and antimonopoly arguments was a third set of economic ideas that proved to be highly influential: the so-called administered prices thesis. Developed by management economists and popular economic commentators, this thesis, a modified oligopoly argument, maintained that although monopoly was the problem, it was only the problem insofar as it had not gone far enough. The appropriate policy response was therefore not to engage in a round of trust busting, as antimonopolists advocated. Instead, administered prices theorists argued that state intervention was needed to promote *further* cartelization. Only this would allow large firms to fix prices at a socially optimal output and halt the deflation.[4]

Yet another contending set of economic ideas stressed the importance of demand and consumption over the regulation of supply and investment. These arguments – which centered upon income distribution, purchasing power, and the role of the state in "pump priming" the economy – were popular among the Democratic Party intelligentsia, New Deal social reformers, and maverick economists. These ideas were initially conjoined with the administered prices thesis in a partial and often contradictory synthesis.[5] Later, by the mid-1930s, these ideas had been divorced from the administered prices framework and formed the basis of a distinctly American version of Keynesianism.

Fifth, and most radically, was the secular stagnation thesis. This theory, popular among certain state elites and academic economists in the late 1930s and 1940s, held that the economy had reached industrial maturity and was overbuilt with plant and equipment. Given this diagnosis, neither the institutional tinkering of the administered prices thesis nor the pump priming of the underconsumptionists would be ineffective in promoting recovery. Instead, a general socialization of the conditions of investment became the policy choice of stagnationists.[6]

[3] See Ellis Hawley, *The New Deal and the Problem of Monopoly: A Study in Economic Ambivalence* (Princeton: Princeton University Press, 1980); *Idem.*, "Economic Inquiry and the State in New-Era America: Anti-Statist Corporatism and Positive Statism in Uneasy Coexistence," in Mary O. Furner and Barry Supple, eds., *The State and Economic Knowledge: The American and British Experiences* (Cambridge: Cambridge University Press, 1990), pp. 287–324.

[4] See, for example, Adolphus Berle and Gardiner Means, *The Modern Corporation and Private Property* (New York: Legal Classics Library, 1923).

[5] See William Trufant Foster, *Business without a Buyer* (New York: Houghton Mifflin Company, 1928); William Trufant Foster and Waddill Catchings, *The Road to Plenty* (Cambridge, MA: Sir I. Pitman and Company, 1929).

[6] See Alvin Hansen, *Fiscal Policy and Business Cycles* (New York: W. W. Norton and Company, 1941).

Finally, following the defeat of these secular stagnationist ideas at the hands of business, there followed a version of the new macroeconomics of John Maynard Keynes that backed away from the policy consequences of the secular stagnation thesis and relied instead upon passive stabilizing techniques to assure slow but steady growth. This passive "growthsmanship," as Robert M. Collins has called it, was developed by business think tanks and postwar state elites. These ideas became dominant in the immediate postwar era and served as the intellectual underpinning of America's version of embedded liberalism until the 1970s.[7]

In sum, the economic ideas that governed American policy responses to the slump of the 1930s followed a particular sequence that began with sound finance and ended with growthsmanship. At various times, the state, business, and labor accepted, appropriated, deployed, and contested different combinations of these ideas both to explain and resolve the crisis. Understanding the construction of America's embedded liberalism therefore requires engaging the ideas that made sense of the depression. Only by doing so can we make sense of the various attempts at institution building undertaken in the name of resolving the crisis.

Hoover, Roosevelt, and the Contradictions of Orthodoxy

The economic boom following World War I proved to be surprisingly buoyant, and by the mid 1920s the American economy seemed oblivious to the crisis already prevalent elsewhere. Despite this, the sheer magnitude of the depression and the uncertainty it generated caught the Republicans, the "party of prosperity," by surprise. The response of the incumbent Hoover administration to this crisis was not one of more and more fiscal orthodoxy, budget balancing, and fiscal retrenchment, at least not initially. Rather, it was one of active management of the crisis, albeit active management in a peculiar form.

President Herbert Hoover's response to the depression was drawn from a mixture of business cycle theory, sound finance, and administered prices ideas. The influence of business cycle theory stemmed, in part, from a conference called by Hoover in 1921 that "influenced the attitudes of public officials and businesses towards public works through most of the 1920's."[8] The conference analyzed the depression from the point of view of academic business cycle theory, which posited that the state of the economy, rather than being one of stability punctuated by crises, was naturally one which oscillated between crisis and stability in a fairly regular

[7] Robert M. Collins, *The Business Response to Keynes* (New York: Columbia University Press, 1981), *passim*.
[8] May, *From New Deal to New Economics*, p. 69.

way.[9] Given this understanding of the economy, it was argued the role of the state during such crises should be limited to providing temporary relief until the inevitable upturn in the economy occurred.

While this may seem rather impractical policy advice, as Alan Sweezy has noted, academic economists during the early 1920s were much more concerned with finding fallacies than finding solutions.[10] As Joseph Schumpeter argued in the introduction to a Harvard monograph that criticized the later Roosevelt recovery efforts, "it was no part of our plan to suggest measures of remedial policy . . . Analysis and criticism have their place quite independently of the existence or nature of alternative proposals."[11] However, given that the depression showed no signs of curing itself, and the idea of the depression as a therapeutic smacked of being patronizing, the deployment of such *laissez faire* economic ideas confined American academic economists to the margins of debate and influence for most of the 1920s and 1930s. Given the practical inadequacy of such ideas, Hoover sought a rationale for a more active policy and began to embrace administered prices ideas more fully. In line with such ideas, rather than break up trusts and cartels, Hoover increasingly sought voluntary cartelization to promote industrial stabilization as the slump wore on.[12]

However, although business cycle theory had been marginalized and the state increasingly turned to administered prices solutions, the financial sector still held sound finance ideas to be the *sine qua non* of recovery. As tends to happen during downturns, government spending grew while tax receipts fell.[13] These problems were exacerbated by the decision of the

---

[9] In an influential monograph, seven senior Harvard economists who criticized the early Roosevelt recovery program argued that, "any revival which is merely due to artificial stimulus leaves part of the work of depressions undone, and adds . . . new maladjustment of its own which has to be liquidated in turn, thus threatening business with another crisis ahead," Joseph Schumpeter, in Douglass V. Brown, Edward Chamberlin, et al., *The Economics of the Recovery Program* (New York: McGraw-Hill, 1934), p. 21, quoted in Byrd L. Jones, "Lauchlin Currie, Pump Priming, and New Deal Fiscal Policy, 1934–1936," *History of Political Economy* 10 (4) (1978), p. 514.

[10] Alan Sweezy, "The Keynesians and Government Policy 1933–1939," *American Economic Review* 62 (1/2) (1972), pp. 116–24.

[11] Joseph Schumpeter, quoted in Sweezy, "The Keynesians and Government Policy," p. 116.

[12] For example, in his 1930 State of the Union Address, Hoover declared that he had "instituted systematic and voluntary measures of cooperation with business . . . to make certain that . . . wages and consuming power would not be reduced." Herbert C. Hoover, *The State Papers and Other Public Writings of Herbert Hoover* (Garden City, New York: Doubleday, Doran & Co., 1934), Volume 1, pp. 145–6.

[13] Hoover spent $1.5 billion on public works in 1929, a figure that rose in 1930 to $1.7 billion. By 1931 overall federal spending was up by a third from its 1929 level. As Herbert Stein put it, "Receipts dwindled by 50 percent and expenditure rose by almost 60 percent." Herbert Stein, *The Fiscal Revolution in America* (Washington: American Enterprise Institute Press, 1996), p. 26.

British to abandon the gold standard in 1931. As confidence in the dollar fell, gold flowed out of the country, interest rates rose, bank failures soared, and the passing of the infamous Smoot-Hawley tariff served to undermine whatever financial sector confidence remained. In such an environment, the further expansion of government borrowing was deemed unsound. Consequently, the importance of restoring business confidence through a policy of sound finance was perceived as being of paramount importance, particularly by financial elites themselves.

If the first measure of such confidence is the state of the budget, then balancing the budget, rather than sponsoring business cartelization and waiting for the upturn in the business cycle, became the number one priority.[14] Consequently, in December 1931, Hoover authorized a tax increase of $900 million to cover budget shortfalls.[15] Unfortunately, this contraction simply served to compound the existing deflation and overwhelm any stabilizing effects that cartelization may or may not have had. Given these contradictory positions, attempting to maintain the convention of sound finance while also seeking voluntary cartelization simply increased the uncertainty of the situation. Responding to this uncertainty and policy paralysis, the voters turned to Franklin Roosevelt rather than returning Hoover in 1932.

However, when Roosevelt came to power in 1932, it seemed that very little was about to change. As William E. Leuchtenberg notes, at the time of the 1932 elections, "National Democratic party leaders criticized Hoover not because he had done too little, but because he had done too much. The main criticism they leveled at Hoover was that he was a profligate spender."[16] As such, it seemed that perhaps "more orthodoxy" was to be the policy of choice. This expectation was to be sorely disappointed. Under Roosevelt, the state's ideas about the crisis underwent a profound transformation as administered prices, and later underconsumptionist ideas, gained prominence over sound finance doctrines.

A clear demonstration of this change in ideas was evident during the first two years of the Roosevelt administration. The state's first reform efforts took place along three fronts: the reform of the banking sector, the reform of industry under the National Industrial Recovery Act (NIRA), and the reform of agriculture under the Agricultural Adjustment Act (AAA).

---

[14] Sponsoring voluntary cartelization in concert with sound finance policies seemed an attractive proposition to both business and the state since cartelization cost consumers money, not business or the state.

[15] As Hoover put it, "we cannot squander ourselves into prosperity." Hoover, *State Papers,* Volume 2, p. 105, quoted in May, *From New Deal to New Economics,* p. 33.

[16] William E. Leuchtenburg, *Franklin D. Roosevelt and the New Deal 1932–1940* (New York: Harper Torchbooks, 1963), p. 3.

Traditionally these reforms have been seen as *ad hoc* or otherwise improvised policy choices.[17] However, when understood ideationally, all three sets of reforms make sense as practical expressions of the administered prices thesis – the set of ideas that became the state's dominant interpretation of the crisis between 1933 and 1935.

Reinterpreting Orthodoxy: Cartelization and Rhetorical Sound Finance

Administering Financial Prices

The Banking Bill that Roosevelt presented to the House five days after his inauguration sought to increase confidence in the banking system in two ways: by increasing liquidity through the issuance of new notes and by giving the president complete control over gold movements. Liquid banks were to be reopened immediately, while those with untenable debt/equity ratios were to be refinanced and reorganized by the government.[18] These crisis measures enabled the state to press ahead with more far-reaching reforms in finance that were to prove central to building American embedded liberalism.

Taking advantage of banking's tarnished image following the Senate's Pecora investigations, the state moved to rein in finance. Following the Banking Bill, the Securities Act and the Glass-Steagall Banking Act were passed by the Senate. These acts separated commercial and investment banking in order to provide a firebreak in the event of any future banking crisis. They also created, against the wishes of the banking community, the Federal Deposit Insurance Corporation (FDIC) to further strengthen this firebreak and guard against future liquidity problems.[19] Once the banking sector was shored up, the thorny issues of confidence and balancing the budget could be addressed more flexibly.

---

[17] See, for example, Arthur M. Schlesinger, Jr., *The Age of Roosevelt: The Crisis of the Old Order 1919–1933* (Boston: Houghton Mifflin Company, 1957), esp. pp. 440–85; Leuchtenburg, *Franklin D. Roosevelt and the New Deal*, pp. 41–62.

[18] For an excellent discussion of New Deal banking reforms, see James S. Olson, *Saving Capitalism: The Reconstruction Finance Corporation and the New Deal 1933–1940* (Princeton: Princeton University Press, 1988).

[19] Leuchtenberg argues that the Securities Act, rather than promoting cartelization as the NRA did in the industrial sphere, instead mandated regulation of restrictive practices. Consequently, he argues that exactly the logic employed in the financial sector was the opposite of that which was supposed to work in the industrial sector. Leuchtenburg, *Franklin D. Roosevelt and the New Deal*, p. 59. However, this conclusion turns upon a level-of-analysis issue. Administering industrial prices is an issue of regulating quantities. Administering financial prices turns on regulating prices *per se*, which is what the Securities Act and the Glass-Steagall Banking Act in fact did. As such, they are both cartelization strategies designed to promote stability and are thus, it can be argued, informed by the same administered prices logic.

In order to square this circle of intervention *with* sound finances, the state essentially began to operate two budgets disguised as one.[20] The regular budget was defined in such a way that emergency expenditures, especially relief payments, were not included in the total. Balancing the budget therefore became more elastic since the state could invoke sound finance ideas while actually behaving more proactively.[21] While this double-counting artifice was attacked by finance, its innovation nonetheless opened up space for the next phase of institution building by setting a precedent for greater federal involvement in the economy. By late 1933, with the stabilization of the banking system, sound finance claims became less compelling. This allowed the space for administered prices ideas to come more to the fore and dictate the institutional forms necessary to resolve the crisis: the institutions of the NIRA and the AAA.

Administering Industrial Prices

The institutional expression of the administered prices thesis in industry, the NIRA posited a particular cause for the depression. Administered prices theorists argued that because of the concentration of plant and equipment required in a modern economy, ever-larger concentrations of capital were the norm. Given such an industrial structure, modern firms had no incentive to respond to decreasing demand in a recession by reducing prices. Instead, businesses could set prices at artificially high levels, since "the policy of holding up price even though volume declined [is] the only sound business policy for the individual enterprise."[22] However, if all firms behaved in this way, such an individually rational choice would prove to have collectively disastrous results. If the main effect of an economic downturn is to lower prices, then such oligopolistic firms, by maintaining administered rather than market prices, would prevent a downward adjustment of prices. The inevitable result of such concentration was an economy that was unbalanced and incapable of maintaining high employment and stable prices. Given such an analysis, the appropriate government response would be to change the institutional context within which business operates, thus helping firms cartelize more efficiently. Monopoly should therefore be

---

[20] Interestingly, this bookkeeping artifice appears again in United States budgetary politics in the 1960s when Walter Heller establishes the practice of calculating the budget by reference to its hypothetical full-employment position, thus making the case for intervention more clear-cut. For an excellent discussion of the politics of budgets in the United States, see James D. Savage, *Balanced Budgets and American Politics* (Ithaca: Cornell University Press, 1986).

[21] As Stein notes, Roosevelt "had shown how small an obstacle the budget-balancing idea was to pragmatic fiscal policy, if the policy was described in such a way that it met the formal requirements of the idea." Stein, *The Fiscal Revolution*, p. 47

[22] Gardiner C. Means, "Notes on Inflexible Prices," *American Economic Review* (26) March (1936), pp. 32–3.

understood as a natural outgrowth of mature capitalism, rather than the exception to be trust-busted by the state. Government intervention could thus be given a rationale if it took the form of making markets more efficient.[23]

However, efficient did not necessarily mean more competitive. Instead, efficient meant the provision of coordination and stability through the development of voluntary codes regulating output and prices. Given such goals, the NIRA was comprised of two separate but complementary elements. The first part of the Act encouraged businesses to cartelize production under a set of coordinating institutions called the National Recovery Administration (NRA).[24] The second part of the plan, influenced by incipient underconsumptionist ideas, facilitated increased public works spending through a host of new state relief agencies. Such spending, it was hoped, would stabilize purchasing power and help cement the cartel arrangements of the NRA. Each of the two parts of the NIRA offered incentives to business and labor respectively. Cooperation over codes would stabilize prices and raise profitability while public works would increase purchasing power and provide jobs.

Business's Rejection of the National Industrial Recovery Act
Right from the start, however, the NIRA encountered a mix of business opposition and cooperation. The most vehement opposition to the NIRA came from the National Association of Manufacturers (NAM). Formerly moribund and decimated by the combined effects of the depression and the euphoria created by the passing of the NIRA, the NAM rebounded when business opposition to the NIRA intensified.[25] Far more important in generating support, and later, stern opposition to the NIRA, however, was the American Chamber of Commerce (ACC).

The ACC began the depression with as close to pure sound finance ideas about the economy as any group in the United States. Chamber President

---

[23] See Robert Himmelberg, *The Origins of the National Recovery Administration: Business, Government and the Trade Association Issue, 1921–1933* (New York: Fordham University Press, 1976); Hawley, *The New Deal and the Problem of Monopoly.*

[24] The NRA was the industrial equivalent of the Reconstruction Finance Corporation (RFC), a Hoover era banking institution that was expanded under Roosevelt and served as the fulcrum of banking system reorganization. For details on the RFC, see Olson, *Saving Capitalism, passim.*

[25] The NAM became the chief opponent of those NIRA provisions that promoted independent labor organization. NAM also highlighted the perceived fiscal dangers of the public works provisions of the NIRA and reiterated the need for orthodox financial stabilization policies, including wage cuts and tax increases. For discussion of NAM policies during the first New Deal, see Collins, *The Business Response to Keynes,* pp. 47–52; Howell John Harris; *The Right to Manage: Industrial Relations Policies of American Business in the 1940's* (Madison: University of Wisconsin Press, 1982); Philip H. Baruch, "The NAM as an Interest Group," *Politics and Society* (14) Fall (1973), pp. 97–130.

Henry Harriman wrote to the House Appropriations Committee on the heels of the Hoover tax increase, arguing that in order to bring about recovery, Congress should cut the federal budget by a further $1 billion.[26] However, as the depression wore on, Harriman allied with other liberal industrialists such as Gerald Swope of General Electric and lobbied for the passage of the NIRA.[27] The increasing uncertainty of the period plus the promise of an end to antitrust activity led the ACC to take a strong stand in favor of the NIRA and the drafting of codes.[28]

A third business organization that was a critical actor at this juncture was the Business Advisory Council (BAC).[29] The BAC was even more fulsome in its support for the NIRA than the ACC. The BAC was composed of some of America's biggest business interests and overlapped with some of the most pro-administration members of the ACC.[30] What attracted this group to the side of the NIRA was the group's belief that only a synthesis of administered prices inspired cartelization, and scientific industrial and labor management would lead the way out of the depression.[31]

Two factors, however, ultimately undermined business support for the NIRA. First, business was itself divided over the root causes of the depression. Specifically, a fault line began to emerge between smaller and larger firms over whether monopoly was the problem or the solution to the depression. As the National Recovery Review Board hearings on the progress of NRA reforms got under way in March 1934, ACC support for the NIRA began to waiver. Specifically, smaller firms in the ACC began to complain that cartelization was hindering, rather that helping, the recovery.[32]

Second, the NIRA contained a *quid pro quo* with labor called section 7a, which reinvigorated both the NAM and ACC's opposition to state involvement in the economy. Section 7a effectively gave labor the right to organize and bargain collectively and the right *not* to join a union (a veiled attack on the policy of company unions), and mandated that the federal government could impose regulations on pay, hours, conditions, and so on. These reforms, in conjunction with the organizational drives of the new

---

[26] Cited in Collins, *The Business Response to Keynes*, p. 26.

[27] For discussion of the so-called Swope plan, which served as the blueprint for the NRA itself, see Arthur Schlesinger, Jr., *The Crisis of the Old Order*, pp. 181–3.

[28] In doing so, the ACC acceded to the title two provisions of the NIRA, the $3.3 billion in public works spending, as a necessary and temporary expedient.

[29] For details of the BAC, see Collins, *The Business Response to Keynes*, pp. 56–62.

[30] Henry Harriman, Gerald Swope of General Electric, and Alfred Sloan of General Motors were among the BAC's founding members.

[31] See Harris, *The Right to Manage*, pp. 91–105.

[32] On the review board hearings and how they ran at counterpoint to the logic of the NIRA itself, see Hugh Samuel Johnson, *The Blue Eagle: From Egg to Earth* (Garden City, New York: Doubleday, Doran & Company, 1935), pp. 272; Arthur Schlesinger, Jr., *The Coming of the New Deal* (Boston: Houghton Mifflin and Company, 1959), pp. 128–34.

industrial unions whose growth was itself partly a result of section 7a, led
to business's disaffection with intervention in general and NIRA associa-
tionalism in particular.[33]

Given these problems, when the November 1934 elections handed to
the state what was widely interpreted as a mandate for change, the ACC
became increasingly defensive. While the state argued for intervention into
ever-wider spheres of activity ranging from labor market reform to general
social insurance, the ACC advocated ever-greater voluntarism among businesses *without* government or labor participation. In response to this opposition, the state became ever more critical of business, and eventually even
the BAC began to dissociate itself from the NIRA. With Roosevelt's rhetoric becoming increasingly antibusiness, and with prominent state officials
such as Tom Corcoran arguing that "fighting with a businessman . . . is like
fighting with a Polack. You can give no quarter,"[34] the NIRA, and the
attempt to forge a coalition with business upon which it was based, began
to fall apart.

Yet, the greatest threat to state action was not business's growing hostility but the Supreme Court's ability to declare a piece of legislation unconstitutional. On May 27, 1935 those fears were realized when the Supreme
Court found the NIRA unconstitutional in the Schechter Poultry case. The
ruling struck down the already weakened NIRA on the grounds that the
Act interfered with interstate commerce, and since the federal government
had no authority to regulate interstate commerce, it had no right to regulate conditions within a firm either.[35] This decision threatened to establish
the legal precedent that regulatory projects such as the NIRA were, by their
nature, unconstitutional.[36] Such a decision struck at the heart of current
forms of state intervention by making state-sponsored cartelization, the
core of the administered prices thesis, largely obsolete. In sum, "[t]he
wishful thinking of the institutional economists . . . evaporated in a flood
of cumbersome regulations, small business opposition, and Supreme Court
hostility."[37]

The ideas of administered prices and "rhetorical" sound finance, the
state's own favored combination, had promoted neither a sustainable coalition between business and the state, nor the new institutions necessary for

---

[33] See Olson, *Saving Capitalism*, p. 157.
[34] Quoted in Collins, *The Business Response to Keynes*, p. 42.
[35] As Roosevelt remarked at the time, all the of the work of the New Deal had been
undone by a "horse-and-buggy definition of interstate commerce." Roosevelt, quoted in
Leuchtenburg, *Franklin D. Roosevelt and the New Deal*, p. 145.
[36] However, as Alan Brinkley has argued, "That the Schechter decision created such alarm in
the administration was mildly ironic, for the NRA by 1935 was a woeful failure." Alan
Brinkley, *The End of Reform: New Deal Liberalism in Recession and War* (New York:
Vintage Books, 1995), p. 18.
[37] Olson, *Saving Capitalism*, p. 223.

economic recovery. As such, it was not until the NRA and the ideas that underlay it were seen by the state to have failed that the state turned to labor for an alternative coalition partner. What made this move toward labor possible was, once again, a change in ideas about the causes of the depression.

After the failure of the NIRA, the state began to see consumption rather than cartelization as the critical determinant of economic activity.[38] These new ideas allowed a rearticulation of the problem of unemployment from being a function of supply to being the result of a collective failure of demand. Such a diagnosis argued for increasing mass consumption rather than a cartelization of production, a diagnosis that made industrial labor part of the solution rather than part of the problem. Unfortunately, what stymied this shift in ideas from producing a new coalition with labor, and thus a new set of governing institutions, was twofold. First, agricultural prices had to be stabilized in order to halt the overall decline in prices. Yet to do so, Southern agricultural labor had to be *excluded* from any new political coalition so that Northern industrial labor could be *included* in one. Second, industrial labor was very much like business: internally divided and suspicious of the state. As such, the first-order task of the state *vis à vis* labor was not to regulate it, but to strengthen and, where possible, educate it. Let us take each of these issues in turn.

Changing Ideas and Partners

Stabilizing and Excluding Agriculture

The depression in agriculture began some five years before collapse of industrial prices in 1929. Following sharp price rises at the end of World War I, agricultural prices fell and continued to fall throughout the 1920s. Given relatively fixed supply and poor farmer organization, which exacerbated control of acreage, farmers' demands for state intervention to halt the deflation took the form of demands for price supports and export subsidies. In line with industrial arguments for tariff support, farmers' allies from the Western and Southern states lobbied behind the McNary-Haugen Bill. The various versions of this bill, which appeared throughout the 1920s, all basically proposed three things: first, that the state set a high domestic price based upon prewar parity levels with industrial prices; second, that the state buy actual output at this price; and third, that any surplus be dumped abroad at the world market price.[39]

---

[38] For an excellent discussion of how ideas changed from focusing on investment and production toward viewing consumption as the root cause of depression, see Brinkley, *The End of Reform*, pp. 65–85.

[39] Apart from the obvious retaliatory consequences of such a policy, it was resisted (and vetoed) by the administration for two reasons. First, as Kenneth Finegold and Theda

The ideas informing both industrial and agricultural recovery in this period were drawn from the same set of ideas, the administered prices thesis, and both institutional projects represented a particular expression of the same cartelization logic. Yet, deriving policy directly from these ideas in agriculture was more problematic than doing so in the industrial sphere, for two reasons. First, the scale economies that would have made NIRA-style cartelization possible were simply not present in most American farms at this time. Second, as Kenneth Finegold and Theda Skocpol argue, for any plan to be successful it would have to meet certain conditions: "that the plan not stimulate production, that it not lead to European retaliation, and that it be voluntary or at least be based on the support of the majority of producers."[40] The only plan that would meet these conditions but not derail industrial recovery under the NIRA was the domestic allotment plan.

This plan paid farmers a premium rate on a domestic allotment, and paid lesser world market rates on whatever excess farmers produced, with this latter provision acting as a tax on increased acreage in production.[41] The 1933 Agricultural Adjustment Act (AAA) that embodied this policy therefore served as the functional equivalent to the NIRA in industry since both were cartelization strategies.[42] The difference between the NIRA and the AAA was essentially that the latter Act worked: Agricultural prices rose, production (relatively) declined, and parity levels stabilized.[43]

The AAA succeeded where the NIRA failed, for several factors. First, farmers, as opposed to businessmen, were too disorganized to mount effective opposition. Second, Northern industrial recovery was believed to be predicated upon the stabilization of agricultural prices, since falling com-

Skocpol note, Hoover thought the bill "the most vicious form of taxation [that] would stimulate production and breed bureaucracy, and was unconstitutional to boot." Second, by dumping abroad, business feared that the United States would provide an export subsidy to European business in the form of cheaper grain to European workers. Kenneth Finegold and Theda Skocpol, *State and Party in America's New Deal* (Madison: University of Wisconsin Press, 1995), pp. 76, 78.

[40] *Ibid.*, p. 81.

[41] Domestic allotment was defined as that portion of a farmer's productive holdings equivalent to that which would cover domestic provision alone.

[42] The Agricultural Adjustment Act, enacted in May 1934 after bitter Senate debate and a near strike by farmers, embodied the domestic allotment plan. What placated farmer opposition to reducing acreage was that farm mortgages were defaulting at an increasing rate due to depressed prices. In June 1934, as a supplement to the AAA, the state passed the Supplementary Farm Credit Act, which authorized the Farm Credit Administration to refinance mortgages and stem the tide of foreclosures. With this *quid pro quo*, which was really the functional equivalent of the 1933 Banking Act's refinancing provisions, farmer support for AAA was assured. See Olson, *Saving Capitalism*, p. 91.

[43] Despite the AAA being declared void by the Supreme Court in the Hoosac Mills case of 1936, the main provisions of the Act were reestablished with the Soil Conservation and Domestic Allotment Act of 1936 and the new 1938 Agricultural Adjustment Act.

modity prices simply pulled other prices down with them. Given this, agricultural price stabilization was seen as a means to an end rather than an end in itself since agricultural labor was deemed irrelevant to the resolution of the crisis. Basically, if the problem facing the state was one of stabilizing the price level, then reaching out to agricultural labor made little sense. Under both the administered prices thesis and the incipient underconsumptionist critique, which informed the public spending provisions of the NIRA, agricultural labor was deemed irrelevant to solving the crisis since such labor could neither cartelize supply nor provide the mass consumption base necessary to stimulate recovery. Consequently, when the recovery of purchasing power became central to the logic of recovery after 1935, it was the purchasing power of industrial labor that was the concern, not agricultural labor.[44]

General price stabilization was therefore predicated upon a prior political exclusion. Building a coalition with industrial labor in the North was predicated upon the exclusion of agricultural labor in the South from any such arrangement. The paternalistic relationships that governed Southern agriculture were to be exempted from the types of reforms undertaken in the North so that class relations and property rights in the South would be untouched, especially where the Democrats were electorally strong.[45] Given Jim Crow laws and other means of disenfranchisement, little could be gained electorally by expending scarce political capital on agricultural labor since no one thought that agricultural labor could play any effective role in stabilizing the economy in the first place. As a consequence, the state may have had to make a trade-off with Southern conservatives to build a new coalition with industrial labor, but the exclusion of agricultural labor demanded was hardly deemed a sacrifice given the ideas that informed those choices.

Strengthening and Including Labor

In contrast to agriculture, where exclusion was the order of the day, industrial labor was actively sought by the state for inclusion in a new coalition.

---

[44] One does not have to see all politics as simply an attempt to get reelected and thereby overemphasize electoral considerations in policy choice. While it is true that unless one is elected one cannot do anything, in situations such as the depression, solving the problem will get one elected and reelected. As such, the ideas that dictate strategy may not have purely electoral derivatives. For a study that emphasizes electoral structures and party politics in the New Deal, see Finegold and Skocpol, *State and Party, passim.*

[45] See Finegold and Skocpol, *State and Party;* Lee J. Alston and Joseph P. Ferrie, "Labor Costs, Paternalism, and Loyalty in Southern Agriculture: A Constraint on the Growth of the Welfare State," *Journal of Economic History* XLV (1) March (1985); Ira Katznelson, Kim Geiger, and Daniel Kryder, "Limiting Liberalism: The Southern Veto in Congress 1933–1950," *Political Science Quarterly* 108 (2) Summer (1993), pp. 283–306.

Unfortunately, the local nature of politics and the fractionalized nature of race and class in the United States meant that the American trade union movement developed along craft rather than sectoral lines.[46] Such an organizational form created a problem for the state since the American Federation of Labor (AFL), the titular organization of craft unionism, effectively kept most industrial workers disorganized by freezing job demarcations as property rights exclusive to individual unions. While this was beneficial for those inside the craft union, it had the side effect of limiting union size and density and thus labor's viability as a coalition partner.

Furthermore, the new and as yet unorganized immigrant industrial workers represented an alternate form of organization that spilled over, and thus undermined, the property rights of craft unions. Fearing large and powerful industrial unions that would effectively create dual organizations, the AFL leadership temporized during the 1920s. Rather than seizing the initiative granted under article 7a of the NIRA, the AFL leadership allowed the union movement to become more polarized because of it.[47] In short, the state's key problem in forming an alternative coalition with labor was that labor was both badly organized and organizing badly.[48] In response to this challenge, the state had to help labor to organize itself.

Key here was the Department of Labor under social reformer Frances Perkins. The Department of Labor advocated minimum wages, health and safety reforms, extensive relief programs, and a variety of other pro-labor measures. In particular, the Bureau of Labor Standards argued for "greater uniformity in respect of labor legislation and to aid in developing modern standards for the health, safety and employment of industrial workers."[49] The Department of Labor also strengthened labor by providing expert opinion on labor's "best interests," whether or not they corre-

---

[46] For a discussion of craft unions and, among other issues, demarcations as property rights, see David Montgomery, *The Fall of The House of Labor: The Workplace, the State and American Labor Activism 1865–1925* (Cambridge: Cambridge University Press, 1987); Joseph G. Rayback, *A History of American Labor* (New York: Free Press, 1966).

[47] Craft union leaders in the AFL were also worried about communist infiltration. In the first half of the 1920s, skilled workers in AFL unions were essentially receiving a tax from nonunionized industrial workers whose wages were falling. Those unions that were most communist were those suffering the most under the present AFL-maintained regime. See Edwin Young, "The Split in the Labor Movement," in Milton Derber and Edwin Young, eds., *Labor and the New Deal* (Madison: University of Wisconsin Press, 1957), pp. 50–1.

[48] While membership gains were made under article 7a, such gains were made primarily within unions that did not fit easily into the existing craft union structure and would shortly form the basis of the new industrial unions in the Congress of Industrial Organizations (CIO). In fact many of these gains were made in company unions, despite the intent of the Act, with membership in company unions doubling between 1932 and 1935 from 1.25 million to 2.5 million workers. Figures from Finegold and Skocpol, *State and Party*, p. 125.

[49] *Twenty Third Annual Report of the Department of Labor* (Washington: Government Printing Office, July 1934), quoted in Murray Edelman, "New Deal Sensitivity to Labor Interests," in Derber and Young, eds., *Labor and the New Deal*, p. 162.

sponded to those expressed by unions themselves. Between 1933 and 1935, the Department of Labor organized a series of conferences between the department and labor leaders, the point of which seems to have been to "sell the union leaders on ideas originating in the department rather than the reverse."[50] Other state agencies, such as the Works Progress Administration (WPA) and the Civil Works Administration (CWA), which organized public works and relief programs, also encouraged the growth of labor as an organized social actor. However, what was to really reenergize the labor movement was Congressional action.

Despite the Congress of the 1930s having an institutional bias against labor, the extent of the depression and the Democratic landslide of 1934 made pro-labor reform more possible than ever. A small pro-labor constituency headed by New York Senator Robert Wagner pioneered legislation that transformed the institutional position of labor. Even before Wagner's reforms were passed, the pro-labor lobby in Congress had made significant progress in strengthening the labor movement. The Norris-LaGuardia Act that outlawed the injunction, section 7a of the NIRA, and the defense of these pieces of legislation from NAM and ACC amendments, all combined to put labor on a firmer institutional footing.

Another factor that promoted this shift toward a pro-labor stance was the increasing grassroots pressure for a comprehensive system of social insurance. This move evidenced the wider ideational shift away from cartelization and toward viewing income redistribution and increased government spending as the way out of the depression. The state was under pressure from both Huey Long's "share our wealth" program and from Dr. Francis Townsend's pensions movement. Of the two, Townsend proved to be the bigger inspiration for, and threat to, state projects of recovery.

Townsend set up an organization called Old Age Revolving Pensions Limited, which proposed that the economic crisis could be cured for the cost of a 2 percent tax on business transactions, which would be used to finance payment of old age pensions. The retirements that these pensions would encourage would facilitate new entrants to the labor market, while the pensions themselves would produce the increase in purchasing power necessary to get the economy moving again.[51] However, what was conspicuous by its absence here was any consistent political pressure from labor for greater reform in any of these spheres. Labor was still disorganized. What remained now was for labor to take advantage of these institutional changes and organize itself, a task the AFL was still singularly ill equipped

---

[50] Edelman, "New Deal Sensitivity," p. 162.

[51] As Long put it in his more radical version, the depression could be cured if "all personal fortunes above a certain amount . . . [were used] . . . to give every family enough to buy a home, an automobile and a radio; old folks would receive pensions and worthy boys would go to college." Leuchtenburg, *Franklin D. Roosevelt and the New Deal*, p. 98.

to do despite the institutional strengthening undertaken by Congress and the Department of Labor.

In response to rejection from business on the right and apathy from labor on the left, the state began looking for a new strategy. That strategy was to come out of the older and overtly antimonopoly tradition of the Brandeisians. Largely at the urging of Felix Frankfurter, Roosevelt more or less explicitly disavowed business-government cooperation and sought to bring business to heel by sending the Social Security Act, the Wagner Act, the Utilities Holding Bill, and a deliberately antibusiness tax proposal to Congress for immediate assent.[52] Of the four items, the Social Security Act and the Wagner Act both clearly articulated the new underconsumptionist ideas that were increasingly informing the state's response to the depression. These institutions were to prove vital components of the emerging embedded liberal order.

Building New Institutions

The Social Security Act
Reflecting the desire to build new institutions both to resolve the crisis and placate the South, the three parts of the Social Security Act – Old Age Assistance (OAA), Old Age Insurance (OAI), and Unemployment Insurance (UI) – were designed to include industrial labor and exclude agricultural labor. However, the notion of general social provision was hardly without precedent. Throughout the 1920s, several states had introduced pension schemes and in 1930 the House Committee on Labor began hearings on a national noncontributory pension proposal sponsored by Representative William Connery. Despite several modifications and fierce business opposition, especially from the NAM, a version of Connery's bill (the Dill-Connery Bill) was passed by the House and almost passed by the Senate.[53]

Apart from federal- and state-supported pension initiatives, business also promoted company pensions as both an incentive to join company unions and as a labor control device. As Jill S. Quadagno notes, nearly all such pensions were discretionary and performance-related and had length of service requirements. Some contained continuous service clauses that barred striking, and some even required retirees to return to the company as strike

---

[52] See Leuchtenburg, *Franklin D. Roosevelt and the New Deal*, p. 150–1. On Frankfurter's role in promoting Roosevelt's defection from business, see Max Freedman, ed., *Roosevelt and Frankfurter: Their Correspondence 1928–1945* (Boston: Little, Brown and Company, 1967), pp. 229–301; Brinkley, *The End of Reform*, pp. 48–52.

[53] Jill S. Quadagno, "Welfare Capitalism and the Social Security Act of 1935," *American Sociological Review* (49) October (1984). My account of the evolution of the Social Security Act draws upon this, Alston and Ferrie, "Labor Costs," and Colin Gordon, *New Deals Business, Labor and Politics in America 1920–1935* (Cambridge: Cambridge University Press, 1994), *passim*.

breakers if ordered to do so by the company.[54] Despite their benefits, such pensions had one severe flaw: They were often financed out of current expenses, and when the depression hit, the majority of these plans went bankrupt. Consequently, the issue of pension reform was not simply the state versus business since certain sections of business were quite favorable toward such reforms. Given that the state was being squeezed by the Townsendites on the one hand and the Dill-Connery Bill on the other, Roosevelt again turned to Gerald Swope, the designer of the General Electric plan that served as the blueprint for the NRA, to design a new set of institutions.[55]

After discussing the issue of social provision over lunch with Swope on March 8, 1934, Roosevelt asked Swope to summarize their discussion for him. "Two weeks later Swope presented the completed proposal to the President, a detailed statistical document which contained plans for unemployment, disability and old age pensions. Roosevelt immediately began pushing for a comprehensive Social Security measure that incorporated both unemployment and pensions."[56] However, seeing the Social Security Act wholly as a business initiative is somewhat simplistic. While such an institutional initiative may have responded to business's perceived interests, it is not reducible to them. Rather, the Social Security Act itself was symptomatic of the changing economic ideas of the period that agents were using to recast seemingly opposed interests as common.

With the ideological failure of the administered prices thesis in the denouement of the NIRA, the ideas underlying the Social Security Act changed focus from cartelization to consumption. These theories – developed by professional economists such as Lachlan Currie and Alvin Hansen, popular commentators such as William Trufant Foster and Wadill Catchings, and some of the more militant sections of organized labor – argued that together with the concentration of industry noted by administered prices theorists, there was a parallel concentration of wealth since the gains from increased productivity outstripped consumption.[57] As George Soule wrote, "Since we have the technical capacity to produce enough for everyone, everyone ought to have a large enough income to buy what he needs."[58] The fact that millions did not strongly suggest that the causes of the depression lay on the demand side rather than the supply side of the

---

[54] Quadagno, "Welfare Capitalism," pp. 636–7.
[55] There was also the more redistributionary Lundeen Bill, but that Bill was never in serious contention.
[56] Quadagno, "Welfare Capitalism," p. 639.
[57] As Jerome Frank argued, the cause of the depression lay in "the fact that the great majority of our citizens were not receiving a sufficient share." Jerome B. Frank, quoted in Theodore Rosenof, *Patterns of Political Economy in America: The Failure to Develop a Democratic Left Synthesis, 1933–1950* (New York: Garland Publishing, 1983), p. 19.
[58] George Soule, *A Planned Society* (New York: MacMillan, 1932), pp. 262–3.

economy. Monopoly concentration and unequal distribution therefore combined to produce two deleterious effects. First, in a mass production economy, mass consumption was a necessity. Yet the increasingly unequal distribution of wealth meant that consumption among wage earners was falling. Second, a greater return to the wealthy meant that savings increased and, in depression conditions, investment fell and the deflation was exacerbated.

Reflecting this shift in ideas, Secretary of Labor Perkins argued before Congress that the point of the Social Security Act was not to facilitate redistribution, but to increase purchasing power. "[B]y paying over moneys to persons who would not otherwise have any income, you are creating purchasing power which will . . . sustain the purchases which will be made from the great manufacturing and mercantile systems of the country."[59] Thus "the stabilization of the economy, not the welfare of workers, was the goal of national welfare programs – a goal that coincided with the interests of monopoly capital."[60]

Despite this attempt by the state to reinterpret business's interests as being in line with increased consumption, business opposition to the whole thrust of the state's reforms was intensifying. While the BAC remained supportive of the Act, the ACC and the NAM began to mobilize opposition, particularly against the Old Age Insurance and Unemployment Insurance provisions.[61] Coupled with this was Southern concern that even though the

---

[59] Frances Perkins in U.S. Congress, Senate. Senate Committee on Finance, *The Economic Security Act*, Hearings, January 1935 (Washington: Government Printing Office, 1935) (Y4.F49:Ec7/7rev). Given the need to have a contributory and nonredistributive system, the Act initially reduced purchasing power by some $2 billion. However, Roosevelt explained why the Act was made regressive. When told about the short-term fiscal implications, Roosevelt replied, "I guess you're right about the economics . . . but those taxes were never a problem of economics. They are politics all the way through. We put those payroll contributions in there so as to give the contributors a legal, moral and political right to collect their pensions and their unemployment benefits. With those taxes in there, no damn politician will ever scrap my Social Security program." Roosevelt, quoted in Arthur Schlesinger, Jr., *The Coming of the New Deal*, pp. 308–9.

[60] Quadagno, "Welfare Capitalism," p. 640. Indeed, the advisory committee created to assist the legislative planning committee charged with implementing the Act, the Committee on Economic Security, had an almost duplicate membership of the BAC and included both Swope and Walter Teagle. Moreover, business was supportive of the creation of Social Security as a means to limit competition. By standardizing welfare costs and externalizing them on the state and labor, the Social Security Act offered business an indirect subsidy for a good that businesses otherwise would have to produce individually. For an elaboration of this theme, see Colin Gordon, "New Deal, Old Deck: Business and the Origins of Social Security, 1920–1935," *Politics and Society* 19 (2) June (1991); Idem., *New Deals*, passim.

[61] The fact of this sustained opposition argues against materialist perspectives that reduce the supply of Social Security to "the work of a motley coalition of business interests grasping

Act excluded agricultural and domestic labor, the precedent of establishing federal standards for a reasonable subsistence compatible with decency and health would jeopardize not just Southern wage scales but the entire labor-repressive Southern regime. Consequently, in deference to the need to garner Southern support, Congress made the Old Age Insurance provisions local rather than federal responsibilities, and also deleted the "decency and health" clause. However, the basic objections of the ACC and the NAM were overridden, and as a consequence, the state's relationship with business became more acrimonious than ever.

The National Labor Relations (Wagner) Act

Whereas business support for the form if not the passage of the Social Security Act was crucial, for the Wagner Act the support of key Congressional legislators and state administrators was essential. Disenchanted with the failure of the voluntarism that section 7a embodied, Senator Wagner tried in 1934 to pass a bill which considerably strengthened article 7a's provisions. Seeing such a controversial proposal in the midst of an election year as divisive, Roosevelt instead opted for public resolution 44, which set up a National Labor Relations Board (NLRB) to investigate disputes, but lacked the ability to force legal compliance.[62] Nonplused by this cooptation of his original measure, Wagner tried again after the 1934 elections, and this time his National Labor Relations Act (Wagner Act) was passed. The Act sought to "encourage the practice and procedure of collective bargaining," to protect "the exercise of workers of full freedom of association . . . and . . . designation of the representatives of their own choosing."[63] Furthermore, the Act specified that the right to strike was not to be interfered with, and perhaps most importantly, the Act empowered the NRLB to compel employers to recognize unions.

The Wagner Act signified a distinct ideational shift toward an under-consumptionist understanding of the depression. As with the Social Security Act, the chief claim for the Wagner Act was that it would increase

for solutions to the ravages of economic competition." Gordon, *New Deals*, p. 279. As Nelson Lichtenstein points out, such a perspective "hardly described political reality during the New Deal years . . . [since] . . . the overwhelming majority of American businessmen fiercely resisted most New Deal reforms." Nelson Lichtenstein, *Labor's War at Home: The CIO in World War Two* (Cambridge: Cambridge University Press, 1991) p. 4.

[62] For different views of resolution 44, see Finegold and Skocpol, *State and Party*, pp. 130–1; R. W. Fleming, "The Significance of the Wagner Act," in Derber and Young, eds., *Labor and the New Deal*, pp. 126–7.

[63] *National Labor Relations Act*, Public Laws of the United States of America passed by the Seventy-Fourth Congress, 1935–1936, July 5, 1935 (Washington: Government Printing Office, 1936), pp. 449–57, quoted in David Plotke, *Building a Democratic Political Order: Reshaping American Liberalism in the 1930's and 1940's* (Cambridge: Cambridge University Press, 1996), p. 92.

purchasing power. As the Wagner Act states, "the inequality of bargaining power between employees . . . and employers . . . tends to aggravate recurrent business depressions, by depressing wage rates and the purchasing power of wage earners in industry."[64] Further normative claims concerning "fairness" and "stability" within an organized framework of industrial relations were advanced in support of the measure.[65] It was also claimed that the Act would reduce the number of strikes. Given that almost 50 percent of stoppages revolved around issues of union recognition, it was argued that mandating that recognition would obviate a significant cause of industrial unrest.[66]

As such, the idea that increasing purchasing power was the solution to the depression gave rise to an institutional innovation: the mandatory recognition of unions. With such recognition, the costs of collective action plummeted. However, instead of the craft-based and moribund AFL taking advantage of these institutional changes, it was the newly formed Congress of Industrial Organizations (CIO) that took advantage and grew rapidly. Support for the CIO also came from an unlikely source, the Supreme Court.

After the election of 1936 strengthened Roosevelt's position, the infamous "Court-packing" incident took place. Briefly, under the guise of an administrative reform to speed up judicial review, Roosevelt threatened to alter the composition of the Court in order to get more progressive legislation passed. Conservatives and liberals alike correctly saw such a move as an attempt to remove older conservative jurists and replace them with jurists more favorable to New Deal policies. While in the short term the incident hurt Roosevelt greatly, it indirectly brought the state and labor closer together.

This convergence occurred because while business strongly opposed passage of the Wagner Act, business's attempts to avoid the Act's implementation were muted. In part this was due to the threat of legal sanction under the NLRB, but it was mainly because business expected the Wagner Act to be found unconstitutional given the precedent of the Schechter case, which invalidated the NIRA. Unfortunately for business, the Court-packing incident actually achieved what Roosevelt wanted insofar as older

---

[64] *National Labor Relations Act,* quoted in David Plotke, "The Wagner Act, Again: Politics and Labor, 1935–37," *Studies in American Political Development,* 9 (1) (1994), p. 125.

[65] See Hawley, *The New Deal and the Problem of Monopoly,* pp. 195–6, 276–7.

[66] Wagner also opined that democracy would be strengthened by strengthening unions. As Wagner said in a *New York Times Magazine* interview, "The struggle for a voice in industry . . . is the heart of the struggle for the preservation of political as well as economic democracy in America. Let men become the servile pawns of their masters in the factories of the land and there will be destroyed the bone and sinew of resistance to political dictatorship." "The Ideal State – as Wagner Sees It," *New York Times Magazine,* May 9, 1937, p. 23, quoted in Fleming, "The Significance of the Wagner Act," in Derber and Young, eds., *Labor and the New Deal,* p. 135.

conservative jurists were cajoled into compliance and found the Wagner Act constitutional.[67] As Edwin Young observed, "The Supreme Court decision to uphold the Wagner Act came at a very precipitous time and gave encouragement to the [CIO]."[68]

Furthermore, the revelations of the Senate's LaFollette Committee regarding the illegal and sometimes murderous practices of business during industrial disputes strengthened Congressional and public support for the Wagner Act. Under its umbrella, the CIO expanded its reach and by October 1937 the CIO could claim 4 million members and count in its ranks unions from all the major industrial sectors. In response to the administration's overture to labor, the CIO (and to a lesser extent the AFL) sought to ally itself actively with the state. Organized labor spent and campaigned heavily for Roosevelt in the 1936 election through a front organization called the Non-Partisan League.[69] While the political fruits of this open alliance were disappointing for labor, and business remained hostile to the whole thrust of reforms, there was no mistaking the coalitional and institutional effects of the Social Security and Wagner Acts. By providing institutional supports, the state had in effect "organized" a disorganized labor movement and provided workers with a set of protective institutions designed to increase purchasing power. Doing so, it was hoped, would reduce unemployment, stabilize expectations, and thus resolve the crisis.

What these new institutions gave labor was strength, autonomy, and most importantly, the right to exist and organize under a state that would not repress such actions. Such efforts were intended to forge a lasting political coalition with industrial labor, and doing so was much more than an electoral expedient. As David Plotke argues, by empowering workers and by redrawing the boundaries as to who a representative agent with rights was (on a micro level with Social Security Act and on a macro level with the Wagner Act), and by excluding business from monopoly privileges over labor and over the use of violence, these Acts fundamentally changed the institutional position of labor.[70] Partly through state initiative and partly through labor's own efforts, the state and labor had redrawn the

---

[67] See Leuchtenburg, *Franklin D. Roosevelt and the New Deal*, pp. 131–6; Leuchtenburg, "Franklin D. Roosevelt's Supreme Court Packing Plan," in Harold Hollingsworth, ed., *Essays on the New Deal* (Austin: University of Texas Press, 1969).

[68] Young, "The Split in the Labor Movement," p. 67.

[69] In 1932 bankers had donated 24 percent of all sums of $1,000.00 or more to Roosevelt's campaign; in 1936 that proportion had shrunk to 4 percent. Given the drop in business support for the Democrats, the support of labor was perceived to be significant even if it turned out to be less than expected in hindsight. See Louise Overacker, "Labor's Political Contributions in the 1932 Election," *Political Science Quarterly* 54 (1) March (1939), p. 60. Direct support of a particular candidate by unions was outlawed in 1943, *before* Taft-Hartley.

[70] Plotke, "The Wagner Act, Again," p. 148.

boundaries of both state action and labor's legitimacy. By late 1936, it seemed that a new and stable coalition between labor and the state had been formed. However, within just a few months, this was to prove to be far from the case. There was to be no American Saltsjöbaden.

By 1937 it seemed that the recovery was well under way. Agricultural prices were rising and New Deal programs were credited with having revitalized the country. Underconsumptionist ideas gained strength when the spending arm of the NIRA was reconstituted and redeployed in a host of "alphabet agencies" that created economic institutions of national reach for the first time. The deployment of these national economic institutions under agencies such as the Civilian Conservation Corps, the Federal Emergency Relief Administration, as well as the numerous agencies originally constituted under title 2 of the NIRA constituted an incremental, but cumulatively radical, change in the relationship between private economic power and the state. Given this challenge to business leaders' very identity as capitalists, it is perhaps unsurprising then that they were far from happy.

Yet, so long as the recovery continued, the struggle over the core ideas behind the recovery program remained in the background. However, the recession of 1937 brought these contending ideas into sharp relief. After the delegitimation of the administered prices thesis, two sets of ideas vied for supremacy: the underconsumption arguments developed and deployed by Marriner Eccles and Lachlan Currie at the Federal Reserve, and the return, once again, to the principles of sound finance and budget balancing, as championed by Treasury Secretary Henry Morgenthau, Jr.

Rediagnosing the Crisis: Ideas and Politics in the 1937 Recession

Until the 1937 recession, the contradictions within the set of ideas governing the state actions were not considered to be a problem, so long as the recovery continued. Thus, underconsumptionist ideas informed the policy of building a coalition with labor, while sound finance principles were deployed rhetorically to persuade business that the state was not an implacable foe of free enterprise. The problem was that in 1937, "[h]opes for retrenchment, balanced budgets, and business confidence collided head on with the most serious economic decline since 1933."[71] Between August 1937 and January 1938, stock prices fell 58 percent, employment fell 28

---

[71] Olson, *Saving Capitalism*, p. 187. In fact, the state's own actions were to blame for the collapse of purchasing power. The state "cut the Reconstruction Finance Corporation and the Works Progress Administration, the Federal Reserve raised reserve requirements, and social security taxes had gone into effect. The result was the recession of 1937–1938." See Olson, *Saving Capitalism*, p. 189.

percent, industrial production fell 43 percent, and corporate profits fell by 78 percent.[72] As May argues, "the recession of 1937 . . . broke the lull of self-confident assurance that the slow, steady pace of recovery had brought."[73] In this context, both spenders and budget balancers argued that the state needed to take action, but that action had to be "part of an overall definition of what the 'New Deal' had been, and where it was going. It must promise consistent coherent solutions to [the] broad range of problems confronting the economy."[74] Once again, in a moment of uncertainty, the crisis had to be rediagnosed before it could be resolved.

Long before the crisis of 1937 buffeted the state, Federal Reserve Chairman Eccles had been the main promoter within the state of an underconsumptionist reading of the crisis. Eccles, a Mormon banker influenced by Foster, Catchings, and other underconsumptionist writers, had as early as 1932 referred to the practice of balancing the budget during a recession as simply compounding deflation. Eccles felt that although such an action may have a limited role in allaying business fears, any recovery predicated upon this action would be overwhelmed by the contraction that balancing the budget demanded.[75] Eccles further warned that orthodox monetary policies that aimed at promoting confidence would fail to bring about new investment because of what Keynes would later term the liquidity preference.[76] As such, only the state could undertake investment of the magnitude necessary to promote recovery.

Indeed, as early as his Senate confirmation hearings in 1933, Eccles proposed "federal insurance for bank deposits, a centralized Federal Reserve system, tax reform to redistribute income . . . unemployment insurance, old age pensions, federal regulation of the stock market and other economic sectors [thereby anticipating] most all of the reforms that would become known as the New Deal."[77] Eccles' ideas were, however, to find their opportunity only in the context of the 1937 recession. What stymied the progress of Eccles' ideas was the fact that until between 1935 and 1937 the recovery seemed to be progressing despite contradictory ideas governing the state's attempts to solve the crisis. Limited spending seemed to have done

---

[72] Figures from May, *New Deal to New Economics*, p. 4; Brinkley, *The End of Reform*, p. 29.

[73] May, *New Deal to New Economics*, p. 14.

[74] *Ibid.*, p. 15.

[75] Marriner Eccles, "Speech to Utah State Banker's Convention," Salt Lake City, June 17, 1932, quoted in May, *New Deal to New Economics*, p. 54.

[76] As May notes regarding the ideas of Eccles, "the multiplier . . . and the propensity to consume . . . were all part of Eccles system, [and were] sufficiently well informed to lead to similar policy conclusions." May, *New Deal to New Economics*, p. 59.

[77] William Greider, *The Secrets of the Temple: How the Federal Reserve Runs the Country* (New York: Simon and Schuster, 1991), p. 309; Olson, *Saving Capitalism*, p. 159.

the trick, and as such, the long-term lessons of underconsumptionist ideas
had not been inculcated. Given this complacency, "sound finance" ideas
reappeared.

The Return of Sound Finance

In his 1936 budget message, Roosevelt once again ploughed the well-worn
furrow of rhetorical sound finance. He argued that given the strength of
the recovery, the time had come to consider balancing the budget once
again. A year later, in his 1937 message, he reiterated this, claiming that
"we expect . . . to be able to attain in 1939 a completely balanced budget."[78]
The logic behind these claims was quite obvious. First, if *ad hoc* measures
and extraordinary expenditures were enough to promote recovery, and if
needed reforms in social insurance, banking regulation, and union activity
that would prevent catastrophic falls in consumption in the future were in
place, then an *eventual* return to orthodoxy seemed warranted. Second,
practicing rhetorical sound finance – that is, constantly promising to
balance the budget and failing to do so – was bound eventually to impact
negatively on business confidence, especially when recovery was under way.
As such, reforming now to reinforce expectations of recovery seemed better
than straining such confidence in the future. Morgenthau thus undertook
to return the state to the canons of sound finance, and unveiled this proposed change in state policy at a meeting of the Academy of Political Science
in New York in November 1937.[79]

To explain why deficits and spending were now to be disavowed after
three years of usefulness, Morgenthau rediscovered classical economics – in
particular, the crowding-out thesis. He argued that at the height of the
depression, such expansionary policies were warranted as they were composed of bank credits and government issues that did not affect business
confidence. However, now that recovery was well under way, it became
necessary to cut back such expenditures, as government demands on credit
would be competing with new private demands and would thus have an
adverse rather than a positive effect on recovery.[80] The wisdom of these
ideas came into question as the recession of 1937 worsened, but nonetheless Morgenthau pressed ahead.

In contradiction to the return-to-orthodoxy signals being communicated
by Morgenthau, Roosevelt decided in October 1937 to signal to Congress

---

[78] Franklin D. Roosevelt, *The Public Papers and Addresses of Franklin D. Roosevelt, with a
Special Introduction and Explanatory Notes by President Roosevelt* (New York: Random
House, 1938–[50]), Volume 5, pp. 643–4.
[79] This was a rather oddly named body since it was composed almost entirely of financers and
manufacturers and had very limited academic affiliations.
[80] For discussion of Morgenthau's desire to balance the budget, see Brinkley, *The End of
Reform*, pp. 25–8; May, *New Deal to New Economics*, pp. 94–6.

that a major package of new reforms would be forthcoming.[81] Business reaction was swift and uniformly negative. Unfortunately this reaction also coincided with a deepening of the recession that made the recession look suspiciously like a Kaleckian capital strike, which, in turn, had the effect of further polarizing sentiment within the state.[82]

Morgenthau thus found himself in a quandary. His "recovery through balancing the budget" idea was predicated upon the assumption that it was now propitious to balance the budget given economic improvement. However, if the recession was worsening, surely balancing would do more harm than good. Rather than resolve these contradictions, Morgenthau instead argued, in line with classical orthodoxy, that a return to sound finance and balanced budgets was needed now more than ever in order to fight recession by "clearing the tracks for the expansion of private business."[83]

Despite the best of intentions of promoting recovery by boosting confidence, this policy failed for two reasons. First, it was not credible. Business simply did not believe Morgenthau's claims to be able to balance the budget. His speech at the Academy of Political Science was met with laughter and derision. Second, such a policy was not only simply deflationary in its own right, it ran contrary to the ideas behind all the new institutions constructed since 1932. Given these patent contradictions, Eccles' refrain that attempting to balance the budget was itself a core problem of the depression began to gain a wider audience.

The arguments for spending had been gaining momentum since 1935, and their deployment in support of both Wagner and the Social Security Acts had strengthened their credibility. Eccles' assistant at the Treasury Department, Currie, was central in further developing the rationale for pro-spending arguments. As Sweezy notes, between 1934 and 1936, Currie calculated a data series eventually called "Net Contribution of the Federal Government to National Buying Power":

This was both a technical improvement on the official deficit ... and even more important [it was] a semantic triumph of the first magnitude. It brought out the common element on all the government's fiscal operations. No one used to

---

[81] There were the so-called little Tennessee Valley Authorities, wages and hours legislation, and an executive reform intended to strengthen the office of the president.

[82] For example, while Morgenthau sought to assuage business's fears rather than curtail business's power, Harold L. Ickes spoke of the recession as the result of a capital strike by an oligarchy of America's top sixty families. Similarly, the Department of Justice's Robert Jackson spoke of an active conspiracy against the state by business. See Brinkley, *End of Reform*, p. 298, fn. 28. For discussion of the 1937 recession as the result of capital strike, see Michal Kalecki, "Political Aspects of Full Employment," *Political Quarterly* 14 October (1944); Brinkley, *The End of Reform*, pp. 48–9, 55–6; Olson, *Saving Capitalism*, p. 188.

[83] Henry J. Morgenthau, *Diaries* (95), p. 127, quoted in May, *New Deal to New Economics*, p. 103.

thinking in terms of the net contribution could advocate promoting recovery by increasing public works spending while at the same time cutting government salaries and raising taxes.[84]

Emboldened by these arguments, Eccles' public remarks during the 1937 recession directly challenged Morgenthau's sound finance ideas. While Morgenthau was sincerely pledging the state to a balanced budget, Eccles was testifying to Congress that a billion-dollar spending package would be the only thing that would halt the new depression.[85] Simultaneously, Eccles, Currie, and others in the spending camp began bombarding the White House with memos advocating greater spending. Indeed, while Roosevelt vacationed at Warm Springs, Georgia, a coterie of pro-spenders encamped close to the president's retreat and formulated the basic elements of the new economic ideas that were to serve as both the intellectual rationale for, and institutional underpinning of, America's embedded liberalism for the next twenty years.

The Triumph of the Demand Side

As Dean L. May has argued, the discussions at Warm Springs centered upon committing the state to shift from a sociofinancial policy – that is, one based upon the "adaptation of economic and production operations to prevailing financial necessities" – toward a socioeconomic policy that would direct government policy toward "the increase in production of goods and services and the elimination of physical and human waste."[86] The telegram the pro-spending lobby sent to Roosevelt suggested, in what was later to be termed *national income accounting*, that the state should calculate the purchasing power necessary to produce full employment. Any deficit projected on this basis should be accommodated through direct spending or tax cuts. This type of active economic management was a radical break from all past New Deal efforts and signaled a sea change in the economic ideas governing the United States.

To make these ideas more politically palatable, the authors of the Warm Springs proposals conjoined their arguments rather creatively with the

---

[84] Sweezy, "The Keynesians and Government Policy," p. 118. Currie also wrote an influential paper called "The Causes of the Recession," which Brinkley has described as the "samizdat" of the New Deal. See Brinkley's essay, "The Idea of the State," in Steve Fraser and Gary Gerstle, eds., *The Rise and Fall of the New Deal Order* (Princeton: Princeton University Press, 1989), pp. 85–122, esp. pp. 96–7, on the importance of the 1937 recession as a moment of ideological struggle.

[85] Marriner Eccles in U.S. Congress. Senate. Senate Special Committee on Unemployment and Relief, *Unemployment and Relief*. Volume 1, Hearings. January 1938 (Washington: Government Printing Office 1938) (Y4. Un2/2 : Un2/v.1).

[86] Henderson-Ruml Telegram, April 1, 1938, *Harry Hopkins Papers*, Box 50, Franklin D. Roosevelt Library, quoted in May, *New Deal to New Economics*, pp. 131–2.

increasingly influential secular stagnation thesis.[87] Rather than arguing that because the growth pattern of the United States had fundamentally changed, permanent increases in government outlays would be necessary to prevent permanent recession – as the writings of Alvin Hansen, and, in places, Keynes, had argued – the authors suggested that such government spending was nothing new.[88]

As Theodore Rosenof notes, the authors harkened back to Frederick Jackson Turner's frontier thesis and argued that in the past the alienation of public lands had performed the same function by massively boosting investment and hence increasing purchasing power.[89] Given that the decline in purchasing power was the root cause of the slump, not only was budget balancing exactly the wrong policy, it actually augured against historical precedent. This Henderson-Ruml thesis made it "inconceivable that there can be any recovery along 'orthodox' lines." To argue so, as Morgenthau did, was therefore anti-American.[90]

The cumulative effects of Morgenthau's rearticulation of sound finance, the continuing decline of the stock market, and the threat of Congressional action to implement a balanced budget combined to strengthen under-consumptionist ideas within the state. By October 1937, how far these new ideas had permeated the state's response to the crisis was heard in one of Roosevelt's radio fireside chats. Blaming the recession squarely on the failure of purchasing power, Roosevelt advocated a new round of expenditures totaling $3.5 billion with the hint of more to come. Roosevelt concluded that, "let us unanimously recognize . . . that the federal debt, whether it be twenty-five billions or forty billions can only be paid if the nation obtains a vastly increased citizen income."[91]

After 1937, spending arguments rapidly took center stage as the rationale for state action. Hansen's secular stagnation thesis was given greater credence by Currie's analysis of investment demand. This suggested that demand would perhaps continue to fall below that necessary for full employment unless government made permanent contributions to national

---

[87] May, *New Deal to New Economics*; Rosenof, *Patterns of Political Economy*.

[88] See, for example, Alvin Hansen, "Economic Progress and Declining Population Growth," *American Economic Review* (29) March (1939); John Maynard Keynes, "Some Economic Consequences of a Declining Population," *Eugenics Review* (29) April (1937).

[89] See Rosenof, *Patterns of Political Economy*, pp. 34–6. Turner's frontier thesis argued that once the frontier was exhausted, new "easy" paths to extensive growth were closed off and the problems of the American economy would become increasingly more acute. See Fredrick Jackson Turner, *The Frontier in American History* (New York: H. Holt and Company, 1920). As Rosenof argues, while the prosperity of the 1920s seemed to demonstrate the futility of the frontier thesis, the onset of the depression resuscitated Turner's ideas among interventionist economists.

[90] May, *New Deal to New Economics*, p. 133.

[91] Franklin D. Roosevelt, *Public Papers*, Volume 7, pp. 236–47.

income. Relatedly, a group of Harvard and Tufts economists broke ranks with old-guard business cycle theorists and published *An Economic Program for American Democracy*. The *Program* authors embraced these new ideas and advocated a proactive and interventionist role for the state.[92] However, at this juncture, these new ideas were most effectively used as weapons to attack existing institutions and thereby to head off the return of some very old economic ideas.

The old economic ideas that made a reappearance here were the Brandeisian antimonopoly arguments that underlay the Sherman Act and other pieces of pro-competition progressive regulation. Older New Dealers in this tradition, such as Robert Jackson and Benjamin Cohen, united with Congressional antimonopoly activists to demand a federal inquiry into the status of monopolistic practices in American industry. After feverish behind-the-scenes efforts, Roosevelt sent a message to Congress on April 29, 1938, requesting both increased spending *and* the antimonopoly inquiry requested by Jackson and Cohen. As a result of this, the Temporary National Economic Committee (TNEC) hearings got under way in December 1938.[93]

Although the principal focus of the committee was the problem of monopoly, the committee hearings and the reports that the committee published were hardly accusatory or indicative of the pathologies of big business. In fact, the hearings served to further the cause of spending advocates much more than that of antimonopoly advocates. As Alan Brinkley notes, the TNEC hearings "served, quite deliberately, as a forum for promoting aggressive federal fiscal policies as a solution to the nation's economic torpor."[94] Aware of the educative function of these hearings, Henderson organized dress rehearsals of key witnesses such as Currie and Hansen. Before the committee, Currie painstakingly made the case for demand stimulating fiscal policies while Hansen used the hearing to campaign for both government spending to supplement private investment, and income redistribution to lower the propensity to save.

The analysis that emerged from the TNEC hearings gave the spenders' ideas the mantle of coherence and generalizability they needed to become the dominant interpretation of the crisis and the solution to it. Increased

---

[92] R. V. Gilbert et al., *An Economic Program for American Democracy* (New York: Vanguard Press, 1938). The position of Keynes and the *General Theory* in actually promoting a change in policy was, like most academic economics in the United States in this period, marginal at best.

[93] Doing so was not so contradictory since, "By late 1937, most antitrusters ... were beginning to fuse the compensatory spending and antitrust proposals." Olson, *Saving Capitalism*, p. 199.

[94] Brinkley, *The End of Reform*, p. 128. Olson, in contrast, views the TNEC hearings as "having little public impact," and having a bias "along Frankfurter-Brandeisian lines." Olson, *Saving Capitalism*, p. 190.

expenditures could now be justified on efficiency as well as humanitarian grounds, while the role of the state in economic life became more certain than it had ever been. There was, however, a dark cloud on the horizon: the threat of war. In such a situation, the need for unity, particularly a rapprochement with business, tempered both the coalitional and redistributionary aspirations of the state. However, the threat of war also served to solidify the new view of the economy and promote the further development of those institutions that would be necessary for its survival, albeit in a tempered form, after the war.

The War and the War of Ideas
Conservative Congressional opposition to these new ideas and institutions began to crystallize just before the outbreak of the war. In 1939 a coalition of Southern Democrats and Republicans defeated the proposed $3.06 billion Works Financing Bill, which was intended to extend the spending cycle that had ended the 1937–8 recession. Electorally, the Democrats had just lost seventy House and seven Senate seats in the 1938 Congressional elections, and seniority rules meant that key committee positions fell to Conservative Southerners who could effectively act as veto points on key pieces of legislation. Also, the new institutions set up to deal with the war, the National Resources Planning Board (NRPB) and the Office of Price Administration (OPA), were often headed by appointed business leaders, many of whom were openly hostile to these new ideas. Likewise, when these institutions were headed by recognizable New Dealers, they were systematically targeted and attacked by the Congress.

These setbacks were often augmented by the actions of the state itself. Antimonopolists, stagnationists, and spenders all became increasingly convinced that, as Paul Douglas wrote, control of monopoly capitalism should not mean jumping "from the frying pan of private property into the fire of an all powerful state."[95] The emergent Hayekian critique of planning and the rise of totalitarianism in both its fascist and Stalinist forms served not only as a lightning rod for conservative opposition, but caused those sympathetic to these new ideas to rethink their position.[96] Once it was admitted that governmental control of the economy could in practice be incompatible with individual liberty, then the possibility of a purely statist solution to the problems of growth and distribution, as advocated by Hansen et al., seemed to be a rather unappetizing solution on its own terms.[97]

[95] Paul Douglas, "Freedom with Security," *The Social Welfare Forum* (1) (1949), p. 150.
[96] On the reception of F. A. Hayek's *Road to Serfdom* in the United States, see Theodore Rosenof, "Freedom, Planning and Totalitarianism: The Reception of F. A. Hayek's *The Road to Serfdom*," *Canadian Review of American Studies* 5 (2) Fall (1974).
[97] It is little wonder that such an analysis as Hayek's found resonance in the United States. As Brinkley notes, "in responding to . . . Hayek, and to the broader discussion of

In this context, rather than providing the springboard for an ever more deeply institutionalized compact between the state and labor, the experience of war tempered the position of labor and reinvigorated business. However, in this process, given extant ideational changes and participation within the new consumption maintaining institutions, business's preferences over the nature of the postwar order themselves changed. In the context of war, policies such as increased consumption and large deficits were to become rather orthodox practices.

"Massive federal spending ended the Great Depression."[98] Unemployment fell from 17.2 percent in 1939 to 1.2 percent in 1944 and it was massive government spending that made the difference.[99] For example, the Wartime Defense Plants Corporation invested more than $15 billion in fixed capital between 1941 and 1943, whereas total private investment in plant and equipment between 1941 and 1945 was only $11 billion.[100] The war forced the state to become more fiscally innovative. First, the state's desire to have as much cheap money as possible mandated that the Federal Reserve underwrite the cost of bond issues. This attempt to create a dependent central bank persisted into the first few years of the postwar era and initially made a cheap money policy possible.[101] Second, by extending the scope of income tax, the 1942 Revenue Act provided an important lever of fiscal control for the state that was lacking until then.

One of the most surprising aspects of this period is that the vitriolic attacks of business against such policies which characterized the 1930s were absent during the war. The reason for this was quite simple. As Collins notes,

> totalitarianism which was permeating virtually all political discourse in the 1940s, liberals were in fact responding to a powerful strain of Jeffersonian anti-statism in American political culture that a decade of the New Deal had done relatively little to eliminate."
> Brinkley, *The End of Reform*, p. 160.

[98] Olson, *Saving Capitalism*, p. 220.

[99] Taking 1929 as the baseline, the percentage of private consumption to overall GDP was 74.8 percent. In 1946 that proportion had fallen to 68.8 percent. Concomitantly over this period, government contributions to GDP increased by 5.4 percent more than this margin, thus making governmental expenditures the main driving force behind both aggregate consumption and gross capital formation. What this demonstrates is that governmental wartime spending, and not private business investment, was the agent of economic recovery. Figures from Harold G. Vatter, *The United States Economy in World War Two* (New York: Columbia University Press, 1985), p. 150.

[100] The Defense Plants Corporation figures are from Brinkley, *The End of Reform*, p. 241. See also Olson, *Saving Capitalism*, pp. 218–19. Nor did this trend reverse itself at the end of the war as the stagnationists feared that it would. In fact, governmental additions to national income continued to grow and by the mid-1950s private consumption had fallen to around 53 percent. Figures from *The Economic Report of the President* (Washington: Government Printing Office, 1984), p. 220.

[101] However, business soon became alert to the dangers of such an institutional arrangement and lobbied hard to break the link that would make a cheap money policy possible.

... businessmen flocked into government service in unprecedented numbers. ... The capitalism that had been damned as bankrupt just a few years before was now celebrated for its prodigious feats of production. The war presented businessmen with the incentive both to re-invigorate their own private organizations and to form new groups in the shadowy areas where the private and public spheres intersected.[102]

These businessmen ran the new institutions of war management, and despite the deep political conflicts over such institutions, the founding and staffing of these wartime agencies both helped to legitimate these new institutions and to establish a pattern of business-government cooperation that was to have far-reaching consequences in the postwar period.

Despite such cooperative aspects, the key struggle over which ideas would shape the postwar order occurred over what the postwar economy would look like – an ideological struggle over which ideas would be the defining ideas of the postwar order.[103] This struggle found its expression in three pieces of postwar legislation: the 1946 Employment Act, the 1946 Administrative Procedures Act, and the 1947 Taft-Hartley Act.[104]

Constructing the Postwar Order

The Struggle over Stagnationism and Full Employment

Perhaps because of the integrative effects of business participation within wartime institutions, business began to use these institutions to head off an even bigger threat than underconsumptionist ideas: the threat of

---

[102] Collins, *The Business Response to Keynes*, p. 81.

[103] The debate formed around whether the world after the war would be the world of secular stagnation or whether it would be a world where instruments such as deficit financing and passive stabilizers would play a role, but where the state would not be predominant in planning investment or structuring distribution.

[104] Of course, the ideational struggle occurred on two levels: domestic and international. On the international level, the struggle was similarly framed. The key issue was whether the United States would return to a *laissez faire* liberalism or whether, as John Gerald Ruggie put it, the liberalism of the future would be "embedded" such that domestic political equilibrium was to take precedence over the international economic equilibrium. The price of reintegrating business into the embedded liberal coalition after the war was to cede ground to business while getting something in return. That *quid pro quo* was to withdraw state support for stagnationist ideas domestically in return for business acquiescence for an international framework that made other national "embedded liberalisms" possible. The key dynamics here were the perceived need to maintain American production after the war, to halt the leftward swing of Western Europe, and to reverse the failure of early convertibility in European currency markets. I do not discuss these international dynamics in detail for reasons of space, and also because the topic has been more than adequately covered elsewhere. See John Gerald Ruggie, "International Regimes, Transactions and Change: Embedded Liberalism in the Post-War Economic Order," *International Organization* 36 (2) Spring (1982); Eric Helleiner, *States and the Reemergence of Global Finance: From Bretton Woods to the 1990's* (Ithaca: Cornell University Press, 1994).

stagnationism becoming the governing set of postwar economic ideas. While the door had been opening ever wider to spending arguments since 1935, such ideas had increasingly placed the issue of corporate power alongside purchasing power. Specifically, it was held that if private economic decisions had collectively suboptimal outcomes, then government intervention would have to go beyond institutionalizing price-fixing or mere pump-priming and move toward the permanent management of the level of consumption and investment in the economy.

For stagnationists such as Hansen, the key to prosperity was sustained growth. This was a function of three factors: the ability to absorb natural resources, population growth, and technical change. Drawing again on Turner's frontier thesis, stagnationists argued that throughout the nineteenth century, America had experienced a period of exogenously driven growth. The ability to add the new resources of the frontier to national income, coupled with ever-increasing population growth and unique one-shot capital investments, had provided spectacular returns. Unfortunately, America had now exhausted such growth-promoting resources and had shifted to an endogenous growth pattern. The frontier was closed, immigration was halted, and it was far from clear that technological innovation alone was going to suffice as the engine of continued prosperity. In this situation, the problem now was how to use existing plant and resources wisely in a permanently stagnant economy. The secular stagnation thesis bespoke a role for the state far greater and more threatening to American business than any of the other ideas about the depression had done before. The problem, according to business, was that the 1937–8 spending debacle and the TNEC hearings had enshrined stagnationism as the key set of economic ideas informing state practices during the war.[105]

Despite piecemeal business opposition, the perceived strength of the stagnationist analysis grew throughout the war. As the business economist George Terborgh noted in 1945, the stagnationist analysis is "now in effect an official creed," with disciples occupying "most of the high policy-making and advisory positions in executive agencies."[106] Indeed, Hansen, Currie, and influential journalists such as Stuart Chase had been vocal in calling for a postwar "Super New Deal" with enhanced planning agencies. What was most troubling, however, was that the government's own postwar fore-

---

[105] It is interesting that Stein, *Fiscal Revolution*, and Schlesinger, *The Coming of the New Deal*, see the TNEC hearings as a showcase for Keynesian economics. In fact, in 1939 Keynesianism as demand management was barely developed. What the TNEC hearings in fact showed was the dominance of a stagnationist interpretation within the New Deal camp.

[106] George Terborgh, *The Bogey of Economic Maturity* (Chicago: Machinery and Allied Products Institute, 1945), p. 13, quoted in Collins, *The Business Response to Keynes*, p. 96.

casts were explicitly framed in terms of a stagnationist analysis.[107] As such, the key institution that drew business ire was the NRPB, the main producer of stagnationist ideas throughout during the war.

As early as 1938, the NRPB was developing ideas about how to create a high-output, high-employment economy. However, its more prominent role during wartime – particularly the publication of its 1943 report *Work, Security, and Relief Policies* – created a firestorm of business protest, with Republican senators, the NAM, and the ACC all denouncing the report. As well as being explicitly stagnationist, the report called for a commitment to full-employment policies and the development of a comprehensive welfare state along the lines of the United Kingdom's *Beveridge Report*. However, the importance of the NRPB report lay not only in its policy recommendations but also in what it signaled. The NRPB report alerted business to the need to challenge stagnationist ideas explicitly rather than simply retreat behind the familiar precepts of sound finance.

Given this wake-up call, business organizations finally became involved in the production and dissemination of alternative economic ideas. Quasireligious opposition to the intellectual developments of the previous decade through the ritualistic affirmation of the tenets of *laissez faire* was simply no longer sufficient; a fight back was needed. As such, the common threat posed to business by stagnationism, plus the reduction in uncertainty generated by wartime institutions, allowed business to overcome its collective action problems and mount a united opposition. In time-honored Smithian fashion, business organizations' opposition was organized by a division of labor. The ACC mounted formal challenges to legislation and lobbied Congress. The NAM provided similar pressure from the grassroots up, while the Committee for Economic Development (CED), an offshoot of the BAC, provided the alternative ideas.

The ACC's attitude to state intervention underwent a transformation during the war from arguing a doctrinaire sound finance line to becoming one of the main postwar advocates of the new macroeconomics.[108] After a backstage *coup d'etat* at the May 1942 ACC convention in Chicago, modernizing forces headed by Eric Johnston usurped the leadership of the ACC and almost immediately began to reorient the activities and structure of the Chamber. By July 1942, the ACC was sponsoring joint meetings with the AFL, the CIO, and the White House aimed at reaching agreements on

---

[107] National Resources Planning Board, *National Resources Development; Report for 1943* (Washington: Government Printing Office, 1943). See also Alonzo L. Hamby, *Beyond the New Deal: Harry S. Truman and American Liberalism* (New York: Columbia University Press, 1973), pp. 11–12. For a discussion of Chase's contributions to the postwar planning debate, see James Schofield Saeger, "Stuart Chase: At Right Angles to Laissez Faire," *The Social Studies* 63 (6) November (1972), pp. 251–9.

[108] Albeit of a particularly passive and restrictive kind.

matters of production, regulation, and representation. The ACC also established an economic research division and a full-time Congressional lobbying organization called the Department of Governmental Affairs during the war. The reasoning behind modernizing these institutions was not just to make sure that business's viewpoint was heard in the Congress, but to also ensure that the ideas shaping the postwar order were, if not business's own, then at least a very limited form of embedded liberalism that was not threatening to American business.[109]

The rallying point for business opposition to stagnationism was Senator James Murray's Full Employment Bill. The Bill was an anathema to both Congressional conservatives and business as it enshrined two principles that threatened to undermine the market basis of American capitalism. First, by guaranteeing all who wished to work a job, the Bill was perceived as threatening the necessity of unemployment for a functioning competitive labor market.[110] Second, by establishing *as mandatory* a consumption gap analysis as the centerpiece of a national full-employment budget, the Act enshrined a stagnationist analysis that *by definition* deemed private initiative and investment inadequate and necessitated permanent compensatory spending.[111] Seen in this light, the Murray Bill, in its original form, heralded Keynes' euthanasia of the rentier and the possible redundancy of American business as the stewards of American capitalism.

However, the ACC, along with the BAC, realized that a return to the unemployment of the 1930s might in fact be far more dangerous than the provisions of the Murray Act themselves.[112] As Johnston of the ACC argued in 1945, "we can't afford to go into another depression . . . [but] . . . I don't think the Murray full employment bill is the answer. We might get full employment . . . but in the process we'd lose our democracy and have a regimented state."[113] As Collins argues, given business's ambivalence between

---

[109] For the official history of the CED that squares with the interpretations offered by Collins' *The Business Response to Keynes*, and Brinkley's *The End of Reform*, but not Stein's *Fiscal Revolution*, see Karl Schriftgiesser, *Business and Public Policy: The Role of the Committee for Economic Development 1942–1967* (Englewood Cliffs, New Jersey: Prentice Hall, 1967).

[110] If this argument sounds like a classic Marxist conspiracy theory, consider that a very similar argument has been made by the ex-chair of the Council of Economic Advisors, Joseph Stiglitz. See Carl Shapiro and Joseph Stiglitz, "Equilibrium Unemployment as a Worker Discipline Device," *American Economic Review*, Volume 74 (3) June (1984), pp. 433–44.

[111] For the classic account of the passage of the Murray Bill, see Stephen Bailey, *Congress Makes a Law* (New York: Vintage Books, 1950). For a less exhaustive account, Stein's *Fiscal Revolution* provides a good summary. See Stein, *Fiscal Revolution*, pp. 198–204.

[112] Collins, *The Business Response to Keynes*, pp. 100–2.

[113] Eric Johnston, General Staff Meeting, ACC, July 18, 1945, quoted in Collins, *The Business Response to Keynes*, p. 102. For similar remarks, see the NAM document by Walter B. Weisenburger, *Challenge to Industry: An Address Delivered before the 51st Congress of American Industry* (New York: NAM, January 1947).

developing a positive engagement with labor and the state on the one hand, and fear of the consequences of that engagement on the other, the approach of the ACC in opposing the Murray Bill was very subtle but very effective in neutralizing its radical potential. At the Congressional hearings on the Murray Bill, Johnston of the ACC did not testify, and this lack of unified business opposition enabled the Bill to escape the Senate largely untouched. However, once the Bill went into committee, business was able to shape decisively the content of the legislation and thus the institutions of the postwar order.[114]

As Collins notes, the key figure in the transformation of the Murray Bill was Southern Democrat Will Whittington. Whittington was the swing vote on the subcommittee charged with hammering together a compromise version of the Murray Bill.[115] Whittington was against any guarantee of employment between the state and labor that would threaten Southern labor costs. Moreover, as Collins remarks, as the former head of the Greenwood, Mississippi Chamber of Commerce, "it was understandable that [Whittington] turned to the Chamber for help in drafting the House substitute."[116]

Armed with three different versions of the amended Bill, all drawn up by the ACC,

Whittington drew up a substitute measure which . . . diluted the bill by extending its scope . . . emasculated the spending provisions by limiting them to loans . . . consistent with "sound fiscal policy" . . . and eliminated the National Production and Employment Budget, replacing it with a less powerful President's Economic Report . . . [and] . . . a Council of Economic Advisers.[117]

Once out of subcommittee, the Bill passed the House and proceeded to a joint conference committee. At this juncture, the ACC's new Department of Governmental Affairs vigorously opposed the Senate's more liberal version of the Bill and strongly endorsed the ACC/Whittington alternative. When the Bill emerged out of the conference committee, it reflected the authorship of the ACC more than that of Murray and Wagner.[118]

---

[114] Where Bailey is suspect on the activities of the CED is in his insistence that "the CED is not included as a pressure group [in his study] as it has made no attempt to initiate direct or indirect pressures on legislators." See Bailey, *Congress Makes a Law*, pp. 136–7.

[115] The "Full" employment nature of the Bill was replaced with "high and steady level of employment" during the passage of the Bill through the Senate.

[116] Collins, *The Business Response to Keynes*, p. 105.

[117] *Ibid.*

[118] As Whittington remarked, "the conference agreement contains the essential provisions of the House bill and it rejects the philosophy of the Senate bill." Collins, *The Business Response to Keynes*, p. 107. The version of events in the CED's official history on the CED's role in the Murray Bill's denouement merely notes that the CED's "thinking" on the Full Employment Bill "fell into the hands of Will Whittington, a moderate conservative from Mississippi." See Schriftgiesser, *Business and Public Policy*, p. 23.

By using conservative Congressional opposition to defeat the Full Employment Bill, the ACC was able to defeat stagnationism as the set of economic ideas governing state actions. However, legislatively heading off stagnationism was only the first step. Business now needed to ensure that the threat of a permanent coalition between an activist state and a strong labor movement was neutralized. To do this, business needed to develop a new set of economic ideas that would present a plausible alternative to stagnationism rather than a simple argument against it. If this did not occur, business would be confined to fighting a permanent rearguard action.

Limiting Labor and Shackling the State

As argued previously, after the failed accommodation with business under the NRA, the state moved to bolster the strength of labor systematically. While the Wagner and Social Security Acts made labor institutionally secure, the war itself did more to strengthen labor than anything else. Union membership rocketed in the course of the war from 8.7 million in 1940 to 14.5 million in 1945. By 1945, one-third of all workers in non-farm employment were unionized.[119] The *quid pro quo* for such an agreement was adherence to the decisions of the National War Labor Board regarding wages. However, under these conditions, wages became politicized.

In the conditions of more than full employment that the war provided, business could pass on cost increases in price rises since prices are less easily controlled than wages. Under such circumstances, the state tends to hold the line on wage increases firmly to avoid a round of inflationary raises. However, the result of this policy is a disparity between wages and prices that in turn creates labor tensions. Due to these pressures, workers in key industries such as coal and steel can strike with relative impunity as the costs of doing so are, given labor market conditions and the necessity of supply, very diffusely spread. Consequently, the United Mine Workers and the United Auto Workers struck in 1942 and 1943 to great effect. Wages were renegotiated, but the price of doing so was to provide business with the political resources it needed to counterattack labor: popular and Congressional discontent with unions, a discontent that business made an issue during the reconversion period.[120]

---

[119] In a compromise over wage controls known as the Little Steel formula, labor received as a *quid pro quo* for a no-strike pledge a membership of maintenance plan that guaranteed union membership for the duration of the conflict. Under this agreement, membership rocketed. See Vatter, *The United States Economy*, p. 120; Lichtenstein, *Labor's War at Home*, pp. 67–82.

[120] This is not to say that the United Mine Workers was greedy. In fact, real wages in the coal industry fell by 10 percent under the Little Steel formula from 1941–5. See Vatter, *The United States Economy*, p. 124.

The first attempt to rein in labor was the 1943 Smith-Connolly Labor Disputes Bill. The Bill mandated a thirty-day cooling-off period before a strike was called and necessitated a vote of the union membership in a strike ballot to determine whether a proposed strike had the support of the workers themselves. Unfortunately for business, this first attempt at reining in labor backfired. As Ruth O'Brien notes, "With the Roosevelt adminis-tration in control of wartime machinery and in charge of implementing the Act, the CIO turned the strike notice and ballot provisions into a union organizing device."[121] By mandating mass participation on the assumption that ordinary union members would not agree to strikes during wartime, the Bill unintentionally facilitated ever greater union organization since the act of calling a strike ballot facilitated avenues for union agitation.

As O'Brien has argued, the failure of Smith-Connolly demonstrated to business and its allies in Congress that such New Deal governmental insti-tutions were able to act *systematically* in favor of labor. As such, the famous checks and balances of the American system were being bypassed by a set of quasicorporatist institutions that threatened to affect the balance of power between business and labor permanently. Realizing this, business and its Congressional allies began to concern themselves with institutional reform as a complement to the direct reform of labor relations. The Act that emerged out of this Congressional effort, the 1946 Administrative Procedures Act (APA), was the key to limiting of the state's institutional reach and achieving the political neutralization of labor.[122]

The logic behind the APA was to delegitimate the ideas, and thus the institutions, of the Wagner Act. The key protective institution set up by the Wagner Act was the National Labor Relations Board (NLRB). The NLRB was designed to protect the right of an individual to join a union, and to create a balance between unions and business. In particular, the Act sought to strengthen the workers position *vis à vis* business given the inability of an individual worker to negotiate a contract freely due to business's dis-proportionate power in such a relationship.[123] In short, it sought to create a level playing field. What Congress sought to do in response was to contest just how level this playing field in fact was.

The point of contention was that as the main protective institution for labor organization against the "unfair" management practices detailed in

---

[121] Ruth O'Brien, "Taking the Conservative State Seriously: Statebuilding and Restrictive Labor Practices in Postwar America," *Labor Studies Journal* 21 (4) (1997), pp. 46–7.

[122] The account here of APA in the postwar order is drawn from O'Brien, "Taking the Con-servative State Seriously." See also David Vogel, *Fluctuating Fortunes: The Political Power of Business in America* (New York: Basic Books 1989), p. 107, for a similar claim con-cerning the APA.

[123] Oddly, the Wagner Act's argument for balancing the capital-labor relationship was phrased almost identically to Karl Marx's observation that the equality of the wage contract was a myth since only one of the parties *had* capital.

the Wagner Act, the NLRB acted as both litigant and legislator in labor disputes. The NLRB was thus seen as having an institutional bias against business, insofar as it established what constituted an unfair management practice and also policed violations of that practice.[124] The challenge of the APA was to restore the legal fiction of the labor contract as a private agreement of equal parties. By re-creating this legal fiction, and by stressing the First Amendment risks associated with the NLRB acting as judge, jury, and executioner in labor disputes, the APA brought judicial review back into labor management relations.

The APA effectively stymied any further attempts by the state to strengthen labor as an independent organized social actor and effectively halted any attempt at corporatist institution building in the United States. After the passage of the APA, state institutions could regulate, but not legislate.[125] Consequently, the capacity of the state to strengthen labor independently of the legislature by developing institutions beyond the orbit of Congress was crippled.[126]

These restrictions on labor were further tightened in 1947 by the Taft-Hartley Act, which achieved the restrictions on labor that the wartime Smith-Connolly Bill failed to implement.[127] Once the legal fiction of the equality of labor and capital in a labor contract had been reestablished, any normative claim or institutional means that the state could deploy to act on behalf of labor had been seriously undermined. Paradoxically, however, by the time both the APA and Taft-Hartley had passed, labor had largely both outgrown and alienated those state institutions that had strengthened it in the first place.

---

[124] In 1939, Congress set up the Smith Committee to investigate the NLRB. The Committee found that by both defining and policing "unfair" practices, the NLRB violated management's right to free speech. O'Brien, "Taking the Conservative State Seriously," p. 41.

[125] As O'Brien put it, the APA "made no distinction between the efforts of an individual worker, the trade union, the trade association or business corporation in the political process. . . . The idea . . . that the state should promote unionization as a counterweight against the strength of big business – was virtually abandoned." O'Brien, "Taking the Conservative State Seriously," p. 37.

[126] Also by bringing judicial review into policy decisions, the interpersonal networks built up between labor and the state were destroyed. Under the guise of "fairness," such associations could be seen as entailing a conflict of interest for state managers. I thank Matt Crenson for this point.

[127] Taft-Hartley was the end result of an attempt by the 1946 Congress to bring the issue of labor reform to the forefront of legislative action rather than an assiduously designed proposal itself. As Robert H. Zieger notes, "in the eighteen months following the Japanese surrender over seventy anti-labor bills were introduced in the House alone." Some of these bills, it might be added, were considerably more restrictive than Taft-Hartley. See Robert H. Zieger, *American Workers, American Unions* (Baltimore: Johns Hopkins University Press, 1994), p. 109. The Taft-Hartley Act mandated what the Smith Committee had earlier suggested, that the governance of unions be treated as an issue of economic regulation.

Postwar Accommodations

The first eighteen months after the end of the war was a period of increasing industrial unrest and increased uncertainty for all parties. For labor, the end of the wartime no-strike pledge combined with the cutbacks in overtime, which was virtually mandatory during the war, to produce wage losses of the order of 30 percent among industrial workers. Moreover, the conservatism of the newly elected 1946 Congress, coupled with the demands by the ACC that all price controls be immediately abolished, led labor to expect an inflationary price hike that would undercut wages even further.[128] In fact, this proved to be exactly what happened. "[B]etween July and December 1946, following the removal of price controls, consumer prices rose at an annual rate of 30 percent and wholesale prices increased 50 percent – the highest rate ever."[129]

President Harry S. Truman unfortunately contributed to this problem by announcing on August 16, 1945, that during the forthcoming reconversion, "there is no longer any threat of an inflationary bidding up of wage rates by competition in a short labor market." This seemed to suggest that the unions were in no position to ask for more. Yet this statement was itself appended to a statement that unions might seek wage increases to make up for real wage gains forgone during the war so long as "they will not be used in whole or in part [by business] as the basis for seeking an increase in price ceilings." As Alonzo S. Hamby remarked, by doing so, "Truman flashed a green light to an era of industrial turmoil."[130]

In response to these signals, CIO unions in particular began to call for 30 percent across-the-board wage increases, and both wildcat and official action intensified. In November 1946, the United Auto Workers struck at General Motors.[131] In January 1946, the Steelworkers shut down United States Steel. In April 1946, the United Mine Workers struck, which resulted in a general economic slowdown, and the situation worsened as a national rail strike took hold and state-sponsored mediation came to naught. By the winter of 1946, meatpacking, rubber, and electrical appliance workers joined the strike wave. Between V-J day and June 1946, there were 4,650 work stoppages, which resulted in the loss of over 116 million manhours.[132]

---

[128] Zieger, *American Workers*, pp. 100–5.

[129] John Snyder, "The Treasury and Economic Policy," in Francis H. Heller, ed., *Economics and the Truman Administration* (Lawrence, KS: Regents Press of Kansas, 1981), p. 25.

[130] Truman, statement on reconversion guidelines, August 16, 1945; quoted in Alonzo S. Hamby, *Man of the People: A Life of Harry S Truman* (New York: Oxford University Press, 1995), p. 375.

[131] On the GM strike, see Lichtenstein, *Labor's War at Home*, pp. 221–8.

[132] Figures cited in David A. Morse, "The Role of the Labor Department," in Heller, ed., *Economics and the Truman Administration*, p. 42.

Truman's impatience with the unions was mounting, as was that of the general population.[133]

Labor had other problems in addition to popular disquiet. As David Plotke argues, although labor was institutionally stronger because of the war, it was programatically weaker, as labor had no clear vision or program to aim for, apart from the repeal of Taft-Hartley. "The labor movement needed to present a positive conception of how its further growth would improve American political and economic life."[134] Labor singularly failed to do this, and the portrayal of union actions by business and Congress as those of self-interested militants played no small part in this failure. Despite continued institutional protection, labor was proving to be less than the coalition partner the state had envisaged. Given these problems, the prospects for strengthening or even preserving the coalition with labor and the institutions of embedded liberalism seemed far from ideal.

However, such a pessimistic interpretation of the fate of labor proved to be somewhat overstated. At the same time as labor was being institutionally reined in, the Truman administration convened a postwar labor-management conference that was designed to ensure uninterrupted production during reconversion. Given the very real fear of a downturn at the end of the war, if not a lapse into the much anticipated stagnationist slump predicted by Hansen et al., this conference marked no mere sideshow.[135]

The conference, held in November and December of 1945, involved labor, business, and the Commerce and Treasury departments. The composition of the conference was particularly significant since it was "dominated by representatives of medium and large-scale manufacturing firms ... [who were] ... overwhelmingly conservative in their politics."[136] Despite this conservative dominance, the conference actually served to strengthen labor's position in the postwar order.[137] As Arthur F. McClure

---

[133] Truman went as far as proposing that striking rail workers be drafted into the army. As Truman noted in a memo to himself (undated, Spring 1946) regarding union policy. "Tell them that patience is exhausted. Declare an emergency – call out troops. Start industry and put anyone to work who wants to go to work. If any [labor] leader intervenes, court martial him. [John L.] Lewis ought to have been shot in 1942!" Quoted in Hamby *Man of the People*, p. 378. These feelings were far from unique to Truman. In a 1945 poll of workers in the industrial belt states, 42 percent of the sample blamed the United Auto Workers for the GM strike, while only 19 percent blamed GM. Poll quoted in Harris, *The Right to Manage*, pp. 140–1.

[134] Plotke, *Building a Democratic Political Order*, p. 253.

[135] Arthur F. McClure, *The Truman Administration and the Problems of Post-War Labor, 1945–1948* (New Jersey: Associated University Presses, 1963).

[136] Harris, *The Right to Manage*, pp. 112–13.

[137] This interpretation challenges that of Nelson Lichtenstein, who sees the conference as "doomed to failure" and devoid of content. See Nelson Lichtenstein, "From Corporatism to Collective Bargaining: Organized Labor and the Eclipse of Social Democracy in the Post-

notes, "The conference demonstrated for the first time that national level representatives from both labor and management could meet together without arguing as to whether or not collective bargaining was desirable."[138] With the acceptance of collective bargaining as a *de facto* state of affairs, the impact of future antilabor legislation would prove to be extremely circumscribed. Rather than seek to destroy unions, management had accepted the legitimacy of their core function and hence their right to exist. As such, the conference was significant not for what was agreed, but for what was *not* argued about.

What this ensured was rather paradoxical. Given tight labor markets and high demand, labor, which had traditionally benefited from the proactive support of embedded liberal institutions, began to argue that unions should be wholly responsible for contract enforcement, thereby cutting the state out. Institutionally secure unions in a period of relative prosperity seemed to prefer accommodation to confrontation.[139] In part this was a response to the negative public image of labor and conservative tenor of the immediate postwar era. Labor began to realize that the institutional support of the state could easily become an institutional constraint on its newly found legitimacy and prosperity.[140]

Business, on the other hand, while traditionally antistatist and the main proponent of the free labor contract, began to change its view of the state. Rather than seeing the state as a biased and unwelcome intervention, business began to see the advantage of the state as a brake on labor. That is, by recognizing unions' core function, business could legitimately limit unions' activities in other areas, hence the logic of Taft-Hartley.[141] As such, a rough meeting of the minds was achieved. This convergence was made possible precisely because both labor and business's ideas about their interests had changed over the past decade through participation in new institutions and through the rearticulation of their interests in terms of new ideas. Consequently, once Taft-Hartley and the APA were passed, business could hardly claim that new legislation to limit the state and unions was

War Era," in Fraser and Gerstle, eds., *The Rise and Fall of the New Deal Order*, p. 131; Lichtenstein, *Labor's War at Home*, pp. 220–1.

[138] McClure, *The Truman Administration and the Problems of Post-War Labor*, p. 63.

[139] See Harris, *The Right to Manage*, pp. 129–58; Michael Goldfield, *The Decline of Organized Labor in the United States* (Chicago: University of Chicago Press, 1987).

[140] As the UAW's Walter Reuther argued, "I'd rather bargain with General Motors than with the government.... General Motors has no Army." Walter Reuther, UAW Press release, "Are We Moving Towards a Government Controlled Economy?" May 30, 1946, quoted in Lichtenstein, "From Corporatism to Collective Bargaining," p. 140.

[141] For a discussion of the evolution of business and labor attitudes in the immediate postwar era, see Harris, *The Right to Manage*, pp. 105–29; Vatter, *The United States Economy*, pp. 125–7. The basis of Taft-Hartley was declaration of principles adopted by NAM at its 1945 annual conference. See Harris, *The Right to Manage*, pp. 121–3, for a list of these principles.

required. Unions, on the other hand, were for the first time institutionally secure, and after the immediate postwar strike wave, they narrowed their goals to that which business was willing to accept.

Given this ideational convergence, major manufacturing firms sought to tie labor into more long-term agreements and thus produce ever more institutional stability. As Nelson Lichtenstein notes, the key to doing so was the COLA (Cost of Living Adjustment) contract. First employed by General Motors in 1948 and unexpectedly accepted by the UAW in 1949, COLA contracts became the industrial norm. Predicated upon improvements in productivity paying for improvements in wages relative to increases in the general price level, COLA contracts constituted the admission by unions that the distribution of surplus, if not fair, was at least acceptable. Given this, union support for expanded state-provided welfare benefits declined.[142]

The failure of postwar labor militancy to provide any real benefits relative to the perceived benefits of accommodation, plus the increasing acceptance by business of the state in the practice of industrial relations, led to a postwar order that was far more restrictive than the one which had appeared possible during the late 1930s. Business had successfully eliminated stagnationism as the governing economic idea of the state and reined in labor. The price of doing so was to accommodate to a weakened and restricted version of embedded liberalism – a liberalism that business had finally begun to author itself.

Limiting America's Liberalism: The Politics of Business's Ideas

Having defeated stagnationism, reined in the state, and limited labor, business still faced the problem of constructing an alternative set of economic ideas that would avoid the pitfalls of *laissez faire* and the political consequences of stagnationism in the future. The key business institution that developed these new ideas as a counter to stagnationism was the Committee for Economic Development (CED). The committee was founded on the assumption that implacable opposition to economic reforms, especially in an economy that was experiencing large profits and income gains for the first time in over ten years, was not going to serve business in the long run. As Ronald Deupree, the chair of the CED, remarked in 1942, "the challenge which business will face when this war is over cannot be met by a *laissez faire* philosophy or by uncontrolled forces of supply and

---

[142] In particular, expanded health care, which had been championed by the CIO, increasingly became an employer-funded rather than state-funded program. Pension and health benefits became privatized and were paid for by incorporation into producer prices, which itself fed the COLA increases, thus returning the ultimate cost back to labor itself. See Lichtenstein, "From Corporatism to Collective Bargaining," pp. 142–4.

demand."[143] The CED "realized that it was no longer enough to resist all proposals for legislated social change on the grounds that they were unconstitutional, immoral, subversive, contrary to human nature . . . etc."[144] In short, a politically relevant alternative set of economic ideas had to be constructed. That alternative was to be found by avoiding distributionary issues and by denying the validity of stagnationism. This was achieved by using a new set of economic ideas: what Collins has termed the philosophy of growthsmanship.

The idea of growthsmanship had its origins in two important CED proposals from 1947. The CED report, *Taxes and the Budget*, marked the first significant attempt by business to coopt the ideas of 1930s and make them more "business-friendly." The second report, *Monetary and Fiscal Policy for Greater Economic Stability*, advocated the shift from a fixed to a flexible monetary policy, a shift that eventually occurred in 1951 with the so-called Fed-Treasury accords. In the immediate postwar period, the former report proved to be the most consequential as it marked a further change in the institutional relationship of business and the state.[145]

Taxes and the Budget skillfully linked the emerging concern over the Soviets and communism to the threat of a new depression. The CED document argued that the only way to safeguard American capitalism in the long term was to accept that the responsibility of the state to ensure the high and steady level of employment mandated by the Employment Act was a permanent and proper feature of contemporary politics. The CED recognized "the crux of the tax problem lay in the reconciliation of the desire for a balanced budget and reduction of the national debt, on the one hand, with the necessity of maintaining maximum employment and production on the other."[146] In fact, rather than reconcile these two objectives, the report scathingly rejected the sound finance doctrine of annually balanced budgets and sought instead to use tax policy as a way of balancing the business cycle. The most consequential part of the report, though, proved to be the call for a "stabilizing budget policy."

Under this formula, unemployment would be targeted at a level of 4 percent and taxes would be set so as to ensure this employment target. In an upswing, revenues would increase, thus allowing a surplus to accumulate, whereas in a downturn taxes would fall, transfers would increase, and

---

[143] Ronald Deupree, meeting of Business Advisory Council Research Committee, April 7–8, 1945, quoted in Collins, *The Business Response to Keynes*, p. 81.

[144] Harris, *The Right to Manage*, p. 182.

[145] Committee for Economic Development, *Taxes and the Budget: A Program for Prosperity in a Free Economy* (New York: Committee for Economic Development, 1947). For commentaries on the CED report, see Collins, *The Business Response to Keynes*, pp. 129–41; Stein, *Fiscal Revolution*, pp. 221–5; Schriftgiesser, *Business and Public Policy*, pp. 27–31.

[146] Collins, *The Business Response to Keynes*, p. 131.

the surplus would be diminished. In short, the CED invented the concept of "automatic stabilizers," so central to postwar economic management. As Collins concludes,

> . . . in providing for the automatic generation of deficits in hard times and surpluses in good, the CED's stabilizing budget offered a middle ground between the positions of those who would balance the budget annually regardless of economic fortunes and those who would vest in the federal government the power to alter revenue rates and expenditures to fit the conditions at hand or those predicted in the future.[147]

This middle ground was where the political imperative of avoiding a return to the depression was conjoined with business's desire to not devolve complete fiscal discretion to the state. Fiscalism was to be passive and be based on the revenue side, rather than the expenditure side. Rather than accept the generation of deficits as a matter of course, as stagnationist ideas argued, the CED proposals emphasized tax rate stability and expenditure generated by growth. These new pro-business ideas constituted a clear repudiation of stagnationism.[148] *Taxes and the Budget* carefully avoided all the radical aspects of the stagnationist analysis – the need for an extension of government, the euthanasia of the rentier, etc. – and instead developed a very limited form of embedded liberalism. Such an order provided business with expectational stability such that investment and profits would be predictable, but at the same time accepted the new political realities of collective bargaining and an expanded state.

Battered by the legislative assaults of business and the indifference of labor, the state readily accepted these proposals. As Herbery Stein notes, the "CED's 1947 statement profoundly influenced fiscal discussion, fiscal thinking, and fiscal policy in the two decades that followed it. Its influence stemmed partly from what it said, partly from who said it, and partly from the effort of the CED to promote understanding of the policy in the economic conditions that unfolded."[149] These new ideas resonated with the state since they allowed the continued development of the state's economic

---

[147] *Ibid.*, p. 135.

[148] For example, the report concluded that by making expenditure dependent upon revenues, "the really frightening possibility of an endless ascent to higher and higher government spending could be avoided." Committee for Economic Development, *Taxes and the Budget*, p. 30.

[149] Stein, *Fiscal Revolution*, p. 227. Stein is rather Whiggish in his interpretation of this whole period. The CED proposals were not merely an attempt to make sense of economic conditions and thus define the optimal policy. They were essentially political in that they were explicitly designed to defeat stagnationism. As Bailey notes in his discussion of the passage of the Murray Bill, the authors of the Bill "shared in the belief that the fiscal ideas stemming from the Keynes-Hansen analysis were basically unsound." Defeating this was business's first priority. Bailey, *Congress Makes a Law*, p. 45.

role, even if that role was to be more passive than active. What cemented this rapprochement between business and the state was an amendment to the CED program that stressed growth over maintaining adequate demand. This amendment was developed and implemented by the newly created Council of Economic Advisors (CEA) under its chair, Leon Keyserling.

The CEA detected what it thought was a flaw in the logic of the Employment Act. That flaw was to focus wholly on employment as the key indicator of economic well-being rather than the economy's level of growth.[150] The reasoning for growth was simple: Growth would simultaneously allow the realization of steady profits and expanding markets while supporting consumption. Growth promised to solve "the ancient conflict between social equity and economic incentives which hung over the progress of enterprise in a dynamic economy."[151]

These themes were latent in the annual reports of the CEA as early as 1947, and by 1950 they had become official thinking. By 1949 Keyserling had produced figures for the new growthmanship model. As Hamby details, "assuming an annual growth rate of three percent and constant dollar values, the gross national product could rise from $262 billion in 1948 to $350 billion in 1958, national income from $226 billion to $300 billion. ... Poverty thus could be eliminated without a redistribution of wealth. Progressive reform did not necessarily mean social conflict."[152] Ironically, in a rerun of 1937, what led to the acceptance of these ideas was an unexpected recession.

Truman wanted to hold the line against postwar inflation and had battled with Congress since 1946 over price controls, tax cuts, and the pace of reconversion. In response to the Republicans voting a tax cut in 1948 that the CEA saw as inflationary, Truman sought to take $4 billion out of the economy in 1949. However, in late 1948, the economy began to slow and fears of a new depression surfaced once again. What served to confirm these new ideas was that the automatic stabilizers argued for by the CED, the tax changes necessitated by war, the transfers promoted by the institutions of Social Security, and the new high-employment budget all came together

---

[150] The point the CEA was making was that national income in 1947 could be lower than in 1945, but the economy may have higher employment. As such, would the economy better or worse off?

[151] U.S. Council of Economic Advisors, *Business and Government: Fourth Annual Report to the President* (Washington: U.S. Government Printing Office, 1949), p. 6.

[152] Alonzo L. Hamby, "The Vital Center, the Fair Deal, and the Quest for a Liberal Political Economy," *American Historical Review* 77 (3) (1972) p. 664, my italics. As Keyserling summarized the rationale behind the new focus on growth, "The principle of economic growth ... is not a chapter in a textbook. Growth is the very meaning of an economy ... more goods and services ... is the source of real wealth." See Leon Keyserling, "The View from the Council of Economic Advisers," in Heller, ed., *Economics and the Truman Administration*, p. 85.

to halt the recession turning into a depression. Active fiscal policy was not needed, as the automatic stabilizers seemed to do exactly as the CED predicted. As Stein notes, "the budget surplus which been running at an annual rate of $3.8 billion in the fourth quarter of 1948 turned into a deficit of $3.9 billion in the second quarter of 1949."[153] The recession passed, and the state did not have to do anything about it.

Flush with this success, the CEA published its 1950 report, which reads like a manifesto for this new and limited version of American embedded liberalism – a liberalism built around the ideas of the CED and the CEA rather than those of the state and labor. The report laid out the four key ideas underlying the new institutional order: that "our economy can and must continue to grow ... [that] ... the benefits of growth and progress must extend to all groups ... [that] ... this growth will not come automatically, but requires conscious purpose and hard work ... [and as such] ... the fiscal policy of the federal government must be designed to contribute to the growth of the economy."[154] Seen in light of these ideational transformations, further institutional projects designed to regulate the economy seemed redundant given a new set of economic ideas that explained why such stagnationist institutions were unnecessary.

By 1950, for the first time in thirty years, business and the state had built a stable coalition around a shared set of economic ideas and supporting institutions that would last a further twenty years. This set of ideas centered on a passive fiscal policy with stable tax rates facilitating positive-sum outcomes for both business and labor. By providing growth through the maintenance of the institutions that supported these distributions, the state would minimize distributional conflicts while regulating the activities of both business and labor. Business received a steady return on investment, expanding domestic and international markets, and relative labor peace. Labor gained legitimacy, recognition, institutional security, and an increasing real wage.

This embedded liberalism was to prove institutionally secure from conservative attacks. There was to be almost no new anti-labor legislation, no serious attempt to repeal Social Security, and calls to reestablish fiscal probity and balanced budgets largely fell on deaf ears.[155] Most important, throughout the 1950s under the Republican administration of Dwight D. Eisenhower, the same institutions were relied upon. While the official position on economic priorities shifted in the 1950s from growth to fight-

---

[153] Stein, *Fiscal Revolution*, p. 239.

[154] U.S. Council of Economic Advisors, *Business and Government*, p. 13. The report goes on to applaud CEA-sponsored management and labor conferences.

[155] Partial exceptions were the 1951 Federal Reserve–Treasury accords that freed the Federal Reserve from its wartime role as a dependent central bank charged with keeping money cheap. This institutional change was to prove extremely important twenty-five years later.

ing inflation and holding the line on the absolute size of the budget, the *de facto* fiscal stance was little different from that developed under Truman. While the state under Eisenhower gave more weight to inflation and pursued a more restrictive monetary stance, when recession hit the economy again in 1954 and 1957–8, there were no radical departures from the ideas and practices established in the late 1940s.[156] In fact, after 1950, growthsmanship did not even need to be actively pursued since the Korean War and the defense buildup under NSC-68 would, as Hamby remarked, "provide stimulus aplenty."[157] Upon the return of the Democrats to power, "John F. Kennedy, working with Walter Heller, would pick up the growth imperative as the basis of his own social-policy engineering."[158] To paraphrase Thomas Kuhn, it seemed that the United States entered a period of normal science when the big questions were no longer up for grabs. However, appearances can be deceptive.

[156] See Stein, *Fiscal Revolution*, pp. 328–45 for a discussion of the Eisenhower administration's response to the 1958 recession.
[157] Hamby, *Man of the People*, p. 500.
[158] *Ibid.*

4

Building Swedish Embedded Liberalism

Swedish economic ideas were markedly different from their American counterparts. Yet, in spite of their different starting points, by 1943–4 both sets of ideas had converged to a remarkable degree. Unlike the United States, where a variety of economic ideas were deployed rather haphazardly, in Sweden the content and sequencing of economic ideas were remarkably clear-cut. The 1920s were, as Benny Carlson notes, "the decade of economic liberalism's gala performance."[1] Swedish academic economics dominated both popular and elite thinking about the nature of the economy and the role of the state. Unfortunately, given the manifest failure of classical liberal doctrines to actually halt the depression, a group of younger scholars based principally at the Stockholm School of Economics began to develop alternative ideas relating underconsumption and unemployment. Due to their institutional links to the Swedish Social Democratic Party, *Sveriges Socialdemokratiska Arbetareparti* (SAP), these new younger economists, many of whom were not Social Democrats, were able to turn these new ideas into state policy quickly.[2] Before analyzing how such ideas effected Swedish institutional development, however, we must appreciate the different political developmental trajectories of Sweden and the United States.

First, in contrast to every leading industrialized nation, the party of the democratic left, the SAP, has been in power in Sweden for over 80 percent of the time since the introduction of the franchise in December 1918. Furthermore, in contrast to other European states, the SAP predated the

---

[1] Benny Carlson, "The Long Retreat: Gustav Cassel and Eli Heckscher on the 'New Economics' of the 1930's," in Lars Jonung, ed., *Swedish Economic Thought: Explorations and Advances* (London: Routledge, 1987), p. 157.

[2] On the adoption of Stockholm School ideas by the SAP, see Sheri Berman, *The Social Democratic Moment: Ideas and Politics in the Making of Interwar Europe* (Cambridge: Harvard University Press, 1998), pp. 164–6; Carl G. Uhr, "The Emergence of the 'New Economics' in Sweden: A Review of a Study by Otto Steiger," *History of Political Economy* 5 (1) (1973).

formation of the first bourgeois party by some thirteen years. As Goran Therborn put it, this gave the SAP a distinct mobilization advantage among the working class compared with the other parties.[3] Second, the lateness of Swedish industrialization meant that the working class grew extremely rapidly. This encouraged the development of a strong trade union movement closely associated with the SAP. Taken together, these two factors enabled the SAP to shape the boundaries of mass politics in Sweden and assume the mantle traditionally occupied by bourgeois parties in other European states, that of the party which most closely represents the "true" national interest.[4] These institutional advantages enabled the SAP to set the agenda of governance for the whole postwar period and cast it within a reformist social democratic framework.

Although the Swedish trade union movement, *Landsorganisationen i Sverige* (LO), was formed in 1898, and the Swedish Employers' Confederation, *Svenska Arbetsgivareföreningen* (SAF), was formed in 1902, both organizations remained weak and reactive in the early part of the century. Thus, despite this mobilization advantage, the SAP at the turn of the century was internally divided and hamstrung by the rules of suffrage. In this context, the SAP set out to mobilize labor, not as part of a struggle for socialism, but as part of the struggle for electoral democracy. Only by struggling for control of the state would reform have many meaning.

Consequently, two developments are particularly relevant for the analysis of institutional change in Sweden. First was the SAP's theory concerning historical materialism and reformism. Second was the party's attitude toward democracy and the state. Just as the Democrats in the United States had to build economic institutions of national reach for the first time in response to the crisis of the depression, so the Swedish Social Democrats had to build political institutions of national reach as the necessary precursor to all other institutional developments.

The SAP and the Idea of Social Democracy

Within the SAP, the Marxist and reformist wings split very early on. By 1910 the SAP had turned away from a class struggle model of revolution toward a model of society based upon humanism and equitable distribution.[5] As early as 1902, leading figures in the SAP were arguing that "Marx

---

[3] Goran Therborn, "A Unique Chapter in the History of Social Democracy," in Klaus Misgeld, Karl Molin, and Klas Åmark, eds., *Creating Social Democracy: A Century of the Social Democratic Labor Party in Sweden* (University Park, PA: Pennsylvania State Press, 1992).

[4] *Ibid.*

[5] See Jae-Hung Ahn, "Ideology and Interest: The Case of Swedish Social Democracy, 1886–1911," *Politics and Society* 24 (2) June (1996); Tim Tilton, *The Political Theory of Swedish Social Democracy: Through the Welfare State to Socialism* (Oxford: Oxford University Press, 1990).

and Engels could not have foreseen the developments of the last years . . .
[and consequently] . . . socialism was a doctrine that could never be proven
. . . [but was rather] . . . an ideal to be implemented."[6] In order to implement this ideal, it was not enough to wait for history to provide the correct
conditions. Socialism would come about only through practical action and
engagement with changing circumstances. Therefore, practically engaging
in day-to-day politics and, in particular, capturing the intellectual high
ground were to prove more important to the SAP than doctrinal purity. As
Per Albin Hansson argued, socialist society "will not come to us . . . before
the masses are educated and . . . ways of thinking have been changed."[7]

Unlike the German SPD, where the ghosts of historical materialism were
not exorcised until 1959, the Swedish SAP eschewed this philosophy during
the struggle for universal franchise at the turn of the century.[8] Under pressure from the left wing of the SAP, which sought to establish socialism
through revolution, and from the newly powerful trade unions, whose
political stance was drifting toward more of what Vladimir Lenin termed
"trade union consciousness," the SAP leadership argued that only with the
development of both intellectual and productive forces would workers'
interests become consonant with that of a common collective action for
socialism. As such, both revolution and retreat came to be seen as
strategic failures.[9]

Given this perspective, the view of the state in capitalist society as simply
the tool of the capitalist class was no longer tenable. By turning away from
this simplistic form of Marxism, the SAP was able to transform the state
from an object of domination to be overthrown into an object of contestation to be captured and used to further the goals of social democracy. As
Hjalmar Branting, the leader of the SAP in this formative period, argued,
"modern socialism has little or nothing left from the theoretical aversion
to the state as such. . . . [as] an organized workers' party could march into
the modern state. . . . [to protect] the socially weak."[10] In order to move
forward, rather than attack the state head on, the SAP sought the right
to win the state from the bourgeois parties. These two strategic decisions,
to downplay the inevitability of class struggle and accept a positive and
reformist role for the state, set the SAP on a course that would enable it to

---

[6] Ernst Wigforss, *Vision och verklighet* (Stockholm: Prisma, 1971), p. 16, quoted in Berman,
  The Social Democratic Moment, pp. 48–9.

[7] Per Albin Hansson, quoted in Berman, *The Social Democratic Moment*, p. 53.

[8] For discussion of the comparison of the Swedish and German social democratic parties'
  intellectual evolutions, see Berman, *The Social Democratic Moment passim*; *Idem*,
  "Path Dependency and Political Action: Reexamining Responses to the Depression,"
  Comparative Politics 30 (4) (1998).

[9] On the evolution the SAP's political ideas, see Berman, *The Social Democratic Moment*,
  pp. 58–63.

[10] Hjalmar Branting, *Tal Och Skrifter* (Stockholm: Tidnen, 1926), pp. 22–8, quoted in Ahn,
  "Ideology and Interest," p. 163.

build a particularly Swedish form of embedded liberalism. In that form, the main source of ideas was the labor movement itself, and as a consequence, business was not able, at least until relatively recently, to challenge those ideas.

The Struggle for Electoral Democracy

As Sheri Berman notes, "The earliest and most consistent demand of the SAP was universal suffrage."[11] The reason for this was quite simple: If the SAP hoped to use the state, it had to win it. Yet before 1919 the electoral system was designed in such a way that even if the entire working class voted for the SAP it would make little headway given tax and property qualifications. Consequently, over the next several years the SAP deployed a two-pronged strategy. First, the party cooperated with, and in large part coopted, the trade union movement to pressure for universal suffrage. Second, the SAP cooperated with elements of the Liberal Party (*Sveriges liberala parti*) to overhaul representative institutions.

The relationship between the SAP and LO was originally quite at arm's length. What overcame this distance was the fact that the SAP was actively proselytizing long before the franchise was meaningfully extended in 1919, and that most of the party's propagandizing efforts for electoral democracy as a core component of social democracy took place within the labor movement itself. At the turn of the century, the LO was structurally similar to the American Federation of Labor (AFL) in the United States. The LO was top heavy with craft unions whose members were part of the so-called labor aristocracy, which traditionally eschewed, or was at best ambivalent to, socialism and social democratic political agendas. In a pattern similar to what would occur in the United States, the structure of the trade union movement began to change as industrialization advanced and cut across craft lines. What was different in the Swedish case was that these changes were directly accommodated by the mobilizing efforts of the SAP.[12]

As Jae-Hung Ahn points out, turn-of-the-century industrialization brought vast numbers of unskilled workers into the cities for the first time. These new workers were mobilized into the new industrial unions that were actively supported and organized by the SAP. Again, as Ahn notes, "twelve out of forty-five unions in Stockholm in 1886 were founded with the help of the [SAP's] union agitation committee. Of fifty unions represented at the first SAP congress in 1889, sixteen labor unions and clubs were established as a result of social democrats' agitation."[13]

[11] Berman, *The Social Democratic Moment*, p. 56.
[12] In the American case, by contrast, the new industrial unions were penned in by "federal locals" run by the AFL, and the Democratic Party was initially much more ambivalent in its efforts to help unions organize. See Chapter 3.
[13] Ahn, "Ideology and Interest," p. 169.

There was of course a backlash against such mobilization within the labor movement. Through a compulsory affiliation clause that the SAP placed in LO statutes, all LO unions would have to be affiliated with the SAP within two years of joining the LO. Naturally, union leaders, particularly craft union leaders, saw these mobilization strategies as a dilution of their strength and resisted this encroachment on their independence. The SAP solved this problem by abrogating this compulsory affiliation clause and instead engaging in a strategy of "reinforcing party-union relationship at the local level."[14] Over time, party and union organization became almost synonymous at the local level, and the personnel of the two organizations became virtually indistinguishable.[15] As such, the normative foundations of the Swedish embedded liberalism, a commitment to positive state action and social progress within a capitalist framework, were there in a prototype form on the side of the SAP and labor as early as 1914.

The electoral alliance with the Liberals was much slower in maturing. Although Branting was elected as the first SAP member of parliament in 1896, it was not until 1902 that he was joined by any other SAP members.[16] Yet once in parliament, the new SAP members worked both within and outside of parliament to force the issue of universal suffrage to the top of the political agenda. The SAP, in alliance with the left wing of the Liberal Party, put forward reform proposals, and in response the state put forward counterproposals in 1896, 1902, and 1906, none of which came close to meeting the demands of the SAP.

In the meantime, the SAP continued to grow electorally through the strategy of treating union and party mobilization as one and the same objective. In 1911 the SAP scored 28.5 percent of the vote for the second chamber of the Riksdag while the liberals scored 40.2. By 1917 and the crisis of World War I, these positions had been reversed. The SAP had increased its share of the vote to 39.2 percent whereas the Liberal Party vote had shrunk to 27.6 percent of the vote.[17] The SAP constituted a majority party for the first time, and at a crucial period in Sweden's political development.

Swedish neutrality during World War I had not stopped the British from blockading their ports. Consequently, the food situation in the cities worsened as the winter of 1917 approached. Prior to this, huge May Day parades demanding the resignation of Conservative Prime Minister Carl Swartz and the extension of the suffrage had badly shaken the Conservative government, eventually forcing Swartz to resign. Despite attempts by the king to block the formation of a new government headed by the SAP, in October 1917 in a protorevolutionary situation, an untested social democratic

---

[14] *Ibid.*, p. 172.
[15] See Berman, *The Social Democratic Moment*, pp. 54–5.
[16] *Ibid.*, p. 98.
[17] Figures from Misgeld et al., eds., *Creating Social Democracy*, p. 451, table 1.

government was formed. What is remarkable is that the SAP did not go the way of its Russian counterpart.[18]

The SAP capitalized upon the popular unrest in the country as a weapon to be wielded against the Conservatives. The LO continually threatened a general strike, and the SAP continually "managed" to moderate their demands. By essentially arguing that "reform now stops revolution later," the SAP managed to push the Conservatives further toward reform. Events came to a head with the armistice in Europe and the subsequent uprisings in Germany. "[T]hreatened with civil war and pressed by the King ... the conservatives finally acquiesced" and the franchise was extended.[19]

It is important to realize, however, that the struggle for electoral democracy was more than an instrumental end in itself. As well as providing a set of enabling institutions for further development in and of themselves, the struggle for democratization in *all* spheres of life became the rationale of SAP activity. Thus electoral democracy was linked to social democracy as a project. Put simply, without capturing the state, the SAP could not act on its reformist goals. Capturing the state was but a means to a broader end that covered all relationships, economic as well as political.

Building Swedish Embedded Liberalism

Governing with Classical Ideas

Having achieved greater electoral democracy, the SAP was now faced with the challenge of putting its ideas into practice. The problem the SAP faced that was although it had clear political ideas concerning how to restructure Swedish society, the party, as yet, had no clear economic ideas concerning how to restructure the Swedish economy. In such a situation, having eschewed revolutionary Marxism, the SAP found itself without any economic ideas of its own with which to further its goals. Unsurprisingly, then, when in power, the SAP behaved like conservatives.

When the SAP was in power during the economic crisis of the 1920s, its interpretation of the economic crisis in Sweden was very much in line with the classical liberal ideas that were the traditional mainstay of orthodox economists. As Erik Lundberg notes, "the strong deflation, the big decline in production (25 percent in the volume of industrial output), and the tremendous rise in unemployment were generally considered to be the natural and unavoidable consequences of the post-war boom of 1918–20."[20] Such an interpretation determined that the downward movement of wages was necessary to achieve equilibrium conditions in relation

---

[18] I refer of course to the government of Alexander Kerensky, not Vladimir Lenin.

[19] Berman, *The Social Democratic Moment*, p. 119.

[20] Erik Lundberg, "The Rise and Fall of the Swedish Model," *Journal of Economic Literature* 23 (1) March (1985), p. 5.

to the world economy. Consonant with this, real wages fell by 30–5 percent from the fall 1920 to summer 1922.[21]

The hegemony of classical economics in the early 1920s stemmed from the dominance of figures such as Gösta Bagge, Eli Heckscher, and later, Gustav Cassel, who were all staunch defenders of both free trade and free markets. Despite their lack of numbers, these academic economists wielded tremendous influence over the conduct of economic policy in this period. As Lundberg argues, "neither before nor since the 1920s have so many Swedish economists played such an active role in the policy debates on current problems."[22] For this older generation of economists, the management of the Swedish economy had to be predicated upon one factor above all others, Sweden's openness to trade. Consequently, the stability of the currency and the general price level was taken to be the fundamental goal of policy.

These economists worked within a strict Marshallian framework that assumed perfect competition and flexible prices. Unsurprisingly, in the context of the rapid inflation and deflation in the aftermath of World War I, economists advocated two policies: First, put Sweden back onto the gold standard as quickly as possible; second, enforce a policy of progressive reductions in the money supply in order to squeeze inflationary forces out of the system – a kind of protomonetarism.[23] It was argued (despite the fact that by the late 1920s the economy was obviously deflating) that this program would reequilibrate wages and prices and restore prosperity.

Under the sway of these ideas, unemployment could only be seen as a secondary problem that would be cured by adherence to the correct market-conforming doctrines, and the SAP in this period did not differ from this line of thinking. Influential economists such as Heckscher and Bagge saw unemployment as the result of insufficient labor mobility, inflexible wages, and obstructions to naturally clearing markets. Thus, the policy responses advocated by these economists were labor exchanges, and a stiff resistance to the demands of combinations (such as unions) that would prevent prices clearing. Consequently, Heckscher argued, as did Cassel, that not only should the supply of useful public works and other relief programs be limited, but such contrivances should pay less than market wages. To pay market rates would hinder adjustment, as such a policy would make the overall price level artificially high. Above all, welfarist policies had to be avoided.[24]

---

[21] Lundberg, "The Rise and Fall," p. 5.

[22] Erik Lundberg, *The Development of Swedish and Keynesian Macroeconomic Theory and Its Impact on Economic Policy, Lectures for the Raffaele Mattiolo Foundation* (Cambridge: Cambridge University Press 1996), p. 7.

[23] See the discussion of Knut Wicksell's monetary policy proposals in Lundberg, *The Development of Swedish and Keynesian Macroeconomic Theory*, pp. 6–11.

[24] Carlson, "The Long Retreat," p. 161.

Consequently, when reformist politicians argued for public works at market rates, they came in for special criticism. For example, when Bertil Ohlin, later leader of the Liberal Party, argued in 1927 that state-financed public works at market rates could have positive multiplier effects that would raise production overall by boosting aggregate purchasing power, Cassel argued that "the notion of abstract purchasing power . . . determined independently of production, must be relegated to the realm of economic mysticism [because] it is manifest that the purchasing power of the community is always sufficient to purchase the entire production."[25] Lacking ideas of their own with which to attack and delegitimate the institutions of classical liberalism, reformists' efforts fell before the rigors of classical orthodoxy.

Throughout the 1920s, Swedish economists vociferously defended other familiar policy precepts of classical liberal economics.[26] Cassel argued that any state-financed investment would crowd out equivalent private investment, and took great exception to the notion of leakages from, or idle money balances in, the savings-investment stream. For Cassel and Heckscher, idle money balances of the Keynesian type simply did not exist since, in line with classical precepts, all savings must equal investment.[27] Likewise, Heckscher continued to argue throughout the late 1920s that Say's Law made the problem of overproduction and underconsumption a similar nonsense.[28] Given the dominance of these ideas, even those members of the SAP who were soon to begin an alternative narration of the crisis, and therefore develop an alternative strategy, were convinced that there was no other alternative but to ride out the deflation. Unsurprisingly, when in power from October 1921 until April 1923, the SAP governed with classical policies.

Given such an ideational context, the SAP accepted the recommendations of the finance committee chaired by Cassel that "deflation, unemployment,

---

[25] Cassel, quoted in Carlson, "The Long Retreat," p. 162.

[26] Indeed, in 1924, in a remarkable anticipation of the policies that Sweden would adopt in the 1990s, Erik Lindahl, later a member of the Stockholm School, advocated an explicit rule-based exchange rate policy as a way of reducing fluctuations in the value of the currency. Lindahl also advocated an independent central bank and a constitutional guarantee of these policies to give them credibility. See Klas Fregeert, "Erik Lindahl's Norm for Monetary Policy," in Jonung, ed., *Swedish Economic Thought*, pp. 127–8.

[27] Carlson, "The Long Retreat," p. 164–6.

[28] In a newspaper article published in June 1927, Heckscher argued that "in the economy, there can never be any question of general overproduction but only of an incorrect alignment of productive power in various fields." Eli Heckscher, letter to *Svenska Dagablet*, June 17, 1927, quoted in Carlson, "The Long Retreat," p. 168. The influence of Heckscher and Bagge outside the state was just as strong as it was inside. After the state refused to take Heckscher's advice and raise the discount rate during the inflation of 1919, he published a newspaper article imploring the Swedish people to exchange their bank notes for gold. The Swedish people duly obliged and cause a run on the Riksbank so severe that the state had to raise the discount rate after all.

falling prices and wages . . . were required" to cure the depression.[29] The policy implications of these ideas were clear. Equilibrium could be reestablished only by a decline in living standards among wage earners. Despite the fact that these ideas and policies attacked the SAP's own goals and constituents, without any alternative economic ideas to narrate the crisis and argue a way forward, the Social Democrats at this time "could offer no alternative explanation. In fact, during this time they were quite passive and politically weak."[30] Indeed, as a part of the government from 1921–3, the SAP fully assented to the report of the Swedish delegation to the Brussels Conference in 1920 that, "The nation that in its financial policy approves a budget shortage treads upon a downward slope that leads to ruin. In order to avoid this no sacrifice is too great."[31] Given the dominance of such ideas, the SAP accepted Sweden's return to the gold standard in 1924, despite the huge secondary deflation this caused.[32]

In sum, without any alternative ideas to govern the economy, social democracy was proving to be little more than a liberal orthodoxy run by the representatives of the working classes. An alternative set of economic ideas with which to defeat the arguments of the classicists and break the cycle of deflation and unemployment thus became an imperative for the SAP.

Developing New Political Ideas

There were alternative social democratic economic ideas around at this time. It was just that they posited at best a zero sum, and at worst an nonsensical solution to the slump. Those ideas, in line with social democratic economic ideas elsewhere, lay in the notion of nationalization. In 1920 the SAP set up a "socialization committee" to pave the way for the nationalization of Swedish industry. However, in contrast to the situation in the United Kingdom, where nationalization became a core party objective written into the Labour Party's constitution, the SAP's attitude toward nationalization was one of profound ambivalence. Given the party's emphasis on democratization in all spheres of life, it was not clear how nationalization would further this goal. State control of the economy had a strongly antidemocratic tenor that went against the notion of a democratic and equal society, while in the short term, given the SAP's adherence to classical doctrines, concrete economic objectives such as halting the deflation through

---

[29] Villy Bergstrom, "Party Program and Economic Policy: The Social Democrats in Government," in Misgeld et al., eds., *Creating Social Democracy*, p. 136.

[30] Bergstrom, "Party Program," p. 136.

[31] Financial Plan, appendix 1, HRH proposition No. 11921, quoted in Bergstrom, "Party Program," p. 137.

[32] Gross Domestic Product (GDP) fell by approximately one-third and unemployment rose by one-third as a result of rejoining the gold standard. Berman, *The Social Democratic Moment*, p. 154.

a program of nationalization made little sense.[33] Moreover, some SAP members openly wondered if it was not the case that "state management is not as economically advantageous as private management," and that in order to provide concrete benefits for workers, the euthanasia of the capitalist was perhaps not the optimal policy.[34] Indeed, the nationalization commission itself became influenced by the work of Gustav Steffan, who argued that "the point of nationalization was to integrate workers into the economic life of society."[35] As such, the transfer of property rights *per se* became secondary to questions of effective control.

As Berman notes, at this juncture the figure of Nils Karleby becomes important within the SAP. Karleby began to argue that policies such as electoral and labor market reforms are not merely means to an end; they are in fact the end of social democratic practice. For Karleby, social democracy constituted an incremental but cumulatively radical strategy through which power relations in society would be transformed. As Karleby put it, "reforms do not merely prepare for the transformations of society, they are the transformation itself."[36] This new focus developed by Karleby and others within the SAP shifted SAP economic strategy away from nationalization and toward a focus on controlling the macroconditions of the economy. This shift was to prove extremely consequential, as it juxtaposed and reinforced set of ideational developments occurring elsewhere.

Developing New Economic Ideas

Advocating wage cuts and defending the currency in the midst of a continuing depression provoked a reaction among younger economists and sympathetic SAP members. A core group of activists who were committed to finding alternatives to classicism formed around Gunnar Myrdal, Erik Lindahl (despite his fondness for nonaccommodatory policies), and Ohlin. The ideas of these younger economists and politicians found their way into public policy through the sympathetic hearing they received from future SAP Finance Minister Ernst Wigforss. Although these ideas served as the weapons with which the SAP could challenge the classical interpretation of the crisis, the original ideas of the so-called Stockholm School marked both a break with, and a partial synthesis of, aspects of the classical tradition.

First, given Sweden's dependence on exports and the influence of younger theorists such as Lindahl who did not fully break with the classical school,

---

[33] See Berman, *The Social Democratic Moment*, p. 161.
[34] Bernhard Eriksson, quoted in Berman, *The Social Democratic Moment*, pp. 160–2.
[35] Gustav Steffan, quoted in Tilton, "The Role of Ideology in Social Democratic Politics," in Misgeld et al., eds., *Creating Social Democracy*, p. 411.
[36] Nils Karleby, *Socialism inför Verkligheten*, quoted in Tilton, *The Political Theory*, p. 82. See also Berman, *The Social Democratic Moment*, p. 163.

the stability of the price level was taken as a fundamental goal that the SAP had to accept. However, stability did not imply sacrificing domestic employment on the altar of international liquidity. Far from being the result of inevitable cycles, the depression was reinterpreted as a qualitatively different phenomenon – namely, a failure of demand. Consequently, since the situation was unprecedented, unprecedented measures to combat the depression such as public works and increased state spending could be tolerated.

Second, Swedish economists, unlike the majority of American ones – business cycles theorists excepted – were already used to working within a macroeconomic framework. Given the influence of Lindahl and Knut Wicksell's earlier work on monopoly and the price level, the notion of aggregate demand, as opposed to individual supply, was far from foreign to the younger generation of Swedish economists.[37] Third, the Stockholm School's economics ideas were generally both more theoretically advanced and more reflationary then their American counterparts. By developing a demand-side model of the economy within a dynamic open-economy framework, the Stockholm School was far ahead of American economists in terms of its studies of the trade cycle, sequence analysis, the effects of uncertainty on expectations and currency values, and the phenomena of crowding in as well as crowding out.[38] Consequently, the theory of underconsumption and the theoretical case for compensatory institutions were developed faster and more readily in Sweden than they were in the United States. Despite the fact that the "old guard" economics profession and economic opinion in general were united in their opposition to them, these new ideas quickly became policy orthodoxy once they were embraced by the SAP.

The opening for these ideas occurred in the mid-1920s when, despite the recovery in exports, unemployment remained stubbornly high. One important avenue for these new ideas was the Committee of Inquiry into Unemployment set up by the coalition government in 1927.[39] The committee was set up with the explicit mandate "to investigate 'the nature and

---

[37] For example, Lindahl's *The Means of Monetary Policy* (Penningpolitikens medel) of 1930 explicitly linked monetary and real economic aggregates. See Fregeert, "Erik Lindahl's Norm for Monetary Policy," pp. 131–4.

[38] See Bjorn Hansson, "The Stockholm School and the Development of Dynamic Method," in Bo Sadelin, ed., *A History of Swedish Economic Thought* (London: Routledge, 1991), pp. 168–214.

[39] Members of the committee included Dag Hammarskjöld, Lindhal, Myrdal, and Ohlin. This account of the work of the Committee of Inquiry into Unemployment is drawn from Eskil Wadensjö, "The Committee on Unemployment and the Stockholm School," Swedish Institute for Social Research, Stockholm University, Occasional Papers Series, reprint (314) May (1991); Carl G. Uhr, "Economists and Policy Making 1930–1936, Sweden's Experience," *History of Political Economy* 9 (1) (1976); Sven Steinmo, *Taxation and Democracy: Swedish, British and American Approaches to Financing the Modern State* (New Haven: Yale University Press, 1993) p. 86; Carlson, "The Long Retreat," pp. 168–9.

causes of unemployment.'"[40] The committee as a whole had a bourgeois bias throughout its eight-year tenure, yet despite this, the traditional liberalism of classical economics was increasingly eschewed for more active strategies. As Eskil Wadensjö notes, while "the majority of the committee was firmly market-oriented, and wage reductions were the expected recommendation from the committee," the actual policy recommendations of the committee turned out to be something very different.[41] The committee reports were distinctly compensatory and interventionist, dealing with such nonclassical areas as new business cycle theories that saw such cycles as manipulable, the relationship between wage formation and unemployment, and the economic effects of active fiscal policies.[42]

Inside the SAP, Wigforss, influenced by the writings of British Liberals, in particular the 1929 liberal publication *Britain's Industrial Future*, began to argue that boosting purchasing power was the key to industrial recovery. His interest in these new underconsumption ideas lead him to anticipate Keynes' *General Theory* by arguing that since individual workers could not affect the market-clearing rate of wages, wage reductions would in fact have no positive equilibrating effect.[43] More important, however, was his insight that general equilibrium, in the sense of all markets being in balance, simply was not possible in the context of a depression. Consequently, imbalances in the labor market logically could not be righted by action in the labor market alone. Wigforss argued that, "It is this automatic price mechanism which is put out of order during periods of crisis. Falling prices fail to stimulate an increase in demand. On the contrary, the price decrease encourages the belief that prices will be even lower later on."[44]

Wigforss also anticipated the Phillips curve. In 1929 he examined the relationship between the inverse of the unemployment rate and the inflation rate and noted that "higher unemployment was combined with lower inflation a quarter later."[45] The implication was, then, as with Phillips thirty years later, that governments could manipulate this relationship, rather than being passive data points trapped within it. In 1930, armed with these new

---

[40] Wadensjö, "The Committee on Unemployment," p. 103.

[41] *Ibid.*, p. 104.

[42] Arguably the most orthodox member of the committee was Bagge, a traditional classicist and later chairman of the Conservative Party. Bagge's first report to the committee even used a classical Marshallian model of the labor market. Yet despite this framework, Bagge concluded that "even if unemployment had been caused by a wage rise . . . a wage reduction was probably not the best antidote." Wadensjö, "The Committee on Unemployment," p. 110.

[43] See Ernst Wigforss, "Prices, Monetary Policy and Unemployment," *Report to the Committee on Unemployment*, May 22, 1929, pp. 20–1; compare, John Maynard Keynes, *The General Theory of Employment, Interest and Money* (New York: Harcourt Brace, 1936), pp. 7–22.

[44] Wigforss, quoted in Wadensjö, "The Committee on Unemployment," p. 113.

[45] *Ibid.*

ideas, the SAP proposed the abolition of public works as temporary relief and advocated instead 20 million krona in new spending for public works at market wages. In 1931 the SAP again raised this demand, yet succeeded in extracting only 3 million krona from the government on a trial basis.[46]

Another member of the committee, Ohlin, later leader of the Liberal Party, made important interventions on public works, but his main contribution was to delimit and separate the thinking of the committee clearly from that of the classical liberal tradition, and thereby help set up this new school as the dominant interpretation of the economy. Ohlin argued in his memo on business cycle theory to the Unemployment Committee that business cycle theorists fell into two schools. The first school contained Keynes, Joan Robinson, and "most ... Scandinavian economists [who] largely adopt the same line. In decided opposition to this ... [is] the so-called Vienna School ... [including] Mises [and] Hayek."[47]

The point of making this distinction was to stress that, "If the Committee should concur with [the Vienna School], it follows that all these memoranda [which embrace the new business cycle theory] cannot provide a basis for the Committee's standpoint in public works, wage policy, monetary policy and fiscal policy."[48] By drawing a line in the theoretical sand, Ohlin was legitimating, and thereby empowering, one set of ideas over another. In sum, this new body of economic thought at last gave Swedish social democracy the alternative economic ideas it needed to narrate the crisis in a new way, build a coalition, and restructure institutions accordingly.[49]

Deploying New Economic Ideas

In 1931 the bottom fell out of the free-trade orthodoxy when Britain went off the gold standard and Sweden followed suit. Naturally, the deflation that hit the Swedish economy worsened the unemployment problem, and the SAP, in power since October 1932, enthusiastically accepted these new ideas. The program of the new government argued that "the state should be given a totally different role than it had before in order to stabilize employment on a high level."[50] However, in contrast to the administered

---

[46] Carlson, "The Long Retreat," pp. 166–7.

[47] Wadensjö, "The Committee on Unemployment," p. 115.

[48] Bertil Ohlin, "Memorandum on the Debate on Business Cycle Theory with Special Regard to Cost Reduction or Consumption Reduction Theory," Report Number Two to the Committee on Unemployment, quoted in Wadensjö, "The Committee on Unemployment," p. 115.

[49] In fact, these ideas were beginning to affect the Liberal government then in office. In 1931, the Liberal finance minister asked Myrdal to attach an appendix to the state budget detailing the feasibility of active fiscal policies. See Lundberg, *The Development of Swedish and Keynesian Macroeconomic Theory*, p. 27.

[50] Bergstrom, "Party Program," p. 138.

prices thesis and later stagnationist ideas in the United States, what enabled the acceptance of these ideas by other groups was their focus on policy goals other than simply getting the economy out of a low equilibrium trap. These new economic ideas promoted the goal of the expansion of the whole economy as the solution to unemployment, falling prices, and lagging profitability, thereby anticipating America's growthsmanship model by some fifteen years.

As Berman argues, "The Social Democrats presented a wide ranging series of proposals to the 1932 Riksdag, containing all the elements of a 'Keynesian' stimulation package."[51] The SAP proposed 93 million krona in spending on public works at market rates. Meanwhile, in order to get support for the package, Wigforss "instructed the skeptical Riksdag members in multiplier theory."[52] Again, anticipating the TNEC hearings in the United States by some fifteen years, Lindahl lectured the Swedish Economic Society on the utility of public works. Lindahl suggested that rather than crowding out investment, if there was idle capacity and idle money balances, then greater government spending would increase overall demand and thus impact positively upon the propensity to invest.

In such public fora, Cassel and other orthodox liberal economists were forced to fight an increasingly rearguard battle against these new ideas. Simply insisting that there was no such thing as an idle money balance, and likewise insisting that because savings and investment had to be in equilibrium, then *by definition* any government spending would result in crowding out, seemed to verge upon the pedantic.[53] According to Carl G. Uhr, such public ideational contests "crystallized public opinion and support for a positive recovery program."[54] By 1933, even the old guard such as Cassel had come around, at least in part, to the new orthodoxy.[55]

This rapprochement was possible because rather than focusing purely on what could be construed as labor-friendly issues, the new orthodoxy took the stability of the price level to be a fundamental policy goal. Inflationary pressures were given a central place in the analysis and protectionism was actively resisted. In the context of the depression, this commitment hardly counted for much economically as deflation rather than inflation proved to

[51] Berman, *The Social Democratic Moment*, p. 170.
[52] Carlson, "The Long Retreat," p. 170.
[53] For a discussion of the classicist reaction to the new ideas, see Carlson, "The Long Retreat," p. 172–3; Uhr, "Economists and Policy Making."
[54] Uhr, "Economists and Policy Making," p. 97.
[55] In 1933, Cassel published a paper in which he makes a distinction between saving in "normal times" and saving in "crisis times," and acknowledges that in crisis times savings do not equal investment. As such, prices fall as the money supply collapses and unemployment rises. Although more a monetarist than a Keynesian explanation, the paper nonetheless shows how some of the core classical assumptions were being slowly stripped away under pressure of these new ideas. See Gustav Cassel, "Monetary Reconstruction," in *Skandinaviska Banken Quarterly Report*, June (1933).

be the problem facing the state. It was, however, politically important insofar as it avoided further alienating business interests.

In 1933 the SAP resolved to strengthen business confidence in these new economic ideas by giving a formal commitment to balance budgets over the whole cycle rather than over a given financial year. In doing so, the SAP accepted that the share of wealth controlled by the government would remain unchanged in real terms. By 1936 this commitment had spawned a commission comprised of Cassel, Lindahl, and Myrdal, who advocated the creation of a budget-balancing fund. This fund would use surpluses accumulated in a boom to reduce government deficits.[56] Relatedly, as we shall see later, taxation was structured in such a way that it was highly favorable to business, and these reforms were coupled with a policy of deliberately encouraging the greater centralization of labor market institutions.

Taken together, these new ideas facilitated a whole new way of envisaging not just the role of the state in the economy, but the nature of the economy itself and the place of the citizen within it. These new ideas were to prove to be central for the acceptance of these new economic ideas by both business and labor. As Rudolph Meidner said of the SAP in this period, "its ideology was to maintain the market economy, to counter short-sighted fluctuations through anti-cyclical policies, and to neutralize its negative effects through fiscal policies. The rallying cry was full employment, economic growth, fair division of national income, and social security."[57]

Integrating and Including Agriculture

Such ideas were indeed revolutionary. However, to implement them, the SAP needed extra parliamentary support. Despite having a majority in the Riksdag in 1932, the SAP was unable to convince the Liberals to go along with its 1932 spending proposals. Given this rejection, the SAP turned instead to the farmers and built a coalition predicated upon the *inclusion* of agriculture.[58] Unlike the experience of the Democrats in the United States, where building a coalition with industrial labor in the North was predicated upon the *exclusion* of agriculture in the South, the SAP's inclusion of agriculture was itself made possible by a prior intellectual shift in the way in which the state saw intervention in agricultural markets. This was wholly at odds with the American experience. Interestingly, here the shift in thinking was made by the Liberals and not the SAP.

As Bo Rothstein has shown, the idea that the success of the Swedish welfare state was a function of the strength of the SAP and the unions alone

---

[56] Carlson, "The Long Retreat," p. 181.

[57] Rudolph Meidner, "Our Concept of the Third Way: Some Remarks on the Sociopolitical Tenets of the Swedish Labor Movement," *Economic and Industrial Democracy* 1 (3) August (1980), p. 349.

[58] For a good summary of this "cow trade," see Uhr, "Economists and Policymaking," pp. 115–16.

is mistaken.[59] A crucial turning point in the way that the state viewed the economy was in fact produced by the actions of farmers rather than workers. For agricultural producers, as well as unemployed workers, the depression meant falling prices for their products as markets simply would not clear at a sustainable threshold. Paralleling the administered prices ideas found in the NRA and the AAA, the Swedish General Agricultural Association (SAL) sent a proposal to the Liberal government in early 1932 suggesting that the organization be granted the right to form a producers' cartel that would put a floor on milk prices, thus perverting the market outcome.[60] This cartel was to be compulsory; even if individual producers remained outside of the SAL cartel, they would still have to pay fees to the cartel, thus "administering" prices.

The Liberal government, which until that time had put its faith in free markets and international trade to restore the Swedish economy, as had the SAP, seemed now to be ready to countenance ignoring the market altogether. As Rothstein notes, "Evidently, the boundary had been reached for how much market economics the Swedish bourgeoisie could tolerate."[61] Consequently, "there was . . . no apparent hesitation in leading bourgeois quarters about a proposition which explicitly disavowed market solutions to structural economic crises."[62]

Given this prior bout of interventionism, the same ideas that had countenanced intervention in agricultural markets were quickly extended to cover labor market regulation. After all, it was hardly tenable to solve the problem of falling prices in agricultural markets by suspending the market mechanism through combination while simultaneously blaming labor combinations for the obvious disequilibrium in the labor market.[63] This intervention in agricultural markets served to legitimize the right of combination in order to achieve price stability. But most important of all, this intervention made the SAP's subsequent coalition with the farmers possible by recasting the interests of workers and farmers as being common.

This reinterpretation of what was possible in the name of legitimate market regulation was crucial since it placed all market participants on an equal footing. Note, however, this footing was *not* the one posited in the liberal understanding of the economy where agents are passive price takers and the macroeconomy is simply the sum of private decisions. Instead, this new understanding portrayed the agent as a citizen apart from his or her

---

[59] Bo Rothstein, "Explaining Swedish Corporatism: The Formative Moment," *Scandinavian Political Studies* 15 (3) (1992).

[60] The Liberals were in power until September 24, 1932, when the SAP took over and announced the crisis package.

[61] Rothstein, "Explaining Swedish Corporatism," p. 179. The account of the turn against the market by the Liberals presented here is based upon Rothstein's rendition of events.

[62] *Ibid.*, p. 180.

[63] *Ibid.*, pp. 182–4.

market position – an agent on whose behalf the state had to intervene and protect regardless of his or her sectoral or class position. This was very much an embedded liberal idea.

This reinterpretation of the relationship between the individual and the market was crucial in facilitating the later development and deployment of the ideas of the Stockholm School and the underconsumption theorists within the SAP. Again, as Rothstein notes, "Social Democracy and the Farmer's League were joined above all in their view of the relation of interest organizations to the state, for they regarded the former not as obstacles, but as instruments for *solving* the economic crisis."[64] These new ideas enabled the SAP and labor to project their ideas as constitutive of the general interest rather than the particular interest of labor and socialists.

Building upon these new economic ideas, in 1933 the SAP budget proposed 160 million krona for public works.[65] Given parliamentary opposition, the SAP had to join with the Farmers Party to get the package through the Riksdag. Despite the Liberal Party's new-found fondness for interventionism in agriculture, it remained for the SAP to convince the farmers to go along with the new spending package. Yet to do so was hardly an easy option given that farmers traditionally saw government spending as zero sum against agricultural rents. The more the state spent, the more taxes would have to be increased, and consequently, the more agriculture would have to be squeezed. Moreover, public spending on schemes for industrial workers seemed to have little relevance for the problems of farmers.[66]

The SAP therefore recast the interests of farmers and workers using the new economic ideas available to them. As Wigforss argued in the Riksdag in 1932

increased purchasing power . . . also means increased demand for agricultural products. . . . No one denies that our exports of butter and meat are suffering from the decreased demand from other industrialized countries . . . but if one recognizes this, then one has to admit that increased purchasing power among Sweden's workers would also benefit Swedish agriculture.[67]

By making this linkage explicit and building upon the precedent set in the milk market by the previous Liberal government, the SAP was able to

---

[64] *Ibid.*, p. 188.

[65] Again, in a striking similarity to what occurred in the United States, in 1936 the state began to run two budgets rather than one – a capital budget and a current budget – thus giving the state greater fiscal flexibility. See Uhr, "Economists and Policymaking," p. 117.

[66] This situation was complicated further by the fact that the SAP and the Liberals together had vetoed moves for effective protection on agricultural products in 1929 and again in 1931. This free-trade policy was pursued because the SAP realized that because of Sweden's dependence on exports, adopting protectionist measures would simply compound the deflation and raise the price of food domestically, thus hitting the SAP's core working-class constituency the hardest. See Uhr, "Economists and Policymaking," p. 115.

[67] Wigforss, quoted in Berman, *The Social Democratic Moment*, p. 171.

build a coalition with the farmers by using these new ideas to redefine their interests in this period of uncertainty. In doing so, the SAP was able to garner enough support to get the spending package through the Riksdag.

In May, the SAP's proposed budget was revised to contain 180 million krona in new spending, of which 100 million krona was earmarked for public works. In return, the farmers were granted import restrictions on dairy products and other nontariff barrier measures to protect prices in the home market.[68] However, getting the spending package through the Riksdag was only the beginning. This so-called "cow trade" was no mere parliamentary *quid pro quo*. In fact, rather than acting as the cement of the so-called "historic compromise," the "cow trade" was merely the first step in fashioning Swedish embedded liberalism. The real work of forming a lasting political coalition with both business and labor still had to be done, and once again, it was the new economic ideas of the 1930s that made this possible.

Bringing Business Back In

What made Swedish embedded liberalism inclusive of business, in contrast to the American experience, was the privileged position of business in the economic ideas developed by the SAP. These ideas enabled the formation of an inclusivist coalition between big business, labor, and the state. Contrary to popular belief, "Sweden has had *lower* marginal income tax rates for the wealthy than have most Western democracies," and such taxes are avoidable for those taxpayers with large businesses.[69] To incorporate business into this emergent order, the state redesigned the Swedish tax system to encourage the use of capital by taxing unproductive wealth. Historically, this made it possible for "some of Sweden's richest businessmen [to] have filed tax returns with zero krona in taxable income in spite of the fact that before deductions, they earned seven figure incomes."[70] The logic of doing so was to encourage reinvestment at the expense of current consumption while keeping the overall fiscal environment mildly restrictive.

Linked to this fiscal policy was the issue of business concentration. Ownership in Sweden exhibits among the highest levels of concentration in the developed world. Again, contrary to what one would expect, under the SAP it was deliberate policy to encourage this concentration. For example, in 1912 large corporations employed 80 percent of all workers.[71] Discounting the government sector, by the 1980s the situation had hardly changed. SAP Finance Minister Kjell-Olof Feldt noted that in 1988, "of all

---

[68] Uhr, "Economists and Policymaking," p. 117.

[69] Sven Steinmo, "Social Democracy vs. Socialism: Goal Adaptation in Social Democratic Sweden," *Politics and Society* 16 (4) Fall (1988), p. 406.

[70] Claes-Gorn Kjellander, "The New Tax Structure Splits the Bloc of Swedish Politics," *Current Sweden* 287 May (1982), pp. 2–9.

[71] Steinmo, "Social Democracy," p. 411.

investments made, 75 percent are made by the twenty-five largest companies, which have around eighty percent of exports."[72]

What these high rates of concentration and low effective tax rates demonstrate is that the SAP deliberately designed Swedish embedded liberalism to
be both labor-inclusionary *and* capital-friendly. As Sven Steinmo notes, "in
Sweden . . . taxes on corporate profits are inversely related to both profitability and size. In other words, the larger and more profitable a corporation, the lower its tax rate."[73] In the eyes of business, it was this arrangement
that made tolerable these new ideas and the institutions they spawned.
However, to understand the details of how it was possible to take an agreement with farmers over dairy tariffs and parlay this understanding into an
encompassing coalition between business and labor, we need to examine the
"historic compromise" worked out at Saltsjöbaden.

Recasting Interests and Building Institutions

As noted previously, high levels of unemployment had not precluded a rise
in labor militancy in the late 1920s and early 1930s. As a response to
this upsurge in industrial unrest, the Conservative government in 1928
"enacted a law that prohibited work stoppages during the term of a wage
contract and made illegal any support to those violating this rule."[74] As the
slump continued into the 1930s, the bourgeois parties resorted to further
repressive labor measures. Given these policies, "the newly elected Social
Democratic government realized the need for reform in light of the economic disruption which such conflicts represented," and it was this issue
that brought labor and business together in the Saltsjöbaden accords of
1938.[75]

The state, in the form of the governing SAP, used these new ideas to convince both business and labor that prosperity could not be achieved with
each group constantly attempting to outflank the other. The state argued
that stability was a public good achieved only through concerted action.
For their part, business and labor feared that unless a bargain was forthcoming between them, the state would unilaterally impose an industrial
relations policy.[76] Given the fact that the SAP could not legislate unilaterally
but depended upon the farmers for support, coupled with the fact that
nationalization had long since ceased to be a viable alternative strategy,
another formulation had to be found that created a positive-sum solution
for all parties.

---

[72] Kjell-Olof Feldt, quoted in Steinmo, *Taxation and Democracy*, p. 181; *Idem.*, "Social
Democracy vs. Socialism," p. 410.

[73] Steinmo, *Taxation and Democracy*, p. 181.

[74] Hugh Heclo and Henrik Madsen, *Policy and Politics in Sweden: Principled Pragmatism*
(Philadelphia: Temple University Press, 1987), p. 111.

[75] *Ibid.*

[76] Steinmo, *Taxation and Democracy*, p. 88.

That solution was to create growth through the success of top corporations inside a system of taxation that was both redistributive and that encouraged productivity increases and investment. As Steinmo notes, "tax reform in favor of larger corporations proved to be the glue that made the historic compromise stick."[77] Those largest corporations were given tax concessions as part of a growth strategy predicated upon the support of these top corporations. By keeping exchange rates very competitive, even if this burden was to be shouldered by wage earners in the short term, the government believed that price stability and growth should be possible.

The SAP rationalized this policy to its constituents by shifting the ideological goal from one of system transformation to one of industrial rationalization. "This meant in effect, that smaller, less efficient producers were to be squeezed out and that capital resources were to be directed towards Sweden's largest . . . corporate enterprises. . . . Unsurprisingly, Sweden's biggest capitalists favored these policies."[78] In return for accepting these pro-business arrangements, labor was given four guarantees. First, the state committed to overall economic growth and the redistribution of income relative to productivity gains. Second, the state committed to full employment as the primary objective of state policy. Third, the state further guaranteed the institutional autonomy of LO in its wage negotiations with the Swedish Employers Federation (SAF). Finally, business committed not to use either replacement workers or mass lockouts as bargaining tools.

In sum, the SAP in the 1930s succeeded in drastically redefining the legitimate boundaries of politics. By eschewing revolution in favor of reform, by embracing the democratization of both the economy and society as ends rather than simply means, and by not challenging ownership, that most fundamental element of capitalist relations, the Swedes were able to develop an embedded liberalism that included business, labor, *and* agriculture. What made this possible was a new set of economic ideas that contributed to the overall goals of welfare and equality through the promotion of consumption-enhancing income transfers. By predicating all this on a positive-sum trade-off for all parties, the SAP redefined the very nature of the Swedish political economy. The deal with the farmers made Saltsjöbaden possible, and Saltsjöbaden in turn brought business into the new institutional order. What made all of this possible was the dominance of new ideas.

Strengthening Swedish Embedded Liberalism

From Elites to Masses

However, agreement by elites does not necessarily translate into mass acceptance. In explaining the broader acceptance of this agreement, the

---

[77] Steinmo, "Social Democracy vs. Socialism," p. 419.
[78] *Ibid.*, p. 420.

further development of the ideas underpinning Swedish embedded liberalism is important. Tim Tilton has identified the major ideological themes that defined SAP politics during this period.[79] First, the SAP has always been an accommodationist party seeking positive sum trade-offs. As already noted, the SAP's conception of democracy was integrative and consensual rather than majoritarian. Key to this was the development of the concept of the "people's home," which was a broader conception of political community than one simply based upon class politics.

The "people's home" envisaged a community of

> ... togetherness and common feeling. The good home does not recognize any one as privileged or misfavoured ... in the good home, equality, consideration, cooperation, and helpfulness prevail. Applied to the great people's and citizens' home this would mean the breaking down of all social and economic barriers which now divide citizens ... into rich and poor, the glutted and the destitute, the plunders and the plundered.[80]

Such a narrative was not mere instrumentalist cover for a temporary alliance with the farmers. The same vision underlined the broader equity and efficiency policy mix of successive administrations and signifies the second theme that typified the consolidation of Swedish embedded liberalism. That is, *accommodation* between business, labor, and the state came to be seen as an end in itself, with positive-sum politics as the norm, rather than a means to an end. The unions' response to the emerging order serves as an example of this accommodation.

The Saltsjöbaden accords were ratified by the LO in its 1941 report *The Trade Union Movement and Industry*.[81] The report endorsed the view implicit in the new economic orthodoxy that improved living standards for all could be achieved only if all parties sought rationalization and productivity increases. This presumed a political compact with business. Such a compact, however, itself presumed central coordination among LO members to overcome coordination problems and thus make the agreements workable as well as desirable. For example, at the Congress of 1941, in part because of wartime emergencies, LO obtained the right to stop all strikes that either "created difficulties or involved more than 3 percent of the association's members."[82] As such, LO could effectively guarantee business that the party could control labor. Furthermore, the state's compact with labor was made in the form of an equally firm commitment to full

---

[79] Tilton, *The Political Theory, passim; Idem.*, "The Role of Ideology in Social Democratic Politics," in Misgeld, et al., eds., *Creating Social Democracy*, pp. 411–27.

[80] Per Albin Hansson, quoted in Tilton, "The Role of Ideology, " pp. 411–12.

[81] On this report, see Tilton, *The Political Theory*, pp. 189–215; *Idem.*, "The Role of Ideology," p. 413; Bergstrom, "Party Policy," pp. 144–7.

[82] Steinmo, *Taxation and Democracy*, p. 92.

employment. Rather than merely a political end in itself, full employment came to be seen as desirable on efficiency grounds insofar as a full utilization of resources facilitated other policy goals.[83] This continuing commitment, which was accepted in turn by the bourgeois parties until the 1990s, served to seal the compact with labor.[84] As such, the exchange of labor peace for growth and investment was made.[85]

The traditional social democratic issue of equity was not neglected in this *quid pro quo*, however. The SAP was to ensure equity by taxing income and consumption and rechanneling these resources into both industry and labor through redistributionary institutions. In line with the new ideas informing its interpretation of the crisis, LO argued that effective control over the investment decisions of business as a whole was more important than questions of formal ownership. Markets were to be made social in their output through establishing the background conditions of production rather than socialized directly. As Wigforss stated in 1938 at the time of the accords, the government "must recognize the need to provide favorable conditions for private investment in all those areas where it is not ready to replace this private enterprise with some form of public activity."[86] Given that the SAP *never* nationalized any of the major Swedish corporations, the sanctity of business was demonstrated over time.

The acceptance of these ideas by labor gave rise to a set of institutions in the postwar period that focused upon policies of industrial democracy and worker co-determination, solidaristic wage policy, and, most importantly in the active labor market, policies enshrined in the Rehn-Meidner model of economic management. For business, equivalent commitments were given in the form of autonomous wage bargaining, state-assisted capital formation, and labor mobility programs. By the end of the Second World War, the new economic ideas of the SAP were firmly entrenched in domestic institutions, and the SAP sought now to extend those institutions. However, similar to what occurred in the United States, the Second World War and the struggle over what ideas would shape the postwar order ultimately produced an interesting challenge from within.

---

[83] As Tilton notes, "unemployment in Sweden has become as delicate a political issue as inflation has in Germany." Tilton, "The Role of Ideology," p. 423.

[84] As Hugh Heclo and Henrik Madsen note, "when unemployment in Europe crept above the 2.0 percent level . . . eventually to reach 3.1 percent, the government was mercilessly attacked by the Social Democrats for abandoning the Swedish welfare state." Heclo and Madsen, *Policy and Politics*, pp. 65–6.

[85] The report also stressed the need for efficiency if business was to adhere the trade-offs established at Saltsjöbaden. "Rationalization must be considered a natural, continuing effort to improve the results of production and to enhance the development of human culture. The trade union committee cannot turn itself against these efforts." LO Conference Committee Report (1941), p. 144, quoted in Tilton, *The Political Theory*, p. 191.

[86] Quoted in Tilton, "The Role of Ideology," p. 418.

The War and the War of Ideas

Just as the war finally ended the depression in the United States, so the war finally brought about a full-employment economy in Sweden. The war demonstrated to the Swedish labor movement that the economy could be run at full-capacity utilization with a full employment of labor and resources. The 1944 SAP party program explicitly made full employment its major policy objective after the war, as it shifted from a strategy of moving the economy out of a low equilibrium trap to one of maintaining full employment. More important, however, was the shift in the economic ideas that took place during the war itself.

Mirroring the United States National Resources Planning Board (NRPB) reports of 1943 and 1944 that enshrined a stagnationist analysis, Swedish economic thinking grew increasingly stagnationist in nature throughout the war. In fact, Swedish research in this period was heavily influenced by the stagnationist reports of the NRPB and the United States Department of Commerce.[87] In line with American stagnationist thought, it was argued that, "as war production was reduced, a short recession would follow; thereupon, as inventories were being depleted and shortages of all kinds still prevailed, a period of economic prosperity would ensue; as effective demand would not be able to keep pace with the rapidly expanding production, a deep depression would occur."[88]

The key figure developing a stagnationist analysis of the Swedish economy in this period was Myrdal, who by 1944, was the head of the SAP's postwar planning commission. This commission, similar to its American counterpart, was charged with providing a blueprint for industrial organization after the war. Again, similar to American stagnationist views, Myrdal's hypothesis was that not only was capitalism inherently unstable, but Swedish capitalism was also largely comprised of over-built plant and equipment.[89] Given this analysis, Myrdal forecast a recurrence of the depression immediately after the war and recommended that trade with noncapitalist countries be expanded to shield the economy from exogenous supply shocks. More threateningly from business's perspective, Myrdal also recommended, *à la* Alvin Hansen and Stuart Chase, that the state should take greater responsibility for planning aggregate investment.

In the 1944 election, the employers' federation (SAF) and the Liberals mounted "concerted business campaign against the idea of a planned

---

[87] Lundberg, *The Development of Swedish and Keynesian Macroeconomic Theory*, p. 43. See also Lief Lewin, "The Debate on Economic Planning in Sweden," in Steven Koblik, ed., *Sweden's Development from Poverty to Affluence 1750–1970* (Minneapolis: University of Minnesota Press, 1975), pp. 282–302.

[88] Lundberg, *The Development of Swedish and Keynesian Macroeconomic Theory*, p. 42. See also Gunnar Myrdal, *The Reconstruction of World Trade and Swedish Trade Policy* (Svenska Handelsbanken, Aktiebolaget: Stockholm, 1947).

[89] Lundberg, *The Development of Swedish and Keynesian Macroeconomic Theory*, p. 44.

economy [and] compelled a reexamination of policy."[90] In particular, Ohlin, now leader of the Liberal Party, echoed American objections to stagnationism that planning was a threat to liberty and that the proposals of the postwar planning commission were well beyond what either SAF or the bourgeois parties were willing to tolerate. However, two factors other than Ohlin's opposition to the stagnationist turn were to prove consequential. First, the mobilization of the Liberals and SAF against the postwar planning commission's proposals did have an electoral impact. In the 1948 election, the Liberals' share of the vote increased at the expense of the SAP.[91] Second, and even more unexpected, the postwar environment continued to be inflationary rather than deflationary.

Given this unexpected inflationary environment, Swedish stagnationism rapidly fell from favor, and as such, the economic ideas of the 1930s had to be modified to take account of these new developments. However, rather than business using these developments to take control of the agenda and rein in the state and labor, as the Committee for Economic Development and the American Chamber of Commerce had done in the United States, the Swedish labor movement, in particular the LO's economic research department, became the powerhouse for the further development of the economic ideas of the 1930s and the institutions they made possible.

Extending Swedish Embedded Liberalism

Rehn-Meidner

As noted in the American case, rather than falling into the stagnationists' predicted slump, the postwar economy continued to boom. As high demand and tight labor markets created inflationary pressures, the SAP quickly abandoned voluntary wage restraint as the optimal policy at the end of the 1940s and embraced what came to be known as the Rehn-Meidner model of economic management. The model was predicated upon the idea that either a recession or mild inflation would affect different sectors' capacity utilization rates to varying degrees. A policy of general stimulation or contraction would therefore have uneven and unpredictable effects across the whole economy. Given these problems, an alternative to a simple underconsumptionist reading of the postwar environment had to be constructed. Rather than business providing these new ideas as they did in the United States, two LO economists, Gösta Rehn and Rudolph Meidner, designed the solution to these problems in Sweden. Rehn and Meidner "broke with

---

[90] Tilton, *The Political Theory*, p. 195; Lewin, "The Debate on Economic Planning," pp. 286–9.

[91] The Liberals' share of the vote increased from 15.6 percent to 22.8 percent, whereas the SAP's vote increased only from 44.4 percent to 46.1 percent. Figures from Misgeld et al., eds., *Creating Social Democracy*, p. 451, table 2.

'the over simplified form of Keynesianism' that relied exclusively on general measures of aggregate demand to maintain full employment," and creatively extended the ideas and institutions of Swedish embedded liberalism.[92]

Rehn and Meidner's solution had three main elements. First, the state needed to practice a somewhat restrictive fiscal policy. This was designed to keep demand at a manageable level and obviate distributionary conflicts. The practice of most embedded liberal states was to develop some type of incomes policy to keep demand under control, inflation being seen as a function of a wage/price spiral. Rehn and Meidner came to a somewhat different diagnosis. Rather than seeing excessive demand as a function of too high wages, themselves being a result of too tight labor markets, Rehn argued instead that the problem lay in too high profits. As Rehn put it, "full employment, and the certainty that it will be permanently maintained, must also tend to result in high profits and thereby give rise to fierce competition for the labor with the help of which profits are to be gained. This would lead to a rise in wages which increase purchasing power, thus leading to further rises in prices, increasing profits still more."[93]

Rehn argued that a policy of keeping profit levels down would encourage employers to resist inflationary wage claims, whereas a policy of general reflation would simply produce inflated profits and wage drift, which would have inflationary consequences throughout the economy and undercut redistributive goals.[94] Capping profit levels through taxation would also have the beneficial effect of transferring private into public savings. These would then be loaned to business at below market rates and used to stimulate the economy in a cyclical downturn. Thus cheap investment funds could be provided as a "sweetener" to business.[95]

The problem with an incomes policy is that it attempts to freeze differentials and it promotes intersectoral comparisons. This inevitably leads to "leapfrogging" wage claims among unions and undermines the centralizing logic of the LO/SAF agreements. Indeed, such leapfrogging became so bad that by 1951 it was SAF, not the LO, that sought greater wage-bargaining centralization.[96] To solve this problem, the LO introduced the second element of the model, a solidarity wage.[97] The unions, through the LO,

---

[92] Tilton, *The Political Theory*, p. 198.

[93] Gösta Rehn, in Erik Lundberg, Rudolf Meidner, and Gösta Rehn, eds., *Wages Policy under Full Employment* (London: William Hodge and Company, 1952), p. 196.

[94] Wage drift is the difference between centrally negotiated and actually obtained wages.

[95] In fact, this latent aspect of the model foreshadowed the development of the wage earner funds proposal by Rudolph Meidner.

[96] Heclo and Madsen, *Politics and Policy*, p. 115.

[97] As well as facilitating the economic goals detailed here, the solidarity wage was explicitly designed by Rehn and Meidner to act as a sweetener to low-paid unions to accept the greater centralization sought by the LO and SAF. See Heclo and Madsen, *Politics and Policy*, p. 115.

would operate a centralized wage-determination policy that stressed the principle of equal pay for equal work across sectors. This policy was designed to force inefficient firms either to increase productivity or go bankrupt, while at the same time furthering redistributive policy goals.[98]

The solidarity wage therefore not only contributed to demand restriction, it also promoted industrial reorganization. As wages were compressed, productivity enhancements emerged as the rational response among firms in such an institutional setting. Either firms innovated and added to productivity or, given profit capping, they stagnated and failed. Thus as well as being socially responsive, by putting a floor on wages this policy also served economic efficiency in that it forced businesses to upgrade production and thereby promote growth. Moreover, such a policy was noninflationary so long as central control of wages prevented leapfrogging wage claims by eliminating high-cost producers rather than cutting wages.

However, the problem with demand restriction was that profit capping and wage compression in isolation drove firms out of the market. Given that the state sought full employment, such a policy would be viable only if the labor freed up from declining low-productivity sectors was productively switched to high-productivity sectors. In the classical world, labor market flexibility is a nonproblem, as labor, as just another factor input, is perfectly mobile in a market with no informational asymmetries. Rehn and Meidner knew that such a picture of flexibility was wholly unreasonable. Yet, in the real world, the problem of how to create such flexibility remained.

Given these restrictions, a third element of the model was designed to balance the other two and overcome the deleterious effects of profit capping. This third element, an active labor market policy, was intended to increase labor flexibility through supply-side training, relocation, and investment programs. Thus, by taking on the responsibility for labor mobility and training, the state was able simultaneously to keep unemployment down and encourage adjustment. As Meidner was later to say,

... labor market policy was to be used to as a means to remove hindrances for a market economy of the type that the classical economic theorists dreamed of. The element of planning in this quasi-liberal ideology was reduced to the method for eliminating these hindrances. When the economy was freed from this it was thought that it could function according to the rules of the market and so do even better than in a consistently non-interventionist society.[99]

---

[98] As the LO report that spells out the Rehn-Meidner model concludes, "to prevent a race detrimental to all groups . . . one must aim at some principle of equal pay for equal work. Work of a similar type should . . . cost the same for all employers." Landsorganisationen, *Trade Unions and Full Employment* (Malmo: Framtiden, 1953), p. 96.

[99] Rudolph Meidner, *I arbetets tjänst* (Stockholm: Tindens forlag, 1984), p. 275.

As well as being entrenched in formal economic institutions such as wage-bargaining arrangements, these ideas were fortified over time by ideological promotion in broader social institutions. For example, the Workers' Educational Association, an integral part of the LO, dominated continuing education in this period, with around seven hundred thousand people attending LO-sponsored courses out of a population of just over 8 million. "Although ... not explicitly committed to political socialization [the association] tends to emphasize the achievements to the Swedish labor movement."[100] Also, in stark contrast to other embedded liberal states, Sweden had a strong pro-labor press, with the Social Democratic daily *Aftonbladet* enjoying a historically high circulation. In short, the SAP formed more than an Olsonian encompassing coalition based on consumption patterns; it forged a political hegemony based upon "dominance in the sphere of values and culture ... [that] ... shaped not only public policies but ... its citizens' personal identities."[101]

The economic ideas of Rehn-Meidner became the institutional centerpiece of the Swedish embedded liberalism and achieved what neither the American labor movement nor the American state could: an extension and deepening of the institutions of the 1930s and the outputs they produced. This model was institutionally viable only because all three parties – business, labor, and the state – shared the same economic ideology.[102] As Andrew Martin argues from the LO's point of view, "the dominating position LO occupies in Sweden's political economy would seem to rest in significant measure on the power of its economic ideas, which have been essential to the effective utilization of the power it derives from its numbers and organizational structure."[103] Just as the SAP managed to frame the "national interest" in terms of social democratic ideas, so LO economists Rehn and Meidner framed the economic ideology that governed the insti-

---

[100] Richard Scase, "Why Sweden Has Elected a Radical Government," *Parliamentary Affairs*, March (1982), p. 47.

[101] Tilton, "The Role of Ideology," p. 426.

[102] Specifically, the most important economics actors – the governing SAP, SAF, and LO – shared the same ideas. For the trade union's view, see the 1951 LO report, *Fackföreningsrörelsen och den fulla sysselsättningen: Betänkande och förslag från Landsorganisationens organisationskommitté* (Stockholm: Landsorganisationen, 1951). For the SAF's perspective, see Sven Anders Söderpalm, *Arbetsgivarna och Saltsjöbadpolitiken: En historik studie I samarbetet på svensk arbetsmarknad* (Stockholm: SAF, 1980). This is not to underrate the conflicts involved in getting to this position, especially given the SAF's fear of nationalization in the 1940s. On the latter, see Jonas Pontusson, *The Limits of Social Democracy: Investment Politics in Sweden* (Ithaca: Cornell University Press, 1992), pp. 50–5.

[103] Andrew Martin, "Trade Unions in Sweden: Strategic Responses to Change and Crisis," in Peter Gourevitch, ed., *Trade Unions and Economic Crisis: Britain, West Germany and Sweden* (London: George Allen and Unwin, 1984), p. 342.

tutions of the Swedish political economy for the next twenty years. As Hugh Heclo and Henrik Madsen put it, "the reformist social democratic vision of society has imparted a quality to Swedish political life that is at once pragmatic and ideological, adaptable and moralistic. Social democrats have captured the idea of the nation – they have successfully interpreted the national identity as one of an ever-reforming welfare state."[104]

Bringing the Middle Classes Back In

This institutional order could, however, hold only if the economic developments sought by the SAP brought a larger base under its mantle. In fact, the economic developments engendered by the institutions of Rehn-Meidner threatened to undermine the class base of the SAP's coalition. First, the very success of the Rehn-Meidner model in forcing productivity enhancements upon firms paradoxically had the effect of reducing the number of workers actually engaged in private sector employment. Active labor market policies could not after all place people in jobs that had been overtaken by improved technology.[105]

Such economic and social developments fractionalized the class basis of the coalition underlying Swedish embedded liberalism by promoting the growth of a new strata of salaried white-collar employees outside the institutional structures of the LO. Consequently, throughout the 1950s, independent unions such as the TCO, the Swedish Confederation of Professional Employees, and SACO, the Confederation of Professional Associations, continued to grow. These were organizations whose perceptions of their interests ran contrary to the solidarity wage policy that discouraged differentials.[106] As Gøsta Esping-Andersen notes, "in order to remain in power the SAP would have to forge a new coalition"; they would have to extend embedded liberal institutions to cover new groups.[107]

The 1959 earnings-related pension reform (the ATP reform) facilitated this realignment. Basically, during the late 1950s, the private sector began to negotiate with the new salaried classes pension agreements that were greater than that available to workers in the LO. Such a development, from

---

[104] Heclo and Madsen, *Politics and Policy*, p. 27.
[105] As Lundberg notes, the very success of Rehn-Meidner meant that replacement rates in industrial employment fell by some 2 percent per year throughout the 1950s and 1960s. See Lundberg, *The Development of Swedish and Keynesian Macroeconomic Theory*, p. 52. This was compounded by the effects that the solidarity wage had on low-productivity sectors, such as shoes and textiles, which were all but wiped out by the policy. See Heclo and Madsen, *Politics and Policy*, p. 118.
[106] See Jonas Pontusson, "At the End of the Third Road: Swedish Social Democracy in Crisis," *Politics and Society* 20 (3) (1992), pp. 305–32.
[107] Gøsta Esping Andersen, "The Making Of A Social Democratic Welfare State," in Misgeld et al., eds., *Creating Social Democracy*, p. 48.

the LO's perspective, cut into the core ideas of Sweden's embedded liberalism, while the state was concerned that such private provisions would effect differentials and thus undermine the centralizing logic of wage-bargaining institutions. In response to these developments, the LO sought to equalize these pension benefits, and did so by narratively linking the equity issue with efficiency concerns.

The LO portrayed the issue of pension reform as one of making the capital market, of which pension funds are a large part, more socially responsive. Indeed, some employers objected to the ATP reforms not because they were against pension equalization *per se*, but because the ATP reform threatened to place huge investment funds in the hands of the state.[108] Despite three years of SAF and bourgeois party opposition, the SAP forced the measure through the Riksdag by one vote. As Esping-Andersen has commented, this intense political battle merely served to entrench rather than weaken the institutions of the day because the ATP scheme was designed to offer compatible, if not better, pension benefits than the private sector. As such, private-sector alternatives offered to the white-collar TCO and SACO were, rather ironically, "crowded out" of the market. Subsequently, these new white-collar unions came under the same institutional structure and tax-and-transfer system as manual workers' unions. Thus the victory over pension reform allowed "ATP to become a vehicle for white collar mobilization" by the SAP.[109]

This realignment with the new middle classes strengthened the SAP electorally and entrenched Swedish embedded liberalism still further. Bringing the middle classes under existing pension institutions safeguarded those institutions against the middle-class tax revolts that arose in Europe and in the United States in the late 1970s. Moreover, the ATP reform, in tandem with the workings of Rehn-Meidner, facilitated greater income equality by making social transfers common to all members of the "people's home" rather than simply manual workers. Social and economic policy came to be seen as one and the same thing. Bringing white-collar labor under one general scheme made these reforms acceptable to some sections of business since this reduced the net volume of business savings and thereby reduced interest rates. As such, the new ATP funds acted as a protocollective capital formation fund that contributed to the subsidization of credit for investment purposes.[110]

Problems with this positive-sum politics of efficiency and equity began to appear in the 1960s. However, such problems were manageable within contemporary institutions of regulation and distribution. Indeed, the Swedish economy seemed to perform comparatively well, even in the reces-

---

[108] See Heclo and Madsen, *Policy and Politics*, p. 163.
[109] Andersen, "The Making of a Social Democratic Welfare State," p. 49.
[110] Pontusson, *The Limits of Social Democracy*, p. 103.

sionary period of 1976–82, with what was essentially more of the same policies.[111] Yet, despite these appearances, Swedish embedded liberal institutions began to destabilize endogenously during the 1970s, when labor challenged what business regarded as the basic ideas underpinning the existing institutional order. The fact that this was done in less than precipitous economic conditions brought about the consolidation of the bourgeois parties' opposition that, with business support, attempted to deligitimate and dismantle Swedish embedded liberalism.

---

[111] This is not to underrate the problems of the large government deficit, inflation, and the burgeoning public sector. See Barry Bosworth and Alice Rivlin, eds., *The Swedish Economy* (Washington: Brookings Institute 1987). However, as this book will show, the economic crisis facing Sweden in the 1970s and 1980s was itself subject to different and conflicting narratives that structured the responses of the state, labor, and business in the 1990s.

5

Disembedding Liberalism: Ideas to Break a Bargain

Unlike the ideas used to build embedded liberalism, the ideas used to break it were not organic responses to an immediate crisis. Whereas the under-consumptionist ideas that came to dominate both American and Swedish actions during the depression were creative responses to the crisis at hand, the ideas used to disembed liberalism were, in many cases, simply a warmed-over version of the ideas that embedded liberalism had seemingly defeated back in the 1930s. By the end of the 1990s, notions of "sound finances" and "budget balances" had once again become the touchstones of economic governance. The ideas used to disembed liberalism in both the United States and Sweden were essentially similar, although the emphasis shifted depending on the context and their time of their usage. As we shall see, the issues of inflation and taxation formed the fulcrum around which the disparate ideas of monetarists, supply-siders, rational expectations, and public choice theorists were brought together in the United States. In Sweden, these same ideas, some ten years after they were deployed in the United States, were instead united around the issues of growth and the need for a credible anti-inflationary policy.

The precise domestic forms that embedded liberalism took in our two cases, growthsmanship in the United States and Rehn-Meidner in Sweden, were in a broad sense both Keynesian regimes. That is, although John Maynard Keynes himself had little or nothing to do with the domestically generated ideas that made these forms of embedded liberalism possible, Keynesianism, particularly in its postwar "neoclassical synthesis" form, became the language through which embedded liberal ideas were trans-mitted and the intellectual masthead to which all such demand-side compensatory economic policies were tied. As such, attacking embedded liberalism meant attacking Keynesian ideas – in particular, the seeming inability of Keynesianism to deal with the problem of inflation.

As emphasized in Chapter 2, neither the supply nor the deployment of such ideas can be reduced to changing material conditions *per se*, since they were around long before the material conditions they diagnosed appeared. Although these ideas found their opening in the inflationary environment of the late 1960s, most of these ideas had in fact been around in some form since the 1950s or even earlier, and their effects were to be felt on many more issues than inflation alone.[1] To appreciate how these ideas were used to disembed liberalism, and by whom, it is first necessary to discuss the changing economic conditions of the late 1960s and early 1970s, and note the uncertainty that these changes wrought. Specifically, we need to understand how the changing international financial position of the United States meshed with domestic overheating to produce uncertainty within embedded liberal institutions both in the United States and abroad. We can then determine which ideas formed the dominant diagnosis for the causes of this new crisis, as it appeared first in the United States, and were then used to attack the existing institutional order.

The Changing International Context: Bretton Woods and Other Unsustainable Structures

The international financial regime that anchored the various domestic forms of embedded liberalism constructed in the 1930s and 1940s was the Bretton Woods exchange rate system.[2] The Bretton Woods system sought to reconcile domestic political stability with an international financial order that facilitated trade in commodities thought to be welfare-improving rather than welfare-diverting.[3] The first lesson that Keynes and his American counterparts learned from the experience of the 1930s was that international financial interests and their adherence to an "unregulated international monetary system [that] . . . impose[d] a contractionary bias on all domestic economies" were to be blamed for the economic collapse of the period.[4] The second lesson was that such contractions did not garner support for capitalism among the lower orders of society since they were forced to bear

---

[1] For early statements of these ideas, see Milton Friedman, ed., *Studies in the Quantity Theory of Money* (Chicago: University of Chicago Press, 1956); Wilhiem Ropke, *Welfare, Freedom and Inflation* (Tuscaloosa, AL: University of Alabama Press, 1964).

[2] So much so that Bretton Woods and embedded liberalism are often seen as synonymous. This is not the case. As Chapter 1 defines it, embedded liberalism is seen here as a particular type of market-reforming domestic regime rather than a particular monetary system. See Chapter 1, fn. 5.

[3] As *The Economist* magazine once put it, welfare-improving things are things that you can "buy, sell and drop on your foot." On the embedded liberal compromise, see John Gerald Ruggie, "International Regimes, Transactions, and Change: Embedded Liberalism in the Postwar Economic Order," *International Organization* 36 (2) Spring (1982); Jonathan Kirshner, "Keynes, Capital Mobility, and the Crisis of Embedded Liberalism," *Review of International Political Economy* 6 (3) Autumn (1999); Eric Helleiner, *States and the Reemergence of Global Finance* (Ithaca: Cornell University Press, 1994).

[4] Kirshner, "Keynes, Capital Mobility," p. 323.

most of the adjustment costs. In sum, these lessons called for a new type of exchange rate system to support domestic-level embedded liberal institutions where trade was "in," but arbitrage and speculation were "out." The Bretton Woods system was specifically designed to allow states to achieve this balance – that is, to attain domestic policy autonomy, especially the ability to practice expansionary policies – without having to keep an eye on the exchange rate.

The Bretton Woods institutions worked while Europe was financially dependent on the United States. So long as European currencies were so weak as to be unconvertible, Europe was dependent upon earning dollars. This meant America could essentially pump-prime the global economy, much as underconsumptionist ideas had demanded domestically, by exporting dollars to promote recovery.[5] However, as Milton Friedman was soon to remind us, there's no such thing as a free lunch. Acting as banker to the world had a cost that the economist Robert Triffin identified. First, if United States capital exports were pump-priming the "rest of the West," then if the United States ceased to run a deficit, the world's money supply would contract, and deflation, the very thing the Bretton Woods system was designed to avoid, would follow. Second, the Bretton Woods institutions were in fact a paper standard masquerading as a gold standard. The dollar was convertible into gold at a fixed rate of $35.00 per ounce. The dollar-gold exchange rate was sustainable so long as no country actually tried to exchange dollars for gold. However, running a permanent deficit meant that the world supply of dollars increased, and when the supply goes up, the price comes down, thus creating a discrepancy between the par and market values of the dollar that opened up arbitrage possibilities.

At this point, capital mobility became an issue. In 1963, in an effort to forestall a devaluation of the dollar that would destabilize the whole system, the United States introduced an interest equalization tax (IET). The tax was meant as a surrogate for higher interest rates and was intended to discourage foreign borrowings in dollars. The IET worked surprisingly well, enabling the United States to slow the flow of dollars without raising interest rates, which would have pushed the world economy into recession. However, the IET had a rather unintended side effect.[6]

Beginning in 1958 with a deposit of Russian oil dollars in London, the Euromarkets came into existence.[7] Being neither physically in the United States nor being the coin of the realm of the United Kingdom, these Eurodollar deposits fell beyond the embedded liberal regulations of both

---

[5] Ironically, then, it may be more accurate to say Bretton Woods worked best precisely when it did *not* work as an exchange rate regime.

[6] See Gregory J. Millman, *The Vandals Crown* (New York: Free Press, 1995), pp. 82–5; Helleiner, *States and the Reemergence*, pp. 83–6.

[7] See Helleiner, *States and the Reemergence*, pp. 81–101; David F. Lomax and Peter Gutmann, *The Euromarkets and International Financial Policies* (New York: John Wiley & Sons, 1981).

states. Because of this regulatory permissiveness, surplus dollars flowed into these Euromarkets where they were lent out without concern about the IET and other regulations. Soon everyone from European regional governments to American corporations were borrowing in these deregulated markets, and consequently, more dollars flowed into them. The United States was happy to let this state of affairs continue as it temporarily eased the Triffin dilemma by providing a kind of international slush fund for excess dollars. However, these booming markets also enabled private finance to use these funds to engage in exactly the type of hot money transactions that the Bretton Woods institutions had sought to eliminate. Given the dollar over-hang, the opportunity for arbitrage profits against the dollar and other major currencies was overwhelming and speculation against the dollar worsened.

What compounded the uncertainty over prices internationally was the uncertainty generated domestically by the inflationary effects of the Vietnam War and Great Society programs. Of course, there was no *a priori* reason for inflation to be the death knell of embedded liberalism in the United States. The ideas underpinning these institutions were not simply "depression economics" and were adaptable to a wide variety of situations, even inflationary ones, with such ideas being interpreted as a function of cost-push and demand-pull factors.[8] The American state in this period, namely President Lyndon B. Johnson and his Council for Economic Advisors (CEA), knew why there was inflation. Unfortunately, Johnson was both institutionally *unable* to deal with inflation and politically *unwilling* to tackle it. Because he failed to tackle these extraordinary pressures, the further weakening of the embedded liberal order became inevitable. The problem of U.S. domestic inflation, in particular the effects it had upon investment and labor market uncertainty, combined with the weakening of international financial institutions to generate increasing uncertainty that existing institutions found difficult to cope with. Given the central role of the dollar globally and the sheer size of the U.S. economy relative to other countries at this juncture, what happened in the United States domestically had great consequences internationally.

The Changing Domestic Context

How Not to Run a War Economy

Six months into the Johnson administration, the effects of Vietnam spending were beginning to be felt. Unemployment had fallen to 5 percent, and under a new method of calculating the budget, it was in surplus.[9] The bad

---

[8] This point had been made as far back as 1947, by Lawrence Klein. See Lawrence Klein, *The Keynesian Revolution* (New York: Macmillan, 1947).

[9] Even though the cash budget was in deficit as calculated on a full-employment basis. This was the main result of James Tobin and Walter Heller's innovations. Like Franklin D.

news was that inflationary pressures were beginning to take their toll in the form of wage and price increases. Johnson nonetheless refused to countenance the most obvious way of lowering inflationary expectations: either raising taxes or the discount rate.[10] In part, Johnson's hesitancy to raise taxes stemmed from his belief that "if Congress had to choose between guns and butter, it would cut back on the butter," and therefore his Great Society programs would be eviscerated.[11]

However, Johnson's inability to control inflation was as much institutional as political. While the 1951 Federal Reserve–Treasury accords (which were inspired by the Committee for Economic Development's 1947 report, *Monetary and Fiscal Policy for Greater Economic Stability*) sought to take fiscal levers from the executive by strengthening the independence of the Fed, such institutional changes did little to encourage Congress, as the sole source of taxation legislation, to actually raise taxes in a boom.[12] As such, the ability of the state to actively regulate the economy was institutionally circumscribed.[13] Therefore, if raising taxes was out of the question, and raising interest rates was beyond the purview of the state given the independence of the Fed, then the only tools that could be used to control inflation were the so-called wage and price guideposts.[14]

Instituted under President John F. Kennedy, the wage and price guideposts sought to tie price and wage increases to productivity increases, and thereby set a norm for wage and price setting throughout the economy.[15] The problem with such a voluntarist solution, in what was effectively a war economy, was that it was bound to create new tensions between business and labor, which was exactly what happened. "Labor leaders denounced management for war profiteering [and] management responded by blaming

Roosevelt's "administrative budget" (see Chapter 3), these innovations allowed more flexible management of state finances. For Tobin and Heller's work on recalculating the budget in the Kennedy administration, see Walter Heller, *New Dimensions of Political Economy* (Cambridge: Harvard University Press, 1966); James Tobin, *The New Economics, One Decade Older* (Princeton: Princeton University Press, 1974).

[10] See Isabell V. Sawhill and Charles F. Stone, "The Economy: The Key to Success," in John L. Palmer and Isabell V. Sawhill, eds., *The Reagan Record: An Assessment of America's Changing Domestic Priorities* (Washington: Urban Institute, 1984), p. 78.

[11] Hobart Rowen, *Self-Inflicted Wounds: From LBJ's Guns and Butter to Reagan's Voodoo Economics* (New York: Times Books, 1994), p. 11.

[12] Committee for Economic Development, *Monetary and Fiscal Policy for Greater Economic Stability* (New York: Committee for Economic Development, 1948).

[13] Moreover, Congress had an incentive not to raise taxes. By not raising taxes, it could effectively pass the buck for monetary stability to the Federal Reserve, and thus avoid the electoral consequences of a tax hike.

[14] As we shall see, once inflation began to hit the economy, the Fed did tighten, but not by enough. Moreover, upon the accession of Arthur Burns to the Fed's chairmanship, the Fed ran a consistently loose policy, which merely exacerbated inflation.

[15] On the wage and price guideposts, see Heller, *New Dimensions*; Tobin, *The New Economics*.

organized labor for all price increases."[16] Unfortunately such finger-pointing did little to cool the economy in the absence of a tax increase.

What further complicated the task of controlling domestic inflationary pressures was that the Council of Economic Advisors discovered in 1965 that the costs of the Vietnam War were not being publicly acknowledged, and these hidden costs were not being factored into CEA economic analyses and policy statements. It was therefore no surprise that actual economic performance and CEA predictions began to diverge rapidly.[17] Because of these constraints, an expected economic slowdown in 1966–7 failed to materialize, and by June 1967 the CEA's projections of the deficit in 1968 were running at $20 billion above their already off-target 1967 forecast.[18]

In this increasingly uncertain policy environment, all the macroeconomic indicators began to move in the wrong direction. "Quarterly demand was increasing by $14 to $16 billion, yet the economy could only maintain price integrity with quarterly increases of $11 billion."[19] Inventories became backlogged and prices continued to increase. This would usually send a signal to business to increase investment. However, as the Consumer Price Index (CPI) was accelerating at nearly twice the rate of the guideposts, the investment that would obviate the inflationary effects of these demand pressures was not forthcoming given uncertainty over expected future returns. Consequently, to make up this investment shortfall, the state increased its share of GDP from 13 percent in 1964 to 14.5 percent and then 15.2 percent in 1966–7, the highest it has been before or since. Concomitantly, the private investment share of GDP fell from 23.8 percent in 1964 to 22.5 percent in 1967.[20] This aborted expansion of supply, itself a function of

[16] Kim McQuaid, *Big Business and Presidential Power: From FDR to Reagan* (New York: Morrow, 1982), p. 239.

[17] As Arthur Okun complained, "everything depends upon Vietnam spending, but we can't get a goddamned word out of [Defense Secretary Robert] McNamara." Arthur Okun, quoted by Hobart Rowen, "Cost of Vietnam? A McNamara Secret," *Washington Post*, June 19, 1966.

[18] Council of Economic Advisors Annual Report, 1967 (Washington: Government Printing Office, 1967), p. 14. Eventually, Congress did pull the deflationary lever in the Tax Surcharge Act of June 1968. It was, however, a Pyrrhic victory. "By the time [the state] got it, Vietnam war spending had risen so high that the remaining federal deficit, even after tax increase and the $6 billion in spending reduction, was $10 billion higher than the $15 billion [deficit] Johnson had estimated in August 1967." In such a circumstance, the tax increases proved to equivalent to locking the door after the horse had bolted. Quote from McQuaid, *Big Business and Presidential Power*, p. 253.

[19] Cathie J. Martin, *Shifting the Burden: The Struggle over Growth and Corporate Taxation* (Chicago: University of Chicago Press, 1991), p. 82.

[20] These figures demonstrate how increasing demand was being reflected in increasing prices that were being funded by government investment and consumption through deficits, rather than being reflected in increased domestic (private) capital formation and the expansion of private capacity. Figures calculated from FRED (Federal Reserve Economic Database) –

increased investment uncertainty, increased international financial difficulties as it led to accelerated capital imports, which in turn worsened balance-of-payments problems. As the government was deprived both politically and institutionally of any means to raise revenues, the deficit ballooned. This lead to ever-higher interest rates, and ever-greater pressure on the dollar.

The Political Consequences of Regulation

While the state was temporizing over inflation throughout the late 1960s, business's uncertainty had been growing during the same period for rather different reasons. Apart from the changing macroeconomic environment, the growth of grassroots organizations such as Common Cause and the consumer movement also exacerbated business uncertainty. Encouraged by the public attention given to new theories of regulatory capture by Grant McConnell and others, Congress enacted a series of regulatory initiatives that were wholly different from regulatory activities heretofore undertaken.[21] Regulatory advocates argued that by getting close to the industry concerned, New Deal era regulatory institutions were eventually captured by the industries they were supposed to regulate. Therefore, to avoid such capture, the new regulatory institutions of the 1970s sought to ensure that there were "widespread and identifiable social benefits and very concentrated industrial costs to provide those benefits."[22] Consequently, over the next several years, a series of new regulatory institutions were set up to enforce regulations on business that focused not upon individual company violations, but upon defining panindustrial responsibilities.[23]

Bandwagoning with the newly vogue environmental movement, in 1969 Congress enacted the Environmental Protection Act. This Act created the Environmental Protection Agency, a huge new federal bureaucracy whose regulations affected almost every conceivable business sector. Similarly, the Occupational Safety and Health Act of 1970 created an Occupational Safety and Health Administration, whose panindustrial mandate required a slew of new regulations that cost business a great deal in compliance costs when their credit reserves were being squeezed by inflation and higher

Federal Government Time Series, and the Penn World Tables v. 5.6, available at http://www.stls.fred.org and http://www.nber.org/penn respectively.

[21] See Grant McConnell, *Private Power and American Democracy* (New York: Knopf Publishers, 1966).

[22] Kim McQuaid, *Uneasy Partners: Big Business in American Politics 1945–1990* (Baltimore: Johns Hopkins University Press, 1994), p. 137.

[23] This discussion of the Environmental Protection Agency and Occupational Health and Safety Administration is based upon the discussion of these agencies in McQuaid, *Uneasy Partners*, pp. 135–51; David Vogel, *Fluctuating Fortunes: The Political Power of Business in America* (New York: Basic Books, 1989), pp. 64–113; William C. Berman, *America's Right Turn: From Nixon to Clinton.* (Baltimore: Johns Hopkins University Press, 1998), pp. 10–14.

interest rates.[24] These regulatory initiatives, beyond their financial cost, were to have far-reaching unforeseen consequences for the political organization of business.

First, these new regulatory institutions constituted a massive transfer of rents from business to the general public. By concentrating costs and diffusing benefits, such institutions quickly became perceived by business, in the context of an inflationary economy, as being part of the problem rather than being part of the solution to the increasing uncertainty of the period. Paradoxically, the regulatory movement actually encouraged business to overcome its own collective action problems and act in a way that it had not done since the 1940s – that is, act as a coherent social actor. In short, as costs became specific to a whole industrial group or set of sectors rather than to an individual violating firm, business began to rethink its own interests.[25]

Second, the policies of the new Nixon administration served to increase business uncertainty since they ran completely contrary to what business would normally expect from a Republican administration. Just before Richard M. Nixon's election victory, Johnson's treasury secretary, Joseph Barr, issued a report on taxation that revealed that many millionaires had an effective tax rate of zero. In response to this report, demands for tax reform became the clarion cry of Democratic senators after the 1968 election.[26] Despite a Republican administration being in power, Nixon jumped upon the tax reform bandwagon and produced what *The New Republic* called "far and away the most anti-rich tax reform proposal ever proposed by a Republican president."[27] The final bill enacted, the Tax Reform Act of 1969, was perceived by business as an ultraliberal measure that restricted business tax shelters such as the oil depletion allowance.[28] Given such a

---

[24] Being the consummate bandwagon jumper, Richard M. Nixon was only too happy to support such seemingly antibusiness measures for the sake of short-term political advantage. As Nixon was to say in his 1970 State of the Union Address, "clean air, clean water, open spaces – these should be once again the birthright of every American. If we act now, they can be." Richard M. Nixon, *Public Papers of the Presidents of the United States: Richard Nixon: Containing the Public Messages, Speeches, and Statements of the President.* January 14, 1970, (Washington: United States Government Printing Office, 1969–74), p. 177.

[25] As Thomas Byrne Edsall has argued, "during the 1970's, business refined its ability to act as a class, submerging competitive instincts in favor of joint cooperative action." Thomas Byrne Edsall, *The New Politics of Inequality* (New York: W.W. Norton and Company, 1984), p. 128.

[26] On the background to the 1969 Tax Reform Act, see Robert Kuttner, *The Revolt of the Haves: Tax Rebellions and Hard Times* (New York: Simon and Schuster, 1980), pp. 232–3.

[27] Edwin L. Dale, Jr., "Its Not Perfect, But Its the Best Yet," *The New Republic*, May 3, 1969, p. 10, quoted in Vogel, *Fluctuating Fortunes*, p. 63.

[28] Moreover, the Bill actually added inflation by boosting consumption in lower tax brackets since it increased personal tax exemptions.

signal as to what to expect from the new administration, stock values and corporate profits fell on the perception that inflation, business's core concern due to the volatility it wrought, was not being dealt with seriously enough.

Adding fuel to the fire was the fact that at the end of 1969, the phenomenon later known as stagflation hit the economy for the first time. When Arthur Burns became the chair of the Fed in 1970, he sought to end the accommodationist stance of the Fed that had persisted throughout the Kennedy and Johnson era. Instead, Burns hoped to control inflation through a combination of higher interests rates and a tighter monetary policy. While interest rates were raised by 3 percent, and this depressed economic activity as unemployment rose, the rate of inflation did not decline. Again, the reason for this was quite simple: Vietnam. "Peace with honor" cost money, and the widening of the war that this policy necessitated simply served to push more inflation into the system. As the state continued to buy more and more plant and material despite high interest rates, further stimulation and inventory growth became necessary, which was reflected in higher end-user prices.

In response to these seemingly intractable problems, Nixon decided to address the nation in a televised speech in June 1970. Nixon devoted his entire speech to the state of the economy. In this speech, he hinted that some kind of wage and price guideposts, or even a mandatory incomes policy, would be necessary to get inflation under control.[29] Nixon was supported in this policy by Burns, who was increasingly discouraged by the inability of a tight money policy alone to control what was effectively a wartime economy. However, the rest of the CEA and the Treasury was split over the use of controls.[30] In the midst of this indecision, the economy continued to deteriorate. Wages were rising at an average of 7 percent per annum, and balance of payments problems were increasing as the pressure on the dollar continued to mount. Seeking a solution, Nixon did two things that simultaneously increased market uncertainty and further weakened embedded liberal institutions.

First, he closed the gold window, which effectively heralded the suspension of dollar-gold convertibility and the end of the Bretton Woods regime. Given these changes, currencies were free to float, and in inflationary conditions, many of them began to sink. This change of regime also constituted

---

[29] Nixon, *Public Papers*, June 18, 1970, pp. 205–19.

[30] Nixon's Council of Economic Advisors was hardly an orthodox Keynesian group. Nixon's CEA chair Paul McCracken described its philosophy as neither Keynesian nor Friedmanite, but "Friedmanesque." McCracken was a Michigan economist, Treasury Secretary David Kennedy was a Chicago Ph.D., as was CEA council member George Schultz, albeit from the Chicago Business School. On McCracken's beliefs and the Nixon CEA in general, see Herbert Stein, *The Fiscal Revolution in America* (Washington: American Enterprise Institute Press, 1996), pp. 532–4.

a massive transfer of exchange rate risk from the public to the private sectors at a moment when private-sector risk-management instruments, such as futures markets, were at best thin on the ground. Uncertainty increased.[31] Second, and perhaps more consequentially, was the domestic side of this policy shift: the imposition of price controls in peacetime by a Republican president. Just as "only Nixon could go to China," only Nixon could implement what business thought it had defeated back in the 1940s: stagnationist Keynesianism as the economic philosophy of the state.

Destabilizing Embedded Liberalism: Supply Shocks and a New Stagnationism

It is a small irony of history that it was almost fifty years after Vladimir Lenin announced the short-lived New Economic Policy, which attempted *to liberalize* the economy in order to prosecute a war, that Nixon announced his own New Economic Policy that was designed *to regulate* the economy in order to prosecute a war. Since the Fed's tighter monetary policy had succeeded somewhat in slowing the rate of inflation from an annualized 6.1 percent in 1969 to 3.6 percent in 1971, by the time this policy of state-mandated controls was announced, unemployment had risen to 7 percent.[32] Yet, when Nixon announced a comprehensive package of controls on August 15, 1971, conservatives and liberals alike were struck by the degree of intervention and regulation that such policies presupposed.[33]

There were to be three phases of controls. Phase one was a ninety-day freeze on wages and prices that was imposed along with a 10 percent surcharge on imports.[34] The logic behind this was threefold. First, it was hoped that such a signal of resolve would relieve pressure on the dollar independent of the suspension of convertibility. Second, it was hoped that the cyclical pay rounds then being negotiated would be limited by the freeze, and as such, after the freeze, inflationary expectations would be revised downward. Third, the import surcharge was intended to combine with the competitive gains brought about through a back-door devaluation and further facilitate inflation control by avoiding extra import inflation. Phase

---

[31] On this aspect of the end of the Bretton Woods order, see John Eatwell, *International Financial Liberalization: The Impact on World Development* (United Nations Development Program: Office of Development Studies, 1996), pp. 5–7.

[32] Figures from Federal Reserve Economic Database at http://www.stls.fred.org/. See also Hugh Rockoff, *Drastic Measures: A History of Wage and Price Controls in the United States* (Cambridge: Cambridge University Press, 1984), p. 200.

[33] As John Kenneth Galbraith, a long-time advocate of controls, is reputed to have said after Nixon's announcement, "I feel like the street-walker who has just learned from Mayor Lindsay that the profession was not only legal, but the highest form of municipal service." John Kenneth Galbraith, quoted in the *Washington Post*, November 5, 1971.

[34] In fact, the import surcharge was really Treasury Secretary John B. Connolly's weapon for bludgeoning the Europeans into submission during the Smithsonian meetings in 1973.

two of the controls began on November 14, 1971, and mandated the establishment of a price commission and a pay board, both of which were tripartite, if not overtly corporatist institutions.[35] Phase two mandated pay increases no larger than 5 percent, tending toward an average target rate of 3 percent, combined with a limitation on profit margins.[36]

Despite bickering between business and labor over the very existence of the controls, the price commission and pay board had a strong and clear effect on the rate of inflation. In the latter part of 1972, the core rate fell to 1.8 percent, but unemployment was proving to be more difficult to shift.[37] In light of this slowdown in inflation, Nixon declared phase two of the controls a success and by early 1972 claimed his economic policy was in fact "just right."[38] Consequently, when phase three of the controls was enacted in January 1973, the shift was made to a semivoluntary regime. In fact, it was wholly voluntary and presumed a manner of business and government cooperation that was not so distant from that of the NIRA of the 1930s.

Under this new voluntary regime, the price commission and the pay board were abandoned and some of the main guidelines were dropped.[39] In particular, business was given the right to administer phase three itself. Unsurprisingly, most businesses ignored the guidelines completely and inflation soared. In the first part of 1973, meat prices grew at an annualized rate of 30.4 percent, and in April the government was forced to place mandatory ceilings on pork, beef, and lamb prices. Similarly, industrial raw material prices shot up as business sought to recoup lost ground. Given these price movements, the stock market sank.

What had also undermined the positive effects of the controls was, once again, the institutional split between the Fed and the Treasury reestablished in 1951. Being institutionally separate meant that rather than sup-

---

[35] Such corporatism was of course completely contrary to the intent of the Administrative Procedures Act passed back in 1946. The price commission was given a relatively free hand in price setting, principally because the Council of Economic Advisors was ideologically opposed to controls. McCracken noted that any attempt at controls was futile because "in the end the market would win out." Schultz grudgingly accepted the notion of controls only after being berated by the Business Advisory Council on the need to "do something." Consequently, CEA member Herbert Stein was only half joking when he said to C. Jackson Grayson, the head of the new price commission, that, "Not much in classical economics seems to be working, why don't you come up with something on your own rather than be prejudiced by our views," which is exactly what the price commission did. C. Jackson Grayson, quoted in Rockoff, *Drastic Measures*, p. 207.

[36] Wage control was the real focus of the controls since they are easier to monitor and police than profits.

[37] The core rate of inflation is the rate of inflation with food and energy prices discounted to control for seasonal volatility. Figures are from FRED database at http://www.stls.fred.org/.

[38] Stein, *Fiscal Revolution*, p. 559.

[39] Specifically, the profit margin limitation implemented in phase one was abandoned, rental properties were exempted, and workers earning less than $3.50 per hour were excluded.

porting the activities of the Treasury and the wage and price commissions, the activities of the Fed undermined the effectiveness of the phase two controls.[40] By devolving responsibility for price control to the price commission and wage board, the controls absolved the Fed of its traditional responsibilities of currency and price stability. Consequently, the Fed was free to respond to other pressures, especially for higher levels of employment and output.[41]

The optimal monetary policy to coincide with controls was a policy of tight money. However, monetary policy throughout the latter Nixon period was consistently loose. The money stock (M2) grew at 2.4 percent in 1968–9 before Burns' ascendance to the Fed.[42] M2 growth shot up to 10.8 percent per annum after Burns' ascendancy to the Fed in 1971–2, precisely when policy should have been tight.[43] Thus, the institutional independence sought by the Committee for Economic Development back in the 1940s to safeguard price stability actually undermined this very goal in the context of controls.

In response to the failure of phase three's voluntarism, the administration announced a second freeze on all wages and prices in June 1973 in the midst of the Watergate scandal. This was followed in turn by a further set of controls in August 1973, phase four. What made phase four and the freeze particularly useless was that they did not cover wages at all, and industry by industry, the price-wage mechanism that tied increases in each category to the guidelines of the New Economic Policy were abandoned. More and more of the economy was being *decontrolled* in the name of price control. Inflation rambled on regardless, and uncertainty increased. What no one expected was the 1973 Arab-Israeli war and the eventual quadrupling of oil prices.

Briefly, the immediate effect of the OPEC price hikes was to increase the price of heavy crude from between $3.00 and $4.00 per barrel in 1971 to $11.65 by December 23, 1973. This had two immediate results: an oil

---

[40] As Hugh Rockoff argues, during previous wartime experiences of inflation, the goal of controls was to prevent fears of inflation from driving prices above those consistent with underlying monetary forces. As such, controls were used to equilibrate the economy. The Nixon controls were different because they attempted to "depress prices below the levels determined by fundamental economic variables." That is, they were used to depress actual inflationary forces and thus *disequilibrate* the economy. Rockoff, *Drastic Measures*, p. 232.

[41] Or perhaps to maximize the reelection chances of Burns' sponsor, Nixon. Whether Burns acted politically to boost Nixon's election chances given that Nixon always blamed his 1960 defeat on tight money at the Fed is impossible to prove. Political business cycle theorists like to point to this episode as a classic case of a political business cycle. See, for example, Alan S. Binder, *Economic Policy and the Great Stagflation* (New York: Academic Press, 1979), esp. ch. 8.

[42] M2 was defined as M1 (currency plus checking deposits) plus noncheckable savings deposits and small time deposits, usually less than $100,000.

[43] Figures from Rockoff, *Drastic Measures*, p. 232.

supply panic and a huge inflationary boost. As oil was one of the most important imported commodities and has a variety of end uses, its inflationary effect was massive. To avoid this inflationary pressure, the state had to do one of three things: reduce imports, reduce consumption, or find alternative energy sources. Finding alternatives was impossible in the short term. Curtailing consumption meant some form of rationing or controls, and curbing imports was nonsensical because domestic supplies could not be increased in the short run.[44]

Given the lack of alternatives, the state enacted the Emergency Petroleum Allocation Act, which promoted panic buying throughout the United States and drove prices ever higher. In response to this supply shock, the Fed and the state belatedly attempted to tighten money and spending simultaneously which led to a collapse in output due to higher input costs and interest rates. Investment volatility grew as the uncertainty surrounding the economy increased. The investment share of GDP of the United States' economy declined from 23.4 percent in 1973 to 20 percent in 1974, an unprecedented 13 percent drop.[45]

In such an environment of increasing instability and uncertainty, Congress searched for an explanation within existing ideas and turned to fiscal stimulation to get out of the slump. However, given that the slump was itself due to increasingly greater institutional incoherence, and with these problems occurring during the Watergate scandal, general policy paralysis remained. By the time Nixon resigned from office, wholesale prices were increasing at an annualized rate of 44 percent, and unemployment had reached 7.6 percent of the workforce. There was indeed a crisis, and the state had lost control of its diagnosis.

Taken together, the failure to confront inflation, increased regulation, peacetime price controls, and volatile commodity, currency, and labor markets represented no mere efficiency loss to business. These policies, especially under a Republican president, violated the core ideas underpinning American embedded liberalism. Growthsmanship may have been objectionable, and may have been viewed as an infringement on the rights of business, but the virtue of those ideas was that they set macroeconomic conditions without interfering in the microdecisions of individual enterprises. Wage and price controls, in contrast, went beyond the pale. John Kenneth Galbraith's warning that, "for some businessmen, the Keynesian remedy

---

[44] It also had one longer-term effect of great importance: It turned the domestic oil industry away from the Democratic Party. The oil industry argued that domestic supply could be increased only if domestic oil prices were decontrolled. This led to accusations that the oil industry was price gouging the American public. Oil executives were dragged up to Capitol Hill and read the riot act by Democratic representatives. See Vogel, *Fluctuating Fortunes*, pp. 124–9.

[45] Calculated from Penn World Tables USA/CI (investment share of GDP in current international prices) on the National Bureau of Economic Research server http://www.nber/pwt.

was at least as damaging as the depression it was presumed to eliminate," seemed to have come true.[46]

The combined effects of these policy failures was to signal to business that the state had expanded its role well beyond the limits established as reasonable in the 1940s and 1950s. Consequently, business reacted against these infringements on what it saw as its fundamental rights and sought to replace the embedded liberal order with one more attuned to its interests, at least as business reinterpreted them in this highly uncertain environment. To do this, business once again had to engage in the politics of ideas. Luckily for business, independent of the uncertainty of the time, there was no shortage of ideas available with which to do this.

Ideas to Disembed Liberalism

Monetarism

The theoretical attacks on embedded liberal ideas began in earnest as early as 1956, when Milton Friedman reformulated the decades-old quantity theory of money.[47] Friedman argued that, in equilibrium, the marginal utility of holding wealth in money form should equal the marginal utility of holding it in any other form – stock, real estate, etc. Thus, if the money supply increased, then consumers would exchange it for other assets and the price would rise on these assets until the demand for money equaled its new supply. This analysis formed the basis the monetarist analysis of inflation.

The first version of monetarism proper appeared in 1959.[48] This time Friedman proposed that if one compared

the timings of the peaks and troughs of the rate of growth of the money supply with peaks and troughs in the level of money income . . . [there was] . . . an average lag of sixteen months for peaks and twelve months for troughs. From this Friedman concluded that fluctuations in the money stock had been a major causative factor in business cycles in the United States.[49]

These findings were supported by the data supplied in Friedman and Anna Shwartz's *Monetary History of the United States*, where in the cases of deep depressions it was postulated that the decline in the money supply was caused by factors independent of the level of money income – that is,

[46] John Kenneth Galbraith, *American Capitalism: The Concept of Countervailing Power* (Boston: Houghton Mifflin, 1956), p. 81.

[47] Friedman, ed., *Studies in the Quantity Theory, passim.*

[48] Milton Friedman, "The Demand for Money: Some Theoretical and Empirical Results," *Journal of Political Economy* 67 (4) (1959).

[49] Michael Bleaney, *The Rise and Fall of Keynesian Macroeconomics* (London: Macmillan, 1985), p. 135.

short-sighted federal reserve policy.[50] The policy prescription that came
from this, the claim that "money matters," became an article of faith for
monetarism and it reversed the causal relationship between money and
income posited in the embedded liberal worldview, where the level of
income was seen to determine the level of output.[51] What amplified this
critique was Friedman's extension of these points in his 1968 presidential
address to the American Economic Association.[52]

Friedman's argument here was that if there was a monetary expansion,
the price of goods would rise, money wages would also rise, but real wages
would fall proportionately due to wages being essentially a fixed cost. At
this point, employers want to expand output and therefore unemployment
would decline. This is in line with standard Keynesian theory. The twist is
that such an improvement cannot last, even over the medium term. Unlike
the embedded liberal idea that unemployment was a function of the failure
of demand, Friedman assumed that unemployment was voluntary. What
Keynes had once argued incorrect, that "the amount of employment is fixed
at the point where the utility of the marginal product balances the disutility
of the marginal employment," was resuscitated by Friedman.[53]

Given this classical reinterpretation, unemployment falls in the short
term because more workers are willing to work at the apparently higher
wage. Of course, money wages have risen, not the real wage, and newly
employed workers either force up wages to equilibrate the real and money
wage rate, or the newly employed withdraw their labor. The effect of
Friedman's model was dramatic, as it called into question one of the key
concepts on which postwar economic theory had relied: the Phillips curve.[54]
Friedman's analysis argued that rather than providing policymakers with a
stable trade-off between unemployment and inflation, the Phillips curve
only showed the supply curve of labor.

Crucial to Friedman's attack on the causal relationships posited in the
embedded liberal worldview was the idea of the natural rate of unemployment. As stated previously, if the government provides a fiscal stimulus,
workers will think that the real wage rate has increased, only to find that
it has not. Workers will consequently withdraw their labor, and unemployment will decrease to its "natural rate," with real variables unaffected

[50] Milton Friedman and Anna Shwartz, *A Monetary History of the United States 1867–1969*
(Princeton: Princeton University Press, 1963).

[51] Bleaney, *Rise and Fall*, p. 175.

[52] Reprinted as Milton Friedman, "The Role of Monetary Policy," *American Economic
Review* 58 (1) March (1968).

[53] John Maynard Keynes, *The General Theory of Employment, Interest and Money* (New
York: Harcourt Brace and World, 1936), p. 6.

[54] A. W. Phillips. "The Relation between Unemployment and the Rate of Change of Money
Wages in the United Kingdom, 1861–1957," *Economica* 25 (100) November (1958).

in the long run.[55] This occurs because the state is successful in reducing unemployment only in the short term, to the extent that it succeeds in duping private-sector agents. Consequently, once workers realize that there has not been a real wage increase, employment will fall once more, but critically, the price level will not since workers will have built current inflation into their future expectations.[56]

Given this failure to achieve a permanent reduction in unemployment, if the state attempts to spend its way to lower unemployment in the future, it will once again succeed only in the short term. However, this time the convention governing market agents' expectations has changed such that these agents are now operating with a higher inflationary expectations baseline. Once labor-market equilibrium is reestablished at the natural rate after the temporary fall in unemployment, expectations will adjust again, and the inflation rate will continue to rise. With the supposed trade-offs that the state sought between unemployment and inflation proving ever more illusory, and with inflation rising ever higher, in the long run the state will have no alternative but to abandon its attempt to control market outcomes.

Friedman's ideas repudiated the core ideas of embedded liberalism. As Michael Bleaney notes, within the understanding of the economy, "ideas concerning lack of effective demand have disappeared out the window . . . we are back in a completely classical world where . . . full employment follows automatically."[57] However, just as the ideas behind embedded liberalism were not static, but were added to over time, the key insights of monetarist theory – the belief in long-run self-equilibration, adaptive expectations, and the deleterious if not perverse effects of government – were taken on board by other theorists and expanded upon. These complementary bodies of theory were rational expectations, supply-side, and public choice theory.

---

[55] The natural rate being defined as the level of employment consistent with market fundamentals.

[56] This proposition hinges on the assumption that agents' expectations are "adaptive" rather than simply a static addition of a weighted function of past observed values. See Friedman, "The Role of Monetary Policy,"; Edmund S. Phelps, "Money Wage Dynamics and Labor-market Equilibrium," in Edmund S. Phelps, ed., *Microeconomic Foundations of Employment and Inflation Theory* (New York: W. W. Norton, 1970). Though Friedman's 1968 address pointed to the role of adaptive expectations, this concept was attacked by rational expectations theorists as a basic flaw in Keynesian models. The monetarist usage, however, seems to have gone unnoticed.

[57] Bleaney, *Rise and Fall*, p. 140, author's italics. As Bleaney continues, "But none of this is argued out; it is simply assumed." Of course, there is a philosophical defense of such a method, that being that the assumptions of a theory can be totally unrealistic so long as its predictions are good. This, however, raises the question of how good predictions actually are. See Friedman's original statement in Milton Friedman, *Essays in Positive Economics* (Chicago: University of Chicago Press, 1953), pp. 17–53.

Rational Expectations

Monetarism had been waiting in the wings since the 1950s to attack embedded liberalism but lacked an opening to do so given the stable institutional conditions of the 1950s and 1960s. Yet, what discredited embedded liberal economic ideas as much as the monetarist critique of inflation was a disciplinary squabble known as the microfoundations critique. This critique states that causal accounts of the behavior of aggregates – for example, income and investment – must be grounded in convincing causal accounts of the behavior of individuals. More specifically, credible theories must be supported by models that are generated from the main assumptions of neoclassical economics: that individuals are self-interested maximizers and that markets clear.[58]

Given this critique, the assumptions underpinning embedded liberal ideas were attacked because they treated aggregates as if they had an independent existence.[59] As the ex-governor of the Minneapolis Federal Reserve Bank, Mark Willes declared, "Because aggregate outcomes are only the sum of individual decisions, the aggregate relationships should have no independent existence, *but they do under the Keynesian approach.*"[60] Focusing upon such aggregates as if they were real was seen to be an error insofar as they provided "arbitrary measures of policy success . . . [that] . . . say nothing about individual welfare." This is in clear contrast to neoclassical models, where "agents are assumed to be acting in their own best interests."[61] Once the challenge of monetarism opened the conceptual door, rational expectations theorists took up this critique of embedded liberal ideas and synthesized their new insights with monetarism. The result was initially hailed as being so successful that embedded liberal ideas seemed completely discredited.[62]

---

[58] For a good discussion of the importance of the microfoundations critique, see Nick Bosanquet, *Economics: After the New Right* (The Hague: Kluwer-Nijhoff Publishing, 1982). On the issue of microfoundations in economics in general, see Maarten C. W. Jansen, "What Is This Thing Called Microfoundations?" *History of Political Economy* 23 (4) (1991).

[59] This is a really odd criticism, given that the Friedmanite unreality of assumptions clause noted previously is a defensive mainstay of neoclassicists. See Friedman, "The Methodology of Economics."

[60] Mark H. Willes, "Rational Expectations as a Counterrevolution," in Daniel Bell and Irving Kristol, eds., *The Crisis in Economic Theory* (New York: Basic Books, 1981), p. 89, author's italics.

[61] *Ibid.*

[62] Among the main contributions to this body of scholarship were John Muth, "Rational Expectations and the Theory of Price Movements," *Econometrica* 29 (3) July (1961); Robert E. Lucas, Jr., "Expectations and the Neutrality of Money," *Journal of Economic Theory* 4 (2) April (1972); Thomas J. Sargent, "Rational Expectations, the Real Rate of Interest, and the Natural Rate of Unemployment," *Brookings Papers on Economic Activity* 2, (1973); Thomas J. Sargent and Neil Wallace, "Rational Expectations, the Optimal Monetary Instrument, and the Optimal Money Supply Rule," *Journal of Political Economy* 83 (2) April (1975).

Rational expectations theorists took issue with the role of expectations in Keynesian models. Such models usually treated inflationary expectations as a weighted function of past averages, usually an inflation-adjusted time series of the price level. The problem with such a view was that it denied that people could adjust their expectations rapidly in response to changes in other variables.[63] Such models assumed "that people had no knowledge of the economic system and did not perceive any interrelationships between the (hypothesized) variables."[64] Thus, rational expectations theorists argued that the agents depicted in these Keynesian models must in some sense be "fooled" all the time for interventionism to work.

However, these new ideas went further than Friedman's injunction that "only surprises matter." Rational expectations theorists' microfoundational focus and neoclassical assumptions insisted that being consistently fooled all the time was impossible because, "If economic agents optimize, as most economists agree they do, they cannot be irrational. Irrationality is unnecessarily expensive – it is more expensive than using the available information efficiently."[65] Given this observation, it could then be argued that "economic agents are completely aware of the true structure of the economy, that is, the form of the equation and the size of the coefficients in the econometric model which governs it, and make full use of this in forming their expectations."[66] This argument directly challenges the role of the state in embedded liberalism since a corollary of this assumption is that the government can be no better informed than the typical man in the street. Therefore, if only surprises matter for interventionist strategies, there can be no surprises. Rational optimizing agents will immediately discount any interventionist strategy pursued by the government.

This conclusion led to what was known as the policy irrelevance proposition. Simply stated, if the government is committed to a specific course of action, such as full employment, and it has demonstrated this preference in the past, then any stimulus to achieve this end will be discounted by agents in the private sector in the present. Agents with the correct model should be able to work out the nominal magnitudes of wages and prices and thereby nullify the effects of an expansionary policy on real variables. The situation is even worse for government if it attempts to do something unique, or more generally, unanticipated. As John N. Smithin notes, "at best, a systematic activist government would be impotent, and at worst, an

---

[63] As Willes noted caustically, "If Washington doubled the money supply, eliminated income tax, named the Ayatollah Khomeini to the Supreme Court, agents in the adaptive expectations economy would expect very little change in the economy." Willes, "Rational Expectations," p. 86.

[64] Bleaney, *Rise and Fall*, p. 142.

[65] Willes, "Rational Expectations," p. 86.

[66] Bleaney, *Rise and Fall*, p. 143.

unsystematic policy would actually contribute to the cycle."[67] These claims about the pernicious role of the state directly contradicted the ideas under-pinning embedded liberalism, and in terms of theory and policy, their results were devastating. Not only was government intervention at best a waste of time and money, it was more likely downright dangerous. Such ideas dic-tated that governments, by definition, can only interfere with the working of the economy; governments *cause* recessions and depressions by their very actions.[68] Left on its own, the economy would not, and indeed could not, produce long-term slumps. Government is not part of the solution. *Government is the problem.*

These ideas not only offered a radically different diagnosis of the crisis facing the state, they also seemed to offer an attractive way out of some tricky political impasses. For example, if government policy causes in-flation, conventional monetary theory demands a deflation that would be electorally undesirable and socially costly. Rational expectations theory, however, provides a nearly costless way out of a deflation. If one accepts that people have rational expectations, then all the state has to do, and *should* limit itself to doing, is announce a policy of tight money and make the claim credible; then agents' expectations will adjust rapidly, thereby pro-ducing a painless deflation without the short-run adjustment costs origi-nally predicted. This, coupled with a credible policy of slow growth in the money supply as dictated by monetarist theory, would then be all that is needed to ensure both economic stability and expectational certainty since the state would no longer be attempting to fool private agents. Once such ideas were accepted, as they were by increasing numbers of policymakers and most of the economics profession in the late 1970s and early 1980s, then any claim that could be made under embedded liberal ideas for the positive and stabilizing role of the state in the economy became utterly redundant.

Supply-Side and Public Choice Theories

While inflation precipitated business's crisis of faith in embedded liberal ideas, it was the issue of taxation that was to provide the rallying point for business's new crusade. The set of new economic ideas that linked concern with inflation to taxation was supply-side theory.[69] The supply-side idea is

---

[67] John N. Smithin, *Macroeconomics after Thatcher and Reagan: The Conservative Policy Revolution in Retrospect* (Brookfield, VT: Edward Elgar, 1990), p. 18.

[68] To jump ahead a little, one can see how such an account fits well with Friedman's account of the Great Depression and public choice accounts of inflation.

[69] A distinction has to be made in this literature between supply-side theory as popularized by economic journalists and "nontraditional" economists such as Arthur Laffer, and supply-side theories of a more orthodox academic persuasion that focused on microeconomic meas-ures to lower the natural rate of unemployment, such as the work of Martin Feldstein and Michael Boskin. It has been maintained that the former body of theory was the product of "cranks" and has little relation with the latter body of thought. Nonetheless, it was this

simple, seductive, and another classical throwback in which Say's Law, the idea that supply creates its own demand, forms the centerpiece of analysis. Supply-side theorists began with the assumption that because supply creates its own demand, a general failure of demand is impossible and as a consequence, markets must naturally clear at an equilibrium price. Individual decisions to work, rest, invest, etc., are therefore affected by one factor over all others: the tax rate. Thus, "if small increases in taxes can have huge effects on the economy, tax reductions can correspondingly have huge positive effects."[70]

The key supply-side idea was that the labor supply curve was extremely sensitive to changes in price. By allowing people to keep more of their income, not only would labor supply increase given the monetarist assumption that unemployment is voluntary, but investment and output would also increase, all reinforcing a virtuous circle. Such a policy obviously suggests the problem of a growing budget deficit given the drop in revenues that such cuts presuppose. However, the supply-side answer to this concern is to insist that the virtuous circle – given the increase in income, investment, and output – would also increase saving, such that a temporary deficit could be financed. In fact, Arthur Laffer went so far as to suggest in his famous curve that the incentive effect was so great that the tax cut would itself increase revenue and bring forth the required tax income to finance the deficit.[71]

One of the reasons that supply-side doctrines became so powerful is that they demanded the same policies as monetarism and rational expectations, and yet had the added bonus of legitimating tax cuts. This was especially true for upper-income tax brackets under the logic of trickle-down economics. In this way, supply-side ideas tackled head on the embedded liberal idea that redistribution was good economic policy by linking concern over inflation eroding financial assets to tax cuts for the holders of those assets. Consequently, under supply-side ideas, redistribution by the state could only be detrimental to the economy since such redistributions would impact negatively on labor supply and investment. In contrast, supply-side theorists suggested that a stable monetary policy, *plus radical tax cuts in the top brackets*, would produce a healthier economy.[72] Supply-side theory shifted

---

version of supply-side theory, the "populist" and "tax-cutting" rhetoric of Laffer et al., that had a tremendous effect on policy discourse and practice. Such a feat was all the more remarkable because although these theorists embraced monetarist doctrine, they were largely shunned by the orthodox economics profession. See Paul Krugman, *Peddling Prosperity: Economic Sense and Nonsense in the Age of Diminished Expectations* (New York: W.W. Norton and Company, 1994), pp. 82–103. The choice of the word "crank" is Krugman's.

[70] *Ibid.*, p. 94.

[71] Laffer and his curve are discussed in Chapter 6.

[72] For some representative supply-side works, see Robert L. Bartley, *The Seven Fat Years and How to Do It Again* (New York: Free Press, 1992); Paul Craig Roberts, *The Supply-Side*

the focus away from the macro to the micro, as did another set of ideas: public choice theory.

Just as the microeconomic focus of supply-side theory marked the denouement of the redistributionary ideas that underpinned embedded liberalism, public choice provided the same microfocused critique of the principal target of business: the state itself.

With the introduction of the concepts, models, and conclusions of public choice theory into popular discourse with terms such as "the political business cycle" and "rent-seeking," the apotheosis of embedded liberalism was reached. Public choice theory argued that inflation was not due to a failure of demand, nor was it due to a monetary surprise, mental "confusion," nor perverse microeconomic incentives, as these other new ideas held. Instead, inflation was the deliberate consequence of the actions of governments, particularly democratic governments.[73] According to public choice theorists, democratic governments are particularly prone to generating inflation.[74] This is because democratic governments are elected to provide goods to constituents. If they do not provide these goods – for example, high levels of transfers and employment – then governments can be voted out of office. As such, assuming politicians are appropriate analogs of market actors and maximize votes, then inflation is the natural consequence of governments meshing their electoral cycle to the business cycle.

Public choice ideas proposed that governments initiated high levels of spending in order to get elected, deflated once in office to stabilize the economy, and then reflated again to fool agents into thinking that "good times" are here again in order to maximize reelection chances. However, because such models rest upon a monetarist theory of inflation, the state cannot simply pick points on a stable short-run Phillips curve and trade them off in a stable way. Instead, it is argued that once the state boosts the economy, *à la* Friedman, expectations adapt and the economy shifts to a new higher equilibrium rate of inflation. Unable to sustain this politically, the government deflates, bringing unemployment down to the natural rate

Revolution: An Insider's Account of Policymaking in Washington (Cambridge: Harvard University Press, 1984); Jude Wanninski, *The Way the World Works: How Economies Fail – and Succeed* (New York: Basic Books, 1978).

[73] I am construing this school more broadly than is traditionally accepted. As well as the Virginia School and its followers, I include here cost-push Keynesians such as Nicholas Kaldor and Samuel Brittan.

[74] The classic contributions to this literature are William D. Nordhaus, "The Political Business Cycle," *Review of Economic Studies* 42 (2) April (1975); C. Duncan MacRae, "A Political Model of the Business Cycle," *Journal of Political Economy* 85 (2) April (1977); Assar Lindbeck, "Stabilization Policy in Open Economies with Endogenous Politicians," *American Economic Review* 66 (2) May (1976); Samuel Brittan, "The Economic Contradictions of Democracy," *British Journal of Political Science* 5, April (1975); James M. Buchanan and Richard E. Wagner, *Democracy in Deficit: The Political Legacy of Lord Keynes* (New York: Academic Press, 1977).

again. Unfortunately, this does not succeed in wringing inflation out of the system as expectations have adapted to the new higher rate, and as a new election fast approaches the state must once again reflate, and so the cycle continues, leading to the increasing inflation and the destabilization of the economy as a function of electoral politics.[75]

Constructing an Inflationary Crisis

Two factors unite all four sets of ideas in opposition to the ideas and institutions of embedded liberalism. First is the belief that inflation is a greater threat to the general welfare than unemployment. Second is the belief that phenomena such as unemployment and inflation are due to the interventions of the state into an otherwise naturally self-equilibrating economy. If the market is seen as naturally self-equilibrating, then any level of employment must accord with the natural rate. As such, there can be no employment policy other than "let the market clear." Inflation, however, augurs no such *laissez faire* solution and requires firm government action.

Inflation is treated differently in this analysis because it is not only regarded as the greatest danger to the stability of a modern industrial economy, but is also seen as being, in some sense, utterly destructive of everything from individual saving to society itself. Such an account accords with common sense, and politicians have always been acutely aware that a perceived drop in the value of currency may be rewarded with defeat at the ballot box.[76] However, what is remarkable about the discussions of inflation that took place in the 1970s was how inflation became public enemy number one, and how one particular theory of inflation as *the* "crisis" of the 1970s became dominant. The inflationary "crisis" of the 1970s was not a situation where the "facts" spoke for themselves. Instead, this was a situation where uncertainty reigned and "facts" demanded a theory. That

---

[75] Public choice theorists expanded the scope of these ideas throughout the 1970s to examine the ways in which politicians maximize votes, thereby giving preference to reelection over aggregate welfare. Bureaucrats earn "rents" from their constituents and generally act to produce suboptimal market outcomes. Where public choice arguments were especially important was in developing the arguments for deregulation and, as we shall see later, in linking the growth of the welfare state with slow growth in Sweden.

[76] Witness the British Prime Minister Harold Wilson's desire to avoid a devaluation of the pound for electoral reasons in the period 1964–6. The real economic effects of a devaluation would have been to lessen balance of payments pressures and to increase export competitiveness. However, Wilson was afraid that people would perceive him as reducing the value of the pound in real terms. As such, when Wilson could no longer avoid devaluation, he appeared on television and went to great lengths to explain that "the pound in your pocket will be worth as much tomorrow as it is today." The point of this example is it shows that if the public believes it to be true, factual, logical, irrational, or not, politicians have to take notice. This is why defining the meaning of inflation and explaining why it constitutes a "crisis" is so central to our discussion.

theory was the synthesis of the ideas of monetarism, rational expectations, supply-side, and public choice theory.

As noted by Matthew Watson, every ten years or so economics develops a new theory of inflation.[77] Each theory is held to be a general theory that applies to all times and places. However, if each supposedly general theory changes every ten or so years, then one must question the extent to which the theory is actually general. If the causes and hence diagnoses of inflation are variable, then the notion that one set of theories can diagnose all inflations as a correspondence theory of the world becomes impossible to sustain. More important, it allows us to see how particular theories become dominant interpretations precisely because they turn present uncertainties into transhistorical facts by appealing to scientific generality. The narration of inflation made possible by these ideas was radical both in terms of the understandings of inflation that preceded, and in terms of the world that such narrations could portray.[78] Only by reference to such ideas, and not to the fact of inflation itself, does the importance of such ideas for attacking embedded liberalism become apparent. No other set of ideas could have constructed such a catastrophe out of what was essentially a rather mild dip in economic performance due to badly handled war financing and unexpected supply shocks.

According to these theories, then, what are the costs of inflation? As Brian Barry argues, "The orthodox interpretation of welfare economics has great difficulty in identifying a welfare loss from inflation at all commensurate with that often loosely attributed to it."[79] One recent survey of the literature on inflation finds that "the costs of inflation, even rates of inflation as high as twenty percent a year, are extremely difficult to find."[80] Indeed, attempts to find such costs by macroeconomists who have built their reputations on the dangers of inflation have reluctantly concluded that "for inflation rates below twenty percent a year ... the relationship between growth and inflation is not statistically significant."[81] Nonetheless, the argu-

---

[77] Matthew Watson, "The Institutional Paradoxes of Monetary Orthodoxy: Reflections on the Political Economy of Central Bank Independence," *Review of International Political Economy* 9 (2) Summer (2002).

[78] In the 1960s, balance of payments disparities were the supposed source of inflation. In the 1970s, technological obsolescence, the social limits to growth, money supply excess, and government largess were all to blame. By the 1980s, labor market rigidities were to blame, whereas by the 1990s a lack of financial market credibility was the villain of the piece. Inflation it seems is many things indeed. See Watson, "Institutional Paradoxes," *passim*.

[79] Brian Barry, "Does Democracy Cause Inflation? Political Ideas of Some Economists?" in Leon N. Lindberg and Charles S. Maier, eds., *The Politics of Inflation and Economic Stagnation: Theoretical Approaches and International Case Studies* (Washington: Brookings Institution, 1985), p. 282.

[80] Jonathan Kirshner, "Inflation: Paper Dragon or Trojan Horse," *Review of International Political Economy* 6 (4) (1999), p. 613.

[81] Robert Barro, "Inflation and Economic Growth," *Bank of England Quarterly Bulletin* 35 (2) (1995), p. 12.

ment that inflation carries real identifiable economic costs was the clarion call of these ideas and went on to become a totem of modern economic thought and practice. Yet such an understanding is far from being either obvious or uncontestable.

Again, as Barry notes, "The assertion that inflation 'can hardly be beneficial to anyone' is extraordinarily implausible. To the extent that inflation is purely redistributive, there are net gainers as well as losers. . . . Against the welfare loss arising . . . [from inflation] . . . must be set the losses of real income and employment created by attempts to reduce inflation."[82] Moreover, if inflation is less than hyperinflation, and if it arises over time, it can be fitted into indexing schemes that allow adjustment of expectations that can both help to stabilize the core rate and maintain the real value of money. The case of hyperinflation seems to be what people have in mind when they think of inflation in general. Yet, there was never any theoretical reason given for any given level of inflation to spiral inexorably into hyperinflation. In short, there is no reason to expect the rate of increase in the rate of inflation to be exponential, especially if agents are assumed to have rational expectations.[83]

Another oft-noted objection is that inflation benefits lenders over debtors. Indeed it does, and this is perhaps a better explanation for why inflation became so feared. Inflation acts as a redistributionary tax on holding debt. Stock prices stagnate and bond prices increase as bond holders demand a premium to guard against the effects of inflation. Investment is hit as inflation eats away at depreciation allowances and stock yields. In response to inflation, investors move out of financial assets and into real assets such as property where the debt to be repaid falls over time. In short, *inflation is a class-specific tax*. Those with credit suffer while those with debt, relatively speaking, prosper. Given then that the benefits of inflation control (restoring the value of debt) are specific while the costs of inflation control (unemployment and economic decline) are diffuse, the reaction of business, particularly the financial sector, to inflation is perhaps best understood as the revolt of the investor class to what it saw as the long-run consequences of embedded liberalism.[84] With this in mind, the apocalyptic pronouncements of the proponents of these new ideas concerning inflation take on a deeper meaning.

[82] Barry, "Political Ideas," p. 294.
[83] This is one of the reasons Alberto Alesina has reformulated business cycle theory to incorporate rational expectations. See Alberto Alesina, *Partisan Politics, Divided Government, and the Economy* (Cambridge: Cambridge University Press, 1995).
[84] For supporting arguments, see Adam Posen, "Why Central Bank Independence Does Not Cause Low Inflation: There Is No Institutional Fix for Politics," in Richard O'Brien, ed., *Finance and the International Economy*, Volume 7 (New York: Oxford University Press, 1993); *Idem.*, "Declarations Are Not Enough: Financial Sector Sources of Central Bank Independence," *National Bureau of Economic Research Macroeconomics Annual* (10) (1995).

For example, public choice theorists James M. Buchanan and Richard E. Wagner maintain that "inflation destroys expectations and creates uncertainty; it increases the sense of felt injustice and causes alienation. It prompts behavioral responses which reflect a generalized shortening of time horizons. 'Enjoy, enjoy!' . . . becomes a rational response . . . where the plans made yesterday seem to have been made in folly."[85] Similarly, Friedman argues that in an inflationary situation, "Prudent behavior becomes reckless and 'reckless' behavior becomes 'prudent.' The society is polarized; one group is set against another. Political unrest increases. The capacity of any government to govern is reduced at the same time that the pressure for strong action grows."[86]

This construction of inflation as an all-encompassing social crisis that was explicable and treatable only in terms of these new ideas fits squarely with what we argued in Chapter 2 concerning the importance of developing and deploying a dominant interpretation of a given crisis as a prerequisite to reducing uncertainty and promoting institutional change. Inflation was a problem, but to maintain that inflation was in some sense "evil" and "benefits no one" is clearly a value judgment designed to promote action against it. Inflation is not a empirical given but a mediated social fact, as is the precise – or, more accurately, vague – understanding of what inflation is that people acquire.[87] In this way, controlling the definition of inflation is inherently political. Responding to inflation is no mere Pavlovian reaction by the public to a crisis. Any crisis, as we saw during the construction of embedded liberalism, has to be diagnosed, deployed, and debated before it can be institutionally resolved. This was precisely why these ideas had such power – the power to change the way the world is seen, by defining what *should* be seen and thus manufacturing new conventions in line with these ideas.

---

[85] Buchanan and Wagner, *Democracy in Deficit*, quoted in Barry, "Political Ideas," p. 284.

[86] Milton Friedman, "Inflation and Unemployment: The New Dimensions of Politics," in Milton Friedman, *Monetarist Economics* (London: Institute of Economic Affairs, 1991), p. 105. Such an apocalyptic view of the 1970s, where the top eight OECD economies had an average annual rate of inflation of 8.8 percent, seems rather exaggerated. As Barry notes, "The fact that academic economists accepted this sort of diagnosis so readily reflects the tendency of positive economics to divide the social realm into one area where the deductive method can be put to work and another that is . . . open to uncontrolled speculation." As Barry continues, "if one is going to maintain such a linkage between socio-cultural change and inflation the causal arrows probably work the other way round, that inflation acts as a safety valve, blurring the impact of incompatible demands." Barry, "Political Ideas," pp. 285, 288.

[87] Especially when one considers that far from evidence for the existence of rational or even vaguely coherent expectations, opinion poll data on public perceptions of inflation show a great deal of confusion about what inflation actually is. See Ben Bernanke, Thomas Laubach, Frederic Mishkin, and Adam Posen, *Inflation Targeting: Lessons from the International Experience* (Princeton: Princeton University Press, 1999), p. 17.

Giving such claims scientific status makes these assertions value-neutral and thus authoritative.[88] What was once merely conservative rhetoric, that in the manner of F. A. Hayek the degree of serfdom was an increasing monotonic function of the level of government, was given social scientific credentials by these new ideas, and these credentials enhanced the ideas' prestige and power.[89] As Paul Krugman has argued,

... a major part of Monetarism's appeal was that it seemed to confirm the conservative prejudice that government activism is always a bad thing. There have without doubt been many conservative thinkers who would have ordinarily been repelled by the crudeness and borderline intellectual dishonesty of Monetarism but were unconsciously moved to overlook its flaws because it fitted their political philosophy. Similarly, many thinkers who would have rebelled at the unrealism bordering on silliness of rational expectations business cycle theory were predisposed to overlook its flaws because of its powerful conservative implications.[90]

Nonetheless, this may still be too sanguine a view of the transformative effects of economic ideas. As argued in Chapter 2, such ideas are not hooks for preexisting interests. Both embedded liberal and neoliberal ideas did not simply provide a justification for preexisting interests. Instead, they succeeded in creating those interests among important sections of the population, that, once promulgated, could be institutionalized and their effects perpetuated across time and space.[91] Both the ideas that were used to make embedded liberalism and the ideas that were used to break it sought to do exactly this. We shall now examine how this was done in the United States and Sweden.

---

[88] Friedman argues that, "Ideological war has raged over these matters, yet the drastic change that has occurred in economic theory has not resulted from divergent political beliefs or aims. It has responded entirely from the force of events." Yet he is also candid enough to admit that, "My own policy position has undoubtedly been affected by the interconnections between value judgments and scientific judgments. Certainly the monetary policy I have come to favor ... is congenial to my preference for limiting government as far as possible." Milton Friedman, "Inflation and Unemployment," p. 110.

[89] See Friedrich A. Hayek, *The Road to Serfdom* (London: Macmillan, 1944), as the classic statement of this thesis, and Albert O. Hirschman, *The Rhetoric of Reaction* (Princeton: Princeton University Press, 1993), as the classic refutation.

[90] Krugman, *Peddling Prosperity*, pp. 52–3.

[91] One need only think of the current trend toward central bank independence as evidence of the increasing institutionalization of these ideas.

6

Disembedding Liberalism in the United States

Building Muscle: The Remobilization of American Business

The policies and practices of the late 1960s and early 1970s detailed in the previous chapter created a new sense of uncertainty among American business. Inflationary pressures, regulatory initiatives, hostile tax legislation, and general policy paralysis combined to convince business that it was under siege within the institutions of economic governance that business itself had designed. Caught between "an avalanche of Congressional, consumer and blue-collar criticism . . . executives became increasingly aware that they needed better negotiating techniques at the federal level."[1] To facilitate this, American business both reinvigorated existing business institutions and developed new ones to protect itself.

For example, the National Association of Manufacturers (NAM) moved its headquarters to Washington, D.C., in 1972 and immediately shifted away from its traditional stance of doctrinaire antireformism toward lobbying, legal research, and closer cooperation with the American Chamber of Commerce (ACC).[2] The ACC went through a thorough revitalization during the 1970s, growing from around sixty thousand member firms in 1972 to two hundred fifty seven thousand by 1982. This quadrupling of members, combined with a sliding fee scale proportionate to income, gave the ACC a budget of $80 million per annum.[3] The ACC also reorganized

---

[1] Kim McQuaid, "The Roundtable: Getting Results in Washington," *Harvard Business Review* 59 (3) May–June (1981), p. 115; *Idem.*, "Big Business and Government Policy in Post New Deal America," *Antitrust Law and Economics Review* (2) 4 (1979); Sar A. Levitan and Martha R. Cooper, *Business Lobbies: The Public Good and the Bottom Line* (Baltimore: John Hopkins University Press, 1984), pp. 34–40.

[2] Principal among NAM's objectives was promoting the research and opinions of a NAM suborganization called the Council for a Union Free Environment (CUFE), which commissioned studies and actively campaigned for a new open-shop drive among employers.

[3] Figures from Levitan and Cooper, *Business Lobbies*, p. 19. Thomas Byrne Edsall gives the ACC operating figures for 1983 at two hundred fifteen thousand members and a budget of $65 million. See Thomas Byrne Edsall, *The New Politics of Inequality* (New York: W. W. Norton and Company, 1984), p. 123.

itself internally and began to operate in three principal areas. First, the ACC began an extensive public relations campaign devoted to countering the public's negative image of business. Second, in response to the move toward class action suits by public interest law firms operating under the new regulatory statutes of the Occupational Safety and Health Administration (OSHA) and the Environmental Protection Agency (EPA), the ACC set up the National Chamber Litigation Center to challenge the litigation brought by activists and the new state regulators.[4] Third, the ACC changed its Congressional lobbying emphasis to focus almost exclusively on grassroots agitation.[5]

A major new business organization that emerged in this period was an outgrowth of the Business Council: the Business Roundtable (BRT). By the mid-1970s, the BRT had largely taken over the Business Council's mantle as the premier business lobbying organization.[6] Though the Roundtable's administrative budget was small, this figure does not begin to capture the BRT's resources.[7] As Mark Green and Andrew Buschbaum argue, "member companies of the Business Roundtable controlled $1,263 trillion in assets and produced $1,265 trillion in revenues in 1978; their collective gross revenues were equal to about one half of the GNP of the United States. If the Business Roundtable were a country, its GNP would be second only to the United States."[8] Given these resources, an individual Roundtable firm's spending on political advertising and public relations could dwarf that of

[4] Levitan and Cooper, *Business Lobbies*, p. 21.

[5] Capitalizing on the Congressional reforms in 1974 that wrested power away from incumbent committee chairs and senior senators, the ACC began to mobilize more from the grassroots up, on the assumption that direct influence at the district level would have a higher payoff as power in Congress was now more diffuse. By 1980, the ACC had set up twenty-seven hundred Congressional Action Committees (CACs) in member districts. These institutional reorganizations were so successful that "within a week [the ACC] could carry out research on the impact of a bill on each legislator's district and through its local branches mobilize a 'grassroots campaign' on the issue in time to affect the outcome of a vote." See Michael Pertschuk, *The Revolt against Regulation* (Berkeley: University of California Press, 1982), pp. 70–1.

[6] The Business Advisory Council reinvented itself as the Business Council during the 1960s and was eventually superceded by the BRT. The same revitalization was not, however, seen in the Committee for Economic Development (CED). The Committee's importance dwindled after 1968 since it suffered from being seen as too weak on labor issues and too closely identified with the Democrats. Once the locus of idea formation began to shift from those organizations with strong links to the state to those outside of it, the CED found itself marginalized. Furthermore, the CED's formal commitment not to lobby but to produce substantive research set it at an institutional disadvantage compared to other more aggressive organizations. See Cathie Jo Martin, "Business and the New Economic Activism: The Growth of Corporate Lobbies in the Sixties," *Polity* 28 (1) Fall (1994).

[7] Its 1979 budget totaled $2.4 million. Mark Green and Andrew Buschbaum, *The Corporate Lobbies: Political Profiles of the Business Roundtable and the Chamber of Commerce* (New York: Public Citizen, 1980), p. 68.

[8] Green and Buschbaum, *The Corporate Lobbies*, p. 68.

all other actors, including the state. Indeed, David Vogel estimates that by 1978 Roundtable firms were spending "between \$850 and \$900 million a year mobilizing their [political] resources."[9]

However, having such vast resources presupposed a strategy of what to do with them, which was itself derivative of why business thought it was under attack in the first place. In answering this question, business

... concluded that the reason [it] had become less popular was because the public was receiving a distorted view of its economic and social performance. Specifically, the institutions responsible for the production of ideas, namely the media and the universities, had become dominated by its critics. Accordingly, business had to learn how to compete more successfully in the marketplace of ideas.[10]

To do this, business developed and deployed a two-pronged strategy. First, it became directly involved in the production and dissemination of alternative ideas. Second, business used these new theories to contest existing economic ideas and the institutions they had spawned. Yet mounting these challenges presupposed another: winning back the state, or at least being able to influence the electoral process to such an extent that further antibusiness legislative assaults would be obviated. What made this possible was the corporate takeover of democracy made possible by the growth of political action committees (PACs).

The Corporate Takeover of Democracy

In 1971 Congress enacted the Campaign Finance Reform Act. This Act sought to increase transparency over the electoral funding process by limiting corporate, union, and private contributions. However, there were exceptions. Businesses and unions could communicate their preferences to stockholders and members respectively, while facilitation of the expenses associated with registration and vote mobilization was also allowed. The most significant exemption, however, was a provision to allow the "solicitation of contributions to a separate segregated fund to be utilized for political purposes by a corporation or a labor organization" – a political action committee, or PAC.[11]

---

[9] David Vogel, quoted in Kim McQuaid, *Uneasy Partners: Big Business in American Politics 1945–1990* (Baltimore: Johns Hopkins University Press, 1994), p. 154.

[10] David Vogel, *Fluctuating Fortunes: The Political Power of Business in America* (New York: Basic Books, 1989), p. 214.

[11] Dan Clawson, Alan Neustadtl, and Denise Scott, *Money Talks: Corporate PACs and Political Influence* (New York: Basic Books, 1992), p. 30. See also Theodore J. Eismeier and Philip H. Pollock III, *Business, Money, and the Rise of Corporate PACs in American Elections* (New York: Quorum Books, 1988).

The logic behind these exceptions was to place business and labor on a level playing field. However, Sun Oil challenged the interpretation of the third exception, and in doing so, at least in the short run, tilted the playing field massively in favor of business. Sun Oil argued that the Act did not preclude business and labor soliciting funds for this fund from anyone, not merely stockholders or members, nor did the Act contain any restrictions on the number of PACs a corporation could set up. Therefore, while limiting any one PAC to a donation of $5,000.00, the Act effectively ended *any* restrictions on corporate donations since the number of PACs could be multiplied exponentially.[12] In 1975 the Federal Election Commission (FEC) upheld this interpretation in the so-called SUNPAC ruling and effectively handed business a license to print political money.

In 1974 there were eighty-nine corporate PACs. These PACs contributed $4.4 million to the 1974 campaigns, with Democrats and Republicans receiving almost equal shares. By 1976 there were 433 corporate PACs, and by 1980 corporate PACs spent over $19.2 million during the single cycle of the presidential election campaign.[13] What is of most significance, however, is not the increase in the scale of funding so much as the change in the funds' distribution.

Beginning in 1978, in response to criticism from pro-market figures such as William Simon and Ronald Reagan, corporate PACs began to shift resources from incumbents to challengers with a clear free-market bias.[14] In September 1978, Democrats received over half of the available PAC funding. *Just one month later*, after the interventions of Simon, Reagan, and others, Democratic incumbents received only 29 percent of available PAC money, and Democratic challengers received less than 1.5 percent of total PAC resources.[15] Business was learning to spend as a class, and such interclass coordination was reinforced by PAC regulations themselves.

Since each PAC was limited to $5,000.00, rather than focusing on marginal changes to benefit individual firms, business increasingly spent as a block.[16] To accomplish this, business developed specific clearinghouse

---

[12] See Clawson et al., *Money Talks*, p. 32; Vogel, *Fluctuating Fortunes*, pp. 119–23.

[13] Figures from Clawson et al., *Money Talks*, p. 33; Vogel, *Fluctuating Fortunes*, p. 207; William C. Berman, *America's Right Turn: From Nixon to Clinton* (Baltimore: Johns Hopkins University Press, 1998), p. 70.

[14] Simon argued, in apocalyptic tones, that business had "betrayed the free enterprise system" by appeasing the Democrats and looking out only for short-term access and political advantage. Reagan argued that giving money to incumbents was simply paying a bribe to make sure that the "alligator will eat you last." Both are quoted in Clawson et al., *Money Talks*, p. 129.

[15] Vogel, *Fluctuating Fortunes*, p. 209; Clawson et al., *Money Talks*, p. 143.

[16] For a discussion of how changes in political opportunity structures facilitate collective action by business, see Dan Clawson, Alan Neustadtl, and James Bearden, "The Logic of Business Unity," *American Sociological Review* 51 (2) (1986); Micheal Useem, *The Inner Circle:*

PACs designed to maximize business's leverage, and the institutions used to do this were the newly invigorated NAM, ACC, and BRT. For example, the NAM's BIPAC (Business Industry Political Action Committee) gained a new lease of life as a coordinating committee for corporate PACs. Meanwhile the ACC's PAC, the National Chamber Alliance for Politics (NCAP), and the most encompassing of all PACs, the National Association of Business Political Action Committees (NABPAC), provided interindustry coordination of spending as well as candidate endorsement, direction, and information.[17] In sum, during this period, business marshaled and expended tremendous resources on the goal of stacking the deck in the legislature.

These new organizations provided the infrastructure and resources to halt simple legislative assaults. However, if business wanted to win the debate over the role and function of business within modern American life, it had to recast the actual terms of that debate. Critical in doing so were three business foundations that provided both the capital and the institutional contacts in universities and the media to develop and deploy alternative economic ideas. The Smith Richardson Foundation, the Scaife Funds, and the Olin Foundation were the prime movers in mounting an intellectual counterattack against embedded liberalism. These funds bankrolled, in whole or in part, a substantial number of policy institutes and think tanks that were explicitly designed to promote free-market and anti-embedded liberal ideas.

Bankrolling Ideas

A division of labor existed among the think tanks that these funds bankrolled. On the one hand, there were institutions tasked to promote a general affirmation of competitive capitalism. Chief among these were the Heritage Foundation; the American Enterprise Institute (AEI); the Hoover Institute on War, Revolution and Peace; and the Center for the Study of American Business (CSAB). Other institutes, chief among them the National Bureau of Economic Research (NBER), received business backing to promote specific projects and provide expert consultancy to business regarding why existing institutions and ideas were inappropriate.

The Heritage Foundation was established in 1973 with a budget of a little under $1 million donated by Joseph Coors, Richard Mellon Scaife, and Simon, Nixon's ex-treasury secretary and head of the Olin Foundation. By 1981 Heritage's budget would rise to $7.1 million per year.[18] The Heritage Foundation grew out of conservative dissatisfaction within the

Large Corporations and the Rise of Business Political Activity in the U.S. and the U.K.
(New York: Oxford University Press, 1984).
[17] Vogel, *Fluctuating Fortunes*, p. 208.
[18] Figures from Edsall, *The New Politics of Inequality*, pp. 117–18.

Nixon administration. The consensus among conservatives working in the Nixon administration was that they were "surrounded by hostile federal bureaucrats and a web of liberal think-tanks," which meant conservatives often went "native" in the federal system.[19] Heritage was founded to counter this trend and quickly evolved into one of the main idea generators across a whole series of public policy issues.[20]

The Hoover Institute, founded in 1919, had the same benefactors as the Heritage Foundation, namely Simon, Scaife, and Coors. Over 40 percent of Hoover's annual operating budget of $8.4 million came from business foundations, specifically the Scaife, Olin, and Smith Richardson funds, which gave the institute over $4.89 million between 1979 and 1982.[21] The Hoover Institute was particularly prominent in both diagnosing and then analyzing the pathologies and perverse effects of welfare provision. In particular, Hoover economist Martin Anderson argued that not only was the welfare system a net drain on the economy, but also that the amount spent on welfare, if left in private hands, would have produced economic growth sufficient to obliterate the poverty that the welfare institutions were designed to alleviate. Such institutions were therefore seen to keep people poor by discouraging risk taking and by creating a cycle of dependency.[22]

The American Enterprise Institute (AEI), established in 1943, was a rather moribund institution by the beginning of the 1970s. However, by 1980, it had been invigorated by a rise in its budget from $879,000 in 1970 to $10.4 million. These sums were provided by the Pew Charitable Trust, as well as Olin, Scaife, Smith Richardson, and other corporate donations.[23] This expansion of funds made the AEI the institutional home of both popular and more policy-focused conservative economics. Herbert Stein, Arthur Burns, Paul McCracken, and a host of other conservative economists took up residency or conducted policy-focused research under the auspices of the AEI. Through a series of books, papers, and policy analyses, the AEI set itself up as the major source of criticism of the policy orthodoxy in the late 1970s. In particular, the AEI campaigned for formal fiscal

---

[19] James Allen Smith, *The Idea Brokers: Think Tanks and the Rise of the New Policy Elite* (New York: Free Press, 1991), p. 196.

[20] Heritage specialized in policy "backgrounders" and "bulletins" for Congress, and began to market these ideas aggressively beyond the beltway. See Berman, *America's Right Turn*, pp. 67–8.

[21] Edsall, *The New Politics of Inequality*, pp. 117–18.

[22] Martin Anderson, *Welfare: The Political Economy of Welfare Reform in the United States* (Stanford: Stanford University Press, 1978), esp. pp. 43–58. This argument formed the core of the 1981 best seller by Charles Murray on the pathologies of welfare, *Losing Ground*. See Charles A. Murray, *Losing Ground: American Social Policy 1950–1980* (New York: Basic Books, 1984).

[23] Edsall, *The New Politics of Inequality*, p. 120; Berman, *America's Right Turn*, p. 67; Vogel, *Fluctuating Fortunes*, p. 224.

restrictions on federal government spending and targeted its products to the media, especially leader writers and Congressional research staff.[24]

The Center for the Study of American Business (CSAB), while smaller than these other institutions, was critical in developing an intellectual reply to the case for regulation. CSAB's chief economist, Murray Weidenbaum, later a Reagan Council of Economics Advisors (CEA) member, produced a series of highly influential monographs that challenged the rationale for regulation. Weidenbaum argued that the total social cost of regulation was greater than the social cost of having no regulation at all. In addition to spawning huge self-perpetuating federal bureaucracies, as public choice theory had argued, such regulations cost business millions of dollars in unproductive activities that not only took away from business's bottom line, but in and of themselves contributed to the falling productivity rates.[25]

However, as Thomas Edsall has noted in his discussion of these new pro-business think tanks, "perhaps most influential in pushing policy to the right has been Martin Feldstein."[26] As the president of the NBER, an organization that in 1983 received over 45 percent of its budget in donations from Fortune 500 companies, Feldstein provided the serious intellectual rationale for the supply-side tax cuts of the late 1970s. Feldstein did not argue for the supply-side effects tax cuts as Arthur Laffer and Paul Craig Roberts were to do later in the decade. Instead, Feldstein focused upon the relationship between productivity growth and the rate of return on capital in an inflationary environment.

Feldstein argued that inflation acted as a tax on investment that reduced its return. Feldstein's econometrics purported to show that because of inflation, the real effective tax rate on investment was as much as 40 percent higher than the nominal rate. Therefore, rather than attempting to defeat inflation by affecting expectations, as the monetarists would shortly try to do, what needed to be done to restore growth was to make an "end run" around inflation and cut taxes by the equivalent amount necessary to obviate inflation's tax effects.[27] Feldstein applied the same framework to

---

[24] Indeed, the AEI spent fully 36 percent of its operating budget on marketing during this period. As William Baroody, Jr., head of the AEI from 1978 to 1986, put it, "we pay as much attention to dissemination of product as we do to the content.... We hire ghost writers for scholars to produce op-ed articles that are sent to one hundred and one cooperating newspapers – three pieces every two weeks." See David M. Ricci, *The Transformation of American Politics: Think Tanks and the Rise of the New Policy Elite* (New Haven: Yale University Press, 1993), p. 171.

[25] Weidenbaum estimated that cost of government regulation net of any benefits by 1979 as $102.7 billion. See Murray Weidenbaum, U.S. Congress, Joint Economic Committee, Subcommittee on Economic Growth and Stabilization. *The Cost of Government Regulation.* Hearings. April 1978 (Washington: Government Printing Office, 1978) (Y4.Ec7:C82/4).

[26] Edsall, *The New Politics of Inequality*, p. 219.

[27] See Martin Feldstein, *Inflation, Tax Rules and Capital Formation* (Chicago: University of Chicago Press, 1983); *Idem.*, "Incidence of a Capital Income Tax in a Growing Economy

capital gains and estimated that in 1973 alone inflation cost United States investors an extra $500 million in capital gains.[28] The optimal policy to beat inflation, restore growth, and increase productivity was therefore to increase investment, and the way to do this was through tax cuts.[29]

Feldstein also contributed to the debate over welfare, stressing in particular the perverse incentive effects of unemployment compensation and social security taxes.[30] Feldstein argued that unemployment compensation acted as a tax on income that workers would otherwise earn. Therefore, to overcome the disutility of work that this promotes, the offered wage would have to be enlarged by the amount of the benefit currently received.[31] Therefore, while inflation was seen to increase the nominal wage, welfare benefits were seen to increase the real wage artificially and hence lower productivity.[32]

In addition to funding these primarily "elite-focused" think tanks, Scaife and Olin were instrumental in bringing these new ideas, particularly the work of Feldstein and Friedman, to the general public. For example, in 1977 the Scaife Foundation gave $650,000 to WQLN in Pennsylvania to produce a television version of Milton Friedman's *Free to Choose*.[33] These funds also supported neoconservative journals such as *Public Interest*, which were a

with a Variable Savings Rate," *Review of Economic Studies* 41 (2) (1974); *Idem.*, "Inflation and Supply Side Economics," *Wall Street Journal*, May 20 (1980). For Feldstein's popular effectiveness, see Ann Crittenden, "Feldstein: The Bull in a Data Shop," *New York Times*, May 20, 1979; Soma Golden, "Superstar of the New Economists," *New York Times Magazine*, March 23, 1980.

[28] Martin Feldstein and Joel Slemrod, "Inflation and the Excess Taxation of Capital Gains on Corporate Stock," *NBER Working Paper Series* (234), February 1987.

[29] Feldstein's arguments were similar to and bolstered by the work of Hoover economist Michael Boskin. Boskin reinvigorated the classical argument that the tax system discouraged saving and hurt growth. See Michael Boskin, "Taxation, Savings and the Rate of Interest" *Journal of Political Economy* 86 (2) April (1978). See also Michael Boskin and Jerry Green, "Taxation and Capital Formation: Missing Elements in the President's Tax Plan," in Rudolph Penner, ed., *Tax Policies in the 1979 Budget* (Washington: American Enterprise Institute, 1978), pp. 47–54.

[30] See Martin Feldstein, "Unemployment Compensation: Adverse Incentives and Distributional Anomalies," *National Tax Journal* 27 (2) June (1974).

[31] In line with the other ideas of this period, Feldstein's model views unemployment as voluntary.

[32] Similarly, Feldstein argued that Social Security taxes were a net drain on capital formation because they were paid out on a pay-as-you-go basis. As such, they constituted a net loss from the savings-investment stream. This was compounded by the fact that by socializing the risk of suboptimal private saving, Social Security actually encouraged individuals to reduce their saving, which further exacerbated the capital shortage. Martin Feldstein, "National Saving in the United States," in Eli Shapiro and William White, *Capital for Productivity and Jobs* (Englewood Cliffs, NJ: Prentice Hall, 1977).

[33] This series was shown widely on public television in the United States and in the United Kingdom in 1978 and 1979. See Milton Friedman and Rose Friedman, *Free to Choose: A Personal Statement* (New York: Harcourt Brace Jovanovich, 1980).

further means of spreading these ideas beyond the D.C. beltway policy community.[34] As Olin Fund President Simon argued, in order to influence the climate of opinion, business should exchange funds in return for "books, books, and more books." The object of doing so was to "funnel desperately needed funds to scholars, social scientists, writers, and journalists who understand the relationship between political and economic liberty."[35] By funding both individual scholars and entire institutions that understood this relationship "properly," business could use these new ideas to delegitimate the institutions of embedded liberalism.

Pushing for tax cuts with a logic similar to Feldstein's was the American Council for Capital Formation (ACCF). The ACCF was primarily focused on influencing Congressional opinion on taxation issues.[36] The ACCF's arguments about taxation were straightforward and resolutely anti-Keynesian. Keynesian models assumed that the level of income determined the level of output and hence investment demand. In contrast, the ACCF, strongly influenced by Feldstein's NBER studies, argued that the level of output determined the level of income, and thus ultimately the supply of investment. Consequently, the main fetter holding back increased investment was the prohibitive tax rates that pertained on investment and perverted incentives. Since high taxation hurt savings, which reduced investment and created a capital shortage, this in turn lowered productivity and reduced growth.

Consequently, according to both the NBER and the ACCF, if the problem facing the state was sclerotic growth, then the answer was simple: Lighten the tax burden. If taxes were cut, capital would be more abundant, and greater investment in plant and equipment would be forthcoming.[37] This in turn would increase productivity and growth, thereby curing stagflation.[38] Despite the dubiousness of these claims, the ACCF succeeded in turning the

---

[34] Scaife funds provided the *National Interest*'s publisher with $380,000 to cover operating costs between 1977 and 1982. See Thomas Ferguson and Joel Rogers, *Right Turn: The Decline of the Democrats and the Future of American Politics* (New York: Hill and Wang, 1986), p. 88.

[35] Simon, quoted in Ferguson and Rogers, *Right Turn*, pp. 86–7.

[36] The ACCF was headed by Simon's assistant at the Treasury, Charls Walker.

[37] This is merely a restatement of Say's Law. Yet, there are good reasons to doubt this automatic translation of savings into investment. Specifically, while savings and investment must be equal in the aggregate, this is merely an accounting contrivance, and not a statement of fact, since the liquidity preference of uncertain investors combines with the interest rate to disrupt this supposed automatic linkage.

[38] For perhaps the clearest statement of the ACCF's logic, see the testimony of David I. Meiselman to U.S. Congress. Joint Economic Committee. Subcommittee on Economic Growth and Stabilization. *The Role of Federal Tax Policy in Stimulating Capital Formation and Growth*. Hearings, July 1977 (Washington: Government Printing Office, 1977) (Y4.Ec7:T19/11). On the ACCF in general, see Robert Kuttner, *The Revolt of the Haves: Tax Rebellions and Hard Times* (New York: Simon and Schuster, 1980), pp. 250–71.

notion of a capital shortage into a Congressional obsession in the late 1970s. The openings that provided business with this opportunity were threefold: the threat of another set of reformist tax changes being passed by Congress in 1978; increasing grassroots resentment and popular mobilization over the issue of property taxes; and the current, but still relatively mild, inflationary state of the economy.

Challenging Embedded Liberalism

Constructing a Capital Formation Crisis

During the 1976 presidential campaign, candidate Jimmy Carter remarked that the United States tax code was a "disgrace to the human race," and that subsidies such as tax-deductible three-martini business lunches could not be tolerated at a time of national hardship.[39] These remarks became the impetus for the next round of reformist taxation. In January 1978 Carter unveiled his tax reform measures. These reforms proposed cutting middle-class taxes and eliminating the three-martini lunch. However, in an effort to placate business, Carter also included a provision to cut corporate tax rates and make permanent the investment tax credit that Congress had offered on and off to business since 1962.

While tax reform in part stemmed from the president's agenda, what really put tax reform back on the agenda of Congress was the growing tax revolt in California and elsewhere over property taxes. Briefly, due to a change in assessment techniques initiated in the 1960s and designed to stop local corruption, the periodic revaluation of residential property in California became automatic and mandatory. Unfortunately, inflation and real estate prices skyrocketed in the 1970s, effectively doubling, or in some cases tripling, the property taxes faced by Californian homeowners. Consequently, because the state did not reduce tax rates, state surpluses built up while homeowners faced seemingly exponentially increasing tax bills. In reaction to this, grassroots efforts by tax activists such as Howard Jarvis put Proposition 13 on the California ballot. This tax reform initiative threatened to slash the tax base of state government. Not only was Proposition 13 passed, it inspired drives in other states, and soon tax reduction, regardless of the form, became a national crusade. As one Oregon state legislator put it, Proposition 13 "was a bullet from a loaded gun that went off in California. . . . But it's still on its way to its ultimate target – the high level of federal spending."[40]

[39] Throughout the campaign in 1976, Carter repeatedly invoked the story of the businessman who reputedly had 338 of these lunches at a cost to the taxpayer of some $10,000. Quoted in, among other sources, Vogel, *Fluctuating Fortunes*, p. 174.

[40] Unidentified Oregon state legislator, quoted in Godfrey Hodgson, *The World Turned Right Side Up: A History of Conservative Ascendance in America* (New York: Houghton Mifflin, 1996), p. 205. See also Kuttner, *The Revolt of the Haves*, esp. pp. 17–107, 273–351.

The ACCF capitalized upon this general hostility to taxation, and business's particular hostility to Carter's proposals, and sought to portray the issue of capital gains taxation as being part and parcel of the general "revolt against government" going on across the country. To counter these proposals, ACCF principal Charls Walker retained fellow BRT member Walter Wriston's Chase Manhattan subsidiary, Chase Econometrics, to estimate the effects of a *rise* in capital gains taxes on growth. Meanwhile, also under ACCF auspices, the Security Industries Association hired Data Resources Incorporated to calculate the positive effects of a capital gains *cut* on growth and productivity. Both studies purported to show that cutting the capital gains tax would spur growth by a margin greater than the value of the tax cut itself, whereas any further increases would actually reduce net revenues as well as depress growth and investment further.[41] Using these studies, the ACCF capitalized upon this popular disquiet over taxes and claimed the issue as its own.

Representative William Steiger was enlisted by the ACCF to sponsor legislation rolling back capital gains taxes.[42] Business rallied around these proposals and extensively lobbied Congress for the legislation's passage. In August 1978 the House passed Steiger's bill, which cut the capital gains tax 25 percent, removed capital gains from exposure to "minimum tax" schedules, and indexed stock and real estate values.[43] This bill was, however, merely the beginning of business's efforts in reversing taxation priorities. The proselytizing zeal of the ACCF and the BRT spread far beyond Capitol Hill, and tax reduction in all forms became the most prevalent and popular political crusade in the nation.

Spreading Supply-Side Ideas

At the same time as the ACCF was rewriting capital gains taxation, Representative Jack Kemp was rewriting other aspects of the tax code. Kemp's first major piece of legislation was the Savings and Investment Act of 1974. This Act proposed to increase business asset depreciation write-offs from 20 to 40 percent and increase and make permanent the investment tax credit at 15 percent. In 1975, after the failure of this Bill in the House, Kemp hired Roberts as his staff economic expert. Roberts joined forces with an economist and consultant to the BRT named Norman Ture. Using BRT funding, Ture constructed an econometric model of the economy based on

---

[41] Data Resources Incorporated, "Tax Policy, Investment and Economic Growth," Securities Industry Association, March (1978); Chase Econometrics, "The Economic Effects of Cutting Capital Gains Taxes," Chase Manhattan Bank, April (1978).

[42] As former Steiger aid Mark Bloomfield remarked at the time, "the Capital Formation Council became a virtual extension of Steiger's staff." Mark Bloomfield, quoted in Kuttner, *Revolt of the Haves*, p. 244.

[43] *Ibid.*, p. 247.

supply-side assumptions.[44] The Roberts-Ture models argued that had the 1974 Savings and Investment Act tax cuts been enacted, the result would have been to *increase* tax revenues by $5.2 billion.[45] Kemp staffers such as Roberts used the studies of Ture and others to turn the terms of debate in Congress. Supply-side advocates used forums such as the Senate Finance Committee and the Congressional Budget Office (CBO) to popularize their ideas, much as underconsumptionists in the 1930s had used the TNEC hearing to spread their message.[46] In particular, Roberts managed to damage severely the Keynesian arguments of the CBO during Congressional hearings on taxation and economic policy in 1978.

In these hearings, Roberts publicized the fact that according to the CBO's econometric studies, GNP was assumed to *fall* if tax rates on business were cut, which was exactly the opposite conclusions to the Roberts-Ture models. CBO chief Alice Rivlin defended this position and disputed the claim that cutting taxes would create any incentive to save or invest.[47] In response, Roberts went on the offensive and argued that the incentive effect of a tax cut would be so great that even if the drop in revenue to the state was sufficiently large to cause a drop in consumption in the short run, this would quickly be obviated by new investment and growth.

What made this position persuasive was that Roberts was able to persuade one of the CBO model's authors, Michael Evans of Chase Econometrics, the same group that had just produced an influential supply-side model for the ACCF, to testify to Congress that the CBO's assumptions about taxes and GDP were in error. Evans testified before the Senate Budget Committee that the CBO model was "bad economics" and that "there is no mention of [supply-side effects] in the CBO model."[48] Despite the complaints of Rivlin that Roberts and Evans were part of "an extreme right-wing clique who should not be given an audience," this criticism of the

[44] Paul Craig Roberts, *The Supply Side Revolution: An Insiders Account of Policymaking in Washington* (Cambridge: Harvard University Press, 1984), p. 31.
[45] What Roberts built into his model, and what Kemp made his own, was the "Laffer" effect – before Laffer's name was attached to it. However, whether Kemp discovered the Laffer effect before the *Wall Street Journal* made Laffer famous is not the point. The point is that two movements, one inside Congress and the other in the financial press, both played supporting roles for each other by spreading supply-side ideas. See Bruce R. Bartlett, *Reaganomics: Supply Side Economics in Action* (Westport, CT: Arlington House Publishers, 1981), p. 127.
[46] See especially Roberts, *The Supply Side Revolution*, pp. 34–69, on the battles between supply-siders and more orthodox economists in the CBO such as Alice Rivlin. For the TNEC hearing, see Chapter 3.
[47] Roberts, *The Supply Side Revolution*, pp. 34–6; Bartlett, *Reaganomics*, pp. 85–90.
[48] See Michael Evans, U.S. Congress, Senate. Committee on the Budget. Second Concurrent Resolution on the Budget, FY 79, July. Hearings (Washington: Government Printing Office, 1978) (Y4.B85/2:C74/979-2).

CBO's model allowed Roberts to run roughshod over objections by Rivlin and others about the validity of the incentive and revenue-raising claims of supply-side ideas.[49] This debacle enhanced the credibility of supply-side arguments in Congress immensely.[50]

It is important to remember that all this occurred despite the fact that the economics profession itself regarded the supply-side thesis with disdain and by and large ignored it. Just as we saw in the 1930s, when academic economists steadfastly refused to recognize the *economic* importance of popular economic ideas such as administered prices and underconsumptionist theories, in the 1970s they refused to recognize the *political* importance of supply-side theory.[51] As Roberts argued, "the fight over economic models went on so long and so hard because more was at stake than economic reputations. *The real issue was political power.* A supply-side tax cut would reduce the power of government relative to the private sector."[52]

In fact, the theory's simplicity proved to be its strongest asset. Whereas supply-side arguments in the capital formation camp were based upon incentive effects and productivity enhancements, the Laffer-Kemp-Roberts version simply stated that a lower tax rate would produce increased revenue. As Hugh Heclo and Richard Penner observed, "as far as treating an ailing economy was concerned, supply-side theory was the equivalent of laughing gas."[53] However, what was needed to solidify these achievements, to "bolt" them into a coherent alternative set of economic ideas, was a synthesis of these disparate elements. Feldstein's work on taxes and incentives, the ACCF's capital gains ideas, and the Kemp-Roberts arguments on income taxes all needed a fulcrum around which they could be articulated as a single coherent package. This synthesis occurred because of two factors: the existence of alternative economic ideas and the political power of the financial press.

A Lafferite Synthesis?

The *Wall Street Journal* acted as both effective synthesizer and chief proselytizer for these disparate ideas. The synthesis of Roberts, Kemp, and the

---

[49] Rivlin, quoted in Bartlett, *Reaganomics*, p. 92.

[50] See Roberts, *The Supply Side Revolution*, pp. 42–4, 53–7; David Meiselman and Paul Craig Roberts, "The Political Economy of the Congressional Budget Office," in Karl Brunner and Allan Meltzer, eds., *Three Aspects of Policy Making: Knowledge, Data and Institutions* (New York: North-Holland Publishing, 1979); Juan Cameron, "The Economic Modelers Vie for Washington's Ear," *Fortune*, November 20, 1978, pp. 102–5.

[51] Indeed, Paul Samuelson reportedly once gave a lecture at Harvard in 1978 called "laughing at Laffer." However, while professional economists were laughing, these ideas were being written into policy.

[52] Roberts, *The Supply Side Revolution*, p. 53, my italics.

[53] Hugh Heclo and Richard Penner, "Fiscal and Political Strategy in the Reagan Administration," in Fred Greenstein, ed., *The Reagan Presidency: An Early Assessment* (Baltimore: Johns Hopkins University Press, 1983) p. 27.

ACCF developed and deployed by the *Journal* was the Laffer curve. Laffer's curve argued that the current tax system not only produced less revenue the higher the rate of taxation, but that, in actual fact, the curve was backward bending; lower rates of taxation would produce greater revenue. *Wall Street Journal* leader writer Jude Wanninski began popularizing Laffer's ideas in the *Journal* as far back as 1974.[54] Wanninski apparently did not meet Kemp until 1977, when he told Kemp about the ideas of Laffer and other supply-side advocates such as Robert Mundell.[55] Kemp immediately saw the relationship between his ideas and those of Wanninski and Laffer, and Wanninski reciprocated by becoming Kemp's biggest supporter.[56]

The Laffer curve united the disparate ideas used to attack embedded liberal institutions. For example, the simple proposition of the backward-bending revenue curve could be coopted by those interested in projects as diverse as monetarism (cutting taxes limits money supply growth and thus reduces inflation) and capital formation (any tax cut has a positive incentive effect). Apart from Wanninski's pieces, the *Wall Street Journal* as a whole became

... a sort of bulletin board for ... commentary by the network of conservative and neo-conservative intellectuals and out-of-power policy makers. But it was on economic matters that [Robert] Bartley's editorial page played out its most active role, the publicizing and popularizing [of] theories that still seemed extreme to people grounded in orthodox economics.[57]

In addition to the *Journal*, Irving Kristol's *The Public Interest* began to actively support the supply-side case. Even Friedman's column in *Newsweek* magazine began to resound very positively to the case for supply-side economics, albeit primarily as a way to cap government spending and thus reduce inflation.[58] Meanwhile, as David Wayne Parsons notes, independent authors such as George Gilder, whose work was bankrolled by business foundations and written in business think tanks, was published widely in

[54] Wanninski's supply-side writings first appeared in the *Wall Street Journal* on December 11, 1974.

[55] On Mundell's relationship to the supply-side theorists, see Paul Krugman, *Peddling Prosperity: Sense and Nonsense in the Age of Diminished Expectations* (New York: W. W. Norton and Company, 1994), pp. 86–9.

[56] On the popularization of supply-side theory in the *Wall Street Journal* and other media sources, see Bartlett, *Reaganomics*, p. 127; David Wayne Parsons, *The Power of the Financial Press* (London: Edward Elgar, 1989), pp. 161–4; William Greider, *The Education of David Stockman and Other Americans* (New York: E. P. Dutton Inc., 1981), pp. 96–101.

[57] Dan Morgan, *Washington Post*, February 15, 1981, quoted in Parsons, *The Power of the Financial Press*, pp. 160–1. For the relationship between Wanninski, Bartlett, and Laffer, see Hodgson, *The World Turned Right Side Up*, pp. 194–8, 208–10.

[58] For a representative example of *The Public Interests'* output, see "The Mundell-Laffer Hypothesis: A New View of the World Economy," *The Public Interest* (39) Winter (1975).

magazines as diverse as *Harper's* and the *Reader's Digest*, thereby adding to the popularization of supply-side doctrines.[59] Finally, all of this occurred within the context of the inflation and tax revolts of the late 1970s. These factors combined with the general perceived antipathy toward government in the wake of Vietnam and Watergate to make the supply-side message all the more effective. Academic concern with inflation, aggressive business lobbing, Congressional supply-siders, press proselytizers, and tax revolutionaries all combined to bring conservative opposition to the political assaults and economic uncertainties of the 1970s under one banner, that of the "supply-side revolution." This revolution's solutions may have been economically dubious at best, but these ideas did successfully diagnose uncertainties, identify causal relationships, encourage new patterns of collective action through the renarration of interests, and advocate alternative institutional solutions to the crisis in a way that the defenders of embedded liberalism could not do.[60]

Destabilizing Embedded Liberalism

The Failure of the State

In a striking parallel to what was occurring in Sweden at this juncture, these intellectual and legislative challenges combined with the failure of the state to destabilize embedded liberal institutions further. This failure was principally ideational. Despite the huge intellectual battles under way inside and outside of Congress, Carter's administration did little to respond to these intellectual challenges and indeed actually furthered them. Carter portrayed himself as a centrist, and rode on the back of popular resentment of government. Despite this self-portrayal, Carter effectively governed as a classical liberal. The basic reasons for this were twofold. First, during the 1976 primaries, Governor Jerry Brown berated President Gerald Ford for creating deficits and supported moves for a constitutional amendment to balance the budget. In an attempt to outflank Brown, Carter adopted the "deficits cause inflation" argument, and after the primaries Carter repeatedly attacked Ford on the issue of deficits, noting that they were "larger than all the Kennedy-Johnson years combined," thus evidencing "the worst fiscal

---

[59] See Parsons, *The Power of the Financial Press*, pp. 163–6.

[60] The critics of supply-side theory in the *New York Times* and the *Washington Post*, such as Hobart Rowen, and academic opponents such as Samuelson, were long on critique but short on alternative ideas or defenses of existing ones. In large part this was a genuine, but unnecessary, intellectual failure. By reducing Keynesianism to the proposition that wages are sticky, Keynesians working within the neoclassical synthesis could not explain what was going on in the economy. They knew that it was not due to a capital shortage – a simple glance at interest rates would tell anyone that – but they were unable to articulate an effective opposition. Moreover, Carter's insistence on a "deficits cause inflation" link effectively discounted whatever room to maneuver the Keynesians had. Consequently, Wanninski et al., came to occupy the intellectual high ground as much by default as by design.

management in our history."[61] Berating Ford for promoting huge deficits served Carter well as an electoral weapon. However, once in power, and despite the OMB and the CEA finding no significant econometric or other evidence to support the proposition that deficits cause inflation, Carter adhered to this idea, and this adherence became increasingly strident in the face of a multiplicity of policy failures in other areas ranging from labor law reform to foreign policy.[62]

However, by accepting this understanding of inflation and the general causes of the instability and uncertainty of the period, Democratic policy options became increasingly narrow over time. Carter's chief economic advisor during the 1976 campaign, Thomas Lance, advised Carter to stay clear of any reinstatement of mandatory wage and price guidelines because of the effect they would have on business confidence.[63] Consequently, Carter sought to control inflation by voluntary means. In April 1977, Carter unveiled a series of voluntary wage and price targets that were to prove to have no effect on inflation. By January 1978, the consumer price index (CPI) reached an annual compounded rate of 9.9 percent, and by April this had shot up to 16.8 percent. Voluntarism was once again proving less than worthless, while legislation was proving to be toothless. In the midst of these multiplying policy failures, Carter's tax reform proposals were hijacked by business, while the economic ideas governing the institutions that Carter was attempting to save were being reshaped by business and the financial press. Given such incoherent and ineffectual policy responses, the financial markets went into a free fall, and in response Carter reluctantly turned to Paul Volker to head the Federal Reserve to appease the markets. Supply-side logics had conquered Congress. Now monetarism was about to dominate the Fed.

Monetarism, the Federal Reserve, and Wall Street

John Kenneth Galbraith once remarked that "what is called sound finance is very often what mirrors the needs of the respectably affluent."[64] Volker's

---

[61] *The Presidential Campaign of 1976*, Volume 1, Part 2, Jimmy Carter (Washington: Government Printing Office, 1978), pp. 749, 755, quoted in James D. Savage, *Balanced Budgets and American Politics* (Ithaca: Cornell University Press, 1986), p. 198.

[62] What complicated this was Carter's sincere belief that deficits did in fact cause inflation and that balancing the cash budget was the most prudent fiscal management the state could follow. As Carter himself noted, "I had inherited the largest deficit in history – more than $66 billion – and it was important to me personally to stop the constantly escalating federal expenditures that tended to drive up interest rates which [were] the root cause of inflation and unemployment." James Carter, *Keeping the Faith: Memoirs of a President* (New York: Bantam Books, 1982), quoted in Savage, *Balanced Budgets*, p. 315, fn. 92.

[63] Hobart Rowen, *Self-Inflicted Wounds: From LBJ's Guns and Butter to Reagan's Voodoo Economics* (New York: Times Books, 1994), p. 169.

[64] John Kenneth Galbraith, *Money: Whence It Came and Where It Went* (New York: Houghton Mifflin and Company, 1975), quoted in William Greider, *Secrets of the Temple: How the Federal Reserve Runs the Country* (New York: Simon and Schuster, 1987), p. 56.

policy choices reflected this privilege. Volker wanted to raise interest rates in order to reduce inflationary expectations through an orthodox credit crunch and deflation. Given the shift in both popular and Congressional economic opinion then under way, Volker jumped upon the monetarist bandwagon and began to stress the need for "credibility" in monetary policy. As monetarism was little more than the quantity theory redux, its policy prescriptions were quite simple. If prices were increasing while real output was lagging, it was because of an expansive money supply. Therefore, to reduce the general price level, one should simply reduce the money supply.[65]

Volker was able to pursue this policy because in 1978, prior to the Fed's monetarist turn, Congress mandated that the Fed publish, publicize, and adhere to a regime of monetary targeting – the essence of monetarism in practice.[66] On August 16, 1979, Volker increased the discount rate to 10.5 percent, and then increased it again on September 18 to 11.75 percent. On September 28, 1979, Volker formally changed Federal Reserve policy over to a regime of money supply targeting, regardless of movements in interest rates.[67]

However, it is not the case that Volker was, like Dennis Healy, a "reluctant monetarist." Volker's and the Fed's Open Market Committee's adoption of monetarism was much more than skin deep. Within the Federal Reserve system, the St. Louis Fed had "made itself into a kind of guerrilla outpost for monetarism" long before Volker's appointment.[68] The St. Louis Fed ran its own monetarist econometric model that worked at counterpoint to the Washington Fed's Keynesian model. This was to prove to be highly influential. For as continuing inflation and policy failures increased uncertainty within markets, so the markets themselves increasingly adhered to a monetarist interpretation of the crisis, and over time, so did the Fed's governing board.[69]

Volker bandwagoned with the monetarists and argued that if the Fed dramatically changed its targeting regime, then as predicted by rational expectations arguments, the new policy regime of targeting M1 (notes and coins in circulation) would become transparent and credibility would be enhanced. Consequently, investors would have less fear of inflation because

---

[65] Volker cloaked himself in this policy as it allowed the raising of interest rates, but it did so indirectly. By restricting the money supply, the policy effectively rationed credit, with the interest rate functioning as the rationing device.

[66] The Democrats in Congress were uniformly eager to jump on the bandwagon with the Republicans on this issue as it shifted the blame for rising inflation and interest rates from the Congress to the Fed.

[67] Figures are from the Federal Reserve Economic Database located at http://www.stls.fred.org.

[68] Greider, *Secrets of the Temple*, p. 97.

[69] *Ibid.*, p. 98.

increases in the money supply could be clearly monitored. Agents would then revise their expectations downward in line with the proposed targets, and the much sought after painless deflation could be brought about.[70] What gave these ideas the opening they needed was just around the corner.

OPEC once again provided that opportunity with a second set of price rises. OPEC increased oil prices by 14.5 percent and then 25 percent in late 1979. These increases combined to help push the inflation rate to 16.8 percent. This gave the Fed the chance to demonstrate its monetarist credentials. While the money supply contracted from a monthly compounded growth rate of 12.8 percent in February 1980 to a decline of −17.2 percent in March, the federal funds rate increased to 18 percent in March 1980, a 50 percent increase since the previous October.[71] In this context, financial markets were suffering heavy losses, and the need for stability and credibility became paramount. Thus financial markets sought, just as Chapter 2 argued, a new convention to govern their expectations.

Another factor promoting the shift of financial markets over to monetarism was a paradox embedded within the "new" classical economics itself. The original rational expectations work done by John Muth noted that being consistently surprised by government policy was unnecessarily expensive for the agents involved since such agents were assumed to have an accurate model of the economy in their heads. Given this, such agents would instead use information efficiently, thereby effectively discounting the actions of government before they occurred. In reality, however, and especially in this period, agents neither had such a mental model nor discounted state actions.[72] What agents possessed instead were multiple and conflicting ideas that sought to define and explain the current crisis. The one narration that made sense to financial markets in particular, due in no small part to its simplicity and resonance with the financial community given the centrality of money, was monetarism.

Monetarism became the new convention governing both the financial markets and the Fed because the financial markets became just as convinced as Carter that monetization of the debt and increasing deficits created inflation.[73] Given their shared beliefs about the causes of inflation, Wall Street wanted explicit money supply targeting by the Fed to become *the* major

---

[70] *Ibid.*, p. 110–11.

[71] *Ibid.*, p. 724, table 2.

[72] For the pedigree of these ideas, see John Muth, "Rational Expectations and the Theory of Price Movements," *Econometrica* 29 (3) July (1961); Robert E. Lucas, Jr., "Expectations and the Neutrality of Money," *Journal of Economic Theory* 4 (2) April (1972), and Chapter 5.

[73] For a succinct discussion of why bond markets fear inflation, see Gerald Epstein, "Domestic Stagflation and Monetary Policy: The Federal Reserve and the Hidden Election," in Thomas Ferguson and Joel Rogers, eds., *The Hidden Election: Politics and Economics in the 1980 Presidential Campaign* (New York: Pantheon Books, 1981), p. 150.

lever of macromanagement because (only targeting) the money supply would demonstrate seriousness about controlling inflation. Such a regime would serve as the benchmark of "credibility" that the financial markets so badly sought in policy. Consequently, financial markets jumped upon the regime of monetary targeting as the sole benchmark of economic perform-ance, and as far as the markets were concerned, the Fed became the pre-eminent governmental institution. In a striking parallel to what we shall see occurred in the Swedish case, American bond market behavior in this period was a perfect example of what Carl Hamilton and Dag Rolander refer to as "cognitive locking" into one "problem description" that makes only one solution possible.[74] As such, the new convention of monetarism became a self-fulfilling prophecy for both the Fed and the financial markets.

Financial markets operate on expectations of future yields. Such markets, particularly bond markets, have increasing leverage over the state the more the state wishes to run or expand its deficit. However, in an inflationary period, to finance the issue of such debt, the state must pay an inflation premium that simply adds to the debt burden overall. In monetarist theory, such a policy inexorably adds to inflation. If monetarism was correct, as the markets believed, then the rate of growth of the money supply should be positively correlated to the expansion of the deficit and thus the future rate of inflation. According to monetarism, the only way inflation can arise is by the state pumping the money supply. Therefore, if the markets held the view that a presently increasing money supply equals future inflation, then simply observing a growth in the money supply, for whatever reason, would paradoxically bring about demands for an inflation premium that would be expressed in higher long bond rates, and thus higher than neces-sary interest rates. The very act of accepting monetarism as the true defi-nition of the crisis created a self-fulfilling dynamic.

This cognitive locking had two effects. First, this adherence to a mone-tarist benchmark enhanced the Fed's short-term goal of promoting a credit crunch. Unfortunately, this cognitive locking had another effect. Once the deflation had begun, it became almost impossible to stop, precisely because the markets were effectively cognitively locked by monetarist market sen-timent. The Fed may have wanted to loosen the money supply and allow interest rates to fall to ease the pressure on unemployment, but to do so would have signaled to the financial markets that inflation was returning as the money supply would have increased. This increase would signal a further devaluation of a debt holder's expected future returns and thus require another inflation premium to maintain the value of the debt instru-ments of the debt holder. This in turn would require the Fed to hold the

[74] Carl Hamilton and Dag Rolander, *Att leda Sverige in I Krisen: moral och politik I negdgångstid* (Stockholm: Norstedts Förlag, 1993). This account of financial market behavior is drawn from Greider, *Secrets of the Temple, passim.*

line ever more firmly on the money supply, thus exacerbating deflation beyond what was necessary for an inflationary correction.

What was important, then, was that the markets believed monetarism was true, since by coordinating expectations through this new convention, monetarism became self-fulfilling. If the markets believed in monetarism, then the markets would demand less of an inflation premium the more closely money supply targets and actual money supply growth correlated. By insisting on this linkage, the Fed found itself a prisoner to money supply targeting. Thus from 1979 until 1985, the state, the Fed, and the financial markets were caught within a deflationary cycle that existed only because the markets believed it to be true.[75] As Treasury Undersecretary Anthony Solomon noted at the time, "notwithstanding the trauma of [1980] . . . we did not basically shake the monetarist view . . . to keep the monetary aggregates as targets. There was still a feeling in the markets . . . that if we stick to this monetary-targeting policy, it would probably work, and *there really was no alternative.*"[76] Monetarism thus became the governing convention of both the Fed and the markets. And as such, it was the Fed, the guardian and interpreter of finance's best interests, that imposed these changes. So long as the markets watched movements in M1-B (adjusted M1) as the key indicator of future yield, then all the Fed could do was to keep M1-B growth very low.[77]

These changes augured the real beginning of the end of embedded liberalism. By binding the autonomy of the Fed with the beliefs of the financial markets, the changes made the state's role in economic management obsolete almost at a stroke.[78] Consequently, the formulation and execution of economic policy moved from the elected representatives of the public to the unelected representatives of financial capital.[79] The structural

---

[75] This is a perfect example of Keynes' ideas about the structuring role of market conventions. See John Maynard Keynes, *The General Theory of Employment, Interest and Money* (New York: Harcourt Brace and World, 1936), pp. 150–4.

[76] Anthony Solomon, quoted in Greider, *Secrets of the Temple*, p. 220, my italics.

[77] Unfortunately, this also had the effect of pushing long-term interest rates above short-term ones, which exacerbated the credit crunch faced by many businesses. Those firms without huge depreciation write-offs began to go bankrupt in alarming numbers.

[78] This is why I find the argument often heard that the Fed "ended the monetarist experiment" by the middle of 1982 to be a classic example of missing the woods for the trees. In fact, the shadowing, rather than the targeting, of M1-B by the financial markets continued until 1985. More important, however, was the institutional change in the role of the state that this abdication by Congress and this preeminence of the bond markets and the Fed signaled.

[79] Ironically, interpreting the crisis through such a lens inevitably saw the general public's interest in stable prices being reduced to the private desires of politicians for inflation. Yet the reality was probably closer to the particular interests of finance in deflation being represented as the general interest of the public as a whole.

consequence of this cognitive locking was that Congress and the state could legislate all day long, but as so long as the Fed and the financial markets were caught within the thrall of monetarism, they could simply hold money tight to obviate any and all democratic control over the direction of economic policy.

This delegation of economic power from the executive and the legislature to the Fed sealed embedded liberalism's fate. Devoid of supporting ideas, and now devoid of the institutions and policy instruments to do anything, embedded liberalism was finally broken. The combined effects of business mobilization and successful ideological contestation had completely discredited the ideas underlying the embedded liberal institutions. Having destabilized and delegitimated the old institutional order, the combined forces of business and the "new" Republican Party had now to construct a new order in its place. The opportunity for doing this was the capture of the state in 1980.

Attacking Embedded Liberalism

The Program for Economic Recovery
Following Carter's defeat, Reagan's campaign team established six economic policy task forces whose purposes were twofold. First, they were to come up with a package of economic reforms that would unite the newly hegemonic ideas of supply-siders, neoclassicists, and monetarists. Second, they were to propose concrete policy initiatives in each of the discrete issue areas they were assigned.[80] The efforts of these six economic policy task forces came to fruition in the new administration's principal policy document, *America's New Beginning: A Program for Economic Recovery*.[81] The

---

[80] Hodgson, *The World Turned Right Side Up*, p. 212. The task forces were staffed by some of the most prominent figures in the intellectual revolt against embedded liberalism. Alan Greenspan, Ford's CEA chief, headed the task force on the budget. McCracken, Nixon's "Friedmanesque" CEA chief, headed the task force on inflation policy. Burns headed the international monetary policy task force, while Weidenbaum headed the task force on regulation. The task force on taxation policy was chaired by Charls Walker, head of the ACCF, the prime mover behind the business tax breaks of the 1970s. In addition to Walker, Congressional and fourth-estate figures such as Laffer, Roberts, and Ture also served as members of the tax policy task force. Other notable committee members included Citibank's Wriston, Representative David Stockman, and Friedman.

[81] *America's New Beginning: A Program for Economic Recovery*, White House, Office of the Press Secretary, Washington, February 18, 1981. This document was also heavily influenced by Stockman's pitch for his Office of Management and Budget (OMB) job, which was cowritten in December 1980 with his sponsor, Kemp, entitled "Avoiding a GOP Economic Dunkirk." For a discussion of this document, see David Stockman, *The Triumph of Politics: How the Reagan Revolution Failed* (New York: Harper and Row, 1986), pp. 71–3. For the text of the memo itself and discussion of its significance, see Greider, *The Education of David Stockman*, pp. 139–59, 87–91.

Program makes clear both the diverse ideas that made up the "Reagan Revolution" and its institutional targets.

The proposals outlined in the *Program* blend public choice/deregulation theory, monetarism, supply-side theory, and "a generous dose of wishful thinking, which is what the administration thought 'rational expectations' meant."[82] The main planks of the program were as follows. First, it was to cut federal spending drastically. Second, the program would enact the main provisions of the 1978 Kemp-Roth Tax Act. Third, it would begin "an ambitious reform of government regulations that [would] reduce *government-imposed* barriers to investment."[83] Fourth, the program was to govern the macroeconomy with a "predictable and steady growth in the money supply." Finally, it was to build a strong national defense. All of these goals were to be achieved while balancing the budget by 1985.

The ideas informing these policies were quite explicit. The need to reduce federal spending was justified in terms of the supply-side idea that "the most important cause of our economic problems has been the government itself," together with the discouragement that results from high marginal tax burdens.[84] Meanwhile, the ideas that diagnosed and sought to deal the crisis of inflation were a hybrid of Friedmanite "adaptive expectations" and Lucasian "rational expectations." Specifically, the problem of inflation was diagnosed *á la* Friedman, but the treatment proposed was Lucasian.

Inflation was seen to result from the fact that "there has been no long run trade off between inflation and unemployment."[85] Second, because people "believe inflation is here to stay[,] they plan accordingly . . . [which] . . . robs the economy of flexibility."[86] Third, "the uncontrolled growth of government spending has been a primary cause of the sustained high rate of inflation experienced by the American economy." Fourth, these factors have been compounded by an accommodationist monetary policy, and since "accommodation is widely expected to continue, inflation has become embedded in the economy."[87] The cure for the crisis was therefore to control the money supply, cut federal spending, and reduce inflationary expectations.

The problem with this solution was that it created a policy dilemma. Cutting spending and reducing the money supply while attempting to increase military spending would generate enormous deficits and compound the deflation. Consequently, the administration sought a way to reduce inflationary expectations painlessly. It was at this juncture that the theory of rational expectations – as popularized by the ex-head of the Minneapolis Fed, Mark Willes, and administration figures such as Beryl Sprinkel and

---

[82] Alan S. Blinder, quoted in Hodgson, *The World Turned Right Side Up*, p. 252.
[83] *America's New Beginning*, p. 2, my italics.   [84] *Ibid.*, p. 4.   [85] *Ibid.*, p. 8.
[86] *Ibid.*, p. 4.   [87] *Ibid.*, pp. 10, 4.

David Stockman – combined with the supply-side arguments of Roberts, Kemp, and Laffer to offer the administration a way out of this impasse.[88]

Sprinkel and Stockman were the prime movers within the administration promoting this "expectations plus supply-side effects" solution to the policy dilemma. As William Greider explains, the supply-side approach assumed that

> ... dramatic action ... especially the commitment to a three-year reduction of the income tax, coupled with tight monetary control, would signal investors that a new era was dawning. ... If economic behavior in a climate of high inflation is primarily based on expectations about the future value of money then swift and dramatic action ... could reverse the gloomy assumptions in the disordered financial markets.

Stockman argued that this was possible because *"the whole thing is premised upon faith ... on a belief about how the world works."* Consequently, once credibility is demonstrated, "the inflation premium melts away like morning mist."[89] In short, Greider suggests, "if the President acted boldly, it would alter the psychological climate surrounding these economic problems" and painless deflation would be brought about.[90]

Simply reducing such expectations, however, would be insufficient to restore growth. It was here that supply-side economics were invoked. As the *Program* details, individual and business tax cuts were combined to do an "end run" around the tax wedge that inflation causes on investment, just as Feldstein had argued. Second, these tax cuts would spur incentives for capital formation, unleash entrepreneurial activity, and thereby restore stable growth, just as the ACCF contended.[91]

To put these ideas into practice, Stockman changed the assumptions behind the OMB's econometric model so that these diverse ideas produced expedient numbers. First, the model's assumptions concerning investment sensitivity to marginal tax rates were changed. Second, in line with his penchant for expectational arguments, Stockman changed the model to show that inflation would not rise in response to a burgeoning deficit due to the

---

[88] Thomas Ferguson and Joel Rogers maintain that the "expectations effect" was developed by William Fellner at the AEI. See Ferguson and Rogers, *Right Turn*, p. 116. Yet Fellner was one of the many popularizers of these ideas. See, for example, the exposition of ex-St. Louis Fed governor Willes, "The Rational Expectations Revolution in Macroeconomics," in *The Public Interest*, July (1978); *Idem.*, "The Future of Monetary Policy: The Rational Expectations Perspective," *Federal Reserve Bank of Minneapolis Quarterly Review*, 4 Spring (1980).

[89] Stockman, quoted in Greider, *The Education of David Stockman*, pp. 7–8, my italics.

[90] Greider, *The Education of David Stockman*, p. 89. On the administration's adherence to this idea, see Isabell V. Sawhill and Charles F. Stone, "The Economy: The Key to Success," in John L. Palmer and Isabell V. Sawhill, eds., *The Reagan Record: An Assessment of America's Changing Domestic Priorities* (Washington: Urban Institute, 1984), p. 71.

[91] *America's New Beginning*, pp. 15, 24.

assumed credibility of the new regime.[92] The function of this set of calculations was not to diagnose the economy as it was, but to maintain the cohesion of the synthesis of ideas that the *Program* represented. The supply-side plus expectations synthesis had to be saved, for otherwise the program as a whole would become little more than a huge self-inflicted depression and tax handout. That, at least, was the theory of Reaganomics.[93]

The 1981 Economic Recovery Act

The 1981 Economic Recovery Act (ERA) was designed to achieve these goals. The ERA combined the 30 percent Kemp-Roth tax reduction with new tax breaks for business. How the Act took in this form is once again a testament to the power of organized business. Walker, the head of the ACCF, was appointed after the election to head the transition tax team inside the White House. However, while doing this, Walker was also building a new business coalition called the Carlton Group to lobby for further changes in business taxation as part of the forthcoming Economic Recovery Act. The Carlton Group was composed of members of the NAM, the ACC, and the ACCF. While each group wanted different forms of tax relief, Walker reasoned that if business was to take advantage of this situation, then it had to be united in its advocacy of a coherent across-the-board program.[94]

Early in 1979, the Carlton Group began to lobby within the business community for a unified tax proposal based upon the Accelerated Cost Recovery System (ACRS). This system envisaged an accelerated depreciation schedule whereby buildings would be written off in ten years, capital equipment in five years, and ancillary equipment such as computers and

---

[92] Greider, *The Education of David Stockman*, pp. 15–19.

[93] Putting these ideas into practice was hardly a simple proposition. As Cathie Jo Martin points out, the divergent ideas behind the *Program* were embedded within different institutional niches within the state. The CEA became the province of both traditional conservative economists and the new deregulators. The Fed was dominated by monetarists while the Treasury became the province of supply-siders. On the one hand, this meant that there were no "institutional holdouts" for opposing ideas. See Cathie J. Martin, *Shifting the Burden: The Struggle over Growth and Corporate Taxation* (Chicago: University of Chicago Press, 1991), p. 112. To combine these ideas practically, Stockman based the calculations for the 1981 Economic Recovery Act and the 1981 budget on some very creative arithmetic. The supply-side faction wanted to show "real GNP growth of around 5 to 6 percent . . . to demonstrate the effect of the proposed tax cut[s]. On the other hand, the monetarists . . . wanted to show the lowest possible numbers for money GNP . . . the litmus test of sound anti-inflationary monetary policy." Stockman described the resulting process of preparing economic forecasts as getting out "our economic shoehorn and try[ing] to "jimmy" the forecast numbers until all the doctrines fit." See M. Stephen Weatherford and Lorraine M. McDonnell, "Ideology and Economic Policy," in Larry Berman, ed., *Looking Back on the Reagan Presidency* (Baltimore: Johns Hopkins University Press, 1990), p. 135.

[94] On the Carlton Group and Walker's role within it, see Martin, *Shifting the Burden*, p. 116–23; Vogel, *Fluctuating Fortunes*, p. 242; Edsall, *The New Politics*, p. 226.

automobiles within three years – the so-called 10:5:3 formula. Once the Carlton Group accepted this proposal, Walker dutifully wrote the ACRS provisions straight into the 1981 tax bill himself.[95]

The new Republican-dominated state accepted ACRS for three reasons. First, it was a logical extension of the capital formation philosophy that the Republican Party had been arguing at business's behest since the mid-1970s. As such, it would have been difficult to say no. Second, Reagan personally accepted the Laffer curve as the new "grand unifying theory" and therefore saw no reason that the same incentive effects that supposedly applied to a personal tax reduction would not apply to a business tax cut.[96] Third, the administration needed business's support for the Kemp-Roth section of the tax bill. Without that support, it was feared that the Democrats would eviscerate the personal reductions. Because the Democrats were desperate to recover from the defection of business support they endured in 1978 and 1980, it was hoped that business's ability to persuade the Democrats to acquiesce to the Kemp-Roth provisions of the tax bill would prove very effective. The *quid pro quo* for this support was the adoption of the ACRS.

In response to these moves, and exactly as the state had expected, the Democrats came up with an alternative tax proposal to curry business support. The Democrats offered a tax bill that proposed a one-year tax cut of $40 billion that was composed of a $28 billion cut in individual taxes and a $12 billion cut in business taxes. However, the Democratic leadership was not willing to back the ACRS provisions.[97] As Cathie Martin notes, after an attempt at a compromise between the two bills failed in May 1981, a bidding war erupted between the Democrats and the administration.[98] The Democrats expanded their own proposal to include refundable tax credits for manufactures and real estate, the equivalent of the ACRS proposal.[99] In response to this, the administration inserted into its version of the bill a refundable research and development credit of 25 percent on labor employed in research and development. The Democrats took this proposal and made the research and development credit 100 percent

[95] Edsall, *The New Politics*, p. 226, fn. 38.

[96] Hodgson cites another reason for Reagan's eagerness to maintain the personal tax cuts come what may. Hodgson asserts, following Anderson, that Reagan took Kemp-Roth on board as a *quid pro quo* to stop Kemp himself running for president. See Hodgson, *The World Turned Right Side Up*, p. 210, fn. 44. Compare, Martin Anderson, *Revolution*, (San Diego: Harcourt Brace Jovanovich, 1988), p. 44.

[97] Martin, *Shifting the Burden*, p. 121; Vogel *Fluctuating Fortunes*, p. 243. However, Democrats on the House Ways and Means Committee and the Senate Finance Committee began to suggest incorporating the ACRS provision into the Democratic alternative.

[98] On the Democrats' bidding war, see Martin, *Shifting the Burden*, pp. 123–31; Ferguson and Rogers, *Right Turn*, pp. 138–62; Stockman, *The Triumph of Politics*, pp. 260–1.

[99] The administration scaled back ACRS by changing the 10:5:3 proposal to a modified 15:10:5:3, with depreciation on buildings being stretched out to fifteen years.

deductible.[100] The administration in turn responded to this Democratic gambit with a new provision called safe harbor leasing. This tax provision allowed firms to buy and sell their depreciation allowances and investment tax credits such that profitable and unprofitable firms would be cross-subsidized by public tax refunds.[101] As Stockman notes, "The hogs were really feeding. The greed level, the level of opportunism, just got out of control."[102]

The end results of this bidding war were fourfold. First, the financial cost of this give-back to business was enormous. A study by Citizens for Tax Justice calculated that as a result of the 1981 Economic Recovery Act, from a sample of 275 major corporations, 129 paid no taxes in at least one year between fiscal years 1981 to 1985. Fifty corporations within this sample of 275 either paid no tax or actually received refunds over the entire four-year period, and in the subsample of 129 firms that paid no taxes in at least one year, their real effective tax rate fell as low as −9.6 percent. This allowed some of America's largest firms to declare pre-tax profits of $66.5 billion while still receiving tax rebates of $6.5 billion.[103] As Kim McQuaid notes, General Electric alone "wiped out most of its 1981 taxes by buying credits up from . . . Chrysler and Ford, and ended up with $110 million in refunds to boot."[104] The combined effects of this bidding war cost the state "$154 billion in lost federal revenues over six years and close to $500 billion over ten years."[105] Given this, any hope of not having a huge deficit without enforcing enormous cuts in the budget became totally unrealistic.[106]

---

[100] Martin, *Shifting the Burden*, p. 127.

[101] Safe harbor leasing "allowed firms earning no profits and paying no federal tax to compute depreciation and other tax benefits that they would have [received] had they paid tax. These benefits were then refunded in the form of credits against future federal taxes. . . . Profitable firms [then bought up these credits] and used [them] to buy their way out of their federal tax obligations." McQuaid, *Uneasy Partners*, p. 169.

[102] Greider, *The Education of David Stockman*, p. 58.

[103] Citizens for Tax Justice, "Corporate Taxpayers and Corporate Freeloaders," Washington, August (1985), cited in Ferguson and Rogers, *Right Turn*, p. 123.

[104] McQuaid, *Uneasy Partners*, p. 169.

[105] Edsall, *The New Politics*, p. 226, fn. 38.

[106] Some mention should be made here of the Tax Equity and Fiscal Responsibility Act (TEFRA) of 1982. The passing of TEFRA is sometimes seen as a reversal of business's political power as it marked an attempt by Congress to reverse the damage of the previous session's bidding war. See, for example, Martin, *Shifting the Burden*, pp. 135, 156-7. Rather, TEFRA marked a strategic withdrawal. TEFRA's goal was to stop financial and product markets collapsing. The combined effects of a domestic recession, huge tax cuts, and sky-high interest rates had increased the deficit from a revised February 1982 estimate of $98.6 billion to an actual deficit of $127.9 billion. While inflation fell threefold from 12 percent in 1981 to 4 percent in 1983, unemployment reached 10.7 percent by the last quarter of 1982. The state was reluctant to give up on the tax cuts for obvious reasons. Without the supposedly stimulating effects of the tax cuts, the program would simply result in an accelerating deflation. Moreover, the state had aimed to use the growing deficits to make the case for ever deeper cuts. The combined effects of the Economic Recovery Act

Second, as M. Stephen Weatherford and Lorraine M. McDonnell argue
regarding the Kemp-Roth portion of the Act, "the tax reductions were
unabashedly regressive, and their cumulative value from fiscal year 1982 to
fiscal year 1985 was about $360 billion."[107] Furthermore, "because of rises
in Social Security payroll taxes already scheduled, between 1980 and 1985
the actual ratio of tax paid on income rose for the bottom 40 percent of
the population and fell for the top 60 percent."[108] Third, the Economic
Recovery Act mandated indexing tax brackets to the rate of inflation. While
this exacerbated the problem of the deficit, it also meant that the state *could
not avoid cutting the budget further*.[109] By indexing brackets, another
source of potential finance (bracket creep windfalls) effectively evaporated.[110] Finally, it must also be noted that by engaging in this bidding war,
the Democrats, being devoid of any other economic ideas with which
to articulate an opposition, "were . . . very effectively destroying any
intellectual credibility they ever had."[111]

The Return of Sound Finance

While attacking redistributive taxation undermined one side of the embedded liberal order, cutting the budget assaulted the other. As Weatherford
and McDonnell argue, "no President since Hoover has called for substantially diminishing the government's role in redistributive social programs;
Reagan accomplished it."[112] The means for doing so was to change public
and Congressional ideas concerning the legitimacy and necessity of spending programs. Given that the 1981 Economic Recovery Act had just given

(ERA) and the Omnibus Budget Reconciliation Act (OBRA) had certainly boosted the
deficit, but the desire to increase defense expenditures at 7 percent per year for the next
five years had exacerbated it. In light of this impending crisis, TEFRA was enacted.
TEFRA's main provisions were fivefold: The ACRS was repealed, safe harbors were
abolished, one-third of other depreciation benefits were taken back, the tax advantages of
mergers and acquisition activities were reduced, and the corporate minimum tax provisions were strengthened. However, all in all, the reforms contained in TEFRA raised only
$57.2 billion in taxes of the estimated $323 billion that business had received under the
1981 ERA. See Michael Meeropol, *Surrender: How the Clinton Administration Completed
the Reagan Revolution* (Ann Arbor: Michigan University Press, 1998), p. 106. TEFRA was
thus as much an exercise in attempting to stabilize market expectations as it was an
exercise in revenue raising.

[107] Weatherford and McDonnell, "Ideology and Economic Policy," p. 131.
[108] Meeropol, *Surrender*, p. 80.
[109] As Roberts notes, "OMB wanted deficits, but not deficits that could be laid at the doorstep
of monetary policy. . . . OMB was determined to use the deficit to focus Congressional
attention on the budget." Roberts, *The Supply Side Revolution*, p. 173.
[110] Berman, *America's Right Turn*, p. 94. For a similar claim concerning the logic of indexing, see Paul Pierson, *Dismantling the Welfare State? Reagan, Thatcher and the Politics of
Retrenchment* (Cambridge: Cambridge University Press, 1994), p. 153.
[111] Richard Rahn, quoted in Martin, *Shifting the Burden*, p. 132.
[112] Weatherford and McDonnell, "Ideology and Economic Policy," p. 131.

away between $600–700 billion in tax breaks, the OMB took advantage of this situation to focus attention on the burgeoning deficit.[113] The fact that these policies caused the deficit was no handicap to blaming the deficit on the institutions of embedded liberalism themselves.

The burgeoning deficit enabled spending reductions to be smuggled into the debate in the name of sound finance. Under the 1981 Omnibus Budget Reconciliation Act (OBRA), Stockman aimed to cut $40 billion from the budget in federal year (FY) 1981 and sought total reductions of $200 billion by 1985 through benefit reductions and tighter eligibility requirements.[114] Although the end result of Congressional bargaining over the OBRA was to cut only $35 billion from FY 1982 and a total of $140 billion through 1985, the 1981 OBRA marked a major change in American distributional politics in two ways. First, such a move was fiscally equivalent to raising taxes in a depression. As such, it compounded the deflation already under way. Second, if reducing a deficit through cutting transfers has the same net effect as raising taxes, then the regressive results of the 1981 ERA's Kemp-Roth provisions were even more pronounced.

Despite such policies actually aggravating the deflation, Reagan affirmed his intention to cut another $63 billion in social programs over the next few years in his 1982 State of the Union Address.[115] Taken apart from the ERA and OBRA changes, what Reagan proposed constituted a 17.2 percent reduction in social spending in real terms from then current budget projections.[116] In his address, Reagan took aim at the plethora of programs created under the auspices of the New Deal and the Great Society and proposed two courses of action: to eliminate what could be defined "unnecessary," and to give the programs back to the states in the form of block grants to finance welfare as they saw fit.[117]

To shift the boundaries of what counted as "necessary," the administration explicitly linked macroeconomic, labor market, and welfare policies.

---

[113] Between 1981 and 1982, the deficit increased from $78.9 billion to $127.9 billion. Gross federal debt increased from $994.8 billion to $1,137.3 billion. The Federal Funds Rate went from a low point in the third quarter of 1980 from 9.8 percent to 17.79 percent in the second quarter of 1982. Unemployment rose from 6.3 percent to 7.4 percent over the same period. Figures from Federal Reserve database at http://www.stls.frb.org/fred.data/business, and from Meeropol's economic database at http://mars.wnec.edu/~econ/surrender/w4.htm#new.

[114] Figures from Greider, *The Education of David Stockman*, pp. 19–21; Berman, *America's Right Turn*, pp. 94–5; Meeropol, *Surrender*, pp. 86–7.

[115] See Reagan's 1982 State of the Union Address in Ronald Reagan, *Public Papers* 1, pp. 174–85.

[116] Calculations from Figure 6.1 in D. Lee Bawden and John L. Palmer, "Social Policy: Challenging the Welfare State," in Palmer and Sawhill, eds., *The Reagan Record*, pp. 185–6.

[117] This latter proposal, known as the New Federalism, was rejected by the states since it was clearly an attempt to reduce the absolute level of spending by passing responsibilities to the states.

The rationale for cutting such programs, as stated in the 1982 State of the Union Address and thereafter, was that such reforms would change the emphasis of federal aid "from the greedy to the needy," with the needy being defined as "unfortunate persons who through no fault of their own cannot be reasonably expected to work."[118] The direct consequence of this linkage was to reaffirm the voluntary nature of both unemployment and welfare dependency. If the only people who legitimately cannot work are those who are physically unable to do so, then anyone who is physically able to work but unemployed is obviously *unwilling to work* at the prevailing wage.[119] At a stroke, the core embedded liberal idea of involuntary unemployment was declared invalid. As such, the state was able to attempt the reform of key embedded liberal institutions.

Dismantling Embedded Liberalism

Reregulating Labor

Concurrent with the supply-side tax battles, business began a coordinated campaign of noncooperation with organized labor. First, business began to use the Wagner Act instrumentally against labor. Second, and most significantly, business sought to further delegitimate the goal of full employment as a core policy goal of the state by hijacking labor's own reform agenda, much as business had done with Carter's tax cuts. The opportunity for this paradoxically presented itself in a last-ditch attempt to strengthen embedded liberal institutions.

In 1975, a group of Democratic economists headed by Robert L. Heilbroner and John Kenneth Galbraith formed the Initiative Committee for National Economic Planning. The Committee advocated the "establishment of an Office of National Economic Planning in the White House ... [that would] ... formulate detailed plans to help the economy reach its long term objectives."[120] Two pro-labor members of Congress, Hubert Humphrey and Augustus Hawkins, introduced a Bill that sought to put these ideas into practice.[121] Under the proposed legislation, the state had to

---

[118] Reagan, *Public Papers* 1, pp. 174–85. For the definition of who constitutes the needy, see Robert B. Carlson and Kevin R. Hopkins, "Whose Responsibility Is Social Responsibility? The Reagan Rationale," *Public Welfare* 39 (4) Fall (1981).

[119] For example, Feldstein's arguments noted previously concerning unemployment compensation constricting the supply of labor were used by the administration to justify reducing unemployment compensation eligibility during the recession. See Meeropol, *Surrender*, pp. 91–2.

[120] Vogel, *Fluctuating Fortune*, p. 143. The recommendations of this Committee were incorporated into an amended Humphrey-Hawkins Bill called the Humphrey-Javits Bill. However, this Bill itself failed to pick up support, and these proposals were rolled back into what might be called Humphrey-Hawkins mark three in early 1977.

[121] This is not the last time the "deficit-challenged" Democrats were seduced by the allure of coordination either. As we shall discuss later, the debates over industrial policy in the 1980s mirror more or less the same dynamics.

bring the unemployment rate down to 3 percent within eighteen months of any given period where this target rate was not attained. The Act also mandated the formulation of an annual "full employment and growth plan . . . [where the state would] . . . act as an employer of last resort if fiscal and monetary policy proved inadequate to reach this goal."[122] Most radical of all, the Bill proposed ending the autonomy of the Federal Reserve. It explicitly called upon the Fed to "bring its policies into line with a national effort for full employment and required the board to prepare an annual statement outlining how its policies for the coming year would be consistent with the goal of full employment."[123] Humphrey-Hawkins signaled to business the last gasp of a set of ideas that business thought it had defeated back in the 1940s: stagnationist Keynesianism. After all, if Nixon could implement mandatory wage and price controls in peacetime, then the idea of the Democrats instituting national economic planning was probably not so far off the mark either.

Unfortunately for Humphrey and Hawkins, the ideas behind the Bill were entirely inconsistent with the new ideas being deployed by business, the financial press, pro-business think tanks, and even Congress itself. In popular and academic economics, unemployment was being reinterpreted as a voluntary phenomena by Feldstein and Friedman. Meanwhile the macroeconomy as a whole was being seen as less a coherent system amenable to manipulation by disinterested experts than as the province of smart and efficient individuals with inviolable utility functions and rational expectations. In such a world, planning was seen as at best, an outmoded, and at worst, a vague and dangerous concept.[124] Indeed, Citibank's Wriston, a major figure in the BRT and the ACCF, called the bill "the first step towards an economic police state . . . [that] would destroy both our personal liberty and our productive power."[125]

Business lobbied vociferously against Humphrey-Hawkins and used these new ideas to challenge its rationale explicitly. Consequently, the final version of the Bill ended up being more influenced by Senator Orin Hatch and monetarism than by Humphrey, Hawkins, or Keynesianism. The target unemployment rate was revised back up to 4 percent, to be achieved by 1983, some five years hence. All of the planning mechanisms and institutions proposed in the original Bill were scrapped, and the employer of last

---

[122] Margaret Weir, *Politics and Jobs: The Boundaries of Employment Policy in the United States* (Princeton: Princeton University Press, 1992), p. 135.

[123] *Ibid.*, p. 135.

[124] As Parsons argues, "when it came to winning over opinion with simple common sense solutions, stop printing money (monetarism), and cut taxes (supply side), it was a non-contest." Parsons, *The Power of the Financial Press*, p. 150. Moreover, the Bill became associated with being a "black" measure and thereby falling prey to all the negative connotations associated with the pathologies of welfare, etc., that were being deployed effectively by the new business think tanks. See Weir, *Politics and Jobs*, p. 140.

[125] Wriston, quoted in *Business Week*, July 23, 1976, p. 72.

resort provision was dropped. Most important of all, Hatch incorporated into the Bill an amendment that called for the reduction of the inflation rate to 3 percent by 1983.[126] Whether one was a Philips-curve Keynesian or not, the purpose of this amendment was clear. If the trade-off implied in the Bill was 3 percent inflation and 4 percent unemployment, the given current rates of unemployment and inflation, only a gut-wrenching recession would reduce inflation to that rate, and only then at the expense of the full-employment target itself. Full employment, a commitment only begrudg-ingly accepted by business and the core of the embedded liberal order, had been eviscerated. As a consequence of this, the state's acceptance of the idea that unemployment was voluntary and of lesser importance than inflation meant that unions, by definition, could be little more than restraints upon trade. Thus, in a parallel to the actions of the state before the Great Depres-sion, labor was "hemmed in" further by direct state action against it.

The most famous example of state-labor confrontation in this period occurred in August 1983 when Reagan fired all 11,400 striking members of the air-traffic controllers union (PATCO) and rescinded the union's bargaining rights.[127] However, what was much more consequential than high-profile union-busting incidents such as the PATCO strike were the institutional and procedural changes that took place within the National Labor Relations Board (NLRB). Under this new confrontational attitude taken by the state, these micro-institutional reforms did more to reregulate labor than overt union-busting ever did.

By law, the board of the NRLB was drawn from business, labor, and the wider public, and historically its decisions exhibited a pro-labor bias. Under Reagan all this changed. Reagan appointees did not constitute a majority of the board until 1983. Once that majority was obtained, "within 150 days, the new majority ... reversed eight major precedents ... [and] ... recast forty percent of the decisions made since the 1970's that conserva-tives found objectionable."[128] Once this majority position was assured, the NLRB's scope of inquiry and authority was considerably narrowed, while the definition of "acceptable employer behavior" was broadened.

By the end of Reagan's first term, the NRLB had passed rulings that would have been unthinkable just a few years previously. On March 22, 1984, the NRLB ruled that a worker who left the place of employment to fetch medical assistance for another worker was voluntarily terminating employment. On June 7, 1984, the board found that an employer, or the employer's agent, taking pictures of workers involved in union activities so

---

[126] Vogel, *Fluctuating Fortunes*, pp. 157–8.
[127] Ironically, PATCO had backed Reagan in the election.
[128] See Terry Moe, "Interests, Institutions and Positive Theory: The Politics of the NLRB," *Studies in American Political Development*, Volume 2 (New Haven: Yale University Press, 1987).

that the employer could have a picture "to remember them by," was not in any way guilty of harassing those workers. On June 13, 1984, the NRLB found that firing laid-off union supporters was legal as it constituted a contractual breach, regardless of whether workers were told they were in breach or not. On top of such rulings, the NRLB sought to weaken the collective bargaining provisions of union contracts systematically by deliberately not enforcing agreements, and all the while the case backlog of the NRLB increased from four hundred in 1981 to seventeen hundred in 1984.[129]

These combined legal and institutional changes had a dramatic effect upon labor as a political actor. By subverting the NRLB, the first and last guarantor of organized labor since the 1930s, the state had effectively removed labor's primary institutional protection and as a consequence labor became "commodified" once again.[130] As William C. Berman notes, by these actions, "Reagan served notice [that] . . . [o]rganized labor would no longer have privileged entrée into the inner sanctum of government . . . nor would its claims be given . . . consideration from an administration eager to convert the National Labor Relations Board into an adjunct of business."[131]

Deregulating Business

While labor was reregulated, business was deregulated.[132] The conventional wisdom concerning the Reagan administration's deregulatory effort is best summarized by ex-CEA member William Niskanen: "The Reagan attempt to reform . . . regulations . . . was a near-complete failure."[133] Such a view, however, misses something very important. If measured in terms of the number of agencies actually abolished, then the deregulatory effort indeed failed. However, such a view of deregulation is problematic. A better way to understand the scope of deregulation lies in the success of the state in halting the growth of regulation and limiting the effectiveness of regulatory institutions. If the Reagan administration's actions are seen as a strategy of

---

[129] See House Committee on Education and Labor, Subcommittee on Labor-Management Relations, *The Failure of Labor Law – The Betrayal of American Workers*, 98th Congress, Second Session, 1984, pp. 17–24, quoted in Ferguson and Rogers, *Right Turn*, p. 254.

[130] For example, unit labor costs fell by 6 percent in 1983 alone and by 1984 work stoppages involving one thousand or more workers in 1984 were only 27 percent of what they had been in 1979. Meanwhile, the number of lost working days due to industrial action declined from 20,409,000 in 1979 to 4,481,000 in 1987, a fivefold decrease. Figures are from the Bureau of Labor Statistics time series dataset at http://stats.bls.gov/sahome.html.

[131] Berman, *America's Right Turn*, p. 98.

[132] For the classic account of the politics of deregulation that has at least an implicit ideational component, see Martha Derthick and Paul J. Quirk, *The Politics of Deregulation* (Washington: Brookings Institution Press, 1985).

[133] William A. Niskanen, *Reaganomics: An Insider's Account of the Policies and the People* (New York: Oxford University Press, 1988), p. 125; Anderson, *Revolution*, p. 117.

changing the boundaries of what could or indeed should be regulated, rather than as a strategy of overt confrontation, one is led to the conclusion that the administration was far more successful in this area than is generally acknowledged.

Among the first actions of the incoming administration was the decision under Executive Order 12291 to subject all new regulatory proposals to cost/benefit analysis.[134] While seemingly neutral, cost/benefit analysis is in fact a very biased standard to apply since costs and benefits are only meaningfully measured relative to their distributional consequences, with such consequences generally being ignored in the calculus. Given this, the moral claim that polluters *should* pay because they do the polluting becomes untenable since there is no room within such a calculus for an external normative standard.[135] Therefore, employing cost/benefit analysis naturally lends itself to market alternatives to formal regulatory structures, which is where most developments in regulatory policy were being made by the late 1980s.

Another highly effective strategy was to staff agencies with political appointees whose ideological convictions were the exact opposite of everything for which the department stood. For example, James Watt, the ex-head of the Mountain States Legal Foundation, a pro-business litigation firm that specialized in the representation of firms that contested EPA rulings, was appointed secretary of the interior. Anne Gorsuch, a Colorado legislator who had campaigned on behalf of mining interests, was appointed head of the EPA itself. Thorne Auchter, the head of a construction firm cited over a dozen times for OSHA violations, was appointed head of the OSHA. Perhaps most consequential of all was the appointment of ex-steel executive Donald P. Doston as the new head of the NLRB. Doston appointed Hugh L. Riley as solicitor to the NRLB. Riley was an attorney for the National Right to Work Legal Defense Foundation, an anti-union public interest law firm that was funded almost entirely by business interests. Indeed, Riley continued to work for the National Right to Work Legal Defense Foundation despite holding the post in the NRLB.[136]

Also efficacious was simply draining funds from the agency in question, or lowering its standards, thereby limiting its effectiveness. For example, between 1970 and 1980, the budgets of federal regulatory agencies increased by 400 percent. Between 1981 and 1984, they fell by 11 percent overall. Between 1981 and 1984, the EPA's budget was reduced by 35 percent and its exposure standards on regulated industrial substances were

---

[134] This order was enforced one month after Vice President George Bush headed the first meeting of the task force on regulatory relief with Weidenbaum.

[135] Consider that the death penalty would never pass cost/benefit analysis, yet this is never taken seriously as an argument for the abolition of that particular penalty.

[136] See Edsall, *The New Politics of Inequality*, p. 229.

raised anywhere between ten and one hundred times. In 1981 the EPA's staff stood at 14,075. By 1982 it had fallen to 10,392.[137] EPA's referrals to the Justice Department for the prosecution of violators fell by 84 percent between 1981 and 1983, and the number of enforcement orders that the EPA issued dropped 33 percent. The Food and Drug Administration likewise had its budget cut by over 30 percent over this period and compliance with its enforcement orders declined 88 percent.[138] Between 1981 and 1984, the absolute number of regulations in the Federal Register declined by 25 percent, and since 1984, no new permanent regulatory department has been authorized or established by the federal government. Business, it seems, got its regulatory relief while labor became, once again, just another factor input.

A Bridge Too Far? Privatizing Social Security

Building upon these successes, the state next took aim at the only embedded liberal institution left: the "safety net" of Social Security. Throughout 1982 Reagan stressed that the social safety net would remain exempt from cuts. However, the program proved to be far from inviolable: The state took aim at the Social Security system in early 1982 and proposed to eliminate it.[139] As Reagan's chief domestic policy advisor Martin Anderson noted, "the term 'safety net' was used . . . to describe the set of social welfare changes that would not be closely examined *on the first round of budget changes* . . . the term 'safety net' was political shorthand that only made sense *for a limited period of time.*" Consequently, the first round of cuts was originally intended as a mere prelude to deeper long-term reductions. To make such reforms possible, a social security crisis had to be created.

The pretext for doing so was to use the slump as evidence for the claim that state commitments had become uncontrollable. Basically, because of the slowdown in growth and the consequent shrinkage in tax receipts that the deflation brought about, changes in the index of consumer prices began to run ahead of the rate of real wage increases. As such, rather than being in their usual surplus positions, the Social Security trust funds had deficits projected for the mid-term future. As the Old Age Survivors trust

---

[137] Vogel, *Fluctuating Fortunes*, pp. 249–51.
[138] *The Democratic Factbook* (Washington: Democrats for the 80's, 1984), pp. 289–99. The same was true for other federal agencies. For example, between 1981 and 1983, the Consumer Product Safety Commission lost 38 percent of its budget, and the National Highway Traffic Safety Board had its budget cut by 22 percent. Between 1981 and 1984, enforcement orders issued by the OSHA fell by 78 percent and the average penalty for a violation totaled a mere $6.50. Ferguson and Rogers, *Right Turn*, p. 134.
[139] Martin Anderson, "The Objectives of the Reagan Administration's Social Welfare Policy," in D. Lee Bawden, ed., *The Social Contract Revisited: Aims and Outcomes of the President's Social Welfare Policy* (Washington: Urban Institute Press, 1984), p. 113.

fund ran low in 1981, Congress permitted cross-subsidization of the various title agency trust funds in order to keep the system as a whole stable. This proved to be the opening the state needed to portray the system as being in crisis.

In response to this constructed crisis, the OMB put forward a plan for reforming Social Security in May 1982. The program contained three main elements: first, to cut the benefits of early retirees by 40 percent; second, to seek a 40 percent reduction in disability allowances and a tightening of disability claim criteria; and third, to change the calculation baseline for Social Security as a whole, with the intent of reducing overall spending by some $200 billion by the year 2000.[140]

Congress saw this as a massive breach of faith given the promises to preserve the safety net and passed a unanimous resolution opposing such changes.[141] Specifically, the Democrats suggested setting up a bipartisan Commission for Social Security Reform. The administration accepted this proposal and appointed Greenspan to chair the Commission. During the reform hearings, business think tanks flooded the press and the Commission itself with proposals to phase out the entire system. Hoover economist Michael Boskin and NBER President Feldstein both testified before the hearings and argued that Social Security both depresses private savings and that private plans could and should replace the current entitlement-based system.[142]

However, coming as it did on the heels of so many other controversial reforms, Social Security proved to be a bridge too far. Yet even though the Commission report emphasized that "the members of the national commission believe that the Congress . . . should not alter the fundamental structure of the Social Security program," Republicans in Congress were still able to weaken the program substantially following the Commission's final report.[143] These reform measures enacted by Congress delayed, and in some cases reduced, cost of living adjustments, increased the retirement age, increased self-employed payroll taxes, increased FICA taxes, and tightened

---

[140] See Merton C. Bernstein and Joan Broadshug Bernstein, *Social Security: The System That Works* (New York: Basic Books, 1988), pp. 34–60. See especially their discussion of how a minor accounting problem garnered under pessimistic assumptions was translated in the press and in the beltway as a huge crisis.

[141] Ferguson and Rogers, *Right Turn*, p. 127. This is not, however, to say that there was no support in Congress for such a move. Senator William Armstrong, the ranking Republican on the Senate Finance Committee, for example, was a longstanding critic of Social Security.

[142] See Bernstein and Bernstein, *Social Security*, p. 41. For Feldstein's argument, see Martin Feldstein, "Social Security, Induced Retirement and Aggregate Accumulation," *Journal of Political Economy* 82 (5) (1974).

[143] Report of the National Commission on Social Security Reform, Government Printing Office: (Washington: January 1983), chapter 2, p. 2, quoted in Bernstein and Bernstein, *Social Security*, p. 49.

eligibility requirements for noncontributory portions of the program.[144] In short, despite not achieving any sweeping changes, Congress accepted Feldstein and Boskin's argument that consumption maintenance in a recession merely hindered market adjustment and labor supply, and acted accordingly.

Yet none of these labor, product, or insurance market changes actually served to halt the recession. The economy continued to fall into a deep recession and by the third quarter of 1983 thirty-one thousand firms had gone bankrupt. Unemployment by late 1982 reached 10.7 percent and the rate of real wage compensation had all but collapsed from an average yearly rate of increase of 8.3 percent between 1973 and 1981 to an actual decline in real wage rates of 1.4 percent per year between 1981 and 1983.[145] What compounded the recession was that the Fed and the financial markets were still caught in the thrall of monetarism.

The Continuing Triumph of Monetarism

As discussed earlier, the financial markets believed that deficits and inflation rates were correlated, thus the Fed had to act as if they were correlated. When the deficit increased, which according to monetarism could only be due to monetization of the debt or an increase in the money supply, the Fed had to keep interest rates high.[146] The markets continued to demand greater monetary restriction because even though the inflation rate was falling, the deficit was still increasing due to the collapse in consumption and the defense buildup. Rather than taking this as a signal that basing market conventions upon a monetarist theory of inflation was actually depressing the economy, the markets continued to insist upon an inflation premium that was no longer warranted given the existing rate of inflation. Being "cognitively locked" into monetarism, the markets continued to demand restriction even when that restriction was unnecessary.

Given this market convention, the Fed insisted that before monetary policy could be eased, Congress had to take action on the deficit – not because deficits cause inflation, but because the markets thought that they did.[147] The Fed did eventually, and unexpectedly, loosen policy in late 1983.

---

[144] *Ibid.*, pp. 41–57, *passim.*
[145] Figures from the Bureau of Labor Statistics time series dataset at http://stats.bls.gov/sahome.html.
[146] This was also compounded by the fact that the Fed could no longer actually control the money supply in the first place. Financial deregulation had thrown all sorts of new financial instruments onto the marketplace that were inimical to Fed control.
[147] To paraphrase that well-known line from the sociologists Berger and Luckmann, "situations *bankers* perceive as real are real in their consequences." See Peter L. Berger and Thomas Luckmann, *The Social Construction of Reality: A Treatise in the Sociology of Knowledge* (Garden City, New York: Anchor Books, 1966), 51–5.

However, what finally made the Fed loosen monetary policy was not any realization that monetarism was part of the problem. Instead, the Fed gave up on monetarism, albeit briefly, because the stability of the whole banking system was at stake.

The Perils of Debt and Deregulation

The 1980 Monetary Control Act reduced banks' reserve requirements and abolished Regulation Q, a New Deal era regulation that set ceilings on interest rates. This encouraged savings and loan institutions to diversify their portfolios in order to remain competitive. In 1982 the Senate passed the Garn-St. Germaine Act, which further deregulated credit markets. The Act decontrolled savings and loan institutions and left them to compete in the marketplace. The problem with this new round of financial deregulation was that it occurred at exactly the worst possible time. Given the policies of the Fed, the interest rates at which the savings and loans had to borrow, and the rates that they could therefore charge their customers, were punitive.[148] Because of this, many savings and loan institutions, and not a few banks, became insolvent either by becoming too exposed on the interest rate yield spreads on existing deals or by investing in assets whose degree of risk proved to be unwarranted.[149]

A second factor destabilizing the domestic banking system was the international debt crisis. Briefly, the OPEC price hikes of the 1970s produced billions of "petrodollars." As a solution to the problem of all this excess cash gaining no returns and thereby depressing the dollar and dollar-denominated assets, Citibank CEO and BRT principal Wriston suggested "recycling" these petrodollars by offering them as loans to developing countries.[150] Given that these loans were taken out in an inflationary period, the real effective interest rate was often negative and developing countries borrowed heavily.

Unfortunately, the monetarist policies of the Fed turned Wriston's solution into a global problem. The deflation that the Fed compounded by its adherence to monetary targeting caused these debtor nations' export earnings to collapse when the United States economy contracted. Meanwhile, the interest rate appreciation that the Fed's monetarist regime demanded simply increased these countries' interest payments and overall debt burden. In May 1982 Mexico discretely let it be known that it was unable to pay back its debt. The state scrambled to assemble an emergency package, and Volker, realizing the seriousness of the situation, finally eased monetary

---

[148] This was especially true when taken in comparison to the sometimes negative real interest rates that pertained when the savings and loans and their customers had taken out the loans just a few years earlier.

[149] Meeropol, *Surrender*, pp. 188–92.

[150] Wriston is in fact infamous for a remark concerning this policy back in 1977. He is reputed to have said, "why not, governments never go bust."

policy. After averaging 14.7 percent from the first quarter of 1980 until the second quarter of 1982, the federal funds rate fell to an average of 9 percent during 1983.[151] Only because the entire world banking system was threatened did the Fed loosen monetary policy, but even then it was still running at approximately twice the rate of a decade earlier.

This confluence of events actually proved rather fortuitous for the state and business. With interest rates down and monetary contraction no longer overpowering the stimulatory effects of the deficit, the economy began to recover just in time for the 1984 election and the declaration that it was indeed "Morning in America."[152] Unfortunately, while unemployment fell and the recovery took hold, the deficit continued to increase, reaching $207 billion in 1983. However, at this juncture something unexpected happened in the markets: They seemed to forget all about the convention of monetarism. Given that the deficit was increasing, the inflation rate should have increased as long bonds were bid upward. Amazingly, with this bidding up of future debt, the "iron law" of monetarism itself disappeared like the morning mist.[153]

This seems to have occurred for two reasons. First, the markets found the value of stocks and bonds to be so depressed by the recession that they were virtually at fire-sale prices. Money exited the bond market and the long bull market of the 1980s began. Second, given that this loosening of policy did not in fact create an inflationary spurt, monetarism was seen by many to have worked and as such was no longer needed.[154] Nonetheless, while the markets seemed to forget monetarism temporarily, the Fed did not. The fear of inflation had become deeply ingrained at the Fed, and fearing a return of inflation, Volker continued to adhere to a policy of tight money throughout the rest of his term.[155] Beginning in December 1983, the prime rate was increased to 12.5 percent and then frozen for fifteen months.

What all this signaled was an important ideational change within the Fed. Until Volker, the Fed had waited for inflation to begin and then acted to suppress it. What the December 1983 policy shift signaled was some-

---

[151] Federal funds data from http://mars.wnec.edu/~econ/surrender/w2.html, calculation by the author.

[152] Given the depth of the recession, it is hardly surprising that the recovery seemed so dramatic.

[153] Long bond rates did in fact go up in late 1983, but in no way proportionate to the response of the Fed. See the figures at Federal Reserve database, http://www.stls.frb.org/fred.data/monetary/.

[154] It is perhaps more accurate to say that given the depth of the recession, even explosive growth would have taken some time to hit capacity constraints and cause inflation.

[155] Greenspan was to do the same with Bush and initially William Clinton. Indeed, if one compares the expected rate of inflation with federal funds rate from 1983, one sees that despite the decline in inflation, the federal funds rate actually increases throughout 1984 and 1985. See federal funds and expected inflation data from http://mars.wnec.edu/~econ/surrender/w2.html.

thing far more revolutionary. It signaled that "the new Federal Reserve approach was to sacrifice economic growth whenever the economy appeared to be 'too close' to 'full employment.'"[156] "Too close" to full employment, an anathema of an idea a mere decade ago, had now become the policy standard. Rather than prices being too high, *unemployment was legitimately being seen as being too low.* Given that interest rates were running at twice their postwar average and unemployment in 1984 averaged 7.4 percent, "Morning in America" was certainly going to be bleak in some parts of the country.

In such a situation, one would expect the opposition to mount a counterattack. Unfortunately, having no alternative ideas of their own to combat the assault of business, and given the Democrats' Coolidge-like aversion to deficits, the Democrats needed a new "big idea" with which to challenge the hegemony of the ideas of business and their allies in the state. In the early 1980s, they found one called industrial policy, and it was a disaster.

The Ideational Failure of the Democrats

To beat an idea, one needs another. As discussed earlier, Carter's penchant for blaming inflation on the deficit served him well as an electoral weapon with which to defeat Ford. However, by making this linkage, Carter effectively discredited the demand-side compensatory economic ideas that served as the basis of American embedded liberalism. By accepting and advocating that deficits caused inflation, the Democrats "[gave] away what had been in their long term interests to defend: the right to use federal funds to promote . . . full employment."[157] As James D. Savage argues, by 1980,

> . . . in the name of short term political gain the Democrats discredited the very foundation of their macroeconomic policy, leaving nothing substantial in its place. By abandoning deficit spending on the basis of a highly questionable economic pretense, the Democrats also discredited their attendant politics. For any new Democratic budget proposal that added a single dollar to the deficit instantly lost legitimacy on the grounds . . . that it helped cripple the economy.[158]

The Democrats therefore needed an alternative set of economic ideas with which to recapture the terms of debate. This proposed solution was, however, wholly different from either the supply-side ideas of Kemp and Laffer or traditional embedded liberal ideas.

In 1979 Carter set up an Economic Policy Group (EPG) headed by Treasury Secretary William G. Miller. In the search for new progressive

---

[156] Meeropol, *Surrender*, p. 105.
[157] Berman, *America's Right Turn*, p. 47.
[158] Savage, *Balanced Budgets*, p. 195.

economic ideas to defend what was left of embedded liberalism, the EPG returned to the ideas of the 1930s, but not the ideas of Eccles and Currie. Instead, the EPG went back to the associationalist ideas of the NIRA. The Democrats had in a sense come full circle. When the economy was in trouble, coordination as a solution once again proved too strong to resist, and this time around the Democrats discovered industrial policy. The meetings of the EPG spilled over into the press through the publications of EPG consultant Amitai Etzioni.[159] Etzioni claimed that America was effectively deindustrializing because the lack of a coherent investment strategy over the past two decades had led to declining industries and sclerotic growth. This idea was picked up by *Business Week*, which published a special issue concerning the "Reindustrialization of America" in June 1980.[160]

The "reindustrialization" idea was that America was being outcompeted in the global marketplace. As other countries entered the same markets as America with lower costs and greater technological advantages, American business was failing to compete. Consequently, to survive, the state had to shift resources from the "sunset" industries of today to the "sunshine" industries of tomorrow. If the state wanted to affect investment from a supply-side angle, rather than cut taxes, it should create institutions that picked winners and encouraged the growth of those firms and industries that would become the leading sectors of tomorrow.[161] Unfortunately, this first call for a Democratic answer to supply-side economics fell on deaf ears as the Carter administration foundered on the second oil shock and the Iranian hostage crisis.

These ideas resurfaced in the writings of Ira Magaziner and Robert Reich in 1982.[162] Magaziner and Reich developed and deployed what could be termed the first globalization argument of the 1980s. They claimed that static Ricardian comparative advantage had given way in the modern world to a situation of "competitive advantage" that could be shaped by the correct government policies. Consequently, *laissez faire*, both domestically and internationally, was a bankrupt strategy. In the "new global economy," only a hands-on "targeted industrial policy" that would promote "winners" would suffice. As Magaziner and Reich put it, "our country's real income can rise only if its labor and capital increasingly flow towards businesses

---

[159] Otis L. Graham, Jr., *Losing Time: The Industrial Policy Debate* (Cambridge: Harvard University Press, 1992), p. 42.

[160] *Business Week, The Reindustrialization of America*, June 30, 1980.

[161] Apart from the *Business Week* piece, see also Lester C. Thurow, *The Zero Sum Society: Distribution and the Politics of Economic Change* (New York: Basic Books, 1980), on the need for an interventionist strategy for investment and the shift from sunset to sunrise industries.

[162] Ira Magaziner and Robert Reich, *Minding America's Business* (New York: Vintage Books, 1982).

that add greater value per employee and we maintain a position . . . that is superior to our competitors."[163]

Such ideas were not without some heavyweight intellectual support. In international economics, a variant of Reich's domestically focused industrial policy, named strategic trade theory, was gaining ground.[164] These strategic trade theorists argued that certain industries generated "external scale economies" that governments could manipulate to achieve Magaziner and Reich's competitive advantage.[165] Taken in combination, domestic industrial policy plus international strategic trade ideas seemed to offer the Democratic Party a supply-side alternative to the ideas of business.

Reich continued to promote his ideas throughout 1982 and 1983. He authored a more popular book of the same lineage entitled *The Next American Frontier* that eventually found its way into the hands of Walter Mondale. Apparently, upon reading the galley proofs, Mondale declared, "This'll do it for the Democrats," and he "offered to plug Reich's forthcoming opus as doing for this generation what Keynes did for the previous one."[166] Indeed, the whole idea was catching on. In Congress in 1983, there were "at least 17 bills [that] proposed an armada of national development boards, commissions on competitiveness, and the like."[167] Concretely, the Democrats proposed the establishment of a National Industry Bank and a Competitiveness Council.[168] The Bank would make loans available to firms to promote cost reduction and investment while the Council would promote competitiveness more generally. It seemed that the "big idea" the Democrats so desperately needed had perhaps been found at last.

Unfortunately, there was a problem. This big idea was going to do nothing to restore American embedded liberalism since it was predicated upon a massive transfer of rents from labor to business. Even if winners could be identified *a priori*, which was problematic in and of itself, then the subsidies needed to generate the strategic gain could come from only

---

[163] *Ibid.*, p. 4 and *passim*.

[164] For a succinct summary of the Strategic Trade Debate, see Paul Krugman, ed., *Strategic Trade Policy and the New International Economics* (Cambridge: Massachusetts Institute of Technology Press, 1983).

[165] Basically, by credibly committing resources to specific sectors, governments not only could steal a lead on the opposition, they could deter new market entrants and thereby gain rents in excess of the resources committed to the sector concerned. Moreover, it was argued that the rent gain to the "strategic" state would be twofold since the barriers to entry that a competitor would face would be so large given the strategic state's commitment of resources that another state would not even try to compete in the same sector. Thus the state playing this type of strategy would gain extra rents to the home country against others. See James A. Brander, "Rationales for Strategic Trade and Industrial Policy," in Krugman, ed., *Strategic Trade Policy*, pp. 22–46.

[166] Mondale, quoted in Graham, *Losing Time*, p. 69.

[167] *Ibid.*, p. 110.

[168] Martin, *Shifting the Burden*, p. 166.

one place, a consumption loss for labor. Consequently, the end result of these policies would be exactly the same as those on offer from the GOP: business gains and labor loses. The advantage that the GOP policies had was that cutting taxes did not require new governmental institutions, the dreaded "big government" that the GOP had so successfully demonized, while industrial policy did.

Yet the fact that the idea was internally incoherent was the least of its problems. For if the success of an idea is contingent upon its plausibility, then the ideas of business that revolutionized economic policymaking in the 1970s should never have had the impact that they did. For political entrepreneurs such as Stockman, "shoehorning doctrines" and "jimmying figures" were far more important than demonstrating the robustness of an idea.[169] *Unfortunately, the Democrats insisted that an idea be correct as well as politically useful.* Thus, in August 1983 at a meeting organized by the Federal Reserve Bank of Kansas at Jackson Hole, Wyoming, "the economic intelligentsia of the Democratic Party (particularly the 'Young Turks' such as Paul Krugman and Lawrence Summers) got together to gun down the industrial policy idea."[170] Following this debacle, the Democratic challenger Mondale shied away from strategic trade and industrial policy arguments in the 1984 presidential campaign. As Mondale put it retrospectively, "the more I thought about it and listened to those guys . . . Reich and the others – I came to see that they were simply advocating more government. . . . So I backed away from it."[171]

Given this lack of any alternative to the ideas of business, the Democrats went out of their way during the 1984 campaign to convince the financial markets of their new-found fiscal probity, while the Republicans went on to become the biggest deficit financers of all time. The height of apostasy was reached when Mondale's main economic platform was reduced to promising to increase taxes in the midst of a recession and making a commitment to cut the budget to get the economy moving again.[172] Hoover, it seemed, was running for the Democrats.

These actions, exposed the crucial intellectual failure of the Democrats. Rather than use the industrial policy idea, regardless of its intrinsic merits, to win the argument and recapture the ideational high ground, the Democrats were still working within the ideas laid out by business and their allies in the state. Big government, regardless of its content, was defined as unquestionably bad. Consequently, any proposal that smacked of increasing the size of the government was *a priori* rejected. Moreover, having given

---

[169] See the comments of Stockman detailed in Greider, *The Education of David Stockman*, passim.

[170] At this meeting, Summers referred to Reich's proposals as "economic laetrile." See Krugman, *Peddling Prosperity*, p. 255.

[171] Mondale, quoted in Graham, *Losing Time*, p. 166.

[172] See Greider, *Secrets of the Temple*, p. 610.

up on their own economic legacy by assigning the cause of all economic ills to deficits, the Democrats found it difficult to advocate a program that, strangely, had nothing to do with deficits, their size, or otherwise.

Rather than use the industrial policy idea in the same way as business and the state had used tax cuts – to win the argument, reap the benefits, and then worry about the economic consequences – the new Democratic economists, the new generation of Walter Hellers and Paul Samuelson, had missed this point completely. As Weatherford and McDonnell put it regarding the Reagan agenda, the "policies proposed as solutions to economic problems appeared . . . to be perverse or mistaken, but . . . they fit neatly as part of a political strategy."[173] The Democrats had still to learn what business had learned back in the 1940s. The point of economic ideas is not merely to diagnose the economy, but is also to win the polity. By not realizing this as late as 1984, the Democrats consigned themselves to another two electoral defeats.

Finishing the Transformation

Democratic Sound Finance
With business having successfully reregulated labor, deregulated business, reinvented the economic ideas of the state, and declared "Morning in America," the revolutionary period of business activity came to an end and a period of consolidation of the achievements of that revolution began.[174] Ironically, despite abandoning monetary targeting, the Fed continued to adhere to monetarist principles, which led to the electoral undoing of George Bush.[175] Basically, in response to the perceived inflationary danger of too strong a recovery, the Fed tightened money throughout Bush's term of office and the economy slowed dramatically. What compounded this slowdown was the budget agreement struck in 1987 under the modified Gramm-Rudman-Hollings Monetary Control Act that sought to limit the growth in the deficit. The new deficit target figures due in 1990 under the modified 1987 budget agreement were projected to be $80 billion above target. To meet these targets, Bush had to go back on his famous campaign

---

[173] Weatherford and McDonnell, "Ideology and Economic Policy," p. 131.

[174] Some observers have made the case that the departure of Feldstein, Ture, and Sprinkel by 1984 shows that "these advisors . . . had only marginal influence." Perhaps a better interpretation is that they had achieved what they had set out to do and therefore left because the job was finished. See Weatherford and McDonnell, "Ideology and Economic Policy," p. 136.

[175] As Kirshner has put it, while "[t]he practical centerpiece of monetarism – control of the money supply – has been jettisoned . . . the essential tenets of monetarist philosophy – conservatism, the primacy of monetary policy, and above all else vigilance against inflation – have won." Jonathan Kirshner, "Inflation: Paper Dragon or Trojan Horse?" *Review of International Political Economy* 6 (4) (1999), p. 613.

promise of 1988 that under his administration he would neither increase taxes nor introduce new ones. On June 26, 1990, Bush reneged on this promise and it cost him the election.[176]

The unexpected decline in the fortunes of Bush opened up the ground for a Democratic alternative. The alternatives on offer, however, were, after twenty years of ideational capitulation, hardly the stuff with which to rebuild embedded liberalism. In the 1991 primaries, Senator Paul Tsongas ran a supply-side campaign that proposed to cut capital gains taxes and loosen antitrust laws to help America compete in the "new global economy." Meanwhile, ex-Governor Jerry Brown, having learned about taxes from the Proposition 13 debacle, proposed a *flat tax* of 13 percent as his main economic platform. Among such company, the candidacy of Clinton – which focused upon rising health care costs, the downsizing of American corporations, and the anemic nature of American economy – actually seemed somewhat radical. Clinton's radicalism was, however, to prove to be very short-lived.

The Clinton campaign did not focus upon the issue of the deficit, as the Democrats had unsuccessfully tried to do throughout the 1980s. Rather, it focused upon the economic consequences of past Republican administrations' assaults on the embedded liberal order. Throughout the campaign, Clinton combined the themes of the distributional effects of Reaganism with the need for investment and modernization in order to compete in the "new global economy."[177] Clinton's major first-term policy document, *A Vision of Change for America*, attempted to retake the ideational high ground from business and the GOP. *Vision* explicitly rejected trickle-down economics and supply-side tax cuts, and, in marked contrast to the efforts of Mondale and Michael Dukakis during previous campaigns in the 1980s, sought to rehabilitate the role of the government in the economy. However, while challenging the economic ideas of business and the GOP, *Vision* made some important capitulations.

Vision accepted the argument that "for more than a decade, the Federal government has been living well beyond its means." As a consequence of this largess, "the projected growth in the economy will be less than the projected growth in the deficit," and "the deficit will become unsustainable unless a credible deficit reduction program is initiated now."[178] Clinton's thinking on this was heavily influenced by Volker's successor at the Fed, Alan Greenspan. In December 1992, Clinton met with the Federal Reserve

---

[176] Figures from Berman, *America's Right Turn*, p. 149.

[177] This constant reiteration of "the challenge of the global" in Clinton's campaign and afterward speaks volumes about the ideological bind into which the Democrats had argued themselves. By giving up on domestic fiscal management and then industrial policy, the rhetoric of globalization was really the only place left to go.

[178] *A Vision of Change for America*, (Washington: Office of Management and Budget, February 17, 1993), p. 8.

chair, who sought to impress upon Clinton the importance of reducing the deficit. In line with the Fed's deeply ingrained monetarism, Greenspan, one of the main developers of the idea that deficits caused inflation during the 1970s, argued that unless long-term interest rates fell, real growth would not take place, as the bond markets would demand an inflation premium. In such a situation, the Fed would have to respond, and any recovery would be choked off by tighter money. Given these constraints, deficit reduction had to come first.[179]

While accepting this argument, Clinton did not want to focus simply on deficit reduction, as this would obviate the rest of the policy goals outlined in *Vision*, including the stimulation of the economy and the establishment of a system of universal health care.[180] In an effort to overcome the bind of the deficit, the Clinton plan stressed investment. As *Vision* argued, "the overarching theme of the Clinton Administration's economic plan is to increase public and private investment in the broadest sense ... [consequently] ... the need to increase investment motivates all three elements of the Clinton plan ... stimulus, investment and deficit reduction."[181] The sequencing of these strategies was important. The primary goal became not deficit reduction, but fiscal stimulus. Once a stimulus had taken hold, greater investment in human capital would follow, and this in turn would be followed by deficit reduction.

Clinton sought a fiscal stimulus of $16.3 billion in actual spending and $12 billion in a temporary investment tax credit to make sure that the recovery was sustained at a high enough level to impact employment and growth. He then sought to reduce the deficit with the receipts of this higher growth. While it briefly seemed as if growthsmanship was making a comeback, the stimulus package was in fact fatally weakened by the Democrats' continued fixation with the deficit.

First, it was impossible to spend without increasing the deficit. By accepting the "deficits cause inflation" logic himself, Clinton simply reinvented the policy dilemma that Reagan had faced. How does one boost growth and reduce the deficit at the same time? In 1993, as in 1981, this question had no real answer, regardless of the sequence of the options. Given this sequencing problem, the proposed spending was carefully packaged to be "a down-payment on longer-run investment" that would be "fast acting and job creating."[182] The problem was that the $16.3 billion in spending advocated was "the amount of appropriations fell short of the combined

---

[179] The meeting with Greenspan is discussed in Bob Woodward's account of the Clinton election. See Bob Woodward, *The Agenda* (New York: Random House, 1994), pp. 69–71. See also Meeropol, *Surrender*, p. 230.

[180] On the effect of this Fed's "deficits cause inflation" thesis on *Vision*, see p. 10 of *Vision*. On health care and inequality, see pp. 7, 11 of *Vision*.

[181] *A Vision of Change*, p. 21.

[182] *Ibid.*, p. 21.

discretionary spending caps in the (1990) Budget Enforcement Act...
[Therefore]...spending [would] not increase the deficit relative to what
was agreed in the 1990 budget agreement."[183] In other words, the stimulus
was at best a restoration of foregone spending, rather than a stimulus *per
se*. Second, the tax credit part of the package was simply a rerun of the
1962 Investment Tax Credit, whose actual investment effects were meager
at best. Third, although *Vision* called for a stimulus that would create
jobs, most of its recommendations centered on educational improvements
designed to make footloose global capital invest in the United States, which,
while admirable if rather implausible, hardly constituted an instant jobs
strategy.[184] Given these contradictions, even if it was passed, the stimulus
was likely to have very little effect on the economy at all.

The question of the desirability, or even the necessity, of the stimulus was
settled rather definitively when Congress rejected the stimulus package. In
a rerun of 1981, albeit in reverse, the administration sent two bills to Congress; one contained the stimulus package, and the other contained deficit
reduction proposals.[185] The former bill was allowed to perish in Congress
in April 1993, and, "With that, the Clinton administration was left with
only one economic strategy, deficit reduction."[186] Consequently, "the
Clinton Council of Economic Advisors pulled out all the stops in identifying deficit reduction as the key element in [the administration's] economic
program."[187] However, in doing so, the 1994 CEA report shows clearly how
much more ideological territory the Democrats had given up over the past
twelve years.

The 1994 CEA report constitutes a reversal of the goals of *Vision* by
claiming that deficit reduction, rather than stimulus and investment, was in
fact the core of the economic strategy of the administration. The report
centers on the effect that a credible deficit reduction strategy would have
on long-term interest rates and growth, just as Greenspan had argued.
Echoing the "wishful thinking" about expectations of the Reagan *Program*,
the 1994 report contends that the very action of putting forward a

[183] *Ibid.*, p. 27.

[184] The appointment of Reich as labor secretary speaks volumes here. It seems that Reich's
argument, that the interdependence of the world economy was such that capital mobility
ensured that jobs were a function of skill premiums alone, was actually listened to at the
highest levels. For some criticisms of this thesis, see, among many others, Robert Wade,
"Globalization and Its Limits," in Suzanne Berger and Ronald Dore, eds., *National Diversity and Global Capitalism* (Ithaca: Cornell University Press, 1996), pp. 78–83.

[185] In 1981 Reagan sent two bills to Congress, one containing tax cuts and the other spending cuts. In 1993 Clinton sent two bills to Congress, one continuing budget cuts and the
other containing spending increases.

[186] Meeropol, *Surrender*, p. 235.

[187] See Meeropol, *Surrender*, p. 236; Council of Economic Advisors, *Economic Report of the
President* (Washington: Government Printing Office, 1994), pp. 35–7.

"credible strategy" would itself cause interest rates to come down.[188] More-over, in a further capitulation to the ideas that had sucessfully disembed-ded liberalism, the report hoped that by pursuing deficit reduction above all else, the Fed would increase the rate of growth in the money stock. In a past era, the Democrats would have hoped that this deficit reduction would increase demand, lower the marginal efficiency of investment, and thus create employment. By 1994 the hope was that a less restrictive policy would increase national saving, leading to an increase in investment that would ultimately reduce the interest rate.[189] Boskin and Feldstein would be proud of the Democrats' economic education.

Despite this capitulation in fiscal policy, there were still sites of resist-ance. One area where Clinton was initially not willing to compromise was on the idea of a balanced budget amendment. A balanced budget amend-ment would abolish Democratic Party politics. The requirement to balance the budget over the financial year would effectively make permanent the fiscal constraints on government spending that the deficit had wrought throughout the 1980s and would constitute the crowning achievement of the revolt started by business in the early 1970s. If such an amendment were passed, then government would be reduced to a truly minimalist form, and any kind of embedded liberal order would be impossible to resurrect. Realizing this, the administration managed to defeat a series of balanced budget amendment proposals in 1994 and 1995.[190] These victories were, however, to prove short-lived. When the Republicans scored heavy victories in the 1994 elections, gaining control of the House for the first time in forty years, they sensed that their moment for counterattack had arrived. As William Feulner, the head of the Heritage Foundation, put it, "Ronald Reagan has been reelected, not once but hundreds of times."[191]

The Republicans proposed a Balanced Budget Act. The Democrats rejected it, but accepted the principle, and eventually a compromise was found. On June 13, 1995, Clinton accepted the goal of a balanced budget by 2005. The Republicans rejected this and insisted on balance within seven years. Unfortunately for the Republicans, their own ideological

---

[188] As the report puts it, "because the Clinton Plan had credibility, financial markets antici-pated these effects . . . [and] . . . long bond rates fell immediately in response." Council of Economic Advisors, *Economic Report of the President* (1994), p. 35.

[189] Meeropol, *Surrender*, p. 237; Council of Economic Advisors, *Economic Report of the President* (1994), p. 36.

[190] In mid-March 1994, a balanced budget amendment failed to pass the House by 271–153, a mere twelve votes short of the two-thirds majority required to pass a constitutional amendment. Earlier, on March 1, 1994, the Senate rejected a similar measure 63–37, only four votes short of the two-thirds figure. In 1995, the administration managed to defeat a proposed amendment in the Senate by one vote.

[191] William Feulner, quoted in Berman, *America's Right Turn*, p. 176.

unity proved as much a liability as an asset, at least in the short term. In November 1995 Clinton vetoed a continuing resolution that had the effect of shutting down the government for three weeks. Rather than consolidating their position, such behavior by the Republicans was widely seen by the public as petulance. Such GOP strategic gaffes, combined with the weak candidacy of Robert Dole for the presidency in 1996, transformed the "lame duck" Clinton into a reelectable president.

But reelected to do what? Clinton no longer had an agenda, let alone a program. Apart from marginal increases in the minimum wage, the extension of the earned income tax credit, and the family leave bill, the Democrats had failed to enact any major reformist legislation.[192] Despite all the discussion of investment in human capital and the inequities of the tax system and income distribution in *Vision*, apart from raising the top rate of tax in the 1993 budget to 39.5 percent *in order to reduce the deficit* (which still made the top tax rate 30.5 percent *lower* than it was in 1979), the Democrats achieved nothing in these areas. The Democrats had lost control of the ideas that made Democratic politics possible. The turn to industrial policy and the later turn to the rhetoric of global competitiveness did nothing to reclaim the ideational ground that business and the GOP had succeeded in constantly expanding despite the election of a Democratic president in 1992. Thus when the new administration began in 1996, there was no attempt to win back that which had already been lost. Clinton, as Michael Meeropol puts it so well, simply surrendered.

Almost in anticipation of a renewed GOP offensive, Clinton's 1996 State of the Union Address declared that "the era of big government is over," and that he would in this session keep a campaign promise made back in 1992, "to end welfare as we know it." That original promise in 1993 was based on a notion of skill enhancements, training, and general active labor market policies – another attempt at a Democratic supply-side alternative. By 1996, the "end of welfare as we know it" was simply the enactment of the ideas of business and the GOP's *Contract with America*.[193] The GOP submitted its Personal Responsibility Act to the House in late 1995. In early 1996, Clinton vetoed the measure as "too extreme" and then announced that he would sign a version of the bill so long as some cuts in Medicaid were restored. The GOP complied and on July 31, 1996, Clinton promised to sign the now modified Personal Responsibility Act in August, which he

---

[192] The hijacking of the health care reform package by business is omitted here for reasons of space. For an excellent account, see Theda Skocpol, *Boomerang: Clinton's Health Security Effort and the Turn against Government In U.S. Politics* (New York: W. W. Norton and Company, 1996).

[193] See United States Congress, House Committee on Ways and Means, *Contract with America: Overview Hearings before the Committee on Ways and Means,* House of Representatives, 104th Congress, First Session, January 5, 10, 11, and 12, 1995.

did. The Act cut straight to the heart of what remained of the ideas and institutions of the 1930s. The commitment of the state to provide Aid for Families with Dependent Children (AFDC) was terminated, and a five-year time limit for the receipt of welfare benefits was established. All told, the Act was estimated to save around $55 billion over five years.[194] The final irony of this capitulation was the fact that the deficit had ceased to be a problem. By 1997 the deficit had shrunk to a mere $21.9 billion, and yet $55 billion in cuts were still being made.[195] The ideas of business had completely triumphed.

Coterminous with these reforms, Clinton finally gave in on the balanced budget. Following on from his June 13, 1995, acceptance of the goal of a balanced budget by 2005, the struggle was reduced to "which path to a balanced budget was more realistic."[196] The GOP proposed tax cuts of $230 billion and spending cuts of $480 billion over the next seven years.[197] The administration countered with $90 billion in tax cuts, but deadlock ensued. Eventually a compromise was worked out, and in November 1996, Congress approved and the president signed legislation that promised a balanced budget by 2002. This legislation "extracted $155 billion in savings over five years from Medicare, and slowed the growth of discretionary spending."[198] In his 1998 State of the Union Address, Clinton celebrated the success of the balanced budget agreement and argued that "turning a sea of red into black is no miracle ... it is the product of hard work by the American people and *two visionary acts by Congress,* the courageous vote in 1993 [the deficit reduction package] and *the truly historic bipartisan balanced budget agreement passed by this Congress.*"[199]

Echoing this ideational failure, the 1998 Council of Economic Advisors attempted to take credit for the achievements of *Contract* and discounted the abject failure of all the main planks of *Vision.* Once again, in a demonstration of the Democrats' ideological capitulation, the economic growth of 1995–8 was wholly attributed to the credibility effects of its deficit reduction strategy.[200] The *Economic Report of the President* in fact gives one the impression that deficit reduction was the only goal the administration ever

[194] Meeropol, *Surrender*, p. 249.
[195] See the St. Louis Fed database at http://www.stls.frb.org/fred/data/business/fygfd.
[196] Meeropol, *Surrender*, pp. 249–50.
[197] Recall that these targets are ten times the nominal figures that Stockman sought to cut in 1981.
[198] Monica Borkowski, "The 105th Congress: A Look Back at a Legislative Term," *New York Times,* October 18, 1998, my italics.
[199] John M. Broder, "State of the Union: The Overview; Clinton, with Crisis Swirling, Puts Focus on Social Security in Upbeat State of the Union Talk," *New York Times,* January 28, 1998.
[200] Council of Economic Advisors, *Economic Report of the President* (Washington: United States Government Printing Office, 1998), p. 22.

had.[201] Similarly, on regulation the *Report* notes that "the administration is also committed to reducing the burden of government regulation and ensuring that the benefits of new regulations justify their costs."[202]

It is perhaps worth recalling the language of the 1981 *Program for Economic Recovery* by way of comparison. Reagan's 1981 *Program* notes that regulatory decisions "should not be undertaken unless the potential benefits to society outweigh the potential costs."[203] The fact that these claims are almost identical speaks volumes to the ideational changes that have taken place since the 1970s, to say nothing of the institutional transformations that those changes made possible. In conclusion, we can observe a final irony. While the Democrats defeated the ideas of business in order to build embedded liberalism, business was able to dismantle embedded liberalism only once the Democrats lost sight of what they were defending. Disembedding liberalism was above all else, then, a struggle over ideas, a struggle that the Democrats lost.

---

[201] Yet a simpler and more accurate interpretation of the long boom lies not in the strategy's credibility effects but in the rather undisguised effort by the Fed to aid Bush prior to the 1992 election. In June 1990, guarding against inflation, the Federal Funds Rate reached 8.29 percent. By December 1992 the Federal Funds Rate had fallen to 3.45 percent. This loosening of policy indeed promoted growth, but it was too late for Bush and too early for Clinton to claim as his own. See Meeropol, *Surrender*, p. 222.

[202] Council of Economic Advisors, *Economic Report of the President* (1998), p. 24.

7

Disembedding Liberalism in Sweden

The Politicization of Labor

Similar to what occurred in the United States, Swedish embedded liberal institutions both generated and became subject to increasing uncertainty during the late 1960s. What brought Sweden to this point was a combination of three domestic level factors: increasing labor militancy, a turn to legislation rather than negotiation in business-labor relations, and increasing state intervention in the economy. For Swedish business, this combination of factors signaled a clear repudiation of the ideas underpinning Swedish embedded liberalism and served as a focal point for the reemergence of organized business as a political actor. How business used the same ideas we saw in the transformation of the American institutional order to break the institutions of Swedish embedded liberalism is once again the key to understanding institutional change.

A new wave of labor unrest hit Sweden in the late 1960s and early 1970s. In December 1969, a strike at the state-owned iron-ore mine at Leveäniemi spread to other mines in nearby Kiruna and Mamberget. As Peter Swenson notes, "the unofficial and illegal character of the strike was widely interpreted . . . as a repudiation of the [Landsorganisationen i Sverige] (LO) affiliated Miners' Union and, perhaps just as much, of centralized . . . control in peak level bargaining."[1] On the heels of this unrest, the number of wildcat strikes shot up precipitously to over two hundred fifty separate instances during 1970.

One of the demands of the striking miners in the Kiruna dispute was parity with white-collar employees outside of the LO wage agreements. What made such claims problematic for the governing Swedish Social Democratic Party (*Sveriges Socialdemokratiska Arbetareparti*, SAP) was

---

[1] Peter Swenson, *Fair Shares: Unions, Pay, and Politics in Sweden and West Germany* (Ithaca: Cornell University Press, 1989), p. 85.

that they seemed to signal that the policy of solidaristic wages was promoting tensions within the unions themselves.[2] The miners' demand for pay equality with white-collar workers would mean that the LO had to make solidaristic pay less egalitarian, and thus less effective as a rationalization strategy. The Kiruna strikes were not merely about wages, however. They were also about poor work environments, the social consequences of the active labor market policies, and most important, shop-floor power relations. As Hugh Heclo and Henrik Madsen put it, "To some extent, the Kiruna strikes represented a traditional action to secure better pay, but more important was the dissatisfaction manifested regarding the prevailing patterns of authority at the workplace."[3]

The issue of shop-floor power relations stemmed back to 1968 when the LO was unable to realize its goal of achieving greater worker decision making at plant level in its negotiations with the Swedish Employers' Confederation (*Svenska arbetsgivareföreningen*, SAF) during the previous year's review of occupational safety standards. By 1970, given concern over these matters and the Kiruna strikes, the LO turned to the SAP for legislative action and proposed "[a] series of legislative proposals known as the democratization of working-life [that] gained broad support in the Riksdag in the 1970's."[4] These legislative proposals fell into three main areas: work-environment reform, codetermination legislation, and the wage-earners funds.[5]

This change from negotiation to legislative fiat bore fruit with the 1973 revision of the 1949 Worker's Protection Act. The following year a more comprehensive modification of power relations at plant level took place under the 1974 Work Environment Act. However, as far as LO was

---

[2] Swenson, *Fair Shares*, p. 91. On the paradox of egalitarian wage policy promoting demands for greater equalization, see Andrew Martin, "Wage Bargaining and Swedish Politics: The Political Implications of the End of Central Negotiations," Harvard University, Center for European Studies, Working Paper Series (36) (1991).

[3] Hugh Heclo and Henrik Madsen, *Policy and Politics in Sweden: Principled Pragmatism* (Philadelphia: Temple University Press, 1987), p. 121. See also the 1971 LO congress report on these issues, *Demokrati I företagen* (Stockholm: Landsorganisationen, 1971).

[4] Victor A. Pestoff, "Towards a New Swedish Model of Collective Bargaining and Politics," in Colin Crouch and Franz Traxler, eds., *Organized Industrial Relations in Europe: What Future?* (Aldershot: Avebury Press, 1991), p. 155.

[5] As Heclo and Madsen put it, "the novel feature in the union's approach to [reforming] the working environment lay in the downplaying of the consultative employer-employee tradition and a greater reliance on the parliamentary process to get results." Heclo and Madsen, *Policy and Politics*, p. 122. Similarly, John D. Stephens argues that "what particularly irked employers was LO's resort to legislation instead of negotiated compromise with SAF." See John D. Stephens, "Is Swedish Corporatism Dead: Thoughts on Its Supposed Demise in the Light of the Abortive 'Alliance for Growth' in 1998." Paper prepared for the Twelfth International Conference of Europeanists, Council for European Studies, March 30–April 1, 2000, p. 6.

concerned, reforming the work environment "proved impossible so long as SAF and its members maintained their unlimited rights at plant level."[6] These unlimited rights, those of ownership and the disposal of surplus that the ideas of the 1930s had established as inviolable, had now become objects of contestation. In response to this perceived lack of progress on the democratization of work life, the state passed the Codetermination Act in 1976, which threatened to give labor a governing voice in the production decisions of firms. Taken together, the work-life proposals constituted a collective legislative assault on business's right to manage, and unsurprisingly, management resisted. Wigforss's slogan from the 1920s that "democracy cannot stop at the factory gates" was fine for business – so long as democracy stopped at the factory gates. Once the LO and SAF began to take Wigforss's slogan seriously, business began to question the value of a set of institutions whose distributions were becoming more and more asymmetric, from business's point of view.[7]

By taking the legislative route, the LO obtained better results in the short run than it could by negotiation. Unfortunately for labor, whatever short-run gains that could be made through legislation were much less than the long-run costs of business's noncooperation. The problem, of course, was that business did not accept obtaining greater job protection, expanding negotiation rights, and having a voice in the disposal of profits as organic extensions of the ideas of the embedded liberal order. Instead, business perceived these claims as an ultimatum to acquiesce in the face of "democracy beyond the factory gates," a demand that business was unwilling to entertain.

Therefore, in parallel to what occurred in the United States, business's sense of being under siege from labor and the state grew throughout this period. As Richard G. Henning puts it,

During the seventies a new law or decree was introduced every eighth hour, and some new regulation applying to companies every 26th hour. A new law restricting the freedom of business life was said to appear every tenth day. This was the image that Swedish business liked to present of the impact of politics on business enterprises during the seventies.[8]

---

[6] Victor A. Pestoff, "Joint Regulation, Meso Games and Political Exchange in Swedish Industrial Relations," in Bernd Marin, ed., *Governance and Generalized Exchange: Self-Organizing Policy Networks in Action* (Boulder, CO: Westview Press, 1991), p. 330.

[7] On business's reaction to the LO's legislative assaults, see Andrew Martin, "The Politics of Macroeconomic Policy and Wage Coordination in Sweden," in Torben Iversen, Jonas Pontusson, David Soskice, eds., *Unions, Employers and Central Banks: Macroeconomic Coordination and Institutional Change in Social Market Economies* (Cambridge: Cambridge University Press, 2000), pp. 232–64, esp. pp. 252–61.

[8] Richard G. Henning, "Sweden: Political Interference with Business," in M. P. C. M. Van Schendelen and R. J. Jackson, eds., *The Politicization of Business in Western Europe* (London: Crook Helm, 1987), p. 29.

However, while the work-life acts promoted business hostility, what really set SAF on a collision course with LO was the 1974 proposal for the wage-earners funds – the LO's proposed solution to the problems of wildcatting and promoting greater economic democracy and investment.

The Wage Earner Funds

The high profit margins that Swedish corporations experienced during the 1972–3 boom had not gone unnoticed by LO. The LO viewed these profits as unacceptable because of a side effect that the solidarity wage has on the distribution of wages and profits during a boom. Specifically, leading sectors were able to employ labor more cheaply than the market rate would dictate since low-productivity workers were paid the same wage as high-productivity workers. While the Rehn-Meidner model was originally designed to promote high-productivity sectoral adjustment, this side effect reduced the cost of high-skill labor as wages were compressed toward the mean. Profits therefore surged at a time when labor in leading sectors was unable to realize its market rate of return, and thus asymmetrically shouldered the costs of solidaristic wages. Just as business began to see the existing institutional order as asymmetrically benefiting labor, labor's demands for greater democracy and control combined with a belief that the distributions of embedded liberal institutions were becoming asymmetrically skewed toward business. As such, the conventions underpinning Swedish embedded liberalism were coming undone. The state sought an answer to this dilemma and embraced LO's proposed solution: the wage earner funds.

As Swen Steinmo notes, "the wage earner funds were initially conceived ... as a mechanism to socialize the economy and reverse the trend toward the concentration of economic power in private hands."[9] The problem with this new strategy was that it constituted a frontal assault on the sanctity of private ownership, the foundational principle of Swedish embedded liberalism. The basic logic of the wage earner funds was that "a 20 percent profits tax was to be imposed on corporations ... [and] ... the revenue from this tax would be used to ... buy out most of Sweden's major capital interests," while the funds were to be controlled by the LO rather than the state.[10] The Meidner plan, the basis of the funds proposal, "sought to even out the differences in the structure of wealth and increase workers' influence over the economy by means of capital ownership. Over the years, a major shift in the social power of ownership would occur, from private holders of capital to collective ownership of capital managed by workers representatives."[11] As a result, the funds would "support solidaristic wage

[9] Sven Steinmo, "Social Democracy vs. Socialism: Goal Adaptation in Social Democratic Sweden," *Politics and Society* 16 (4) Fall (1988), p. 431.

[10] Steinmo, "Social Democracy," p. 431. See also Swenson, *Fair Shares*, p. 140.

[11] Heclo and Madsen, *Policy and Politics*, p. 269.

policy, counteract the wealth and power concentration which results from profit-based self-financing, and strengthen wage earner influence via co-ownership."[12]

Despite what was being proposed, the LO did not see the funds as an assault on the rights of business. Rather, it saw the funds as an extension of the existing order. Again, similar to what was seen in the United States, a capital formation crisis was narrated, but in this case it was labor rather than business doing the narrating. The LO argued that a particular weakness of current embedded liberal institutions, apart from generating excessive profits, was that they precipitated a decline in the rate of investment. The LO reasoned that the funds could solve this problem as they could supplement capital formation. Therefore, as far as the LO was concerned, the funds did not constitute a fundamental challenge to business since the original Rehn-Meidner proposals in the early 1950s had opened the door for collective capital formation through credit subsidization, while the 1959 ATP pension reform strengthened this investment-augmenting principle.[13] Moreover, the funds were hardly a new idea; as far back as the 1961 LO congress, the unions had argued for the need for rationalization funds that would strengthen the role of the LO in both guiding and even providing investment.[14]

Yet, what the LO did not take into account was a more general problem with embedded liberal institutions: how to best stabilize differing conventions among business and labor as to the appropriate determinants of investment. For business, retained profits at whatever level are defined as investment, while for labor, profits beyond a politically determined level were deemed inherently "excessive" and were thus candidates for political control rather than market allocation. This dispute over the appropriate role of the state and the market in investment policy formed the crux of the disagreement between business and labor over the funds. Under the logic of embedded liberal institutions, "transforming public savings into corporate investment must be done through indirect forms of lending that curtailed public steering of corporate investment decisions."[15] In other words, the right to manage and invest had to remain a micro-level managerial prerogative. The work-life legislation and the funds proposal signaled to business that labor and the state had abandoned this understanding.[16]

Business's discomfiture over this issue was heightened by the slowdown in growth that occurred across all the OECD countries during the early

[12] Quoted in Swenson, *Fair Shares*, p. 167.
[13] See the 1976 LO report *Kollektiv kapitalbildning genom lötagarfonder* (Stockholm: Landsorganisationen, 1976).
[14] Heclo and Madsen, *Policy and Politics*, pp. 163–4.
[15] Jonas Pontusson, *The Limits of Social Democracy: Investment Politics in Sweden* (Ithaca: Cornell University Press, 1992), p. 103.
[16] See Martin, "The Politics of Macroeconomic Policy," p. 255.

1970s. One of the unexpected effects of this slowdown was that companies' time horizons shortened. Given the concomitant collapse of the Bretton Woods order and attendant uncertainty, companies' debt management structures changed to accommodate greater financial volatility. Consequently, the financing sought by business changed in content from debt financing, which is subject to interest rate fluctuations, to equity issues.[17] Such a change meant that the primary responsibility for the supply of credit fell no longer to the state, acting as the creditor of cheap money, but fell instead to stockholders more concerned with the short-term financial bottom line of the company. In this new and uncertain context, the idea that the funds could assist in capital formation struck business as an obsolete idea at best and political camouflage for nationalization at worst.

In short, the SAP was landed with a political albatross, the SAF was furious, and at last, the bourgeois parties all had an issue around which they could collectively mobilize. As Olof Ljunggren, director of the SAF, summarized business's perspective on the funds issue, "the wage earner fund proposal is brutal and will lead to a direct socialization. Additionally, it is presented in a fraudulent manner. I can guarantee that employers will use all legal means of opposing the fund socialization scheme."[18] Not surprisingly, the SAP lost the next two elections to a center-right coalition.

The Failure of the Bourgeois State

Despite being in power for the first time in forty-four years, the bourgeois administrations of 1976–81 surprisingly did not attempt to alter fundamentally the institutions of Swedish embedded liberalism. Apart from disavowing the wage earners funds, the bourgeois parties offered no real alternative to SAP policies. In fact, during the economic downturn of the period, the bourgeois parties nationalized several major industries and allowed the government deficit to grow exponentially. Yet, while the economic downturn of the period obviously played a part in limiting the bourgeois state's freedom of action, there were also strong ideational reasons behind such odd policy choices.

Foremost among them was that "for two generations, the Social Democratic Party . . . had warned the public about the dismantling of social commitments that would occur should a bourgeois government ever come to power."[19] Given these ideological constraints, "the bourgeois coalition found itself continuing to improvise from crisis to crisis."[20] As the LO's chief economist Per Edin observed,

---

[17] On this issue, see John Eatwell, "International Financial Liberation: The Impact on World Development," UNDP Office of Development Studies Discussion Papers Series (12) May (1997).

[18] Olof Ljunggren, July 1, 1983, quoted in Jan-Erik Larsson and Jon-Henri Holmberg, *Vändpunkt* (Stockholm: Timbro Forlag, 1984), p. 6.

[19] Heclo and Madsen, *Policy and Politics*, p. 61.

[20] *Ibid.*, p. 66.

... for the first time in forty four years there was a bourgeois government. Every conservative person, politicians, and employers said "why couldn't our government, the bourgeois government, rule by bourgeois policies? Why did they have to be social democratic policies?" And the answer was given by Ullsten, the Liberal Prime Minister, [he said] "we were the prisoners of LO."[21]

Ullsten was right, but not in the most obvious sense. What really mattered was that the bourgeois governments of 1976–82 were prisoners of the ideas of the LO.

There are several reasons why the bourgeois parties accepted the governing ideas of embedded liberalism at this time and did not seek to break them. First, although the ability of the LO to call disruptive strikes was not in doubt, the bourgeois government was not held back by the threat of industrial action. As we shall see later, SAF was not afraid of provoking LO, and indeed SAF actively sought such confrontations during this period. As such, the bourgeois state was not hamstrung by the threat of industrial action since this was beyond its control in the first place. Second, any attempt to go against the ideas of the LO took place in the midst of a sharp economic downturn. Given this, the ability of the LO to call industrial action was reduced by the threat of greater layoffs. Third, and perhaps most important, during the elections of this period none of the bourgeois parties actually articulated any desire to depart radically from traditional social democratic policies during their campaigns.

How the bourgeois parties thought about taxation policy is illustrative of this ideational path-dependence. In the 1981 election, the Conservative Party (*Moderata Samlingspartiet*) argued that "tax pressure encourages invisible transactions and thereby undermines the civic spirit and solidarity which keeps society together."[22] Therefore, "easing the tax burden ... becomes paradoxically a means of defending the welfare state."[23] The Conservatives also campaigned throughout the 1970s and early 1980s that high marginal personal taxation was bad for growth, not because of its disincentive or Laffer effects, but because high taxes were beneficial to business, the low-wage earner was hardest hit. Thus, the tax system had become a new source of poverty. When the Conservatives did try to challenge these ideas head on, they were roundly defeated. For example, in 1985 the Conservatives attempted to break with existing ideas and adopted a neoliberal agenda that proposed a Thatcherite assault on the welfare state. Their 1985

---

[21] Per Olof Edin, interview with the author, Stockholm, June 6, 1997.

[22] Daniel Tarschys, "Public Policy Innovation in a Zero-Growth Economy: A Scandinavian Perspective," *International Social Sciences Journal* (31) 4 (1987), p. 699.

[23] *Ibid.*, p. 699. See also Erik Åsard and W. Lance Bennett, "Regulating the Marketplace of Ideas: Political Rhetoric in Swedish and American National Elections," *Political Studies* 43 (4) December (1995).

platform called for "a 'system change' to replace the social democratic order with the market economic alternative." This alternative included "lowering tax pressure, opening the public sector to competition, and privatizing publicly owned enterprise."[24] Mounting such a direct ideational challenge as a purely electoral gambit proved costly in that the Conservatives' vote share in 1985 did not recover to its 1982 level.

In sum, the only way the Conservatives could advocate tax changes was to frame them in the embedded liberal terms, and in doing so, they strengthened rather than challenged those terms. Given these three factors, the state was not simply hamstrung by the LO's ability to man the barricades. In a rerun of the situation facing the SAP in the 1920s before the ideas of the Stockholm School were available to them, the bourgeois parties could not practice bourgeois politics precisely because they had no alternative ideas with which to govern when actually in power.

With the failure of the bourgeois state to advance bourgeois policies, business realized that the existing institutional order, in particular the ideas it rested upon, had to be challenged and replaced. Business interpreted the legislative assault by labor and the failure of the bourgeois government of 1976–82 as the point of no return and began to deploy new ideas to change the terms of debate and thus attack the institutions of Swedish embedded liberalism directly. The institutional changes and policy shifts of the late 1980s and early 1990s become explicable only with an understanding of the politicization of business and the politics of ideas in which business engaged.

Coordinated action by the SAF was key in turning the tide against embedded liberal ideas and institutions. While for most of the 1950s and 1960s the SAF was largely an apolitical organization, once the encroachments of labor and the state began, a new generation of SAF leaders – Sture Eskillsson, Olof Ljunggren, Curt Nicolin, and later Ulf Laurin – revitalized SAF structures and contested the ideological terrain once wholly owned by the LO and Rehn-Meidner. In short, "SAF ventured into the marketing of capitalism."[25]

Building Muscle: The Remobilization of Swedish Business

The Structure and Resources of Swedish Business
In the late 1970s, the increasing concentration of Swedish business was reflected in changes in SAF's organizational structure. While the number of small firms in SAF increased during the 1980s, the percentage of the total firms that employ over five hundred people also increased, thus reflecting

---

[24] Martin, "Wage Bargaining and Swedish Politics," pp. 94–5.
[25] Heclo and Madsen, *Policy and Politics*, p. 126.

the overall trend in industry toward concentration.[26] The political relevance of such concentration is that voting rights in SAF, and thus a voice in policy, are directly proportional to the number of employees and the total wage bill. Decisions therefore get concentrated in very few hands, principally those of very large firms. Moreover, SAF statutes prohibit independent action of member firms on either collective wage agreements or strike/ lockout policy. Such prohibitions are backed up by hefty fines for non-compliance. This hierarchical structure enables the SAF to target its financial resources precisely.

SAF's resources dwarf those of all the Swedish political parties combined. Between the late 1970s and 1987, SAF dues, and thus SAF resources, doubled. Beginning in 1978, dues increased every other year, and by 1987 "SAF's total income reached ... 986 million crowns."[27] SAF annual accounts in 1987 detailed two main funds: the insurance fund, which exists as a reserve for industrial conflict; and the guarantee fund, which acts as a reserve for long, drawn-out conflicts and a disciplinary mechanism over member firms.[28] In 1987 these funds were valued at 5,400 million and 4,259 million krona respectively. This gave Swedish business the ability to bring, in 1987 prices, over 1.5 billion dollars, to influence any given dispute or issue area. Such financial leverage, given the size of the economy, simply dwarfs the resources available to any other business organization in the world.

Research by Victor A. Pestoff reveals that the SAF employed its financial resources in three main areas: conflict remuneration, administration, and propaganda.[29] Beginning in the late 1970s, spending in the last of these categories increased dramatically, jumping from 15 percent of SAF expenditure to 25 percent, where it leveled off in the following decade.[30] This pattern, argues Pestoff, "represents a shift in emphasis in SAF's role from collective bargaining to one of political influence ... [and] ... corresponds with the struggle against wage earner funds."[31] According to Pestoff's estimates, in 1982 SAF spent 55–60 million krona in propaganda on the single issue of the wage earner funds. In comparison, in the 1982 Riksdag election, all five major political parties spent a combined total of 69 million

---

[26] For figures, see Victor A. Pestoff, "The Politics of Private Business, Cooperative and Public Enterprise in a Corporate Democracy – The Case of Sweden" Unpublished manuscript, University of Stockholm, Department of Business Administration (1991), pp. 25–7.

[27] Ibid., p. 71. To put this in perspective, SAF fees took in over $155 million in 1987 prices.

[28] Ibid.

[29] While the SAF does not detail the category "propaganda" in its accounts, a surrogate measure is the category "other administrative expenses." "Other administrative expenses can cover anything not covered under other headings, including political activities such as ad hoc campaigns, public opinion formation, meta organizations etc." Pestoff, "The Politics of Private Business," p. 75.

[30] Ibid.

[31] Ibid., p. 76.

krona. By 1988 annual SAF expenditure had risen to some 200 million krona.[32] This organizational structure, plus the huge financing at its disposal, provided SAF with a crucial resource for transforming Swedish embedded liberalism.

To achieve this goal, Swedish business, like its American counterpart, developed a two-pronged strategy of institutional withdrawal and ideological contestation. That is, business aimed to weaken institutions of economic governance by subverting their corporatist underpinnings. However, as detailed in Chapter 1, to account for such an institutional withdrawal is merely to describe the destabilization of the existing order and not explain the rise of its replacement. Business crested new institutions by combining this strategy of noncooperation with a sustained ideological campaign aimed at delegitimating and dismantling the institutions of Swedish embedded liberalism. However, it took a while for SAF to realize that in order to beat LO, it had to beat the LO's ideas, not its numbers. As such, the SAF's efforts to disembed Swedish liberalism began rather traditionally.

Using Muscle: Mass Lockouts and Other Labor Market Measures
In response to the passing of the Codetermination Act in 1976, the SAF declared the Saltsjöbaden agreements dead. Shortly afterward, in 1977, "SAF planned to lock out 220,000 salaried employees for two weeks, but a major labor-market conflict was averted at the last minute."[33] Resistance to the lockout stemmed from two main sources. First, SAF's organizational reforms on voting rights and independent action by member firms had yet to be completed at the time of the 1977 lockout. Consequently, many firms, especially small firms, were able to free-ride on the lockout without threat of sanction. Second, 1977 was the low point of the economic downturn of the period. In such an uncertain environment, many firms were unwilling to risk a protracted labor conflict, a consideration that was especially important for many large firms dependent upon state subsidies. At the onset of the downturn, the governing SAP "introduced subventions for companies which agreed to continue production and to stock commodities."[34] As a lockout would rather obviously have halted the production of commodities, and hence have jeopardized subsidies, many large firms were unwilling to risk it. Given such an environment, the SAF's policy of proactively generating industrial conflict was judged to be simply too radical for many of its own members. Consequently, "in response to this [failure] SAF director Curt Nicolin decided that the existing machinery for collective bargaining needed to be shipwrecked before it could be scuttled."[35]

---

[32] Pestoff, "Towards a New Swedish Model," p. 163.

[33] *Ibid.*, p. 157.

[34] Joachim Israel, "Swedish Socialism and Big Business," *Acta Sociologica* 21 (4) (1978), p. 351. Such subventions constituted up to 20 percent of the value of the commodities stocked.

[35] Pestoff, "Towards a New Swedish Model," p. 157.

Scuttling began in 1980 when the SAF rejected the so-called EFO model of the Swedish economy. This model was used in wage bargaining since it forecast the ability of the economy to absorb wage rises based upon projected investment rates, relative to the economy's competitive position.[36] The SAF argued that because corporations did not wish to finance investment out of debt to the extent that they did before, the EFO model was redundant. While one could maintain, as noted previously, that such a move was simply part of a larger shift in corporate finance in the post–Bretton Woods era, it must also be noted that the disavowal of this mode of finance effectively destroyed the logic for the wage earner funds as represented by the LO and the SAP. Similarly, with the withdrawal from agreements based upon the EFO model, the solidarity wage and the logic of Rehn-Meidner, the institutional framework of labor power, likewise becomes redundant, bypassed by seemingly neutral market forces.[37]

Also in 1980, SAF managed to provoke the lockout it failed to get in 1977. In response to what began as a strike, the SAF enforced a lockout of nearly 3 million workers in the name of "employer solidarity," despite opposition from SAF's own members. At the time, SAF Director Nicolin described this conflict as "an investment for the future."[38] Despite being costly to SAF in the short run, this conflict galvanized SAF for action in the longer term. As Per Olof Edin notes concerning SAF strategy, "they lost [the lockout] and they realized that they could not beat LO. So what could they do? The right thing to do was not to make the SAF strong, but to make LO weak."[39] Weakening the LO meant weakening its constituent parts, and the next blow to collective bargaining institutions was dealt by the defection of the metal workers' union from the LO's central agreements in 1983. Several scholars have analyzed this defection as a rational response to wage drift.[40] However, this defection also fits well the overall political strategy behind SAF activities in the 1980s.[41]

---

[36] The model was designed in 1968 by three economists each representing the SAF, the LO, and the white-collar union TCO, respectively.

[37] On these points, see Pontusson, *The Limits of Social Democracy*; Martin, "Wage Bargaining."

[38] Quoted in Victor A. Pestoff, "The Demise of Concerted Practices and the Negotiated Economy in Sweden," in Tiziano Treu, ed., *Participation in Public Policy Making: The Role of Trade Unions and Employers Associations* (New York: Walter de Gruyter, 1992), p. 238. The strike itself was provoked by the SAF, which took the line that "any increase in wages presupposed public sector cutbacks." Pontusson, *The Limits of Social Democracy*, p. 110.

[39] Per Olof Edin, interview with the author, Stockholm, June 6, 1997.

[40] For discussions of the 1983 metalworkers defection as due to wage drift, see Andrew Martin, "Trade Unions in Sweden," in Peter Gourevitch, ed., *Unions and Economic Crisis: Britain, West Germany, and Sweden* (London: Allen & Unwin, 1984); Swenson, *Fair Shares*, pp. 171, 227; Jonas Pontusson and Peter Swenson, "Labor Markets, Production Strategies, and Wage Bargaining Institutions: The Swedish Employer Offensive in Comparative Perspective," *Comparative Political Studies* (29) 2 (1996).

[41] See Stephens, "Is Swedish Corporatism Dead," *passim*.

In 1983, prior to the annual round of SAF/LO negotiations, the SAF "announced its refusal to negotiate centrally any more . . . with the ultimate aim of merely reaching company wide agreements."[42] The defection of the metal workers was apparently prompted by side payments made to the union in the form of an agreement with the engineering employers federation over and above what SAF was offering in the central negotiations, and what LO had tabled as its initial bid. The leader of the metal workers' union at the time of the negotiations, Lief Blomberg, was a new leader with no firm constituency of support within an already divided union. In such an environment, he was unable to say no to the employers' offer.[43] Thus, the SAF was able to undermine collective bargaining institutions using a divide-and-conquer strategy. However, such institutions had not been weakened enough to delegitimate them. To do that, the SAF had to challenge the ideas behind the current order directly. Yet here, once again, the SAF acted in a traditional manner.

Using Muscle: Denouncing the Funds

Challenging the ideas behind the old order initially took second place to labor market confrontation. Of initial efforts in this direction, two incidents stand out. First, following its 1977 declaration of the death of the Saltsjöbaden agreements, SAF went public with its new pro-market agenda at its new annual conference in that same year. Ostensibly, the desire to establish an annual conference was a response to claims of smaller companies that the SAF was not doing enough to represent their interests. However, given that voting rights within the SAF are a function of dues as dictated by the size of the wage bill, this conference was hardly a democratic forum. In fact, it was never intended to be. Its main function was to generate wide media coverage and focus public attention on the pro-market agenda being developed by the SAF. The annual conference has served this function well by receiving wide press coverage once a year, every year, since its founding.

Six years later, in 1983, the SAF bussed nearly one hundred thousand businesspeople from across Sweden to rally in Stockholm against the wage earner funds. Though portrayed as a spontaneous outpouring of opposi-

---

[42] Pestoff, "Joint Regulation," p. 327.
[43] See Pontusson, *The Limits of Social Democracy*, pp. 171–2. This defection also has a political basis in that the SAF had been trying to get the engineering unions to defect since 1977. See Martin, "The Politics of Macroeconomic Policy," pp. 255–6; Stephens, "Is Swedish Corporatism Dead," p. 5; interview by the author with LO chief economist Edin, Stockholm, June 6, 1997. By 1991 Blomberg's reaction toward the SAF was somewhat different: "People [in SAF] who supported the 'Swedish Model' have been replaced by spokesmen for the market . . . SAF is emphasizing political opinion formation rather than taking responsibility for wage formation. . . . Neo-liberals, who have the US and the UK as their ideal . . . don't give a damn about wage differentials and inequality is increasing at a catastrophic rate." Blomberg, quoted in Pestoff, "Towards a New Swedish Model," pp. 157–8.

tion, the demonstration was in fact highly orchestrated under the guise of an *ad hoc* group called the Fourth of October Committee. As the SAF's publishing house and think-tank Timbro notes in its account of the October 4 rally, "no manifestation of close to 100,000 people is possible without careful planning, careful organization [and] preparatory work. Who was responsible?"[44] The report then goes on to note that the committee "consisted of 24 people – major industrialists like Mr. Matts Carlgren of MoDo, Mr. Gøsta Bystdet of Electrolux, and Mr. Ulf Laurin of PLM, as well as executives from small and medium sized firms."[45] Other examples of this strategy included the provision of "public information" on the costs and benefits of the wage earners funds and similar campaigns against public provision and public spending called "Give Yourself a Chance" and "Inflation." These *ad hoc* political campaigns and attacks on the institutions of central bargaining throughout the late 1970s and 1980s did much to ensure that by 1983, when the funds passed into law, they were rendered cosmetic at best. However, despite defeating the funds proposal, SAF was just beginning to enact its agenda on the ideational front in 1983, since defeating the funds proposal was merely the immediate objective. While the SAF did much of this idea promotion directly, it also used a number of think tanks on the American model that operated with direct financial support from SAF and/or SAF members.

Challenging Embedded Liberalism

Business and the New Stockholm School
During the 1930s and 1940s, SAF members regularly convened an *ad hoc* body called the Club of Directors. The Club of Directors exercised a dual strategy. On the one hand, given the Saltsjöbaden agreements and fearing SAP dominance of the political agenda in the future, the club decided that business should adopt an apolitical stance with political parties and actively cooperated with the SAP throughout the postwar period. However, as noted in Chapter 4, members of this club also became worried about the reemergence of planning and a Swedish version of stagnationism as a possible alternative economic strategy for the SAP in the run-up to the 1948 election.

In cooperation with other business organizations such as the Association of Swedish Bankers, the SAF founded the Joint Committee for Private Commerce and Industry (NÄSO) and enlivened another somewhat moribund business association, the Swedish Free Enterprise Foundation (NÄFO), in 1947 in order to head off this stagnationist threat. After the defeat of the nationalization and planning proposals in the 1948 election, these organizations reverted back to their apolitical stance and became

[44] Larsson and Holmberg, *Vändpunkt*, p. 26.
[45] *Ibid.*

passive observers of developments rather than active participants. However, during the upheavals of the early 1970s, these organizations were revitalized and served the SAF well as the organizational means for attacking embedded liberalism.

Using these organizations, SAF propaganda activities in the 1980s operated on multiple levels. The most obvious means of propagandizing was the use of *ad hoc* committees to organize public education on specific issues such as the Fourth of October Committee discussed earlier. Arguably, though, the SAF's most influential institutions were formal think tanks and publishing outlets. Among these, two organizations stand out, both of which were directly funded by NÄSO and NÄFO: the Center for Business and Policy Studies (SNS) and Timbro. The importance of SNS and Timbro in understanding the transformation of embedded liberalism in Sweden cannot be overemphasized. However, what made SNS so influential was a prior shift in the ideas held by Swedish academic economists and opinion makers, similar again to what occurred in the United States.

The key figure in Swedish economics in the early 1980s was Assar Lindbeck. Although Lindbeck resigned from the SAP in 1976 over the wage earner funds, he remained resolutely Keynesian in his academic writings and more popular pronouncements.[46] By the early 1980s, however, Lindbeck's writings began to incorporate more of the basic assumptions of monetarism and rational expectations, which were, particularly in this period, anticollectivist and pro-business in their analysis and policy conclusions. As Edin notes regarding the changes in economic thinking that took place in Sweden at this time, "There was an enormous pressure on almost all economists inside the Swedish system. If you go to the middle seventies, almost all Swedish economists were Keynesian. The first to shift was Assar Lindbeck, and he was very dominant, but he didn't go all the way. But the others [the younger economists] went all the way."[47] Once Lindbeck shifted, the discipline as a whole shifted, and what was once unthinkable was fast on its way to becoming a new orthodoxy.[48]

Given this neoliberal ideational shift, Swedish academic economists embarked upon a wholesale critique of Swedish embedded liberal institutions that gave force to the new agenda of SAF. Agneta Hugemark has summarized the changes in academic discourse surrounding the welfare state in Sweden, tracing the evolution of neoliberal, pro-market ideas in official

---

[46] See, for example, Assar Lindbeck, *Inflation: Global, International and National Aspects* (Leuven: Universitaire Pers Leuven, 1980). However, see also *Idem.*, *The Political Economy of the New Left: An Outsider's View* (New York: New York University Press, 1977).

[47] Interview with Per Olof Edin by the author, Stockholm, June 6, 1997.

[48] This shift in Swedish economic thought and Lindbeck's role therein are detailed in Johan Lonroth, *Schamamerna: Om ekonomi som forgylld vergdag* (Stockholm: Bokforleget ARENA, 1993); Torsten Sverenius, *Vad hände med Sveriges ekonomi efter 1970? en debattbok* (Stockholm: Fakta info direkt, 2000).

government reports and in the main "debate journal" of Swedish economists, *Ekonomisk Debatt*.[49] Hugemark notes how these new economic ideas permeated the Swedish debate over welfare provision in three discrete phases.

First, "the public sector has, from the beginning of this period, been defined as constituting a problem," and economists have gained scientific credence for their ideas about the institutions of welfare through their ability to "describ[e] different activities in terms of the neoclassical theory."[50] Originally such institutions were seen as part of a general macroeconomic problem of growth. However, the focus in academic and popular economic writings shifted throughout the 1980s, as it did in economic theory elsewhere, from macro to micro, as public choice frameworks became the dominant approaches to the analysis of the welfare state. Once such ideas became the framework for discussion, the focus of the debate shifted from arguing that the welfare state constituted an efficiency loss to measuring that loss, and finally to developing concrete proposals to obviate that loss.

It was against this background of shifting academic ideas about the nature of the economy and the role of the state within it that the SAF-affiliated think tank SNS rose to prominence. SNS sponsored economic research that criticized the institutions of the Swedish model and then disseminated these new ideas to an elite but influential public. By doing so, SNS proved to be very influential in setting the course of Swedish policy and institutional development during the late 1980s and early 1990s.

Spreading New Ideas
Although SNS was founded in 1948 by NÄFO as a deliberate counterweight to the influence of LO economists on government economic policy, this business research organization has really come into its own only in the past twenty years. SNS describes itself as "a private non-profit organization with the aim of promoting research on economic and social issues of importance to public decisionmakers."[51] SNS does not see itself as a think tank in the sense that the American Enterprise Institute or the Heritage Foundation are think tanks. Indeed, it sees itself as a politically neutral organization whose function is to tell the scientific truth about the Swedish economy and polity.[52] However, SNS economic publications have consistently taken a

---

[49] Agneta Hugemark, *Den fängslande marknaden: Ekonomiska experter om välfärsstaten* (Lund: Arkif Förlag, 1992).

[50] *Ibid.*, p. 210.

[51] *SNS: The Center for Business and Policy Studies* (Stockholm: SNS, 1992), p. 1. Such research is conducted through one of seven standing research groups on topics such as "the public sector," "economic policy," and the "political system." SNS also issues a very influential annual economic report discussed later in this chapter.

[52] Indicative of the fact that this scientific appearance is important to SNS is the fact that it has a standing Scientific Advisor Board comprised of two economists and three historians.

very orthodox neoclassical line arguing that any form of social organization other than a market exchange among private individuals is inefficient, and consequently that the role of the state should be kept within circumscribed limits.

Most influential on the thinking and practice of the SAP in the late 1980s and the Conservative administration of the early 1990s were the writings of SNS's chief economist, Hans Tson Söderström. Söderström advocated a norm-based, nondiscretionary macroeconomics that would bypass and indeed render obsolete traditional social democratic institutions.[53] Söderström has been vocal regarding the need for noninterventionist strategies since the late 1970s. Originally, SNS's argument was that full employment "accommodates" the demands of trade unions and this inevitably produces inflation. Later, in line with the general shift in macroeconomic thinking, the government itself came to be seen as causing inflation directly. As a result, SNS advocated adherence to an expectations-reducing external "norm policy" (normpolitik) centered around a nonaccommodatory fixed exchange rate.[54]

Normpolitik, like credibility arguments in general, maintains that the basic problem with government is that it is democratic. Normpolitik, much like public choice theory discussed in Chapter 5, posits that because politicians have to respond to sectional interests rather than the general interest, suboptimal and inefficient government spending patterns become entrenched. The particular problem in the Swedish case is that because embedded liberal institutions ensure employment above the "natural rate," all sorts of allocative distortions occur throughout the economy. In turn, such distortions cause slower growth and higher inflation. To cure such pathologies, the state must therefore give up any attempt to improve the short-run performance of the economy through the manipulation of the interest rate, the exchange rate, and the budget – the three main levers of macromanagement.[55] Instead, the optimal policy is to make the central bank independent and enforce a credible inflationary norm, which states that the government will maintain an exchange rate of X and an inflation rate of Y come what may. The point of such a policy is to enhance the credibility of the expectation that the government will not run an inflationary policy.

This point was also reiterated to the author by Hans Tson Söderström in an interview with the author, Stockholm, June 5, 1997.

[53] See Hans Tson Söderström, "Den nya skepticismen," *Ekonomisk Debatt* 2 (1) (1978).

[54] For an excellent discussion of normpolitik and its consequences, see Carl Hamilton and Dag Rolander, *Att leda Sverige in I Krisen: moral och politik I negdgångstid* (Stockholm: Norstedts Förlag, 1993), pp. 33–61. For Söderström's own view, see Hans Tson Söderström, *Normer och ekonomisk politik* (Stockholm: SNS, 1996).

[55] For representative examples of SNS's positions, see Ingemar Hansson, Hans Tson Söderström, et al., *Vägen till ett stabilare Sverige* (Stockholm: SNS, 1985); Magnus Henrekson et al., "Disinflation, Integration and Growth: The Swedish Economy in 1992 and Beyond," SNS Occasional Paper 37, June (1992).

Once such credibility is established, rational agents will adjust their expectations downward, prices and wages will fall, and inflation will be painlessly reduced. As we shall see in this chapter, SNS's ideas were highly influential on Swedish economic policy in the late 1980s arguing for this normpolitik.

Meanwhile, SAF's other main idea generator, Timbro, attempted to influence the quality and financial press, in particular *Dagens Industrie* and *Dagens Nyheter*. Timbro does not conduct in-house research *per se*. Instead it acts as "a platform, a forum, we act as brokers, idea brokers, [by bringing] in people who we think have an interesting contribution to make and let them stand up for their messages."[56] Timbro has excelled in bringing public choice arguments into the mainstream of Swedish public debate beyond the environs of top policymakers.

Two versions of public choice theory underlie the critique of the welfare state that has become known in Sweden as the "systems failure" thesis. The first, associated with Assar Lindbeck and some SNS-affiliated economists, focuses upon hypothesized long-run nonlinearities (lags) in the return to the institutions of the welfare state. Over time, the argument goes, as the institutions of the welfare state became more encompassing and complex, and the public sector as a whole grew, such institutions ceased to benefit the economy and became a drag upon it. While there has been some attempt to model this process and/or provide econometric evidence for it, the debate remained, until recently, somewhat open.[57]

As mentioned previously, Timbro excelled in taking this debate to a broader public as well as to the decisionmaking elites. Timbro took the coincidence of the growth of the welfare state and the apparent contemporaneous decline in growth rates and applied public choice analysis to the data to argue that the state's rent-seeking activities inherently conflict with efficient market principles and allocations. As Timbro's president commented, "I think that one of the major contributions Timbro has made is to produce public choice economics outside the closed circle of academic economists . . . to a broader audience of opinion makers."[58] Timbro coined a term for Sweden's problems as seen from their perspective, "Suedo-Sclerosis," a term that has gained wide public currency.[59]

[56] Interview with P. J. Anders Linder, president of Timbro, by the author, Stockholm, June 13, 1997.
[57] For its closure, see the exchange between Walter Korpi and Magnus Henrekson, "Economists, the Welfare State and Growth: The Case of Sweden," *Economic Journal* (106), November (1996).
[58] Interview with P. J. Anders Linder, president of Timbro, by the author, Stockholm, June 13, 1997.
[59] See, for example, Ingemar Ståhl and Kurt Wickman, *Suedo-Sclerosis: The Problems of the Swedish Economy* (Stockholm: Timbro, 1995). Indeed, Walter Korpi has argued that by "largely borrowing lines of argument from their American counterparts, Swedish econo-

One measure the success of Timbro and SNS in broadening the audience for these ideas is Kristina Boréus' study that examined shifts toward pro-market discourse in Timbro's chief target, the quality press.[60] She found that in the op-ed pieces in the conservative daily *Svenska Dagbladet*, the proportion of notations for what she termed "new liberal" ideas increased from 30 percent to 70 percent in the period 1975–89. Similarly, such notations increased from 15 percent to 30 percent in the liberal daily *Dagens Nyheter* between 1971 and 1989, although the fluctuations were much wider.

While these figures point to a dramatic effect on elite opinion, it must be recalled that SNS and Timbro were part of a much larger assault waged by business as a whole. Again, as Timbro's president noted, "Timbro's not the only thing that happened, the really important thing that happened is that SAF itself raised its voice and started communicating with the general public, because they have the financial muscle to do that."[61] In summary, when taking account of the importance of the politicization of business, the resources at its disposal, and the ideas it promoted, there emerges a rather different picture of the transformation of Swedish embedded liberalism.

Resuscitating Embedded Liberalism?

The "Third Way"

As noted previously, the period of bourgeois rule broke two of the foundational ideas of the old order: first, that the government should manage market conditions, not industrial concerns; second, that the budget should always be balanced over the business cycle. The bourgeois government broke both these tenets when the supply shocks of the period caused it to undertake a massive nationalization program. Consequently, between 1976 and 1979, government spending on industrial policy quadrupled.[62] Such

---

mists managed to convince Sweden's political decisionmakers to base their policies on the Sclerosis diagnosis." Walter Korpi, "Eurosclerosis and the Sclerosis of Objectivity: On the Role of Values among Economic Policy Experts," *Economic Journal* (106) November (1996), p. 1741.

[60] Kristina Boréus, "The Shift to the Right: Neo-Liberalism in Argumentation and Language in the Swedish Public Debate since 1969," *European Journal of Political Research* (31) (1997); Idem, *Högervåg: Nyliberalismen och Kampen om språket I svensk debatt 1969–1989* (Stockholm: Tidens förlag, 1994). Note that while Boréus' study focuses upon what she calls "new liberalism" and includes moral elements that are not strictly part of the economic debate, her work is still a good indicator of the discursive and ideological shift at an elite level. Boréus' research demonstrates the importance of gaining proprietorship over concepts in ideological struggles. Gaining the ideological high ground is often a function of whose definition of a word such as "liberty," for example, is accepted.

[61] Interview by the author with Linder, Stockholm, June 13, 1997.

[62] OECD, *Economic Surveys: Sweden, 1976–1982* (Paris: Organization for Economic Cooperation and Development, 1982). For the 1976 crisis and its effects, see Peter Walters, "Sweden's Public Sector Crisis before and after the 1982 Elections," *Government and Opposition* Summer 18 (1) (1983), p. 26. Indeed, Nils Asling, the Liberal minister of

extra expenditure was financed by borrowing, and the government deficit
rose to 13 percent of GDP in 1981 while public expenditure rose from 52
percent to 65 percent of GDP.[63]

In this already uncertain environment, the defeat of the bourgeois
coalition led to the decision by the SAP to find a "third way" between the
deflationary policies of Margaret Thatcher and the inflation of Francois
Mitterand. For the SAP, the solution lay in increasing growth of GDP, and
given Sweden's trading position, growth would have to be export-led.
Moreover, the SAP accepted the bourgeois government's argument that the
public sector deficit and debt had to be reduced because they were inflationary.[64] The idea of a devaluation as the core of this attempt to negotiate
a third way came from the so-called reformist wing of the SAP, specifically
from Kjell Olof Feldt, Klas Eklund, and Ingvar Carlsson.

The third way emerged out of a 1981 "crisis report" authored by Feldt
and Carlsson that was circulated around SAP local branches. The report
suggested that rather than rely on the wage earner funds to promote public
investment, the state needed greater austerity and budget cuts instead to
stabilize the economy and stimulate private investment. These claims were
amplified in a 1981 letter to the SAP paper *Arbetet* entitled "Here Is the
Bitter Medicine." Authored by Eklund and other young SAP-affiliated
economists, the letter advocated a thoroughgoing revision Sweden's
embedded liberal institutions.[65]

Eklund et al., argued that consumption had to be sacrificed in favor of
production, and as such, wage growth had to be reduced in order to increase
international market share through cost reduction. In making these claims,
Eklund et al., were quite open about the fact that "such a development
must lead to increased profits that the labor movement must accept."[66] The
distribution of national income implied by such a policy meant that
demand, particularly import demand, would have to be curtailed and transferred into the export sector. Therefore, in a modern-day version of the classical "crowding-out" thesis, it was thought that both the budget deficit and
the public sector as a whole would have to be reduced in order to stop the
preemption of resources by the public sector away from the revenue-
generating private sector. Influenced by these new ideas, the SAP sought a
policy to increase demand through foreign consumption of Swedish goods,
and a devaluation seemed the only way forward. Thus, the centerpiece of

---

industry during this period, was known as the minister for the casualty ward. See Henning,
    "Sweden: Political Interference with Business," p. 23.
[63] Richard Scase, "Why Sweden Has Elected a Radical Government," *Parliamentary Affairs*
    March (1982), p. 45.
[64] Neil Fraser, "Economic Policy in Sweden: Are There Lessons from the Swedish Model,"
    International Review of Applied Economics 1 (2) (1987), p. 218.
[65] "Här är hästkuren," *Arbetar*, February 18, 1981.
[66] *Ibid.*

this third-way policy was a 16 percent devaluation coming in the wake of a 10 percent devaluation in 1981.[67]

At first the devaluation succeeded remarkably well, and that was the beginning of the problem. Exports rose 10.7 percent in 1983 and by 6.5 percent in 1985, while investment grew in 1984–5 at an average of 16.2 percent. By 1985 the growth in government expenditure had been all but halted, the deficit had declined to a mere 2 percent of GDP, and unemployment had fallen back to 2.9 percent.[68] However, the problems that the SAP was soon to face did not lie at an economic level. Implicit within the third way was a political redistribution that served to increase business-labor tensions and destabilize the existing order further.

The New Politics of Distribution

As Peter Walters has argued, "the third way hinge[d] on a strategic redistribution: a long-term rise in profit levels, in order to provide for investment, at the expense of wages. Such a shift in resources from income to capital could not be justified as equitable, only as economically necessary."[69] The third way thus constituted an attempt by the state to redefine the content of embedded liberalism away from the efficiency and equity combination of the Rehn-Meidner institutions toward a neoclassical view of efficiency and price stability as the state's primary policy goals.

At this juncture, the state's efforts to make the LO accept this redistribution were complicated by the fact that the SAF was, as noted earlier, simultaneously attempting to rid itself of its relationship with the LO over wage determination in the wake of the wage earner funds debacle. Traditionally, LO's autonomy over wages was as sacrosanct as business's over ownership. Now, just as the LO had challenged business's autonomy over ownership, the state began to pressure the LO over its autonomy in wage setting, a move that inevitably produced conflict between the state and the unions. Wage restraint, due primarily to effective political pressure, was initially successful in avoiding the import inflation associated with devaluations, despite the defection of the engineering workers. However, high profit levels of major export concerns and wage drift outside of the LO institutions among white-collar unions in 1984 made the LO take a less cooperative stance with the state.

---

[67] The original policy called for a one-time devaluation to improve competitiveness and then to tie the krona to the deutschmark to ensure that inflation did not eat away the competitive advantage thus gained. Unfortunately, in this pre-EMU environment, the Bundesbank balked at the proposal while the LO rejected its deflationary implications. Consequently, the krona was instead allowed to float.

[68] Figures from Fraser, "Economic Policy in Sweden," p. 218.

[69] Peter Walters, "Distributing Decline: Swedish Social Democrats and the Crisis of the Welfare State," *Government and Opposition* 20 (3) Summer (1985), p. 362.

Compounding these political tensions, the third way, as an attempt to resuscitate the economy, was almost too successful. By 1985 it became apparent that the devaluation was too large and had overshot its target. This made the economy vulnerable to import inflation, which cut into real incomes and exacerbated labor's distributional anxiety. In such a situation, when the state was seen by labor to be abrogating its commitment to equality and universalism through its new distribution policy, when the burden of the solidarity wage and increased import costs fell all the more heavily on the unions, and when business was seen to be reaping profits from what LO perceived as a zero-sum redistribution, the unions themselves started to turn against the third way.[70]

By 1985 union agitation had resulted in the rate of real wage increases reaching 12 percent per year.[71] The competitive effects of the 1982 devaluation were thus being undercut, and industrial unrest was increasing. Meanwhile, record industry profits were met with calls for wage restraint. By 1986, while Lief Blomberg, the head of the Swedish metalworkers' union who had defected from the LO's central agreements in 1983, was arguing that "it is the capitalists, not the workers who need to be clobbered," GDP growth had fallen to 1.6 percent.[72] Given such a slowdown, it was no surprise that the third way was not reaping the investment dividend it was supposed to.

Politically, the net effect of the third way was to politicize distribution and further stress the institutions of Swedish embedded liberalism. However, what was finally to dismantle these institutions was not economic problems *per se*. Instead, the continuing campaign of ideological contestation and institutional withdrawal begun by business in the late 1970s performed this function by focusing on three specific areas of institutional change: financial deregulation, tax reform, and exchange rate politics. As was stressed in Chapter 1, while "brute" economic factors may weaken an institutional order, ideas play the crucial role in determining both how to break such an order and how to shape the institutions that replace it.

---

[70] As Martin argues, "The redistribution from labor to business, was larger than necessary, making the burden of securing agreements by organized claimants ... larger than it had to be." Andrew Martin, "Macroeconomic Policy, Politics and the Demise of Central Wage Negotiations in Sweden," paper prepared for the Peder Sather Symposium, Center for West European Studies, University of California, Berkeley, March 21, 1996, p. 10. See also Magnus Henrickson, "The Devaluation Strategy and Its Effects on the Structure of the Swedish Economy," Research Report 34 (Stockholm: Trade Union Institute for Economic Forecasting, 1990), table 1, p. 46.

[71] Figures from *The Economist*, March 9, 1985, p. 117.

[72] Blomberg, quoted in *The Economist,* February 1, 1986, p. 58, figures from the same issue.

Transforming Embedded Liberalism

Ideas to Build a Bubble: Free Markets and Fair Taxes

Given the desire to support embedded liberal institutions, Swedish monetary policy had historically largely consisted of keeping interest rates low and avoiding overheating through credit controls. However, because Sweden had an open export-driven economy, credit and capital controls were always a second-best strategy. Moreover, growing external imbalances in the late 1960s called for a tightening of credit market regulations at the same time as the deepening of embedded liberalism sought by labor demanded greater liquidity for housing construction and other social spending. A consequence of these credit market controls was that "bank portfolios were increasingly concentrated in fixed-interest government and housing bonds at the expense of regular loans to households and business."[73] Such a pattern of lending led to the creation of a so-called gray market of finance companies that tapped into the potential market for consumer borrowing but fell outside of official bank regulations. This gray market grew rapidly during the late 1970s and early 1980s and, in vogue with the call for deregulation in the United States and elsewhere, Swedish financial interests began to agitate for a deregulation of domestic financial markets to take advantage of this latent demand.

Deregulation presented the governing SAP with both a cost and a benefit. The cost was that monetary policy would be harder to control after deregulation since the state's ability to ration credit would be undermined. The benefit was that deficits would be easier to finance. Given the perceived short-run costs of the third way, the finance ministry acquiesced to this deregulatory impulse while the central bank enthusiastically embraced it. The state began to issue securities to take advantage of its new credit position while private finance houses began to pump more and more money into the economy.

Rather than regulate to offset these imbalances, the government instead abolished the bond-holding requirements for banks in 1983, further adding to credit market liquidity. Soon afterward, restrictions of foreign and domestic purchases of shares were lifted and in May 1985 the Riksbank abolished interest rate regulation. Paralleling the 1981 abolition of Regulation Q in the United States, in November 1985 the so-called November revolution occurred when the Riksbank abolished limits on loan ceilings.[74] Just as the abolition of Regulation Q led to the destabiliza-

---

[73] Peter Englund, "Financial Deregulation in Sweden," *European Economic Review* 34 (1990), p. 385.

[74] This account draws on Torsten Svensson, *November-revolutionen: Om rationalitet och makt I beslutet att avreglera kreditmarknaden Rapport till expertgruppen för studier I offentlig ekonomi* (Stockholm: SOU Finansdepartment, 1996).

tion of the United States credit system in the savings and loan debacle, so
the deregulation of Swedish credit markets was to have similar deleterious
effects.

The SAP's Eklund, now one of the main supporters of deregulation in
the finance ministry, referred to the existing regime as "Swiss cheese, with
more holes than cheese."[75] Given that the gray market was undermining
the efficiency of the old regulations, the best thing to do was to appeal to
Gresham's Law and "let the good money drive out the bad" by allowing
the market to decide credit worthiness.[76] The possibility that this policy
could create a situation of profligate loans and a credit bubble was expected
to be obviated by a device called the *ranttetrappan*, or "interest rate ladder,"
which would automatically increase interest rates in line with a greater
volume of transactions occurring at the central bank. Unfortunately, the
ranttetrappan proved to be totally ineffective as a policy tool.

As Torsten Svensson notes, given the pent-up demand for credit, the
situation among banks and finance houses became similar to a multiplayer
prisoner's dilemma. The rational thing to do was to loan first and get the
good debt. However, given the lack of regulations in going after the best
loans, the banks' exposure to credit risk increased, which made the imperative of getting the good loans to cover the bad all the more important.[77]
Rather than the *ranttetrappan* regulating a slowly increasing volume of
loans, the banks fell over each other to give money away as fast as possible. This created a huge volume of credit in a closed environment where
exchange controls were still in place. Given such controls, capital could not
exit the domestic market to find additional returns to repay the original
loans borrowed. As a consequence, asset prices and commercial real estate
prices skyrocketed.[78]

In a booming real estate market, huge speculative profits can be made.
As demand for loans increased and assets were sought to collateralize
those loans, asset prices were bid upward. This rise in asset price made
these same properties an ever-hotter commodity, and the demand for them
further increased, raising the demand for loans again. However, those
new loans were secured against those same mortgaged assets, so to service
debt, asset prices had to continue to rise. As Dwight M. Jaffee notes, in
such a situation, "the perceived real rate of interest on real estate loans
falls even further as investors extrapolate the high current rates of
asset appreciation into the future . . . [creating] a self-fulfilling cumulative

[75] Eklund, interview with the author, Stockholm, June 16, 1997.
[76] *Ibid.*
[77] Dwight M. Jaffee, "The Swedish Real Estate Crisis," SNS Occasional Paper (59)
November (1994), pp. 81–2.
[78] By 1990, at the peak of the speculative cycle, Stockholm's office space was second only to
Madrid in cost. See Bank of International Settlements Annual Report 1994 (Basle: Bank of
International Settlements, 1994), p. 54, table 3.

expansion."[79] In this environment, it became possible for debtors to borrow against assets to pay the loans that had bought the assets in the first place. Meanwhile, it became necessary for banks to loan in ever greater amounts as the decline in real interest rates meant that the return on banks' assets were falling at an accelerating rate.[80]

In such an environment where real interest rates fall and the cost of borrowing becomes cheaper, the demand for credit becomes self-fulfilling, as asset inflation leads to demand for credit, which leads to further inflation. Consequently, a classic speculative bubble was formed, and as with all bubbles, short-term performance of the economy seemed to be very good as unemployment fell to 1.4 percent by 1989.[81] However, as with all booms, there was also a bust just around the corner. What burst the bubble was tax reform and the side effects of normpolitik.

In line with the new ideas about taxation being imported from the United States and elsewhere, "The debate about tax policy in Sweden took a new direction in the beginning of the late 1980's. More emphasis than before was placed on efficiency and incentives and less on the goal of an equitable distribution of income."[82] Indeed, tax reform became a personal crusade of Feldt, who was now SAP finance minister. Feldt argued that, "our party program states that a market economy can only yield acceptable results under certain conditions. It should be described as the other way around. Only under certain conditions and in certain markets is economic planning better than market solutions."[83] Beginning in 1987, Feldt advocated a battery of tax cuts on the top marginal rates. In 1988 tax cuts were announced that intended to do away with central income taxes in favor of local ones, and in 1989 the much heralded "tax reform of the century" was unveiled. These reforms cut the basic rate for most taxpayers to 30 percent and further reduced top marginal rates. Coterminous with such tax reforms, foreign exchange controls were also removed.

The combined effects of the tax reforms, which were underfunded and implemented in the middle of a hothouse boom, and the lifting of exchange controls simply added fuel to the fire of the credit market boom. Unfortunately for the government, the bubble was about to burst. At the same time as these underfunded tax reforms were being implemented, the finance

---

[79] Jaffee, "The Swedish Real Estate Crisis," p. 78. It is interesting to note that rather than conclude that the deregulation itself was at fault, Jaffee concludes that the economic fundamentals of the market caused the crisis. I really have no idea what this means in this context, given that it was a bubble.

[80] *Ibid.*, p. 83.

[81] Figures in this section are drawn from Martin, "Macroeconomic Policy," p. 29.

[82] Jan Sodersten, quoted in Sven Steinmo, *Taxation and Democracy: Swedish, British and American Approaches to Financing the Modern State* (New Haven: Yale University Press, 1993), p. 185.

[83] Fledt, quoted in Steinmo, *Taxation and Democracy*, p. 186.

company Nyckeln "suspended payments following major losses on real estate loans. . . . Soon thereafter, the banks themselves began to suffer major losses themselves" [84] Once Nyckeln collapsed, the banks attempted to call in their debts, and as Keynes had said sixty years ago, what was rational for an individual banker can often be collectively suicidal for the financial system as a whole.

Just as lending had the characteristics of a prisoner's dilemma, so did calling in the debt since an individual bank wants to get its creditable loans recalled before any other bank does the same. In this manner, the credit crunch began. By calling in loans and increasing interest rates, Swedish banks began a general deflation from a very exposed position. This lead to "a general collapse of real estate prices and construction activity."[85] The bust following the boom had arrived, and by the end 1993 the total cost of bailing out these financial institutions was to be anywhere between 74 and 153 billion krona, depending on the estimate.[86]

In 1990, however, the imminent bursting of the bubble was not yet apparent and the state was preoccupied with the dangers of inflation, not deflation. The SAP aimed to cool down the credit boom and sought to take 2 percent of GDP out of circulation to encourage a general deflation. Furthermore, in late 1990, the SAP executed its most radical policy U-turn just before the bubble burst by setting inflation fighting, with inflation currently reaching 11.5 percent, as the number one policy priority rather than full employment. In line with SNS's normpolitik ideas, the SAP instructed the Riksbank to be concerned only with maintaining parity between the European Currency Unit (ECU) and the krona as an external currency anchor – in other words, implementing normpolitik. This, it was hoped, would foster credibility and reduce inflationary expectations. Unfortunately, the timing of this Policy adoption could not have been worse. In August 1990, Iraq invaded Kuwait, oil prices shot up, the market optimism of the late 1980s evaporated, and the economy crashed.

The net effect of these changes was to make the effective real interest rate and the exchange rate of the krona much higher than they would have otherwise been. Meanwhile, the deficit increased as the tax reforms reduced state revenues just as expenditures were increasing. The markets viewed defending the ECU/krona peg at this level as "incredible" rather than credible given the concurrent domestic deflation. However, since a devaluation to relieve pressure was now deemed unthinkable due to the abolition of

---

[84] Jaffee, "The Swedish Real Estate Crisis," p. 88.

[85] *Ibid.*, p. 78.

[86] The 74 billion krona figure is given by Jaffee, "The Swedish Real Estate Crisis," p. 89. The 153 billion krona figure is given by Tor Wennerberg, "Undermining the Welfare State in Sweden," *Z Magazine*, June 1995, located at
http://www.lbbs.org/Zmag/articles/june95wennerberg.htm.

controls and the commitment to normpolitik, currency speculators began a feeding frenzy. Money poured out of the country, and the Riksbank was forced in response to raise interest rates as high as 500 percent on the overnight rate and 17 percent as the nominal rate at the height of the collapse. Unfortunately, interest rates of such magnitudes were completely incompatible with an ongoing domestic deflation. Adoption of the ideas of SNS at this point turned a bad contraction due to speculation, bank failure, procyclical disinflation, and historical accident into a massive economic collapse. The only people in Sweden who said from the beginning that these policies would lead to exactly these consequences were the LO economists. However, when they issued their warnings about the perils of deregulation, no one was listening to the unions. No one thought these old ideas were of any relevance.[87]

Continuing Institutional Withdrawal

Coterminous with these changes, SAF launched a final assault on the remaining institutions of embedded liberalism: those of representation. In January 1990, SAP finance minister Feldt invited the SAF, the LO, and the white-collar union TCO to Haga Castle to discuss what would be needed to get a new version of collective bargaining up and running. While the unions cooperated, "SAF's board rejected the very idea of the talks."[88] Indeed, SAF Chairman Ulf Laurin had said before the Haga Castle proposals were tabled, "after a long illness, the Swedish Model is dead. The historic decision made by SAF on February 2nd [1990] means that there is no return."[89] In response to SAF's refusal to participate, Feldt proposed a crisis package of austerity measures designed to shock the parties into agreement. Despite this shock, the SAF refused to cooperate, which in and of itself provoked a governmental crisis and worsened the political position of the SAP.

SAF then turned its attention toward representative institutions that depended upon tripartite cooperation. In Swedish policymaking, the opinions of different interest organizations were solicited by the state and incorporated into legislation through a remiss procedure. Beginning in 1985, the SAF began to challenge these governing arrangements by publicly questioning business's role within such corporatist institutions. In 1990, following SAF's refusal to countenance a return to centralized

---

[87] It was not until much later that those academic economists who had been favorably disposed toward deregulation admitted the problems with the strategy. See Lars Calmfors, "Lessons from the Macroeconomic Experience of Sweden," *European Journal of Political Economy* (9) (1993), esp. p. 50.

[88] Pestoff, "Towards a New Swedish Model," p. 157.

[89] Ulf Laurin, quoted in *SAF-Tidningen*, February 16, 1990, p. 11, translated and quoted by Pestoff, "Towards a New Swedish Model," p. 160.

bargaining, SAF's Chairman Laurin "relieved the Director of the Negotiations Division [of SAF] of his responsibilities" the week after the Haga Castle crisis.[90] In all, some six thousand business representatives were withdrawn, thus paralyzing these representative institutions.[91]

Instead of cooperating to repair Swedish embedded liberalism at this moment of economic vulnerability, the SAF offered "a detailed plan for the complete privatization of the welfare state by the turn of the century."[92] As SAF's Laurin noted at the time, "the center of gravity in SAF's work has shifted to idea and opinion formation. It is ideas that change the world. [If] SAF can . . . successfully spread tomorrow's thoughts then its role will be larger than ever. SAF is the driving force in changing the system."[93] Indeed, just two years later Laurin could argue that "[i]t's almost embarrassing. The program SAF adopted in 1990 provided a strategy until the turn of the century. [However,] most of our ideas have already been put into practice . . . so next year we will spell out what needs to be done in the remainder of the decade."[94] The program included calls for the privatization of education and health care. Just as the Democrats had done in the 1980s in the United States, by advocating and implementing tax cuts and deficit reduction, the SAP itself undermined both the ideas and the supporting institutional framework that had kept the party in power since 1932. As the state rejected its own ideas, it changed its supporting institutions in such a way that benefited business and isolated labor from the SAP.

The SAF's declaration that the sacred cows of collectivism were dead simply would not have been possible without the consistent attacks on embedded liberal institutions waged over the previous ten years. An attack began by labor was exacerbated by business and completed by the state. Indeed, the leader of the Conservative Party, Carl Bildt, was incorrect when he said on election night that "the winds of political change blowing across Europe have finally reached Sweden."[95] In fact, the SAP policy agenda by 1985 had already prepared the ground. The state, with the help of business, had managed the institutions of the old order to the point to destruction. Unsurprisingly, the Conservatives emerged in the midst of this crisis as the majority party in a governing bourgeois coalition for the first time since the 1920s. Once in power, the Conservatives used the

---

[90] *Ibid.*
[91] Stephens qualifies this conclusion by arguing that such collective modes of representation were actually replaced by individual representatives from the same sectors. Thus, nothing much actually changed. See Stephens, "Is Swedish Corporatism Dead," pp. 7–8.
[92] Pestoff, "Towards a New Swedish Model," p. 153.
[93] Laurin, quoted in *SAF-Tidningen*, February 16, 1990, translated by Martin, "The Politics of Macroeconomic Policy," p. 258. See also Henning, "Sweden: Political Interference with Business," pp. 30, 34.
[94] Laurin, quoted in Pestoff, "Towards a New Swedish Model," p. 165.
[95] *Financial Times*, November 8, 1990, p. 2.

ideas of SAF to put the blame for the collapse on Sweden's embedded liberal institutions, and thereby advocated the need for the further reform of those institutions.

Replacing Embedded Liberalism

Den Enda Vägens Politik

In November 1991, the new Conservative government closed the ministry of housing and pushed for the privatization of the housing stock and those state enterprises nationalized during the bourgeois administrations of the 1970s. The Conservatives' macroeconomic strategy centered upon formally linking the krona to the ECU, just as SNS's ideas mandated. This norm-politik was supplemented by proposals to increase saving through tax incentives. This, it was argued, would dampen domestic demand and reduce inflation. The problem was that by the time Bildt stepped into office, infla-tion was no longer the problem, deflation was, and the policies of the Con-servatives simply served to make the situation far worse than it had been.

As Carl Hamilton and Dag Rolander argue, the Conservatives saw infla-tion as a function of three things: trade unions, social democratic govern-ments, and the public sector. Unfortunately, none of these factors had anything to do with the inflation of the late 1980s.[96] The government nevertheless set itself two tasks: first, to deal with inflation as the number one economic threat by following the normpolitik ideas of SNS; second, to break embedded liberal institutions by subjecting the public sector to the strictures of a tight nonaccommodationist monetary policy.

This approach encouraged in the Conservatives what Hamilton and Rolander call "kogntiv förankring" – a "cognitive locking" that made the situation amenable to only one "problem description." This locking had the effect of "rendering the government incapable of seeing any other alter-native."[97] In the environment of 1991 and 1992, such a policy meant that "Sweden got a government pledged to fighting inflation, but there was no longer any inflation to fight."[98] This strategy took absolutely no account of the deflationary state of the Swedish economy. "Fight inflation" became an ideological mantra to be repeated and applied no matter what the actual conditions were. Bildt even echoed Thatcher's claim that "there is no alter-native," by declaring that he offered "den enda vägens politik" – the "only way policy." The Conservatives also shared the SNS view that the crisis was not the result of deregulation, tax reform, and normpolitik. Indeed, such market-conforming policies had to be, by definition, good things.

---

[96] This section draws on the analysis of the Bildt administration provided by Hamilton and Rolander, *Att leda Sverige.*
[97] Hamilton and Rolander, *Att leda Sverige,* p. 10.
[98] *Ibid.,* pp. 12–13.

Embedded liberal institutions, plus the "nonlinearities of the welfare state" and a dependent central bank, were to blame instead. Policy therefore had to be designed to wring inflation out of the system, inflation that was and could only be generated by such institutions.

Out of this diagnosis of the current collapse, the Bildt government decided SNS's norm policy was still the only way forward.[99] As noted earlier, normpolitik effectively meant giving credibility to the fixed value of the krona to reduce inflationary expectations. However, the further attraction of a credibility regime to the Conservatives was that it allowed the state to obviate domestic groups' claims for higher wages and transfers, as accommodation is deemed *ultra vires*. Inflation fighting through a restrictive monetary policy becomes the only way forward. However, converting these ideas into actual policy caused considerable problems.

Like the United Kingdom's experience with the European Exchange Rate Mechanism (ERM), tying the krona to the ECU to foster credibility forced a huge interest rate appreciation in the face of speculation. Eventually, the currency was floated on November 19 and promptly sank. Sweden had tied the krona to the ECU, as noted previously, both to provide stability and indicate commitment as normpolitik dictated it should. However, when hit by a wave of speculative pressure in 1991, "Sweden appeared to be locked into a hopeless circle. Defense of the Krona demanded high interest rates. These in turn slowed down growth, increasing the budget deficit. Tackling the deficit by cutting down the budget meant a further slow-down in growth."[100]

As Hamilton and Rolander argue, the policy response of the new government to this situation was doctrinaire adherence to the ideas of business. Rather than stabilizing the economy by accommodating the deflation, the government announced in the fall a crisis package that lowered sick pay, decreased housing allowances, and increased taxes, thereby taking approximately 40 billion krona *out* of the economy. This was pure classicism from the 1920s and was as wholly inappropriate for a slump in the 1990s as it was in the 1930s. Yet the state's cognitive locking into the ideas of business made any other outcome impossible.

As Hamilton and Rolander note, a particular problem in Sweden is that "the corps of economists is so homogeneous [that] no Swedish government has been able to follow an economic policy that goes against the general ideas of economists."[101] It was this homogeneity of personnel and ideas,

---

[99] See *Ibid.*, pp. 33–61, for details on SNS's norm policy and its impact on the Conservative government.

[100] Graeme D. Eddie, "Sweden: Krona Crisis Stalls 'New Start,'" *World Today*, January (1993), p. 11. See also Geoffrey Garrett, *Partisan Politics in the Global Economy* (Cambridge: Cambridge University Press, 1998), p. 143.

[101] Hamilton and Rolander, *Att leda Sverige*, pp. 100–1.

coupled with the politicization of business, that thrust these new ideas onto the agenda and ultimately led to the transformation of Swedish embedded liberalism. Like *laissez faire* everywhere, Sweden's was planned. However, the consequences of this institutional transformation were never part of the blueprint.[102] By November 1992, Swedish industrial output had fallen by 12 percent and unemployment had risen, despite labor market policies, from just over 4 percent when the SAP left office to around 9 percent.[103] Nonetheless, the state pressed ahead with further institutional reforms. However, given the depth of the recession, there was, to paraphrase Bo Rothstein, a limit to how much free-market economics the Swedish people could tolerate, at least all in one dose.[104] Given this, the Bildt administration realized that if it did not want to be remembered as a repeat of the failed bourgeois experiment of 1976–81, then it would have to reform embedded liberal institutions further in such a way that even if the SAP came back into power, it could not change course.[105] That other way was through European integration.

The Turn to Europe

The Conservatives' attempt to replace embedded liberal institutions was hamstrung by the economic downturn that these ideas had both precipitated and exacerbated. Sweden's attempt to join the EU was therefore perhaps best understood as an attempt by business and the Conservatives to let the economic ideas and institutions of the EU achieve by international convergence what they had failed to do through domestic reform.[106] Defeating the LO was only part of the struggle. Now that the unions were on the

---

[102] Lars Calmfors notes concerning this period as a whole, "Sweden opted for the same disinflation as did most other Western European countries already in the early eighties." This is in fact exactly what the Conservatives did, despite the fact that it was absolutely the wrong time to deflate. Furthermore, even in the best of conditions, this strategy implies that adjustment in the labor market will be more or less instantaneous. This naive interpretation of labor market responsiveness was exactly what the Conservatives were betting upon occurring, despite other "supply-shocked" European economies having demonstrated that labor markets do not clear quite so easily. Thus, Calmfors errs on the side of caution when he says that "the responsiveness of real wages to unemployment is likely to have been overestimated." The "cognitive locking" of the Conservatives could hardly assure otherwise. See Calmfors, "Lessons from the Macroeconomic Experience of Sweden," pp. 53, 55, 57.

[103] Figures from *The Economist*, November 28, 1992. This figure includes those in labor market training schemes.

[104] Bo Rothstein, "Explaining Swedish Corporatism: The Formative Moment," *Scandinavian Political Studies* 15 (3) (1992).

[105] Hamilton and Rolander, *Att leda Sverige*, p. 115.

[106] On European monetary integration as a conservative project designed to instantiate neoliberal practices in member states, see Kathleen R. McNamara, *The Currency of Ideas: Monetary Politics and the European Union* (Ithaca: Cornell University Press, 1998).

defensive, institutions that would guarantee this reapportionment of power still had to be constructed. Consider the Bildt administration's policies toward Europe and how joining Europe was expected to affect the institutions and goals of domestic taxation and unemployment.

As Graeme D. Eddie notes,

> In an address ... to representatives of the EC Commission, Bildt described the decision to submit an application for membership of the EC as a decisive, epoch-making event. In terms much stronger than those used by the previous government, Bildt wanted to assure the Community that Sweden was prepared to adhere to the political aims of the Treaties of Rome and the Single European Act, and that the country was ready and willing to carry through whatever decisions on economic, monetary and political union might be agreed upon at the Maastricht summit.[107]

Bildt similarly commented that EU membership would make tax cuts "more or less inevitable."[108] In this, Bildt was quite correct. To allow for the free flow of goods, services, and persons as envisaged in the Maastricht Treaty, Sweden would have to undergo a thorough reform of the tax system – not just on the marginal tax rates of individuals, but of the complete tax, credit, and investment system that defined Swedish embedded liberalism. In sum, international economic integration would promote those domestic institutional changes that were otherwise impossible to attain.

An example of this reformation by convergence lies in the area of unemployment policy. As noted in Chapter 4, until the early 1990s, all Swedish parties accepted the commitment to full employment as the primary policy goal of the state. Despite this cross-party abrogation, unemployment has neither dropped out of the Swedish political lexicon nor from the public's list of priorities. Indeed, one of the main reasons that the SAP lost the election in 1991 was that it underplayed unemployment as an issue and publicly declared inflation to be more important than unemployment.[109] As Steven McBride has observed, "the fact that Sweden pursued full employment policies under bourgeois governments and that [in comparison] Britain lapsed into high unemployment policies under a Labour government is significant in that their behavior was shaped by a hegemonic consensus not entirely of their own making."[110] Given this commitment, it would be very difficult for the Conservatives to eschew this policy goal and remain

---

[107] Eddie, "Sweden: Krona Crisis," p. 9.
[108] Paulette Kurzer, *Business and Banking: Political Change and Economic Integration in Western Europe* (Ithaca: Cornell University Press, 1993), p. 120.
[109] See Klas Åmark, "Afterword: Swedish Social Democracy on a Historical Threshold," in Klaus Misgeld, Karl Molin, and Klas Åmark, eds., *Creating Social Democracy: A Century of the Social Democratic Labor Party in Sweden* (University Park: Pennsylvania State University Press, 1992), pp. 429–45.
[110] Steven McBride, "The Comparative Politics of Unemployment: Swedish and British Responses to Economic Crisis," *Comparative Politics* 20 (3) April (1988), p. 318.

in power, unless the institutions that made this policy goal possible were substantially restructured. If the Conservatives wished to transform these institutions, then that policy consensus would have to be broken. European integration could conceivably have supplied the sufficient conditions for such changes.

Sweden remains an open economy whose firms must obey international price signals. Given this pressure, some analysts have extrapolated that "when the sum of imports and exports exceeds the GDP, national economic measures become either impossible, ineffective, or costly. At that point, reliance on market mechanisms becomes the most feasible alternative."[111] How such a claim relates to Sweden is difficult to see given that Sweden's degree of openness is nowhere near this level. Although by 1986 Swedish multinationals' share of total exports had risen from 42 percent to 56 percent, and concentration among these multinationals had increased, this in itself does not explain the desire by business to break existing domestic institutions.[112]

In contrast to arguments that consider these institutional upheavals a determinate function of the changing structure of Swedish business, or the degree of export dependence, it is worth recalling that in such arguments the effect precedes the cause. First, business's attempts to transform these institutions *preceded* the change in export-dependence of the state and the increased multinationality of Swedish firms. Second, by 1992, at the height of the Swedish debate over Europe, Swedish exports had collapsed. Sweden's "openness" to trade, the inverse of which is the degree of policy autonomy that the state has *vis á vis* international trade flows, had plummeted to just over 54 percent, which was on par with openness in 1974–6.[113] Yet this was exactly the point at which business pushed the hardest for EU membership using globalization arguments to justify joining Europe.[114] Therefore, the motivation for business in gaining access to European markets, from which Swedish businesses were hardly excluded in the first place, must be seen in relation to the other goal that business shared with the Conservatives, the dismantling Swedish embedded liberalism. The two goals are entirely complementary. Joining the EU would have facilitated the policy goal of abrogating any commitment to full employment by making it technically, and practically, impossible to fulfill such a commitment and remain within the EU.

---

[111] Paulette Kurzer, "Unemployment in Open Economies: The Impact of Trade, Finance and European Integration," *Comparative Political Studies* (24) 1 April (1991), p. 11.

[112] Figures from Martin, "Wage Bargaining and Swedish Politics," p. 97.

[113] The exact figures are (X + M)/CGDP (1975 55.87) (1992 54.05), calculated from Penn World Tables v. 5.6 on NBER server, http://www.nber.org/pwt.

[114] It is also the same rhetoric that Clinton used in the 1992 election to attempt to promote a more active state role, despite the fact that the United States is the world's least globalized economy.

The key attraction of the EU to business and the Conservatives in the early 1990s was the operation of the European Monetary System (EMS).[115] The EMS was a credibility-based regime predicated upon monetary coordination in defense of parity among member states. The 1991 experience of the krona being tied to the ECU, but being in fact outside of the system, demonstrated that there was no one except the Swedes themselves to defend the krona, which is why its credibility failed. However, if Sweden joined in the EMS, so the argument went, then other European states would also defend the krona and credibility would be enhanced.[116]

However, joining facilitates another policy goal. As Paulette Kurzer has correctly noted, joining the EMS constitutes a *de facto* relinquishment of monetary sovereignty, that is, no more free-riding devaluations nor other aspects of a stabilization policy.[117] The consequences of this for full-employment policy are profound. As Ton Notermans emphasizes, "Tying macroeconomic policies to external balance implies that the corporatist logic of political exchange . . . becomes inoperative."[118] Joining the EMS abrogates a state's commitment to any full-employment policy, the fundamental principle of embedded liberalism. What was achieved in the United States domestically was to be achieved in Sweden internationally.

As intervention to defend parity is costly, there is an incentive for states to aim for external equilibrium to avoid such constant interventions. However, equilibrium can be achieved only by "influencing domestic expenditures, which usually implies curbing public and consumer spending."[119] Traditionally, such pressure would be offset at a domestic level by manipulating interest rates or devaluing the currency. However, in the EMS such a strategy would no longer be feasible since "credit policies [we]re aimed at establishing parity with the D-Mark."[120] As such, cutting consumption would appear to be the only way forward, and thus Sweden's commitment to a full-employment policy would be outflanked by the EMS.

Moreover, the convergence criteria outlined in the Maastricht Treaty further dictate that budget deficits and inflation rates must all be kept under strict control, preferably independent central bank control, which Sweden also established in the early 1990s. In such an environment, capital cannot be regulated, as that would contradict the basic freedoms of movement

---

[115] See McNamara, *The Currency of Ideas, passim.*
[116] It must be recalled that this attraction was predicated on the assumption that the EMS would be stable and around until the full European Monetary Union succeeded it. No one saw "Black Wednesday" coming.
[117] Kurzer, "Unemployment in Open Economies," *passim.*
[118] Ton Notermans, "Abdication from National Policy Autonomy: Why Has the Macroeconomic Policy Regime Become So Unfavorable to Labor," *Politics and Society* (21) 2 (1995), p. 134.
[119] Kurzer, "Unemployment in Open Economies," p. 13.
[120] *Ibid.*

enshrined in the Maastricht Treaty, nor could tax policy be used to facilitate redistribution, as capital would simply exit. Thus, joining Europe would not only rule a policy of full-employment *ultra vires*, it would in fact facilitate a further institutional reformation. As a leading LO economist remarked, "In 1993–1994 we became EU members and essentially adopted a neo-liberal strategy as neoliberalism is built into EU institutions. It takes away all your strong means to combat unemployment."[121]

Despite joining the EU, however, Sweden found that such an exogenously driven institutional transformation was not to be. Neither Bildt nor the SAP, which began the drive for European integration in 1988 in part because Feldt was attracted to the effect it would have on tax rates, could have foreseen the breakup of the EMS. The Conservatives originally perceived European integration as part of a three-pronged strategy: First, fight inflation through norm policy. Second, rein in the public sector and create the conditions for noninflationary growth. Third, prevent a return to stabilization policy by locking in these changes into an external disciplinary environment that demanded uniform taxes, spending commitments, and an overall credible noninterventionist macroeconomic policy. Unfortunately for the Conservatives, the first strategy was inappropriate given existing deflationary conditions. The second strategy was outflanked by the collapse of normpolitik, and the third strategy ended because of the very currency speculation it was originally intended to avoid. One would think that after such a clear demonstration of the failure of a set of economic ideas to deliver the goods, it would be discredited. However, as Volker's monetarist experiment proved, mere empirical failure is not enough to discredit a mode of thought. The same strategy of reform continued in Sweden after the return of the SAP to power in 1994.

The Art of Paradigm Maintenance

The Return of the SAP
The policy stances that the SAP has taken since its reelection in 1994 highlight the continuing salience of the ideas of business. Rhetorically, the attitude of the reelected SAP since September 1994 toward the need for domestic restructuring has been one of positive acceptance. However, such restructuring was to be on wholly different terms from the previous administration, terms that would strengthen the existing institutional order rather than weaken it. However, the reality of the SAP in power has been somewhat more path-dependent.

Fearing a return to stabilization policy upon the return to power of the SAP, shortly before the 1994 election, five of Sweden's largest multinational

---

[121] Unidentified LO economist interviewed by Stephens. Quoted in Stephens, "Is Swedish Corporatism Dead," p. 10.

firms warned jointly in a newspaper article that they would reconsider plans to invest domestically an estimated 50 billion krona (around $6.5 billion) per year if taxes were raised after the election and the budget deficit not stabilized.[122] Unfortunately for these firms, the main result of this very public threat seems to have been to increase support for the SAP since it was returned to office in September 1994 with 45.4 percent of the vote. The return of the SAP was "interpreted in Sweden as . . . a fierce determination among the voters to protect the extensive welfare system, which came under sustained attack during Bildt's tenure."[123] Yet, this is only partly the case. In fact, the SAP had followed a dual strategy since its return to power, a strategy very similar to that pursued by New Labour in the United Kingdom: First, dampen expectations as much as possible while anticipating the reactions and accommodating the preferences of business.[124] Second, maintain in public that the welfare state is safe while pursuing almost as reformist an agenda as the Conservatives.

An example of this duality was seen in one of the first tasks of the new SAP administration. The SAP's response to business's very public exit threat was to attempt to reintegrate business into what remained of the old cooperative institutions, which business had unilaterally scuttled, by creating a so-called "wise men" industry panel containing precisely those companies that threatened an investment strike. In a statement after the first meeting, the wise men announced that approximately 50 billion krona were planned for domestic investment over the next five years after all. However, they gave no guarantees that such investment would be forthcoming, and moreover, given the efforts of business and the Conservatives prior to this declaration, the wise men detailed no institutional means to realize these investments. As this entire integrative strategy relied upon the good will of business, some saw the whole exercise as a public relations move to improve business's image after it had threatened a capital strike.[125]

Similarly, the SAP's attitude toward Europe seemed to be different from the Conservatives'. By the time Sweden joined the EU, the political make-up of Europe had changed in a manner that could have conceivably helped traditional SAP objectives. Specifically, the leftward swing of Europe in the mid-1990s meant that the commission may have been less worried about pleasing international business and more sympathetic to goals such as full

---

[122] See *Svenska Dagablet*, September 24, 1994.
[123] See *The Guardian*, October 1, 1994.
[124] See Colin Hay, "Anticipating Accommodations, Accommodating Anticipations: The Appeasement of Capital in the 'Modernization' of the British Labour Party, 1987–1992," and the rejoinder by Mark Wickham Jones, "Social Democracy and Structural Dependency: The British Case. A Note on Hay," both *Politics and Society* 25 (2) June (1997), on the issue of how far social democratic parties need to accommodate business's preferences.
[125] Interview with an SAF official (unattributable comment) by the author, June 1997.

employment. Moreover, the voting structure agreed to at Maastricht gave small states disproportional advantages: Finland, Denmark, and Sweden can together outvote Germany. Given such changes, the SAP voiced an intent to restructure Maastricht from within and make unemployment the top policy priority, perhaps even at the expense of inflation. At the Essen summit, Carlsson pushed for action on infrastructural investment, active labor market policies, and worker retraining, and while being in favor of being inside Europe, the SAP declared itself not to be in favor of monetary union.[126]

The reasons for this reticence were twofold. First, there was the issue of the convergence criteria. Until very recently, Sweden simply was not able to meet the EMU admission criteria. Second, the Riksbank has repeatedly stressed the need to correct structural imbalances before such integration could occur. Given these factors, one could plausibly claim that the SAP does in fact wish to return to stabilization policy and conclude that Sweden has no intention of using Europe to restructure domestic institutions. However, such a conclusion is too sanguine. As noted previously, the SAP's actual strategy has been to carry forward the policies and reforms of the Conservatives – that is, to extend market-conforming ideas into new policy areas.

In terms of labor market policies, the SAP promised the LO that on returning to power in 1994, it would restore the labor legislation passed in the 1970s that was disavowed by the Conservatives. However, while making these commitments, the SAP was also trying to get the LO to accept new flexible working practices, practices long sought by the SAF that would have significantly undermined the LO, as the *quid pro quo* for reinstating these laws.[127] Similarly, EU membership continues to ensure fiscal probity by the state, just as the Conservatives thought it would. For the SAP, deficit reduction, inflation control, and balanced budgets, rather than full employment and an equitable distribution of income, became the cornerstones of macroeconomic policy after 1994. The privatization of the pension system, the public good that brought the middle classes into embedded liberal institutions, has been discussed in the Riksdag, and private provision has been *de facto* accepted. In short, the SAP is still cognitively locked into these new economic ideas, thereby obviating any chance of rebuilding the old institutional order.[128] Given that the economy had improved from its 1992–3 low

---

[126] Reuters Money Report, Bonds, Business Market, November 18, 1994, p. 14.

[127] Rianne Mahon, "Death of a Model? Swedish Social Democracy at the Close of the Twentieth Century," unpublished paper, September 1998, pp. 24–6.

[128] There is another reason for this adherence of the SAP to these new ideas. Because all the major political parties were complicit in accepting the new SNS version of economic policy, no one had any incentive to turn against it, even when it became clear that it was economically suicidal. As Linder noted, "Everybody was in on it. We (the Conservatives) were there in this big pact with the Social Democrats to defend the krona . . . everybody's guilty

point and that the 1994 election clearly signaled that the public did not want any more *laissez faire* policies, the question remains why the SAP accepted these policy commitments. Once again, the effect of institutionalized ideas is to promote path-dependence in policy.

The Continuing Triumph of Business's Ideas

The reason for the SAP's adoption of business's ideas and conservative policies lies not in the new, and exaggerated, nature of the constraints of the global economy.[129] Instead, it is more aptly summarized in Hamilton and Rolander's observation that due to the homogeneity of economists and economic opinion in Swedish public discourse, it appears that in both boom and bust, "in Sweden there is only one choice on the menu."[130] Despite the disastrous experiences of the early 1990s, elite economic opinion in favor of the "system change" has remained constant. The highly influential SNS surveys of the Swedish economy are an excellent example of what Robert Wade has termed "the art of paradigm maintenance."[131] The SNS reports of the 1990s match almost perfectly with the policy choices detailed previously and allow us to see how, despite empirical failure, these new ideas have been reinforced over time.

SNS's 1991 report notes that Sweden was "on its way to an acute costs crisis" that could only be obviated by "a norm-based stabilization policy that implements clear, stable and credible rules for households, companies and organizations."[132] However, three key developments – the deregulation of credit markets, EU membership, and commitment to a price stabilization norm – have meant that "we have now come to the journey's end of the Swedish policy of accommodation and that policies must be more *European* in the future."[133]

The overall thrust of the 1991 report was that the problems of the Swedish economy were produced by an insufficient level of credibility, an oversized public sector, and a lack of the kind of flexibility that would

---

in a sense." Interview with Linder, president of Timbro, by the author, Stockholm, June 13, 1997.

[129] On the extent of this exaggeration, see Colin Hay, "Globalization, Competitiveness and the Future of the Welfare State in Europe," paper prepared for presentation at the European Community Studies Association's International Conference, Madison, WI, May 31–June 2, 2001; Robert Wade, "Globalization and its Limits," in Suzanne Berger and Ronald Dore, eds., *National Diversity and Global Capitalism* (Ithaca: Cornell University Press, 1996), pp. 78–83.

[130] Hamilton and Rolander, *Att leda Sverige*, p. 103.

[131] By this, Wade means the ability to maintain the coherence of a set of beliefs, regardless of any amount of disconfirming information to the contrary. See Robert Wade, "Japan, the World Bank, and the Art of Paradigm Maintenance: The East Asian Miracle in Political Perspective," *New Left Review* (217) May–June (1996).

[132] SNS Economic Policy Group Annual Report 1991, "The Swedish Economy at the Turning Point," SNS Occasional Paper (26) May 1991, pp. 4–5.

[133] *Ibid.*, p. 9.

restore growth.[134] Therefore, the report argued, the key to restoring growth was "to declare an anti-inflationary policy and then persist in upholding it, *no matter what the consequences*, be they bankruptcies, financial crises, or unemployment."[135] Finally, it was argued that the credibility of a price stabilization norm could be enhanced by association with the Exchange Rate Mechanism (ERM). As we saw previously, these recommendations were basically adopted *in toto* as government policy by the Conservatives and led to the biggest deflation to hit the economy since the 1930s.[136]

The 1992 report was written just as the real extent of the slump was becoming apparent. However, for SNS, the causes of the near collapse of the Swedish economy were the world recession, the punitive and correctional "need" to undergo the disinflation that other European states underwent some ten years earlier, and the fact that Sweden has a large public sector. The two main themes of the report are that harmonization with the rest of Europe will rule out a return to stabilization policy, and that the reason for the slump is the size of the public sector.

As well as considering EU membership as economically restrictive for the reasons noted previously, the SNS report opines that "mobility across national borders places limits on the taxes that can be imposed and the benefits that can be offered." As such, "when households decide where to reside, they choose a bundle of goods consisting of a tax system and a set of social benefits [although] a high tax burden in one country does not inevitably lead to emigration."[137] This Tiebout model from welfare economics – a model that assumes no externalities, completely mobile individuals with perfect information, and sufficient demand for all job seekers – is generally not regarded as a good guide to policy. However, it does enable the authors to conclude that "the main point of our analysis . . . is that the [European] integration process invalidates arguments in favor of large-scale national welfare systems," since free and complete mobility allows people to choose where to live, to pay taxes, to invest, and to retire.[138] At a time when the total number of claimants upon Sweden's national welfare system was higher than it had been at any time since the 1930s due to the collapse that normpolitik, deregulation, and tax reform

---

[134] The report does not spell out why a country that pioneered active labor market policies should be in need of additional flexibility.

[135] SNS Economic Policy Group Annual Report 1991, p. 16. My italics.

[136] The report goes on to advocate the privatization of services that are "intrinsically private," such as health care and education, and concludes that only by the application of these policies can the long-term structural problems associated with a bloated welfare state be corrected and economic growth restored to Sweden. The definition of an intrinsically private service, however, is left open to interpretation.

[137] SNS Economic Policy Group Annual Report 1992, "Disinflation, Integration and Growth: The Swedish Economy 1992 and Beyond," SNS Occasional Paper (37) June 1991, p. 9.

[138] *Ibid.*, p. 10.

had brought about, SNS was reaching back to welfare theorems from 1956 to justify welfare state rollback.

The 1993 report reinforced these themes and avoided any suggestion that the current deflation may in fact be a function of the deployment of SNS's own ideas. The 1993 report argues that the crisis is "the result of the interplay of many factors." However, above all else, "the crisis is deeply rooted in *structural and secular problems* in the Swedish economy [that were] created by the economic policies of the past decades."[139] Specifically, rather than seeing the krona crisis as a result of normpolitik, SNS was now arguing that the reason for the collapse was that normpolitik had not been applied with sufficient vigor.[140]

The report argued that abandoning the fixed exchange rate regime on November 19, 1992, shattered credibility in normpolitik, despite the fact that "before the krona fell, the nonaccommodation policy . . . gave rise to several positive results. Inflation and inflationary expectations [had] been forced down."[141] However, by SNS's own figures, inflation was plummeting due to the bursting of the property bubble.[142] Norm policy was applied with vigor *after* the deflation began and simply made the situation worse. Furthermore, the 1993 report makes no mention of financial deregulation as in any way contributing to the collapse. In fact, the collapse is seen as a punishment "which may be regarded as belated extra cost for many decades of credit market regulation."[143] Therefore, the way forward was greater deregulation of the private sector.[144]

By 1994, as noted previously, there was considerable nervousness that the return of the SAP might mean a return to old policies. Consequently, the 1994 SNS report reiterates that the blame for the turmoil of the past five years should be laid squarely at the door of the welfare state and the public sector.[145] The 1994 report begins by noting that because the Swedish

---

[139] SNS Economic Policy Group Annual Report 1993, "Sweden's Economic Crisis: Diagnosis and Cure," SNS Occasional Paper (43) February 1993, pp. 2–3.

[140] This is hauntingly similar to Karl Polanyi's comments concerning the arguments espoused by classical liberals when liberalism was seen to have failed in its application: "its partial eclipse may have strengthened its hold since it enabled its defenders to argue that the incomplete application of its principles was the reason for every and any difficulty laid to its charge." Karl Polanyi, *The Great Transformation: The Political and Economic Origins of Our Time* (Boston: Beacon Press, 1944), p. 143.

[141] SNS Economic Policy Group Annual Report 1993, p. 8.

[142] *Ibid.*, p. 9, figure 6.

[143] *Ibid.*, p. 15.

[144] The logic behind this policy recommendation is pure rational expectations. As the report continues, given "the difficulty of making forecasts, insufficient knowledge about the effects of economic policy measures as well as shortcomings . . . in the political decision making process, make it hard to stabilize the economy through discretionary economic policy intervention. As such, the best policy is of course, to let market mechanisms allocate." *Ibid.*, p. 23.

[145] What unfolds is what Hirschman refers to as a "perversity thesis" where the unintended consequences of benign actions end up producing malign consequences. Albert O.

welfare state has ballooned in recent years (largely as a function of the collapse of the 1990s, which is not acknowledged), then the only way to restore growth is to transfer resources from the public sector to the private sector because "there is ample evidence of a statistical correlation between a large public sector and slow growth."[146]

What causes this slowdown in growth is a hypothesized catch-22 of welfare provision that owes its pedigree to the arguments of Martin Feldstein, Norman Ture, and Jude Wanninski. SNS argued that a high social safety causes impaired incentives, and as the safety net is broadened, expenditures increase. Consequently, the tax revenues needed to support this burden were also increased, thus broadening the tax base. This broadening led to reduced activity, which in turn led to a further slowdown in production. This incentive-driven slowdown exacerbates the problem of slow growth by increasing the number of claimants, and so a vicious circle was created.[147] The report concludes that "the mere size of the welfare state inhibits economic growth in general. The social security system poses a severe threat to full employment. The rapid increase in the budget deficit causes economic insecurity on both an individual and collective level."[148] Thus the report narrates the crisis of the early 1990s without ever addressing any of the actual causes of the collapse.

In 1985 Barry Bosworth and Alice Rivlin of the Brookings Institution undertook a study of the Swedish economy that hailed the third way policy as a success.[149] In 1995 SNS set up a new study of the Swedish economy with the NBER and the University of Chicago. The NBER/SNS joint study took a more even-handed approach to analyzing the Swedish economy than SNS's annual surveys did themselves. However, the SNS/NBER study is remarkable for the frame of reference it applies regarding the way forward for the Swedish economy from this point on.[150]

The NBER/SNS team analyzed the crisis of the early 1990s from three perspectives. First, they outlined the systems failure–sclerosis thesis of SNS and Timbro regarding the long-run effects on economic growth of the growth of the welfare state. The SNS/NBER team concluded candidly that "to accept this hypothesis we need both a model and supporting evidence.

Hirschman, *The Rhetoric of Reaction: Perversity, Futility, Jeopardy* (Harvard: Belknap Press, 1994).

[146] SNS Economic Policy Group Annual Report 1994, "The Crisis of the Swedish Welfare State," SNS Occasional Paper (55) May 1994, p. 10. There is also ample statistical evidence refuting this proposition.

[147] *Ibid.*, pp. 10–13.

[148] *Ibid.*, p. 31.

[149] Barry Bosworth and Alice Rivlin, eds., *The Swedish Economy* (Washington: Brookings Institution, 1986).

[150] Richard B. Freeman, Brigita Swedenborg, and Robert Topel, "Economic Troubles in Sweden's Welfare State – Introduction, Summary and Conclusions to the Project: The Welfare State in Transition," SNS Occasional Paper (69) January 1995.

... But at present we have no such model."[151] Next, the study discusses a version of the policy failure thesis outlined previously, minus its ideational aspects, but comes to no conclusion regarding the validity of this thesis. Finally, the NBER team hypothesizes that perhaps change is painful regardless of the conditions and that the collapse was somehow "inevitable." As the authors conclude,

... we do not take a position with respect to these (possibly overlapping) explanations. While critical for some purposes to assess why the Swedish economy did so poorly ... it is perhaps even more important to realize that the crisis changed the basis for the Swedish welfare state ... The issue for the 1990's is not *whether* to reform the welfare state, but *how* to do so.[152]

This conclusion that the causes of the collapse no longer matter is vitally important on an ideational level, for it constitutes a declaration that the old institutional order is now no longer an option, *regardless of how it was undermined.* The point stressed is that the old order is completely untenable now that the country has arrived at this postcollapse position. As such, the ideological struggle is over, and the economic ideas that specify what an economic problem is and how to deal with it are set. The rest is arguing over the details.[153]

As an example as to how far these new economic ideas have permeated SAP policymaking, consider the following speech by the Riksbank Governor Urban Bäckström to the SAF annual conference in May 1997.[154] Bäckström begins by noting that since unemployment is high it must be a function of wage formation. As such, "unduly high wage increases can lead to a higher path for inflation ... [while] ... combating inflation is the central bank's primary function." However, low unemployment is not a

---

[151] *Ibid.*, p. 10.

[152] *Ibid.*, p. 11. The authors note that, "changes in the tax system, in wage setting, in the rules for benefits, in regulation of industries, including credit markets, were all in the direction of economic efficiency, but this did not prevent a major economic downturn." *Ibid.*, p. 24. It never seemed to occur to the authors that precisely these efficient policies may have in fact caused the crash.

[153] For reasons of space I shall not detail the 1997 SNS annual report. Suffice to say that it opens with a comparison of Tanzania and Sweden on the grounds that they are both victims of a Hayekian tyranny of the welfare state. This comparison leads to the conclusion that Sweden will end up an economic disaster unless it reforms. Other claims include the claim that South Korea succeeded in growing while others stagnated because of its adherence to free-market principles, and the claim that Chile's brutal dictatorship under Augusto Pinochet was worth it from a fiscal standpoint. See SNS Annual Report 1997, "The Swedish Model under Stress: The View from the Stands" (Stockholm: SNS Förlag, 1997) pp. 16–21, 72–9, 124–5, respectively.

[154] All quotes in this section are from Bäckström's speech at the SAF conference, May 22, 1997. While Bäckström himself is a liberal and the Riksbank is itself independent, his comments still give a candid appraisal of government policy.

good thing in itself. It is only good insofar as "a favorable trend for jobs and unemployment helps to strengthen the long-term credibility of a low inflation regime." Unemployment does not actually help reduce wages because "increased unemployment does not seem to be able to instill wage restraint." This situation "illustrates what economists refer to as the theory of labor market insiders and outsiders." Given this analysis, "the problem of poorly functioning wage formation and other economic problems were veiled and too many people were lulled into believing that inflation and over-expansion had rendered Sweden immune to economic laws."[155]

Given this diagnosis, the crisis of the 1990s was not the result of ideologically driven policy, but was instead the result of problems "which could no longer be concealed," such that "by the 1980's the Swedish economy was in urgent need of changes." Despite the collapse that adherence to these ideas generated, the government has "preserved and displayed [its] determination by working to consolidate government finance . . . keeping interest rate policy tight in pursuit of price stability." The governor closes with a note that "the Riksbank inflation target is clearly supported by society in general," in the context of a eulogy to the virtues of the gold standard.

Note how each of these statements embodies the ideas advanced by SNS, business, and the Conservatives over the past fifteen years. Wage increases cause inflation, not profits or supply shocks, as under Rehn-Meidner, nor can the blame be laid at the door of a credit boom and an underfunded tax reform. Combating inflation and guaranteeing price stability must be the foremost policy goals of the state, and these should be achieved with a fixed exchange rate policy backed by a credible anti-inflation norm. This is advocated despite the fact that this very policy led to a huge disinflation just a few years previously when there was no inflation left to fight. Similarly, high unemployment is not caused by insufficient demand throughout Europe due to the self-enforced constraints of Maastricht and the Sado-Monetarist stances of European central banks. Instead, unions are still to blame despite business's deliberate weakening of the LO and central bargaining institutions. Meanwhile, the insider-outsider model is merely a rediscovery of the classical argument put to rest by the Swedish Unemployment Committee in 1927 that unions interfere with price setting and hence cause unemployment.[156] Finally, the root cause of all this lies in believing that Sweden could

---

[155] In many of the interviews I conducted with SAP policymakers, I encountered this refrain that Sweden thought itself immune from economic laws operative elsewhere, yet never once was this said by SAF spokespeople. It is interesting to note that adherence to these laws gave Sweden its worst economic performance in decades. Perhaps, then, ignorance was bliss?

[156] Other hysterisis models that focus on search costs and effectiveness as reasons for European unemployment are not promoted with the same vigor, probably because they bespeak

avoid the economic "laws" operative elsewhere despite the fact that in this case, and comparatively speaking, this ignorance supported a distributional coalition and set of stabilizing and supporting economic institutions that lasted a generation and a half.

Finishing the Transformation?

Observers of Sweden are fond of saying that Sweden is currently at a "cross-roads." This analysis maintains that Sweden is well past the crossroads and is accelerating up the block. However, such a conclusion may be too deterministic. After all, nothing in the theory outlined in the earlier chapters says that states *must* go all the way from a pure market-conforming to a pure market-reforming institutional order. Indeed, one does not wish to criticize Polanyi for positing an end of history and then go on to posit one's own historical end. Perhaps sources of resistance may be found in the very narrow social base of the coalition that these new ideas made possible. Rather than building a coalition by inclusion, as the ideas of the 1930s and 1940s did, these new ideas created a coalition by exclusion from the people's home and a protective welfare state. Thus the public sector, unions, and welfare recipients were discursively marginalized from the mainstream of successful market participants.

Moreover, this new order rests on a false premise. Supporters of the new order, such as Jan-Erik Lane, argue that, "During the 1980s a general swing towards market values has taken place in Scandinavian societies. There is hardly any support for more public sector solutions to social problems." He concludes, "The Northern lights no longer shine as they used to. Nordic economies are characterized by increasing institutional sclerosis."[157] If Lane is correct, if there really is no longer any support for more public sector solutions to social problems, then the pendulum *must* swing the whole way from market-reforming to a market-conforming regime.

In principle at least, people get what they vote for in a democracy. So, if they want less interventionism and state-funded protection, then it will be provided by rational vote-maximizing parties. However, such a view is mistaken on two levels. First, political parties compete within and over economic ideas within which the political middle is not an exogenous given but is a political construction.[158] If the only choice on the menu is "the market" or "the untrammeled market," then while it may seem that people are in fact supportive of these policies, they in fact are merely forced to

---

an interventionist solution. The insider-outsider model simply invites further "deregulation," and as such, it discursively fits well with these new economic ideas.

[157] Jan-Erik Lane, "The Twilight of the Scandinavian Model," *Political Studies* (61) (1992), pp. 318, 324.

[158] Mark Blyth, "Moving the Political Middle: Redefining the Boundaries of State Action," *Political Quarterly*, July (1997).

choose within very circumscribed limits. Second, such market-conforming ideas may not be successfully institutionalized over the long term in Sweden. The problem lies in Lane's observation that "during the 1980's . . . a general swing towards market values has taken place in Scandinavian societies."[159] Indeed, this view is often supported in the Swedish media. For example, the 1991 election survey cited a key reason for the loss of power by the SAP as "an ideological shift among the voters . . . from socialism to [a] market economy."[160] However, the work of Stefan Svallfors is particularly instructive in this regard in dispelling this assessment.

Svallfors' data, drawn from attitude and opinion surveys, show that while there has been a rise in support for market solutions on certain questions such as the provision of child care and care for the elderly, this has *not* been at the expense of state and local authorities. In fact, the rise in private provision has been almost wholly at the expense of *family* provision. Support for state provision for these services, and also for education and social work, has been remarkably stable. Moreover, support for state provision dwarfs support for private provision by as much as a 20 : 1 margin on some issues. Support for the private sector may have doubled, but to double 4 percent is still little more than a marginal improvement.[161] Svallfors finds that "On the question of how to finance welfare policies we find even greater stability." In fact, by Svallfors' measures, support for the state financing of education, health, and dependent care actually increased between 1986 and 1992.[162] Svallfors concludes that "the sudden loss of legitimacy for welfare policies envisaged by some interpreters is hard to detect at the level of ordinary citizens' attitudes. The present crisis of the Swedish welfare state is not emanating from any grass-roots revolt against the present organization of welfare policies."[163]

This analysis suggests an interesting conclusion that I shall return to in the final chapter. In Sweden, these new economic ideas may have become the *lingua franca* of policymaking, but only at an elite level.[164] Mass public

---

[159] Lane, "Twilight of the Scandinavian Model," pp. 318, 324.

[160] Mikael Gilljam and Sören Holmberg, eds., *Väljarna inför 90-talet* (Stockholm: Norstedts, 1993), quoted in Stefan Svallfors, "The End of Class Politics? Structural Cleavages and Attitudes to Swedish Welfare Policies," *Acta Sociologica* (38) (1995), p. 54.

[161] Svallfors, "The End of Class Politics?" p. 59, table 2.

[162] *Ibid.*, table 3.

[163] *Ibid.*, p. 69.

[164] That is to say, as Boreus' data show, support for market economics among the readership of *Svenska Dagablet* may have doubled, but only a small minority of Swedes read *Svenska Dagablet*. Crucially, though, those readers are the ones setting policy. Elite resistance to these ideas seems largely to have collapsed by the late 1980s. One notable exception was the work of the prominent sociologist Walter Korpi. Korpi had argued against the SNS-Timbro Suedo-sclerosis thesis in the debate pages of *Dagens Nyheter* and elsewhere throughout the 1990s. In 1996, Korpi was invited to put his objections in the form of an article for the *Economic Journal*, which he did. Korpi argued that the key to SNS and Timbro's analyses was not the numbers. Rather, it was the values behind those numbers.

support for state-financed provision of public goods is as high now as it has ever been. Thus, parties such as the SAP that portray themselves as the representatives of a large coalition of interests find themselves caught within a set of economic ideas which deem impossible, or at least detrimental, most of the policies that those constituencies support. Like the Democrats in the United States, the SAP appears simultaneously as the heir of the embedded liberal order and yet as the party most likely to dismantle it. The key question for Sweden is, will the lack of public support for these new ideas and the policies they augur prevent their consolidation, or will such an order be constructed *despite* the wishes of the majority?

This initial outlook suggests that Sweden's second great transformation, which was so successfully carried out in the United States, may indeed be hamstrung. Despite the persistent attacks on embedded liberal institutions and the delegitimation of the ideas governing those arrangements, the results of the 1998 election suggest, in line with Svallfors' findings, that there are limits to how far a neoliberal transformation will proceed. The SAP's continuation of conservative policies from 1994 until 1998 resulted in a huge drop in support from 45.4 percent of the vote in 1994 to 36.5 percent in 1998. But such an electoral reversal cannot be seen as support for the Conservatives either, since their share of the vote also plummeted, thus allowing the SAP to govern in coalition with the left.

In sum, it seems that despite the SAP's new-found predilection for austerity policies and market solutions, the party was forced by a popular demand to "restore" the welfare state and to promise more money for health care and social services. As the *New York Times* noted on the 1998 election campaign, "the most repeated claim in this election was not the

Korpi argued that by "largely borrowing lines of argument from their American counterparts, Swedish economists managed to convince Sweden's political decisionmakers to base their policies on the Sclerosis diagnosis." Walter Korpi, "Eurosclerosis and the Sclerosis of Objectivity: On the Role of Values among Economic Policy Experts," *Economic Journal* (106) November (1996), p. 1741. Korpi notes that the same arguments concerning the effect of taxes on incentives have been trotted out for the past two hundred years, despite the fact that economic growth continued unabated. As Korpi put it, "although political measures affecting market processes certainly may have negative efficiency consequences, social scientists should be seriously concerned when theoretical arguments are recycled generation after generation without the addition of empirical evidence increasing the precision as to the size of these negative effects and the conditions under which they are likely to occur." *Ibid.*, p. 1742. Despite their reasonableness, Korpi's views were ridiculed and disparaged. In the introduction to the follow-up issue of the *Economic Journal* where economists responded to Korpi's thesis, the editorial opined that, "it is worth pointing out that Korpi is a Professor of Sociology and Social Policy, and not an Economist." Huw Dixon, "Controversy: Economists, the Welfare State and Growth: The Case of Sweden," *Economic Journal* (106) November (1996), p. 1725. This of course disqualifies Korpi from saying anything sensible. As Korpi said to this author, "I naively thought all I had to do was show them the facts and that would be that." Korpi, interview with the author, Stockholm, June 13, 1997.

dynamic pledge to bring about change common to campaigns elsewhere in Europe, but a solid promise to restore what was."[165] Perhaps, then, Sweden may not go all the way, nor even nearly as far as the United States, and other countries, have gone. Nonetheless, when taken together, the cases of Sweden and the United States demonstrate just how far the second great transformation of the twentieth century has progressed, and how important both the power of ideas and the power of organized business were in promoting these institutional transformations. I return to these issues in the next and final chapter.

[165] Warren Hoge, "Swedish Party Pledging Expanded Welfare Gains Slim Victory," *New York Times*, September 21, 1998.

PART III

CONCLUSIONS

8

Conclusions

The "end of ideology" is never possible: no social order is given once and for all.

– Adam Przeworski, *Capitalism and Social Democracy* (Cambridge: Cambridge University Press, 1985), p. 146.

The aim of this book has been to demonstrate that large-scale institutional change cannot be understood from class alignments, materially given coalitions, or other structural prerequisites. Instead, it has been argued that institutional change only makes sense by reference to the ideas that inform agents' responses to moments of uncertainty and crisis. This is not to claim structures irrelevant; far from it. But it is to claim that the fact of structural change does not on its own create a particular politics. Regardless of the structurally given interests one assumes agents to have, such structures do not come with an instruction sheet. This conclusion strengthens these claims in four ways.

First, this chapter revisits the five hypotheses about ideas posited in Chapter 2. These hypotheses, and the more general claim that institutional change follows a particular sequence, are reexamined. Where appropriate, counterfactual logics are used to support the claims made. Second, this chapter discusses the relevance of this study for existing theories of institutional change. In particular, likely objections to the theory presented here and the limits of such ideational explanations are explored. Next, we consider whether the second great transformation was as great as the first, or indeed, whether these institutional changes constitute a simple return to the market-conforming institutions of the 1920s. Finally, Karl Polanyi's concept of the double movement is reexamined. It is argued that when reformulated as a problem of institutional supply under Knightian uncertainty, the double movement indeed provides the analyst with a powerful tool for understanding institutional change in capitalist societies. However, such a tool is powerful only to the extent that analysts rethink the relationships among ideas, interests, and institutions.

Five Hypotheses about Ideas – Revisited

Hypothesis One
In periods of economic crisis, ideas (not institutions) reduce uncertainty.

In both of our cases, the hypothesis that ideas, rather than institutions, reduce uncertainty finds strong support. The cases demonstrate that these moments of economic crisis could not be institutionally resolved until agents on the ground had some idea as to what the causes of these crises were. Institutional supply in such conditions could not simply be a function of structural changes since these uncertain conditions hardly demanded an obvious response. That these economies were in crisis was not in doubt. Rather, what was in doubt was the nature of these crises.

During the 1930s, the American state's first attempt to resolve the crisis institutionally occurred under the auspices of the National Recovery Administration (NRA). The NRA was based upon a diagnosis of the depression as a function of industrial cartelization. Given this diagnosis, the institutional solution proposed was to further that cartelization by administering prices. While such ideas were efficacious in reducing uncertainty, they were less successful in providing institutional stability. Cartelization disaffected smaller firms that did not have the economies of scale to benefit from such institutions, while the *quid pro quo* of cartelization, section 7a labor organization and spending on public works, served to convince business as a whole that continued uncertainty was perhaps a lesser evil than continued cooperation. The NRA thus failed to support a workable coalition with business, which in turn delegitimated the ideas underpinning these institutions.

Counterfactually, the design of the NRA as an institutional response to uncertainty makes little sense without reference to the ideas informing it. Unless one posits that the depression was caused by the ability of large firms to set prices regardless of demand, then the idea that voluntary cartelization and price setting would produce stability makes no sense. There was, after all, nothing in the fact of falling prices that axiomatically led to cartelization as the optimal policy response.[1] The example of the NRA

---

[1] For examples of approaches that do assume such an unproblematic relationship, see Peter A. Gourevitch, *Politics in Hard Times: Comparative Responses to International Economic Crises* (Ithaca: Cornell University Press, 1986); Jeffry A. Frieden, "Sectoral Conflict and U.S. Foreign Economic Policy, 1914–1940," in G. John Ikenberry, David A. Lake, and Michael Mastanduno, eds., *The State and American Foreign Policy* (Ithaca: Cornell University Press, 1988), pp. 59–91. For a critique of these models, see David Plotke, *Building a New Political Order: Reshaping American Liberalism in the 1930's and 1940's* (Cambridge: Cambridge University Press, 1996), p. 90, fn. 44.

clearly demonstrates that the precise form that institutions take is not a derivative function of a self-apparent crisis. Instead, both the crisis and its institutional response make sense only in terms of the way that ideas were used to diagnose the crisis and reduce uncertainty.

In the Swedish case, the state's adherence to classical liberal ideas dictated that adjustment to external conditions should take precedence over any interventionist policies. Such ideas proved to be of little help in reducing uncertainty. First, as a price-taking economy, the restoration of equilibrium conditions was predicated upon stabilization elsewhere, conditions that the state had no control over. Second, as the 1920s wore on, support for such *laissez faire* ideas waned as the deflation continued and unemployment worsened. In this uncertain environment, new ideas that bespoke interventionist solutions to the crisis were creatively, not axiomatically, generated by the SAP and the Stockholm School. Once again, what made these new economic ideas efficacious was not so much their immediate practical application, but how they managed to reduce uncertainty and recast seemingly contrary interests as common.

For example, in contrast to American underconsumptionist ideas that stressed the importance of industrial labor as the base for recovery, the SAP's *political* ideas stressed the need for the inclusion of all sectors. This led to the development of a set of *economic* ideas that actively sought to incorporate business and agriculture along with labor as integral components of recovery. Therefore, it was the state's ability to narrate the crisis in a specific way and recast interests as common that made possible the reduction of uncertainty and subsequent institutional construction. The importance of ideas in reducing uncertainty again finds counterfactual support in the instance of the SAP's experiences in government during the 1920s. Governing with classical ideas meant that when in power, "the SAP were . . . politically weak."[2] Such weakness was not simply a function of electoral numbers, considering that the SAP was the majority partner in a coalition government four times during the 1920s. Instead, such weakness stemmed from having no alternative economic ideas about the causes of, and possible resolutions to, the crisis that the state faced.

Given this analysis, the supporting counterfactual is, could the SAP have governed differently in the 1920s had the ideas of the 1930s been available? This counterfactual can be supported. The Unemployment Commission, the key institution through which reflationary ideas were transmitted, was present in the 1920s, and at that time advocated *deflation*. Thus, had reflationary ideas been available earlier, then it is reasonable to assume that

---

[2] Villy Bergstrom, "Party Program and Economic Policy: The Social Democrats in Government," in Klaus Misgeld, Karl Molin, and Klas Åmark, eds., *Creating Social Democracy: A Century of the Social Democratic Labor Party in Sweden* (Pennsylvania: Penn State Press, 1992), p. 136.

the SAP could have promoted change earlier. In sum, how agents think about a crisis is no trivial matter if the crisis presents no self-apparent solution.

Hypothesis Two
Following uncertainty reduction, ideas make collective action and coalition building possible.

Once ideas have reduced uncertainty, specific distributional coalitions can be constructed in line with those ideas. This hypothesis gives support to recent theoretical work on the role of increasing returns in politics. Such dynamics, not only play a role in reducing uncertainty, as argued in Chapter 2, but also have important role in facilitating collective action. As Paul Pierson has argued, "understandings of the political world should themselves be seen as susceptible to path dependence."[3] Given that collective action is predicated upon the mutual recognition of collective ends, the representation of those ends through ideas becomes the prerequisite of successful collective endeavors. Therefore, if one accepts that, "Once established, basic outlooks on politics . . . are generally tenacious," and path-dependent, then ideas and collective action must be theorized together since it is the intellectual path-dependence that such ideas encourage that makes collective action possible.[4]

For example, when the American state's coalition with business failed and underconsumptionist ideas came to prominence, the state sought to ally with industrial labor to the exclusion of agricultural labor. While this made political sense in terms of obviating the Southern veto in Congress, such a coalition also made *ideological* sense. Within the framework of these new ideas, agricultural labor was seen as being simply unable to provide the mass consumption base deemed necessary to bring about recovery. Consequently, institutions were designed to support industrial labor's consumption patterns while excluding agricultural labor from any such settlement. As such, the diagnosis of the crisis dictated who was a potential partner and who was not. Ideas pushed the politics of coalition building down some paths and not others.

In contrast, the inclusive focus of the SAP's political and economic ideas made possible an encompassing coalition of business, labor, and agriculture. By narrating the crisis as a function of a failure of demand that affected all sectors equally, and by portraying full employment as the prerequisite of both price stabilization for business and as the source of adequate

---

[3] Paul Pierson, "Increasing Returns, Path Dependence, and the Study of Politics," *American Political Science Review* 94 (2) June (2000), p. 260. See also Andrew Polsky, "When Business Speaks: Political Entrepreneurship, Discourse and Mobilization in American Partisan Regimes," *Journal of Theoretical Politics* 12 (4) (2000).

[4] *Ibid.*

demand for agriculture, the SAP was able to build a coalition wholly different and more resilient than its American counterpart. Through such economic ideas, the SAP's political coalition became both more encompassing in distributional terms and more open to later extensions than was possible in the United States.

These conclusions also find counterfactual support. As the example of the Agricultural Adjustment Act (AAA) demonstrated, the desire to exclude agricultural labor and include industrial labor stemmed from the fact that the AAA was informed by both administered prices *and* incipient underconsumptionist ideas. In contrast, the Swedish state's more inclusive underconsumptionist ideas viewed agricultural demand as a significant source of stability and sought to incorporate such labor into new institutions. The appropriate counterfactual is, therefore, "if the ideas informing institutional construction in both cases did not matter, then could such different coalitional forms be predicted by agents' hypothesized material interests or sectoral alignments?" Again, such an outcome is unlikely. Without reference to the differences in the ideas informing each of these projects, and thus how these ideas shaped perceptions of possible coalition partners, the precise form that these coalitions and their supporting institutions took is very difficult to explain. In sum, changes in ideas about the causes of a given crisis made constructing certain coalitions possible and others impossible.

Ideas as resources for building coalitions were also vitally important during the denouement of embedded liberalism. However, it is important to note that in this period the nature of the coalitions necessary to capture the state and effect institutional change had themselves changed substantially. In the United States, the concerns of business – inflation, regulation, and corporate taxation – were hardly the stuff of mass coalitional politics. With the costs of such problems being rather diffuse, such issues were hardly likely to inspire marches in the streets.[5] However, by the late 1970s, it was no longer necessary to build a mass supporting coalition in either America or Sweden in order to affect political change because of some unexpected institutional changes that served both to limit the scope of coalition building and to concentrate the effects of ideas.

In the United States, the reasons for these changes in coalitional politics were some unexpected side effects of the 1970s campaign finance reforms. As discussed in Chapter 6, the Campaign Finance Reform Act of 1971 and the 1976 SUNPAC ruling effectively ended all restrictions on corporate donations.[6] Given these changes, the need to build a mass base to effect

---

[5] Except, as we saw in Chapter 7, on October 4, 1984, in Stockholm.

[6] See Dan Clawson, Alan Neustadtl, and Denise Scott, *Money Talks: Corporate Pacs and Political Influence* (New York: Basic Books, 1992), p. 30; David Vogel, *Fluctuating Fortunes: The Political Power of Business in America* (New York: Basic Books, 1989), pp. 119–23.

change in the American political system was obviated. By heavily funding pro-business candidates, the ideas of business could become concentrated within the Congress and the executive branch. Once individuals no longer constituted a mass resource base for politics, except as direct-mail targets, the need to bring them into a coalition of the type built in the 1930s disappeared.

Similar changes occurred in Sweden, albeit for different reasons. While the institutional logic of Sweden's embedded liberalism dictated that decisionmaking was concentrated in very few hands, the political logic of democracy pulled in the other direction. Specifically, the institutions of Rehn-Meidner created a self-reinforcing compact among the titular members of business, labor, and the state, which reduced the Riksdag to the role of a spectator. Medium-term economic decisions were handled on an *ad hoc* basis by small informal bodies such as the so called "Thursday club" and "Harpsund" group, where these titular representatives would meet secretively and agree policy among themselves.[7]

Despite disquiet over the antidemocratic nature of such arrangements, such a pattern of rule persisted.[8] In fact, it seems that practically all the major decisions regarding economic policy in Sweden since the 1970s were taken by no more than five people at any given time. The wage earner funds proposal, the 1982 devaluation, the 1987 credit market deregulation, the 1989 tax reform, and the 1991 decision to abolish exchange controls all conform to this pattern.[9] Given such concentration, the coalition that needed to be held together by such ideas could be made much more limited and specific to members of elite institutions. As the example of the Conservative government of the 1990s demonstrated, within very hierarchic state structures such as those found in Sweden, ideas can become institutionalized very quickly. Moreover, such institutions are most likely to produce a path-dependent cognitive locking since they circumvent outside influences on policymaking.

This comparison of how coalition politics changed in both the United States and Sweden during the second great transformation suggests an interesting modification to a well-known historical institutionalist argument

---

[7] On the Thursday club and Harpsund democracy, see Sven Steinmo, *Taxation and Democracy: Swedish, British and American Approaches to Financing the Modern State* (New Haven: Yale University Press, 1993), p. 126.

[8] As Steinmo notes, "The technocratic nature of Swedish policymaking during these years did not make everyone happy. Many were beginning to question the nature of a democratic political system in which many of the most controversial issues of the day were, in fact, settled behind closed doors by unelected representatives of interest organizations and technocrats." Steinmo, *Taxation and Democracy*, p. 126.

[9] That these decisions were made by so few was confirmed in interviews by the author with SAP, LO, and SAF principals in Stockholm in July 1997.

about ideas. In their famous study of the policy responses to the Great Depression, Theda Skocpol and Margaret Weir argued that the degree to which existing institutions were open or closed to new ideas was the critical factor that explained variation in policy responses.[10] That is, state structures and policy legacies acted as filters for policy-relevant ideas.[11] This analysis gives specificity to this insight by arguing that specific types of state structures may be more prone to ideational capture and intellectual path-dependence than others. Moreover, this variation can be explained theoretically.

Occupying one extreme, the case of the United States suggests that very open polities nonetheless contain key veto points. For example, key congressional committees, the Federal Reserve, etc., are particularly important sites for ideational capture. If a particular ideological faction gains control of these critical nodes, then structural openness to ideas may paradoxically amplify the effect of such ideas throughout governing institutions. As the example of the Democrats' "bidding war" over tax cuts demonstrated, this concentration of ideas may set up tipping game dynamics where the cost of being a holdout to these new ideas rises *pari passu* with the number of defectors. As such, despite the apparent openness and fluidity of such a polity, ideas can become concentrated and their effects amplified. At the other extreme, the Swedish case suggests a simpler model where concentration of ideas in very few heads within extremely hierarchical institutions can similarly amplify the effects of ideas and further obviate the need to build a broad supporting coalition.

Comparatively speaking, this suggests a U-shaped relationship, with openness to ideas along the horizontal axis and strength of ideas along the vertical. In such a distribution, Sweden and the United States represent very closed and very open polities respectively – the contrasting peaks of the curve. Meanwhile, states that are neither as open nor as hierarchic would be distributed around the trough of the curve.[12] In sum, while ideas have remained important elements of coalition building, both the nature of those coalitions and the effects that ideas have upon them seem to have varied across time.

---

[10] Theda Skocpol and Margaret Weir, "State Structures and the Possibilities for Keynesian Responses to the Depression in Sweden, Britain and the United States," in Peter B. Evans, Dietrich Rueschemeyer, Theda Skocpol, eds., *Bringing the State Back In* (Cambridge: Cambridge University Press, 1985), p. 109.

[11] As Skocpol and Weir put it, "we must ask not about the presence of individual persons or ideas in the abstract, but whether key state agencies were open or closed to the use or development of innovative perspectives." Skocpol and Weir, "State Structures," p. 126.

[12] This suggests why polities prone to coalition governments, particularly Southern European states, seem to be strangely unaffected by ideational developments elsewhere. I thank Jonathan Hopkin for this insight.

Hypotheses Three and Four
In the struggle over existing institutions, ideas are weapons (and blue-prints).[13]

Ideas were used as weapons and as institutional blueprints during both transformations. During the 1937 recession and the subsequent TNEC hearings in the United States, underconsumptionist ideas were used to defeat the sound finance ideas of business and the Treasury Department. These new ideas were used by the state to delegitimate business's demands for a return to orthodoxy and served to establish underconsumptionist ideas as the rationale for greater state intervention in the economy. Such ideas also contained within them clear institutional blueprints. During World War II, these new ideas, as expressed in the National Resource Planning Board reports of 1943 and 1944, bespoke an expanded role for the state within a new institutional order that deemed private investment insufficient for the maintenance of full employment. Business realized that it needed its own ideas to defeat these ideas, and through organizations such as the Committee for Economic Development deployed alternative ideas to limit the nature and scope of postwar embedded liberalism. In the Swedish case, the example of SAP policies during the 1920s demonstrates that having no weapons of one's own – that is, governing with classical ideas – severely limited the ability of the SAP to challenge and change existing institutions. It was only once the state adopted reflationary ideas that it proved possible for the SAP to challenge the existing order.

During the second great transformation, business also used ideas as weapons to promote institutional change. The ideas of monetarists, new classical macroeconomists, and public choice theorists were used to attack and delegitimate existing institutions. Inside Congress, supply-side tax ideas were used to narrate a capital formation crisis, while the OMB used supply-side ideas allied with expectations arguments to promise painless deflation and increasing revenue from smaller tax rates. In the financial markets, monetarist ideas gained dominance and established new conventions governing market behavior.

The actual economic efficacy of these ideas – that is, the extent to which they constituted useful technical knowledge – was not the issue. The ability of these ideas to affect change was. In this respect, the importance of ideas as weapons is revealed in how the Democrats, the heirs of embedded liberalism, singularly failed to deploy any ideas to defend their legacy. By accepting the ideas of business that deficits caused inflation and taxation retarded growth, the Democrats found themselves devoid of any weapons to contest the institutional changes wrought by business and the GOP. They were unable to articulate a defense of what was, after all, their core achievements.

---

[13] I have condensed the discussion of weapons and blueprints into a single section for reasons of space.

How the downturn of the 1970s was narrated in the United States as a capital formation crisis offers further counterfactual support for the importance of ideas as weapons. The idea that there was a capital formation crisis in the United States due to excessive taxation was dubious at best. First, retained earnings are not a significant source of investment in the United States, which is why stock markets exist. Second, if there was a shortage of capital, then the price of capital – crudely speaking, the interest rate – should rise. Once the equation takes inflation into account, however, the effective real interest rate in this period tended toward zero. Therefore, if there was a lack of investment, it was because business was choosing not to invest rather than the federal government voraciously consuming all available capital. As such, a crisis of capital formation had to be constructed, and the ideas of Martin Feldstein, Michael Boskin, Norman Ture, and Paul Craig Roberts made this possible.

In Sweden, these same ideas were used to effect institutional change, albeit with more emphasis placed on the deleterious effects of the welfare state institutions on growth and the perceived need for credibility in macroeconomic policy. Here the ideas developed and deployed by pro-business think tanks built upon the new market-conforming ideas of influential academic economists to demand a "system change" in Sweden.[14] The ideas developed and deployed by these institutions dictated that practically any and all economic dislocations were generated by existing embedded liberal institutions. Given such a diagnosis, existing institutions had to be reformed.

As the 1980s wore on and the third-way devaluation strategy created domestic overheating, the governing SAP reformed taxation and credit market institutions in line with these new ideas. These reforms had the unfortunate side effect of creating a credit bubble in the midst of an underfunded tax reform. Ironically, at the same time as the bubble burst, the Conservatives were elected. Armed with the same market-conforming ideas, the Conservatives sought to solve the crisis of inflation and used these ideas as weapons to squeeze inflation out of the system, despite the fact that the economy was deflating all around them. In sum, both of the cases examined here provide ample support for the hypotheses that ideas are both weapons with which to contest existing institutions and blueprints for their replacements.

Hypothesis Five
Following institutional construction, ideas make institutional stability possible.

---

[14] For a good example of the system change literature, see Assar Lindbeck et al., *Turning Sweden Around*, (Cambridge, MA: MIT Press, 1994).

Building upon John Maynard Keynes' understanding of market stability, Chapter 2 argued that while ideas reduce uncertainty and act as institutional blueprints, it is the institutions constructed from those blueprints that in the longer run produce market stability.[15] Again, the cases provide empirical evidence for this claim. During the first great transformation, deflation weakened existing institutions and destabilized the conventions governing investment expectations.[16] Under these conditions, the prerequisite of reestablishing market stability was the supply of new institutions.

As the case of the United States demonstrated, the consumption-maintaining institutions constructed during the 1930s combined with the passive stabilizing institutions built in the 1940s to reinforce business's expectations of limited slumps, steady growth, and labor peace. Such conventions were relatively stable, and as a consequence, these outcomes persisted as long as the economy performed within the boundaries of these established conventions. Once the problems of dollar overhangs, regulation, controls, and policy failures increased business's uncertainty during the late 1960s, these conventions came unstuck. The uncertainty this engendered impacted negatively upon expectations, thereby slowing down investment.[17] To reestablish stability, business's conventions had to be restructured. The key to doing this was to attack, delegitimate, and replace embedded liberal institutions with neoliberal ones. Such institutions would produce new market-conforming conventions that enshrined business's diagnosis of the crisis and disavowed those past practices by the state that business blamed for the crisis.

The same stabilizing role of conventions can be found in the Swedish case. In the 1920s, the convention that deflation would produce equilibrium conditions became increasingly untenable as the depression wore on. Existing institutions could not produce new stabilizing conventions while the supply of new institutions to manage expectations was stymied by the lack of alternative economic ideas. It was not until the state accepted and acted on a new narration of the crisis that new institutions to stabilize expectations were constructed. Similarly, the legislative assaults visited

---

[15] On Keynes' understanding of conventions, see John Maynard Keynes, *The General Theory of Employment, Interest and Money* (London: Harcourt Brace and World, 1964), pp. 147–65.

[16] This is the mechanism that Keynes posits to control the liquidity preference. See Keynes, *The General Theory*, pp. 170–4.

[17] The state's share of GDP increased from 13 percent in 1964 to 14.5 percent and then 15.2 percent in 1966–7. Meanwhile, the private investment share of GDP fell from 23.8 percent in 1964 to 22.5 percent in 1967. These figures demonstrate how increasing prices reflected increasing demand. Such price rises were fueled by government investment and consumption through deficits, rather than reflected in increased domestic (private) capital formation and the expansion of private capacity. Figures are calculated from FRED (Federal Reserve Economic Database) – Federal Government Time Series, and the Penn World Tables 5.6, available at http://www.stls.fred.org, and http://www.nber.org/penn.

upon business in the midst of the downturn of the 1970s destabilized existing conventions as to what possible futures business should expect. In response to this uncertainty, business used new economic ideas to blame the slump on existing institutions and sought to replace them with a new market-conforming institutional order.[18]

The period of bourgeois rule in Sweden from 1976–81 and 1991–4 offers counterfactual support for these propositions.[19] In the Swedish case, one of the main reasons business attempted to reform domestic institutions was the failure of the bourgeois governments of 1976–81 to implement market-conforming policies. In explaining these policy failures, it was stressed that these bourgeois governments were unable to pursue market-conforming policies not simply because of the unions' ability to veto such policies through strikes. Rather, the bourgeois parties in this period were cognitively locked into the ideas of the existing institutional order and were therefore unable to offer any alternative ideas to explain the current downturn, or indeed to suggest what to do other than offer "more social democracy." Likewise, when the Conservatives returned to office in 1991, they could understand what was happening to the economy only in terms of the ideas they held. In this context, the belief that the role of the state should be limited to inflation fighting, a goal the Conservatives followed in the middle of a deflation, led to policies that produced an economic collapse.

The supporting counterfactual in these two instances is therefore quite simple. Remove the ideas of the LO from the practices of the Liberals in the 1970s and remove the ideas of business from the practices of the Conservatives in the 1990s, and the policy responses of these governments make no sense. After all, why would the first bourgeois government in forty years *not* adopt bourgeois policies when it had the opportunity to do so, and why would the first Conservative administration in an even longer period insist on an anti-inflationary stance in the midst of a deflation unless the locked-in effects of such ideas were not causally important?

In sum, taken both on their own terms and counterfactually, the cases analyzed here provide evidence for the five hypotheses about ideas detailed in Chapter 2 and the more general claim that institutional change follows a particular sequence.[20] Indeed, a final supporting counterfactual can be

---

[18] The point here in both cases is that whether or not these institutions were to blame for the slump is secondary to the fact that business *thought* they were to blame. As such, once they were reformed, uncertainty would be reduced, regardless of whether or not those institutions in fact generated this uncertainty.

[19] How American financial markets' monetarist understanding of the dislocation of the 1980s led to M1-B watching and punitive interest rates in the midst of a rapidly deflating economy can also be adduced as a supportive counterfactual in this case. See Chapter 6 for a discussion of this episode.

[20] For kindred attempts to understand institutional change as a sequence of discrete events, see William H. Sewell, "Historical Events as Transformations of Structures: Inventing Revolution at the Bastille," *Theory and Society* 25 (6) December (1996); *Idem.*, "A Theory

posited to strengthen these claims overall. If one assumes that business-people are rational actors, one must question why they bothered to spend millions of dollars and thousands of hours over such a long period in each of these cases attempting to change these ideas unless *they* thought there was some payoff in doing so? That is, why did they alter the conditions of policy choice rather than merely heading off one legislative assault after another? After all, if *they* did not think ideas mattered, why did they act as if they did?[21]

Comparing Materialist and Ideational Explanations of Institutional Change

When examined with the theory developed in this chapter, the symmetry of the two cases is remarkable. These ostensibly very different forms of liberal capitalism underwent essentially similar sequences of change. Both countries began as market-conforming regimes, both became market-reforming regimes, and both were then transformed once again into market-conforming regimes. Obviously, the degree to which each country conformed to the ideal type varied. The United States was always the weakest embedded liberal state, while the Swedes' deeply embedded liberalism meant that its market-conforming turn, though extensive, was incomplete. Nonetheless, such surprising symmetry is apparent only if these cases are examined sequentially and temporally. Only by doing so can we appreciate how such seemingly polar examples of advanced capitalism underwent such surprisingly similar institutional transformations. Indeed, this comparison raises an interesting issue concerning the value added of ideational theories of change over materialist theories. An important branch of scholarship has recently emerged that serves as a useful point of comparison in this regard.

The so-called varieties of capitalism literature investigates the persistence of distinct types of capitalism despite pressures to converge on one "best practice" capitalist model.[22] While taking international economic variables

---

of Structure – Duality, Agency, and Transformation," *American Journal of Sociology* 98 (1) (1992); Paul Pierson, "Not Just What, But *When*: Timing and Sequence in Political Processes," *Studies in American Political Development*, 14 Spring (2000).

[21] Accepting this turns on a particular understanding of explanation. One can argue that business may have done these things, but that they had no effect. Rather, some other hypothesized factors can be seen to have done the work instead. However, such an explanation implies that history is made "behind the backs" of the agents who think that they are making it, and that businesspeople are somehow rational in the economic realm and irrational in the political. I find these propositions to be discomfiting at best.

[22] See Herbert Kitschelt, Peter Lange, Gary Marks, John D. Stephens, eds., *Continuity and Change in Contemporary Capitalism* (Cambridge: Cambridge University Press, 2000); Torben Iversen, Jonas Pontusson, David Soskice, eds., *Unions, Employers and Central Banks: Macroeconomic Coordination and Institutional Change in Social Market Economies*

seriously, this literature rightly contests the view that globalized financial and product markets, class fragmentation, and new technologies axiomatically create pressures for such convergence.[23] Instead, this literature examines how different countries' domestic institutions combine to form distinct national production regimes that refract global economic pressures. By stressing how international competition remains uneven and how national production regimes exhibit increasing returns, this literature offers a welcome corrective to the "globalization changes everything" literatures of the early 1990s.[24]

However, this literature poses an important questions for this study. To put in terms of the analytic categories used by varieties theorists, this study maintains that the quintessential national coordinated market economy (CME), Sweden, and the exemplar liberal market economy (LME), the United States, have undergone essentially the same institutional changes, at more or less the same times, with more or less similar results. As such, rather than see the persistence of national models, this study sees essentially similar transformations of those models. What then are the points of convergence and divergence between this body of scholarship and the approach developed here?

First, much of this variation in result turns on a methodological issue: the choice of starting point. The varieties literature takes the high point of the embedded liberal order as the common starting point for all states and then plots both convergence and divergence from that point over time. This study, in contrast, takes as its starting point the pre-embedded liberal order where CMEs did not exist.[25] Both the United States and Sweden were very much LMEs in the 1920s, and the whole point of the 1930s and 1940s was to turn them into CMEs. Furthermore, the struggles of the 1970s and 1980s were intimately concerned with turning these states back into LMEs. As such, whereas the varieties literature maps a lack of convergence, reasonable given its temporal focus, this study maps essentially similar transformations where the two states under study move in the same direction at the same time. The contrasting result is an artifact of the choice of starting point.

(Cambridge: Cambridge University Press, 2000); J. Rogers Hollingsworth and Robert Boyer, *Contemporary Capitalism: The Embeddedness of Institutions* (Cambridge: Cambridge University Press, 1997); Suzanne Berger and Ronald Dore, eds., *National Diversity and Global Capitalism* (Ithaca: Cornell University Press, 1996). I concentrate here on the Kitschelt et al., volume for reasons of space and similarity in the level of analysis.

[23] See especially Kitschelt et al., *Continuity and Change*, pp. 427–60.

[24] The Kitschelt et al., volume also notes that agents' perceptions of global pressures for convergence will vary according to institutional location, but the authors actually do very little with this insight analytically. *Ibid.*, pp. 440–1.

[25] Arguably one type did, the German model, but the national CME is clearly a postwar invention.

Some aspects of the varieties literature support the findings of this study. As Kitschelt et al., note, "we would expect convergence to become more probable when, in the face of similar challenges, the relevant policy or institution is less closely tied to deeply embedded other institutions . . . [and is] . . . less determined by deep-seated beliefs."[26] This is indeed what this study found in its cases. Strong ties within a dense network of institutions with deeply held beliefs were precisely the factors that hamstrung Sweden's second transformation. In contrast, since the institutions of American embedded liberalism were neither strongly tied to other institutions nor protected by deeply held beliefs, their transformation was much easier. As such, many aspects of this literature are supportive of the findings reported here. However, where these two studies do differ, and quite fundamentally, is on the actual causes of these institutional changes. Specifying such causes is where the strength of an ideational approach is demonstrated.

In the varieties literature, the proximate causes of institutional transformation are exogenous changes in the global economy, and since such changes are mediated by institutions with increasing returns, divergence remains. For this study, the proximate causes of institutional transformation are domestic agents, not international changes. Therefore, the approach taken in the varieties literature is exactly the type of analysis criticized in Chapter 1. Such an approach rests on a model of institutional equilibrium → punctuation (changes in technology, finance, and product markets, as mediated by existing institutions) → new institutional equilibrium.[27] As was argued in Chapter 1, such a model is unsatisfactory for two reasons.

The first reason is that *post hoc* does not necessarily lead to *proptor hoc*. As Pierson has argued, "The varieties of capitalism analysis persuasively illuminates distinct equilibria in different economies, but it does not address how these distinct equilibria emerge."[28] Without specifying such a mechanism of emergence, the theory, at base, relies on "that which comes after" being a function of "that which comes before". The approach lacks a theory of institutional origins and therefore has to rely upon exogenous causes. Second, and as a consequence, such an account lacks a focus on agency. This promotes a rather thin notion of politics as, at best, an intervening rather than an independent variable.[29] For example, Kitschelt et al., find that "there has been a clear tendency for national CME's to converge

[26] Kitschelt et al., *Continuity and Change*, p. 442.
[27] See the model presented in Kitschelt et al., *Continuity and Change*, p. 48, figure 15.3.
[28] Pierson, "Increasing Returns," p. 264.
[29] For a notable exception to this statement within this literature, see Andrew Martin, "The Politics of Macroeconomic Policy and Wage Coordination in Sweden," in Torben Iversen, Jonas Pontusson, David Soskice, eds., *Unions, Employers and Central Banks: Macroeconomic Coordination and Institutional Change in Social Market Economies* (Cambridge: Cambridge University Press, 2000), pp. 232–64, esp. pp. 252–61.

towards sectoral CME's."[30] This finding is supportive with this study's conclusion that Sweden's institutions of wage bargaining and representation were transformed during the 1980s as the SAF-LO agreements came apart. However, in the varieties rendition of events, such changes are a derivative function of changes in the values of exogenous international economic variables. Such a model reduces agents to being the passive bearers of institutionally mediated international price changes. When prices change, preferences are transformed and institutions are reformed in line with these price changes, a finding that is at best rather self-confirming. Politics, if present, appears in the model only as an intervening variable to explain the observed lack of convergence.

For example, the varieties literature commonly posits three variables as promoting convergence: technological changes that lead to a reorganization of production, an intensification of market competition due to the rise of new market entrants, and the growing internationalization of finance.[31] All of these are international-level variables, and politics intervenes only to refract the influence of these international factors. As Kitschelt et al., argue, as a *result* of such international changes, "business has been more willing and better able to challenge existing basic frameworks of industrial relations and to seek to restructure "class compromises" to its advantage."[32] Yet, when seen in this way, the politics of business can only be a function of *prior* international level changes.[33] What this book argues is that the varieties literature and structural models of institutional change in general temporally confuse political causes and economic effects. Specifically, there are four reasons to doubt the veracity of such materialist models.

First, the convergence of the United States as an LME on itself makes no sense. Therefore, if there has been institutional change in the United States, it has to have occurred for reasons other than convergence to international-level pressures since the institutional changes that took place in the United States all occurred *before* technology, competition, and especially financial liberalization became important causal variables. Second, there are currently no satisfactory theories of how technology affects institutions beyond rather broad increasing returns models. Absent such a theory, we can

---

[30] Kitschelt et al., *Continuity and Change*, p. 444.

[31] *Ibid.*, pp. 445–7.

[32] *Ibid.*, p. 446.

[33] As Kitschelt et al., continue, the supposed inevitable convergence to the LME "ignores the politics of political economic change. The existing diversity of production regimes implies different distributions of socioeconomic and political power among actors with different stakes in current and possible . . . institutional configurations." Kitschelt et al., *Continuity and Change*, p. 448. This observation is undoubtedly correct, but politics is still seen here as an intervening variable that refracts the independent variables of structural change in the international economy. The idea that domestic politics can be constitutive of these changes is not entertained.

neither prove nor disprove technology's importance. Third, trade competition, as highlighted in the case studies, only became an issue for the United States in the 1990s, and according to some important commentators, it is still an minor irritant at best.[34] For Sweden, trade openness actually *declined* during the mid-1980s and early 1990s.[35] As such, increased competition cannot be the cause of institutional change if that competition *declined* while those changes took place. Fourth, the liberalization of finance in Sweden undoubtedly put pressure on domestic institutions. Yet business attacked such institutions for a whole decade before financial deregulation was undertaken. Such deregulation was argued for and applauded by business agents who had been trying to scuttle the existing order, and given that the credit market reforms that were undertaken certainly furthered that end, the causes of Swedish institutional change seem to lie much more in the domestic political arena than in the international economy. While international economic variables are obviously important in a whole host of ways, they cannot be invoked to explain satisfactorily domestic institutional changes when *the timing in such theories is wrong*. The political decisions taken by business to dismantle such institutions and the shift in ideas that made these actions possible, in both of our cases, *preceded* these hypothesized material changes.[36]

Thus, the comparison of this book with the varieties of capitalism literature demonstrates how ideas are *essential* components of explanations of institutional change. As argued in Chapter 1, exogenous punctuations do not automatically produce new, stable equilibria.[37] Rather, any new equilibrium has to be defined, debated, and implemented, none of which is a given function of changing structural conditions. Looking for the causes of these institutional transformations solely within such international material factors may encourage the analyst to miss the temporal woods for the

---

[34] Paul Krugman, "Competitiveness: A Dangerous Obsession," *Foreign Affairs*, March/April (1994).

[35] Sweden's 1975 level of openness was 55.87. Though this increased rapidly (and briefly) during the third-way period, it began to decline in 1986 and by 1992 had fallen to 54.05. As such, there is no linear relationship between trade openness and domestic institutional change. Figures are calculated from Penn World Tables v. 5.6 on the NBER server, http://www.nber.org/pwt.

[36] One could argue that this claim is itself *post hoc ergo proptor hoc* and is therefore really no better than the materialist alternative. However, such a claim would be incorrect given that it is generated by a theory of institutional change and not simply based upon the observed fact of the temporal sequencing of events. The materialist alternative discussed here has no endogenous theory of change.

[37] The varieties approach partially obviates this difficulty by noting that since the shocks of 1973–82, "none of the democratic capitalist market economies appears to have achieved stability." Kitschelt, et al., *Continuity and Change*, p. 460. Yet if this is the case, one must wonder how long a switching point must continue to switch before it is considered an equilibrium.

structural trees. Taking the politics of ideas seriously and sequentially obviates such difficulties and shows the strength of the approach taken here.

Identity and Uncertainty in Institutional Change

We can now ask a question that perhaps must remain speculative: Why were the ideas used to attack and dismantle embedded liberal institutions in both cases essentially the same ideas discredited a generation before? One possible answer is that in moments of crisis when agents are uncertain about their interests, they resort to repertoires of action that resonate with their core identities. Whereas Charles Tilly has discussed repertoires of collective protest, it is possible that market agents also have repertoires of collective belief that affirm their identities during moments of uncertainty.[38] The Swedish wage earner funds debacle provides an interesting example of this dynamic.

The original Meidner proposal discussed in Chapter 6 provided business with a reasonably good deal once the provision that company shares be bought with business's own profits was dropped. Essentially, the state offered business a leveraged buy-out on reasonably good terms. Yet this was no ordinary market transaction. In pursuing this policy, the state effectively challenged Swedish business's right to exist as capitalists and questioned business's very identity as a class. In this uncertain and unprecedented situation, business responded as a class and sought to defend its identity, not its interests (if interests are defined as simple profit maximizing) and did so by reaching back into its repertoires of belief.[39] Specifically, the identity of capitalism and capitalists is built around the mythology of competition, individualism, and markets. When challenged during the 1970s, Swedish business drew from its repertoire of collective beliefs those ideas that were delegitimated during the 1930s and used them to defend itself. A similar phenomenon may have occurred with American business during the same period given its perception of the massive growth of regulation and government intervention. While speculative, this argument may offer some insight on this issue.

Another important question that the case studies raise is the extent to which both periods of transformation were in fact constituted by Knightian uncertainty. Recall it was argued in Chapter 2 that Knightian uncertainty characterized these moments of economic crisis. Such moments were unique situations where agents could not rank prior probabilities over the causes of the uncertainty they faced. In such an environment, agents could not take institutions "off the shelf" to resolve the crisis since they

---

[38] See Charles Tilly, *Popular Contention in Great Britain, 1758–1834* (Cambridge: Harvard University Press, 1995).

[39] I wish to thank Robin Varghese for first mentioning this aspect of the Swedish case to me.

could not know which institutions would perform this function, or even what their interests were in such a situation. Evidence that the presence of this type of uncertainty led to the construction of embedded liberalism lies in the fact that the crisis of the period was a crisis of deflation.

Basically, deflation generates Knightian uncertainty. Falling prices lead to increased competition, which hits profits and thus lowers investment. Growth slows, unemployment rises, and this in turn leads to a fall in demand, which reinforces the slump already under way. As such, action by any one set of market agents to protect itself tends to be zero sum against all others. This is how the downturn of the 1930s generated Knightian uncertainty. Actions undertaken to protect oneself served only to worsen the overall situation by causing greater uncertainty. Consequently, one's own interests became increasingly uncertain since following them only seemed to make things worse. Such uncertainty made collective action ever more problematic, and hence the downward movement of prices became cumulative. To paraphrase Keynes, what was individually rational proved to be collectively disastrous.

This is also why the state emerged as the key actor in this period. If agriculture, business, and labor were unclear as to what their interests actually were, then only the state could develop new ideas and narrate a way forward. Yet this analysis of how Knightian uncertainty is generated begs another question, namely, was the uncertainty that caused the decline of embedded liberalism also Knightian? After all, not only was it business rather than the state that took the lead promoting in institutional change, the situation facing market agents in the 1970s was one of inflation rather than deflation. The answer to this question is yes, the uncertainty of the 1970s was Knightian, but there is a caveat: Such uncertainty did not affect all parties uniformly, and this is why business rather than the state came to the fore during this period.

There is indeed a marked difference between inflations and deflations: Inflation disproportionately affects business. As Chapter 5 detailed, inflation is a class-specific tax that disadvantages the holders of financial wealth.[40] In contrast, mild inflations of the order of less than 20 percent seem to have little effect on growth and actually serve to redistribute incomes from wealth holders to debtors.[41] Consequently, although the causes of the dislocation of the 1970s were multifarious and far from obvious to all agents, the fact that they impacted so disproportionately on business combined with the legislative assaults then under way to convince

[40] For excellent discussions of why the financial sector fears inflation, see Adam Posen, "Central Bank Independence and Disinflationary Credibility," *Oxford Economic Papers* 50 (1998); *Idem.*, "Declarations Are Not Enough," *NBER Macroeconomics Annual* (1995), pp. 253–73.

[41] Jonathan Kirshner, "Inflation: Paper Dragon or Trojan Horse?" *Review of International Political Economy* 6 (4) (1999).

business that it, rather than the state, needed to resolve this crisis. However, admitting as much does not simply reduce the second great transformation to the *a priori* material interests of business.

First, the causes of the crises of the 1970s, like those of the 1930s, were far from obvious and had to be narrated. Similar to a situation of *falling* prices, there is nothing in the fact of *rising* prices that demands specific policies. As such, the control of the money supply or tax cuts to promote investment do not appear as unambiguous policy responses. Nonetheless, the fact that those dislocations affected business more than other groups did lower business's collective action barriers. Yet as our theory suggests, collective action is far from automatic and depends upon the representation of particular interests as universal. This, once again, is why ideas are important. While the ideas of business had seemingly been delegitimated by the consolidation of embedded liberalism, the fact that such market-conforming ideas were available for business to use "off the shelf," gave business a tremendous mobilization advantage. Whereas the state in the 1930s and 1940s had to invent its own ideas, business was able to take these ideas, which resonated with business people's identities as capitalists, deploy the ideas as a new narration of the crisis, and facilitate their collective action.

Such a usage, while instrumental, still does not reduce ideas to given material interests. The fact that a few conservative business elites wished to reestablish sound finance principles as the governing economic ideology of the state says nothing about how such beliefs were created among other agents, both labor and state, whose cooperation or at least acquiescence in such a reformation would be necessary. Moreover, since these ideas were far from being accurate correspondence theories of the crisis at hand, it is far from clear why the policies that they demanded represented a universal interest. While inflation may have been an unmitigated "bad" for some section of business, as Chapter 5 details, it had to be constructed as such for everyone else.[42] This is why business mobilized such extensive resources and mounted such lengthy ideological campaigns. Just as occurred during the 1930s, other agents' interests had to be reinterpreted so that they became homologous with business's, a homology that was neither obvious nor *structurally determined*. The fact that such ideas effectively transformed elite opinion in both states meant that, for example, Democrats could no longer argue for spending and Social Democrats could argue for norm-politik. Absent the transformative effect of such ideas on agents' perceptions of their self-interest and the policy choices of the heirs of embedded liberalism make little sense. This demonstrates that the necessary condition for both the rise and fall of embedded liberalism was the presence of

[42] For example, labor has no obvious interest in deregulation, unless labor's interests are recast as those of consumers rather than as producers. Transforming identity, and thus interest, has no structural prerequisites. I thank Adam Sheingate for this observation.

Knightian uncertainty, situations where agents' interests are always structurally underdetermined.

Structure and the Limits of Ideational Explanation

Given such an analysis, interests must be seen as intrinsically bound up with
ideas. Yet, in recognizing this fact, the danger is simply to move from a
materialist reductionism to an ideational essentialism, which would be a
mistake. While many structural models do not accurately specify interests,
to go to the other extreme and deny self-interest is equally pointless. Although it has been argued throughout this book that agents cannot have
interests without reference to their ideas about their interests, this is not
equivalent to saying that agents have no interests *apart from* the ideas that
inform them. It is not plausible to deny *either* intersubjectivity *or* instru-
mentality, but to argue *a priori* that "interests trump ideas," or vice versa,
is to maintain an untenable separation. All agents have interests. The point
is to recognize that while such interests may be structurally given and may
make logical sense, this in no way implies either that such interests will be
unambiguous, particularly during moments of Knightian uncertainty, or
be acted upon in a politically significant manner. This is why understanding the relationships between ideas and interests sequentially is so important. Ideas are instruments of change, yet they are also conditions of choice.
The question, as Pierson has formulated it, is therefore "not just what, but
when?"[43] When, and under what conditions, are ideas powerful? When,
and under what conditions, are interests unproblematic? Only by viewing the relationships among ideas, interests, and institutions synthetically
and sequentially can these distinctions be made and meaningful questions
be asked.

The condition of the social world is mainly that of institutional stasis
and path-dependence, not rapid change. Given that this book focuses upon
periods of great institutional upheaval, it perhaps gives the impression that
the transformative effects of ideas and the underdetermination of material
interests are commonplace. But to accept this as a general condition would
be to overstate the position taken here. As our fifth hypothesis argued,
during periods of institutional stasis, ideas reinforce expectations and contribute to the generation of stability. This situation pertains most of the
time. It is only in those moments when uncertainty abounds and institutions fail that ideas have this truly transformative effect on interests.

Therefore, rather than argue that the social world is "ideas all the way
down," to use Alexander Wendt's phrase, this book takes the position that
the world is constituted by ideas all the way through.[44] Agents' interests are

---

[43] Pierson, "Not Just What, But *When*," *passim*.
[44] This is not to suggest that "ideas all the way down" is the position that Wendt adopts;
    far from it. See Alexander Wendt, *The Social Theory of International Politics* (Cambridge:
    Cambridge University Press 1998), esp. pp. 92–138.

themselves social constructs that are open to redefinition through ideological contestation. Ideas permeate all aspects of materiality and determine
agents' orientations to social objects. But none of this means that institutions are "up for grabs" all the time. As such, the ability to determine the
dominant narration of "the way the economic world works" is powerful
only to the extent that such ideas can reach across consumption categories
in moments of uncertainty and transform supposedly given interests. This
is exactly what occurred during both periods of institutional transformation examined here.

Was the Second Great Transformation as Great as the First?

Beyond strengthening the claims made for ideas as important explanatory
and causal factors, this conclusion addresses two final questions. First, was
the second great transformation as great as the first? Second, do these great
transformations constitute a simple return to the institutional *status quo
ante*, or do they represent a more complex pattern of institutional change?
In attempting to answer the first question, some theorists have concluded
that the depth and scope of these institutional changes were not all that
great. For example, writing in 1994 regarding the institutional transformations wrought under Ronald Reagan and Margaret Thatcher, Pierson
observed that, "in neither country has there been a marked curtailment of
social expenditures or a radical shift towards residualization."[45] From the
perspective of the mid-1990s and the election of William Clinton and more
centrist Conservatives such as John Major in the United Kingdom, such a
perspective may have seemed reasonable, particularly if one focuses upon
the absolute level of transfers as the key indicator of change. However, this
view may be misleading. Once one factors in taxation changes, the less
obvious effects of financial deregulation, and the cumulative effects that
these changes have had on inequality, there can be no doubt that a great
transformation of both institutions and patterns of distribution has indeed
occurred. A brief examination of such changes in the United States illustrates this point.[46]

First, the deepening of the 1979–81 recession caused by the Fed and the
financial markets' monetarist turn disproportionately benefited those in the

---

[45] Paul Pierson, *Dismantling the Welfare State? Reagan, Thatcher, and the Politics of Retrenchment* (Cambridge: Cambridge University Press, 1994), p. 181.
[46] Swedish data are omitted for reasons of space. The basic finding of the HINK (*Hushållens
inkomster*) surveys conducted by Statistics Sweden is that the net result of the institutional
changes in taxes, transfers, and assets that took place in the past two decades was to
"increase [wealth] in absolute and relative terms for the most wealthy households while the
lowest decile has increased its debts." further, "The inequality of wealth has increased . . .
[and] . . . the GINI coefficient for extended wealth has increased by some ten percent." See
Lars Bager-Sjögren and N. Anders Klevmarken, "Inequality and Mobility of Wealth in
Sweden 1983/84–1992/93." Unpublished manuscript, Department of Economics, Uppsala
University, November 1998, pp. 9, 20.

upper half of the income distribution. Under a policy of tight money and high interest rates, those with little or no financial assets are those most exposed to the effects of a credit crunch. Meanwhile, those who derive their incomes from financial assets experience increasing returns from those assets.[47] Because of such institutional changes, the percentage of total rents and dividends held by the top 1 percent of families in the United States increased from 26 percent in 1980 to 30.5 percent in 1990. Meanwhile, the percentage of total capital gains realized by the top 1 percent of families increased from 57.7 percent to 68.5 percent over the same period.[48] By 1992, the top 1 percent of families owned 52.4 percent of all investment in real estate and unincorporated businesses, 28.7 percent of all stock and financial securities, and 62.4 percent of all bonds.[49] As Edward N. Wolff puts it, "the share of marketable net worth held by the top one percent, *which had fallen ten percentage points between 1945 and 1976,* rose 39 percent by 1989."[50]

Apart from showing shifts in income, wealth data reveal even more extreme redistributions. By 1989, "U.S. wealth concentration was more extreme than [at] any time since 1929. Between 1983 and 1989 the top half of one percent of the wealthiest families received 55 percent of the total increase in household wealth."[51] As Wolff notes, "to put it succinctly, the top quintile received more than three quarters of the increase in income and essentially all of the increase in wealth."[52] The tax and benefit changes of the early 1980s that built upon the changes already achieved by business in the 1970s simply accelerated this trend. The 1981 Economic Recovery Act alone ensured that those in the bottom quintile of the income distribution received an average tax break of $3 per year once benefit cuts were included. In fact, once the effects of the ERA and TEFRA and changes in eligibility and funding for social programs are taken into account, those with incomes *under* $30,000 actually *increased* their tax burden. In contrast, the top quintile received an average tax break of $2,429 and an effective 15 percent tax reduction.[53] By 1985 real take home pay was as much as 12.5 percent lower than it been in 1972 for those earning less than

---

[47] Furthermore, those in higher tax brackets could deduct more than those who were in lower tax brackets, giving greater effective relief.

[48] Figures are from Michael Meeropol, *Surrender: How the Clinton Administration Completed the Reagan Revolution* (Ann Arbor: Michigan University Press 1998), p. 331, fn. 78, table N-17.

[49] Edward N. Wolff, *Top Heavy: The Increasing Inequality of Wealth in America and What Can Be Done about It* (New York: New Press, 1996), pp. 62–3.

[50] *Ibid.*, p. 10, my italics.

[51] Edward N. Wolff, "The Rich Get Increasingly Richer: Latest Data on Household Wealth during the 1980's," Unpublished Paper, the Economic Policy Institute, (1992), p. 1.

[52] Wolff, *Top Heavy*, p. 27.

[53] Thomas Ferguson and Joel Rogers, *Right Turn: The Decline of the Democrats and the Future of American Politics* (New York: Hill and Wang 1986), p. 123.

$30,000, and by 1991 real mean family income had fallen by 5.3 percent for the lowest quintile of the income distribution from its 1977 level.[54] Because of such changes, banking and finance became the most profitable sectors of the economy.[55] Meanwhile, the burgeoning federal deficit further compounded the regressive effect of these changes on incomes.[56]

All in all, "$120 and $160 billion per annum was transferred to the wealthiest 5 percent in America."[57] As William Greider put it,

> ... if one viewed the Federal Reserve's policy of high interest rates as an implicit government program for redistributing incomes, its magnitude by 1982 was approximately as great as all the government's other income transfer programs combined. . . . The flow of money distributed through Social Security . . . welfare, and the rest, came to $374 billion . . . [whereas] . . . the income redistributed to wealthholders through high interest rates [was] $366 billion.[58]

When one adds to these institutional changes the fact that a *de facto* "monetarism without targets" was followed by the Fed from 1979 until 1998, then the second great transformation appears to be just as dramatic as the first; what varied were the beneficiaries.[59] As then–Federal Reserve

[54] *A Vision of Change for America*, (Washington: Office of Management and Budget), February 17, (1993), chart 2–10, p. 18.

[55] "Profitability of Insured Commercial Banks in 1984," *Federal Reserve Bulletin*, November (1985); "Financial Developments in Bank Holding Companies in 1984," *Federal Reserve Bulletin*, December (1985). The crucial thing here is the effect that tight money has on the real interest rate. So long as the interest rate on a loan is greater than the inflation rate, then when inflation declines, banks can still hold the loan at the higher rate, thereby increasing the spread and the return to the loan. The debtor in such a situation has to borrow more to meet the payments, which merely compounds the debt and the class-skewed nature of the credit crunch.

[56] The reason for this had little to do with the reborn classical crowding-out arguments popular in the Fed and in the financial markets. The deficit had this regressive effect because those financial institutions that benefited from high interest rates also benefited from the inflation premium demanded to hold bonds. As the deficit continued to increase throughout the 1980s, the returns to holding federal debt increased in lockstep. Therefore, far from being a net drain on the economy, the deficit proved a bonanza for bond holders. Rather than the state having to bribe investors into accepting government debt, the demand for bonds never faltered. Not once during the "crisis of the deficit" did the Fed ever fail to sell the bonds that it issued, so long as the markets received high interest rates as inflation cover.

[57] William C. Berman, *America's Right Turn: From Nixon to Clinton* (Baltimore: Johns Hopkins University Press, 1998), p. 106.

[58] William Greider, *Secrets of the Temple: How the Federal Reserve Runs the Country* (New York: Simon and Schuster, 1987), p. 457.

[59] After the federal funds rate averaged a mere 3 percent in 1993 because of the weak state of the economy, the Fed increased the rate to 6.21 percent on July 5, 1995, and maintained it at between 6.5 and 5.5 percent until the October 28, 1998, when it fell below 5 percent for the first time in three and a half years. The rationale for this move was to stop the recovery from getting out of control. Similarly, the prime rate remained frozen at 6 percent between August 1992 and February 1994, again because of the weak state of the economy.

Chairman Paul Volker reportedly told a Senatorial delegation from the Farm Belt who complained about the distributive effects of these institutional changes, "look, your constituents are unhappy, mine aren't."[60]

Ideas and Institutional Change: Pendulum Swings or Forward Movements?

Given such distributional changes, the conclusion that the second set of transformations was not as consequential as the first seems less assured. While embedded liberal institutions of some type remain in place in all advanced capitalist states, the context within which they operate has changed radically. When one combines these domestic-level changes with concurrent international changes designed to facilitate the free flow of capital, the increasing independence of central banks, and the growing interpenetration of markets, then it seems that the second set of transformations may be as consequential as the first in many respects. However, this in no way implies a simple return to the principles of sound finance and the institutions of 1920s. In fact, such an institutional "swing of the pendulum" is impossible.

Political economies are not closed systems where institutional reversals can be made. They are instead evolutionary systems populated by agents who learn and apply those lessons in daily practice. As such, any attempt to simply "turn back the clock" within such an environment cannot work since the institutions that make up such systems are constantly modified by the agents who inhabit them. Although great transformations can be effected, the objects of such projects are moving targets pushed along by factors that are seldom repeated or replicable.[61] While Chapter 2 argued that it is precisely this quality that makes ideas particularly influential in promoting institutional change, this is also what makes any attempt to restore extinct institutions impossible. While liberal capitalism has indeed been "disembedded" once again, this does not mean that the disembedded market of the early twentieth century has simply been put back in its place. Institutions can be transformed, but they cannot be restored.

Given such conclusions, the double movement as Polanyi conceived it needs to be rethought. In this book, I have attempted to do this by problematizing structural notions of institutional change and by highlight-

---

Once unemployment began to get "too low," the prime rate shot up to 9 percent in February 1995 and did not fall below 8.5 percent until September 1998. Figures are from the Federal Reserve Bank of St. Louis monetary database at http://www.stls.frb.org/fred/data/monetary/fyffr and http://www.stls.frb.org/fred/data/monetary/fypr.

[60] Paul Volker, quoted in Greider, *Secrets of the Temple*, p. 676.

[61] For one of the few books in political science that attempts to theorize such dynamics, see Robert Jervis, *Systems Effects: Complexity in Social and Political Life* (Princeton: Princeton University Press, 1997).

ing the constitutive role of ideas within such transformations. Given this theoretical reconstruction, the message of this book is really quite simple: It is only by reference to the ways that agents think about their condition within an uncertain evolutionary order that the actual path of institutional change can be fully explained. Such ideas do not inform agents' interests willy-nilly, however. Nor should this study be taken as a denial of self-interest, for it is not. Agents who see an existing institutional order as asymmetrically benefiting someone else over themselves will try to change that order. This much is the politics of "normal times." However, what is important to realize is that moments when the opportunity for fundamental change occurs, moments of deep uncertainty, do not lay courses of action bare to agents with given interests in reaction to self-apparent crises. There is nothing in such assumptions or the static models of change that they generate that enables one to explain how agents react in such moments. Only the examination of the ideas used by agents to diagnose the uncertainty around them and construct specific institutional solutions to that uncertainty can do this.

In summary, then, this book has sought to make the case that ideas are much more than an adjunct to materialist explanations and should instead be seen as causal variables in their own right. While power, money, and self-interest should not be discounted in the haste to proclaim ideas triumphant, it should be remembered that such material resources and "structural factors" are powerful only to the extent that they can be mobilized to specific ends. However, neither material resources nor the self-interest of agents can dictate those ends or tell agents what future to construct. Ideas do this, and this is ultimately why they are important.

Index

Made in the USA
Lexington, KY
08 August 2013